Driving Down
Health Care Costs

STRATEGIES AND SOLUTIONS

1993

A PANEL PUBLICATION

Copyright © 1993

by
PANEL PUBLISHERS
A division of Aspen Publishers, Inc.
A Wolters Kluwer Company
36 West 44th Street
New York, NY 10036
(212) 790-2090

ISBN 1-56706-002-1

Printed in the United States of America

About Panel Publishers, Inc.

Panel Publishers derives its name from a panel of business professionals who organized in 1964 to publish authoritative, timely books, information services, and journals written by specialists to assist business professionals in the areas of human resources administration, compensation, and benefits management, and pension planning and compliance as well as owners of small-to-medium-sized businesses and their legal and financial advisors. Our mission is to provide practical, solution-based "how-to" information to business professionals.

Panel's list of publications that are designed to assist professionals in the areas of human resources, compensation and benefits, and pension and profit-sharing includes:

Managing Employee Health Benefits
Medical Benefits
Employee Benefits Answer Book
Employee Assistance Law Answer Book
The Americans With Disabilities Act
State by State Guide to Human Resources Law
Health Insurance Answer Book
Hiring Handbook
Sexual Harassment
Employment Law Answer Book

All Panel publications are supplemented periodically to ensure that the information presented is accurate and up-to-date. If you would like to receive updates for this volume, please contact our Customer Service Department at 1-800-457-9222.

PANEL PUBLISHERS, INC.
Practical Solutions for Business Professionals

SUBSCRIPTION NOTICE

This Panel product is updated on a periodic basis with supplements to reflect important changes in the subject matter. If you purchased this product directly from Panel Publishers, we have already recorded your subscription for this update service.

If, however, you purchased this product from a bookstore and wish to receive future updates and revised or related volumes billed separately with a 30-day examination review, please send your name, company name (if applicable), address, and the title of the product to:

Subscription Services
PANEL PUBLISHERS
A division of Aspen Publishers, Inc.
A Wolters Kluwer Company
36 West 44th Street
Suite 1316
New York, NY 10036
(212) 790-2090

Preface

The 1993 edition of *Driving Down Health Care Costs* presents comprehensive coverage of the cost control strategies that have recently proven successful for many of America's leading corporations. Inside, you will:

- Learn how First Chicago Bank has used the data management plan to cap some of the most rapidly rising health care costs;
- See how Xerox and General Electric have focused on quality;
- Find out why Cleveland's health care coalition has recently obtained cooperation from hospitals in efforts to control rising costs;
- Learn how Campbell's Soup's new, innovative employee assistance program is controlling mental health costs;
- Find out about the little-noticed cost-shifting approach pioneered by Allied Signal, Equitable Financial Co., and American Savings Bank, and how Sears and Marriott are using audits as key parts of their cost control strategies.

Driving Down Health Care Costs has been prepared specifically for corporate benefits planners who must design and implement cost containment strategies in the face of steep increases in medical costs. You'll get the best thinking available on the hottest subjects in the field:

- Considering point-of-service plans? Find out what they can do to control costs—and what they can't do.
- Worried that you may have to sacrifice quality of care to reduce health benefit costs? See why leading corporations have concluded that better quality care is actually more cost effective.
- Wondering what to do next about postretirement medical benefits? Before you do anything, learn what other companies have already done, and make sure you understand all of the options.
- Not sure how a flexible benefits plan will affect medical costs? See how managed care can be integrated into a flex plan.

Whether it's direct contracting or prescription plan cost control, risk management or case management, employee communication or worker's compensation, *Driving Down Health Care Costs* offers you more than just theory. The contributors to this year's edition include experts who know why cost control efforts succeed—and why they fail. These experts can provide you with the ideals, the analytical background, and the real-world experience that you need to design and manage benefit plans in today's turbulent health care climate.

From audits to wellness plans, *Driving Down Health Care Costs* is your guide to the best practices in the field today.

Contributors

David J. Blume is Partner in charge of the industry practice for the Hartford, CT, office of Andersen Consulting. He acknowledges the assistance of James T. Thorton in the preparation of this article.

Joseph A. Brislin is Staff Attorney and Director of special services for Timber Operators Council, Inc. Tigard, OR. He advises association members on all aspects of labor law and serves as adviser and trustee for several health and welfare and pension funds in the forest products industry. Mr. Brislin, who is a graduate of Paul Smith's College, received BSF and master's degrees from the University of Washington and a JD from the University of Oregon School of Law. He has served on the International Foundation of Employee Benefit Plans' board of directors and Research Committee and has spoken at a number of its educational conferences. Mr. Brislin is a contributing author of several books published by the Foundation and has written previously for the *Employee Benefits Journal*.

Wayne N. Burton, MD, has been Vice President/Corporate Medical Director for First National Bank of Chicago since 1982. He is Associate Professor of Clinical Medicine and Psychiatry at Northwestern University Medical School and Assistant Clinical Professor of Preventive Medicine at Rush. Prior to joining First Chicago he was with the World Headquarters of International Harvester Company. Dr. Burton is a Fellow of the American College of Physicians and the American College of Occupational and Environmental Medicine. He is a member of the Board of Directors of the Midwest Business Group on Health, Central States Occupational Medical Association and the Mental Health Association of Greater Chicago.

Daniel M. Campion has been an Associate with the Alpha Center since June 1989. He is deputy director of the technical resource center, funded by The Robert Wood Johnson Foundation in collaboration with the Health Care Financing Administration (HCFA), that supports the Essential Access Community Hospital/

Rural Primary Care Hospital Program. The center provides technical assistance to states that have received grants from HCFA under this $20-million federal program to develop regionalized health care delivery systems and implement a new licensure category for rural health facilities. Mr. Campion assists in directing The Robert Wood Johnson Foundation's State Initiatives in Health Care Financing Reform Program and provided technical assistance to grantees under the Health Care for the Uninsured Program. He also assists in developing and producing policy workshops for state and local government officials on behalf of the Agency for Health Care Policy and Research's (AHCPR) User Liaison Program.

Shari Caudron is a freelance writer.

Douglas G. Cave, PhD, MPH, is a consultant for Hewitt Associates in Santa Ana, CA.

Maureen Corcoran is an attorney in the San Francisco office of the law firm of Pillsbury, Madison & Sutro and provides counseling on the full range of legal issues related to the health care industry.

Barbara Creed is head of the Employee Benefits and Health Care Practice at the San Francisco office of the law firm of Pillsbury, Madison & Sutro and specializes in employee benefits and executive compensation.

William Custer, PhD, is Director of Research at the Employee Benefit Research Institute (EBRI) in Washington, DC, where he conducts research related to employer health benefits and the health care delivery system. Dr. Custer has investigated a wide range of topics in health care, including the market for hospital services, hospital–physician relationships, Medicare's Prospective Payment System, and alternative physician payment mechanisms. He is currently directing studies of private health plan cost management incentives, the impact of health care reform proposals, and quality assessment in health care services. Prior to joining EBRI, Dr. Custer was an economist in the Center for Health Policy Research at the American Medical Association and was an assistant professor of economics at Northern Illinois University.

Helen Darling is a principal and senior consultant in health care with the firm of William M. Mercer in Stamford, CT. She served as senior health policy adviser and legislative assistant for Senator Dave Durenberger (R-MN) from October 1986 to November 1988.

Arthur G. Dobbelaere, PhD, is an associate professor at Loyola University and Director of the Institute of Human Resources and Industrial Relations. At the Institute, he teaches graduate level courses in labor economics, compensation management, cost analysis in human resource administration, quality of work life and computer application in human resource administration. In the management consulting firm of D. G. & Associates, he consults frequently in strategic planning development, human resource management, benefit and compensation design, and team building. Dr. Dobbelaere is a member of the Academy of Management and many other organizations. He also lectures and publishes frequently in the area of human resource management.

Mary Jane England is president of the Washington (DC) Business Group on Health (WBGH). A psychiatrist, she was previously vice-president for group medical services at the Prudential Insurance Company.

Alain C. Enthoven, PhD, teaches in the Graduate School of Business at Stanford University.

Madelon Lubin Finkel, PhD, MPA, is clinical associate professor of public health at Cornell University Medical College, where she focuses on research in health care cost management and epidemiology. Dr. Finkel is also president of Second Opinion Consultants, Inc., of Millwood, New York, a nationwide health care organization dedicated to health care cost management. She earned her BA at University College, New York University, and her MPA and PhD at the Graduate School of Public Administration, New York University. Dr. Finkel has served as consultant to numerous corporations and trust funds in the area of health care cost management. She has written extensively in this area and is the author of the first and second editions of *Health Care Cost Management: A Basic Guide* and co-author of *Retiree Health Care: A Ticking Time Bomb*, all published by the International Foundation of Employee Benefit Plans.

John D. Fortin is an actuary in the Dallas office of The Wyatt Company. As Practice Director, he provides actuarial consulting services in employee benefits, particularly in the area of group insurance benefits and flexible compensation. Since joining Wyatt seven years ago, Mr. Fortin has focused his attention on the evaluation of group life, health, and disability plans with respect to both plan design and funding vehicle analysis. Prior to joining Wyatt, Mr. Fortin was Vice President-Corporate Planning for Southwestern Life Insurance. Mr. Fortin is a fellow in the Society of Actuaries and is an Enrolled Actuary under ERISA.

Joyce Frieden is Senior Washington Editor of *Business & Health.*

John C. Garner is president of Garner Consulting. He began his career in employee benefits in 1972. Before founding Garner Consulting, he was a principal in the Los Angeles office of TPF&C. Mr. Garner has served as technical advisor on flexible benefits for the Family Economic Policy Task Force of the League of California Cities and County Supervisors Association of California. He has special expertise in the area of cost containment.

Virginia M. Gibson is a principal with the MG Group, a Baltimore-based employee benefits consulting group.

Kathleen H. Goeppinger, PhD is an associate professor at Loyola University of Chicago, Institute of Human Resources and Industrial Relations, where she teaches graduate level courses in benefits, compensation, human resource management, quality of work life, and advanced compensation/benefit theory. She has been involved in the employee benefits field for 20 years. She is Chairman of the corporate board of Chicago Osteopathic Health Systems, and former chairman of the Midwest Business Group on health, as well as the Chicago Association of Commerce and Industry. As a partner in the management consulting form of D. G. & Associates, Dr. Goeppinger consults, speaks, and publishes frequently on a wide variety of employee benefits and human resource management issues.

Ellen Goldstein is Director of Health Policy at the Association of Private Pension and Welfare Plans in Washington, DC. In that capacity, she is responsible for the development and coordination of APPWP health policy through its Health Care Issues Committee and manages legislative and regulatory activities in the health area. She also serves as Staff Director for the new APPWP Action Center for Quality Health Care, and directs the Association's public affairs programs, including the annual legislative conference. Prior to coming to the APPWP in 1985, Ms. Goldstein worked on state regulatory policy for MCI Communications in Washington, DC. From 1977 to 1981, she served on the Domestic Policy Staff at the White House during the Carter Administration. As an Assistant Director for Human Resources, she was responsible for developing budget, policy, and legislative recommendations for the President on a wide range of federal human services programs.

Jack B. Helitzer is a vice president of Metropolitan Life Insurance Company. From 1983 to 1985, when the National Association of Insurance Commissioners' (NAIC) group model coordination of benefits (COB) regulation was developed, he served as the chairman of the Industry Advisory Committee to the NAIC Task Force on Coordination of Benefits.

W David Helms, PhD, has directed the Alpha Center since it was established in 1976. He has directed a wide range of health policy and planning projects for federal and state governmental agencies, state and local health planning agencies, and private foundations. Dr. Helms serves as a Project Director for a contract with the Agency for Health Care Policy and Research's (AHCPR) User Liaison Program. He also serves as Program Director for The Robert Wood Johnson Foundation's State Initiatives in Health Care Financing Reform program and as Director of the technical resource center funded by The Robert Wood Johnson Foundation to support the Health Care Financing Administration's Essential Access Community Hospital/Primary Care Hospital (EACH/ PCH) program. Dr. Helms received his doctorate in public administration and economics in 1979 from the Maxwell School of Citizenship and Public Affairs, Syracuse University.

Donald A. Hoy is the Vice President and Manager of Benefits Planning and Administration in the Human Resources Policy Section for First Chicago Corporation/The First National Bank of Chicago. He has over 20 years of experience in the employee benefits field, including plan design, funding, communication, and administration. His current responsibilities at First Chicago include planning, design, and administration for the retirement and welfare plans, as well as postretirement benefits administration. Prior experience includes design and administration of the international benefits program and salary administration. He is a member of the Society of Human Resource Management. He has coauthored articles for the Journal of Occupational Medicine on psychiatric case management and health care cost control. He received his BA in psychology from Elmhurst College and his MBA in Human Resources Management from Loyola University.

Carol Johnston is the Director of the claim audit practice in the Chicago office of Coopers & Lybrand's Actuarial, Benefits and Communications group. Ms. Johnston has over 23 years of experience in the health care and benefits consulting areas and leads the Chicago office's practice group in the design and delivery of claim and utilization review audits and evaluations.

Donald W. Kemper is Founder and Executive Director of Healthwise, a nonprofit organization whose mission is to help people do a better job of staying healthy and taking care of their health problems. Healthwise was founded in Boise, ID in 1975.

Paul J. Kenkel is a reporter for *Modern Healthcare.*

Louise Kertesz is an associate editor of *Business Insurance.*

Sharon Klingelsmith is an associate in the Employee Benefits group of the Philadelphia law firm of Drinker Biddle & Reath and concentrates on a full range of employee benefits programs, including welfare and cafeteria plans.

Richard Kronick, PhD, teaches in the Department of Community and Family Medicine at the University of California, San Diego.

David Lally is Marketing Communications Manager for ITT Hartford's employee benefits division.

Marcia Leitner is an attorney in the San Francisco office of the law firm of Pillsbury, Madison & Sutro and practices in the areas of employee benefits and health care law.

Raymond A. Lenhardt is partner is charge of the insurance industry practice for Andersen Consulting's Washington, DC office. He acknowledges the assistance of James T. Thorton in the preparation of this article.

Michael J. Lotito is managing partner of the San Francisco office of Jackson, Lewis, Schnitzler & Krupman. He is a member of the Society of Human Resources Professional's (SHRM) board of directors as National Vice President At-Large.

Irene McKirgan is Assistant Director of Worksite Programs at the national office of March of Dimes Birth Defects Foundation, a non-profit organization committed to improving the health of babies by preventing birth defects and infant mortality. At the foundation, she is responsible for developing and managing maternal and infant health initiatives for the workplace. Before joining the March of Dimes, she implemented cancer education and screening programs for employees in major corporations while with the American Cancer Society and managed a comprehensive worksite health promotion for IBM while with US Corporate Health Management.

Daniel N. Mendelson, MPP, is a project manager at Lewin ICF.

Dr. Rich Miller is an associate professor in health education, Department of Human Services, George Mason University. He is formerly the Manager of Health Management at the Xerox Corporation. Dr. Miller was also the Manager of Occupational Health at the University of Rochester's Medical Center. He specializes in the study of employee health services.

Paul M. Millholland is Employee Benefits Research Director at The Upjohn Company. Over his 32-year career with Upjohn, he has served in various employee benefits capacities including Manager, Benefits Administration; Manager, Benefits Planning and Development; and Director, Corporate Benefits. In his current position, he serves as an EBRI Fellow at the Employee Benefits Research Institute in Washington, DC. He also represents The Upjohn Company on the National Association of Manufacturers (NAM) Health Care Subcommittee and the Business Roundtable (BRT) Health, Welfare and Retirement Income Staff Committee. Mr. Millholland is also past president and a current board member of the Council on Employee Benefits (CEB) and Treasurer and a member of the board of the Midwest Business Group on Health (MBGH).

Jim Mishizen is Assistant Vice President-Disability Marketing for CIGNA Special Benefits Companies in Philadelphia.

Ronald J. North, CEAP, is president of North, Clawson and Bolt, Ltd., an independent EAP and managed behavioral health care consulting firm based in Sacramento, California. The firm designed Campbell's Quality Care Program.

Margaret E. O'Kane is the President of the National Committee for Quality Assurance (NCQA). NCQA is an external quality review organization for HMOs. Previously, as the Director of Quality Management with the Group Health Association (GHA), a staff model HMO with approximately 150,000 members, Ms. O'Kane served as the principle staff person for GHA's quality improvement initiative. Prior to that she was Director of the Medical Directors Division for the Group Health Association of America (GHAA). Ms. O'Kane also functioned as Special Assistant to the Director of the National Center for Health Services Research and Health Care Technology Assessment and as a Research Associate on state health policy issues at the Intergovernmental Health Policy Project at the George Washington University, in Washington, DC. She has a Master's degree from the Johns Hopkins University School of Hygiene and Public Health.

Arthur E. Parry, PhD, is Manager of Risk Management Services for The Wyatt Company, Dallas, TX. Dr. Parry has had 25 years of experience in the insurance industry and is a frequent contributor to industry publications on risk management matters.

Brenda Ballard Pflaum is an Associate in the Chicago Office of William M. Mercer, where she specializes in group benefits and health care cost management consulting.

Richard Pimentel is senior partner of Milt Wright & Associates in Northridge, CA.

Anna M. Rappaport, FSA, is a Managing Director of William M. Mercer. She is an actuary and futurist with 30 years of business experience and has a broad background in pension and benefits consulting, corporate research, and life insurance company management. Her special interest has been social and economic change and how it affects benefits and human resources management. She has published in the *Harvard Business Review, Inquiry,* the *Journal of Pension Planning and Compliance*, and *Compensation and Benefits Management,* for which she is a regular columnist.

Matthew Schwartz is a staff writer on health care issues for *National Underwriter.*

William B. Schwartz, MD, is Professor of Medicine at the University of Southern California.

Bruce Shutan is Managing Editor of *Employee Benefit News.*

Ellis Simon is a contributing writer to *Risk & Insurance.*

M Daniel Sloan is the president of Quality Health Systems of America, Inc. in Seattle, WA. He has a bachelor's degree in psychology form Baldwin-Wallace College in Berea, OH. Sloan is a member of the American Society for Quality Control (ASQC).

Joseph CH Smith, PhD, is Executive Vice President, The Townsend Group, Inc. (TTG). Dr. Smith founded TTG in November 1991 with the objective of working with federal and state governments and private sector companies to design and implement health care cost containment programs. The company's focus includes both general health benefit programs and workers' compensation programs. Prior to founding TTG, Dr. Smith was Manager, Health Policy Research Program, Workers Compensation Research Institute (WCRI) in Cambridge, MA.

Kenneth L. Sperling, CEBS, is a managing consultant in the health care practice of Hewitt Associates in Rowayton, CT. He specializes in the design, financing, and administration of indemnity and managed care arrangements and has more than ten years' experience in the field. He has been published in the *Journal of Compensation and Benefits*. Mr. Sperling is a graduate of Duke University and received his MBA in management from New York University. He is also a Certified Employee Benefit Specialist.

R Philip Steinberg is a partner in the Employee Benefits group of the Philadelphia law firm of Drinker Biddle & Reath and concentrates on a full range of employee benefits programs, including welfare and cafeteria plans.

James Studnicki, ScD, is Professor and Chairman, Department of Health Policy and Management, College of Public Health, University of South Florida. Previously, he was associate professor and director of the Program in Health Finance and Management at the Johns Hopkins Medical Institutions. Dr. Studnicki has also been a hospital executive and consultant to organization in both the public and private sectors. He was the project director of an International Foundation of Employee Benefits Plans-funded project to develop a national comparative database for analyzing health care utilization and costs.

Roger Thompson is a senior editor for *Nation's Business*.

Larry J. Tucker is a Partner of Hewitt Associates in Santa Ana, CA.

Veronica Vaccaro is Manager, Mental Health Promotion, at the Washington, DC Business Group on Health (WBGH).

Beth F. Vorwaller is an Associate in the Chicago office of William M. Mercer. Ms. Vorwaller is a senior actuary with ten years of experience at Mercer. Her experience includes consulting on actuarial and plan management issues for pension, health care, and casualty insurance benefit programs for both active and retired employees.

Victoria D. Weisfeld, MPH, currently holds the position of Senior Communications Officer at The Robert Wood Johnson Foundation (RWJF) in Princeton, New Jersey. She graduated from the University of Michigan with a Bachelor of Arts degree and from the University of Pittsburgh with a Master's Degree in Public Health. She is responsible for a wide range of communications activities that support RWJF grants and programs and the dissemination of their findings. Ms. Weisfeld serves on the Communications Committees of the Council on Foundations and the Independent Sector, and is Editor of *Update*, the quarterly newsletter on the Communications Network in Philanthropy. Before coming to the Robert

Wood Johnson Foundation, Ms. Weisfeld was a Senior Associate with the Institute of Medicine, Division of Health Promotion and Disease Prevention, at the National Academy of Sciences in Washington, DC, and also wrote a weekly freelance newspaper column on federal health policy, medical research, and trends in health care services delivery. She has authored numerous articles on health care and edits a quarterly health services research newsletter for RWJF.

Gary S. Wolfe, RN, CNA, is Director of Case Management for Pacific Review Services and has over 20 years of experience in a variety of health-care settings. He is an officer of the Case Management Society of America and a member of the Government Affairs Committee for that organization. He is also on the advisory board of the Individual Case Management Association and the Editorial Board of the Center for Consumer Health Care Information.

Dale Yamamoto is a health care consultant and group actuary with Hewitt Associates, located in the firm's general office in Lincolnshire, IL. He manages a group actuarial unit that specializes in a broad range ofted in the firm's general office in Lincolnshire, IL. He manages a group actuarial unit that specializes in a broad range of technical consulting services.

Contents

Introduction: Understanding Health Care Costs

William S. Custer

National health care expenditures have been increasing at twice the rate of general inflation for almost the entire decade. With medical expenses estimated at almost $817 billion in 1992, the United States now spends 14 percent of its gross national product (GNP) on health care. For employers, health benefits have grown into a major component of labor costs; in 1970, health benefits comprised 2.4 percent of total compensation and 23 percent of total benefits, but by 1989 they accounted for 5.8 percent of total compensation and 36 percent of all benefits. It should be noted that these are national averages which include employers that do not offer any health benefits. A survey of employers that do offer health benefits found that the average cost per employee in 1991 was $3605, almost 11 percent of payroll.[1]

Health care cost inflation has resulted in health care benefits becoming the fastest growing component of total compensation for employees, and the fastest growing component of federal expenditures for taxpayers. Federal, state, and local governments account for about 42 percent of national health expenditures. The remaining 58 percent come from direct out-of-pocket patient expenditures and insurance payments.[2]

The reactions of different employers to increases in health care costs has varied depending on the labor market each employer faces, the amount of competition in the product market, and the level of market power the employer has in its specific health care services markets. In general, employers have adopted four types of cost management strategies: cost sharing, utilization review, packaging provider services, and selectively contracting with providers. These strategies have been combined in the various managed care plans now used by many employers. Individual employers have achieved lower rates of cost inflation by employing these strategies, but to date they have had little impact on the rate of increase in national health expenditures.

The widespread use cost management strategies has affected the practice of medicine. Caregiving has moved out of the hospital to a variety of sites, referral patterns of physicians have been affected, the relationship between hospitals and their medical staffs has been altered, and the way providers market themselves have changed due to changes in the way payers purchase health care services. A cost management industry has arisen composed of utilization review firms, provider networks, data analysis firms, and other vendors whose services track medical decision making.

The fundamental question is whether the public and private cost management strategies now being developed and employed can slow the growth of health care costs in a pluralistic health care system. Some have argued that health care cost inflation can be controlled only by capping national health expenditures, employing a single purchaser of health care services, and imposing an explicit rationing scheme.

SOURCES OF HEALTH CARE COST INFLATION

The increased use of health insurance in the period from the end of World War II through the early 1980s has been an important component of health care cost inflation. Unlike other types of insurance, health insurance benefits are based on expenditures for health care services rather than the actual loss due to a particular ailment. As a result, health insurance lowers the effective price of medical services to insured individuals, increasing patient demand for health care. This change in consumer behavior due to the presence of insurance is a form of moral hazard, and is one source of health care cost inflation.

The characteristics of the provider reimbursement policies of private and public insurers have also had important implications for health care cost inflation. Hospitals have been regarded as quasi-public institutions, and as such were traditionally reimbursed on a cost-plus basis to ensure that they were able to maintain high quality services. However, reimbursement under fee-for-service for physicians or cost-plus systems for hospitals gives providers little incentive for limiting the potential range of diagnostic and therapeutic services available to a patient or the quantity of services provided.

Health insurance also helped to weaken the relationship between the cost of health care services and the demand, a relationship important to the control of cost. Physicians have long considered price competition unethical, and have instead competed in the area of quality—or, more accurately, the perception of quality, since patients generally lack the information needed to evaluate objectively the quality of a particular caregiver and so focus on signals they believe relate to quality, such as location, office attributes, and hospital affiliations.

Hospitals are in a similar position, competing with each other for physicians and patients by offering the ability to perform more procedures and to deliver more amenities, since these are often perceived as important signs of quality.[3] The costs of the more expensive new technology required to perform new procedures are often spread across all other procedures.[4]

The increasing demand for health care services led to a corollary increase in the demand for new medical technology, and medical researchers, with financial assistance from the government and other sources, responded impressively. The number of available diagnostic tools for a given set of symptoms and the number of potential therapeutic procedures for a given diagnosis have increased dramatically in the last 25 years. In short, new technology both lengthens the list of procedures a physician can perform for a given condition and increases the number of conditions a physician can treat, increasing the total number of services purchased. Unfortunately, much of this new technology is introduced with little or no evaluation of its benefits relative to costs. Without such information, and with no other disincentives, providers adopt practices based on personal preferences, as proved by the well-documented variation in practice patterns among physicians working in the same geographic area.[5]

Another factor in a caregiver's treatment decisions is the potential threat of litigation. Malpractice proceedings are intended to punish incompetent providers, but with the current system, it is left to lay juries to decide the appropriate medical practice for a given condition in order to determine the accused's competence. The threat of malpractice suits may lead physicians to be overly cautious, performing more procedures than they deem necessary or cost-effective.

Tax policy spurred the spread of private health insurance and encouraged employers to accommodate health care cost inflation. The costs of employer provided health benefits are deductible as a business expense for employers and are not included as personal income for employees. Although most researchers agree that this tax preference has affected the provision of health insurance benefits by employers, it is not clear how much of the increase in private health insurance coverage (and thus in health care costs) results from tax policy. In general, the tax subsidy of health insurance benefits has increased both the number of individuals with health insurance and the breadth of coverage, although its effects differ by employee group.

Most large employers who offer health insurance would likely continue to offer it in the absence of a tax preference. Group insurance is less expensive than individual policies because the costs of administration and the problem of adverse selection. If sold individually, the people most likely to use health insurance would also be the people most likely to purchase it, increasing the cost. Pooling eliminates adverse selection by providing insurance for a group of people with mixed health care needs, thereby decreasing the cost of coverage per individual. Employers are thus able to provide more insurance per dollar than the employee could purchase individually. As an employee benefit, employer sponsored health insurance may also decrease turnover and increase productivity.

The effects of changes in tax policy on national health care expenditures are unclear. Removing the tax preference would probably reduce the number of individuals with employer sponsored health insurance, and reduce the breadth of services for those with employer sponsored coverage, but the magnitude of these reductions is unknown. However, research into the relationship between tax policy and the demand for health insurance, and between insurance and health care demand, suggest that the magnitude may be small.

The exact impacts of insurance coverage on technological advances, the quality of care, and the intensity of care are not well understood.[6] It may be that, over time, changes in health insurance induced by changes in tax policy could have profound impacts on the health care delivery system.

In summary, the sources of health care cost inflation all relate back to the allocation of risk. Tax policy not only encouraged the spread of health insurance, but aided the accommodation of health care cost inflation. The increased costs of health care coverage were offset by the greater value of the tax preference as employees were pushed by general price inflation into higher marginal tax brackets. The spread of health insurance and the characteristics of health insurance (in which the insurer bears the risks associated with the uncertainty in the efficacy of treatment) increased the demand for health care services and stimulated the development of new procedures. Since it is the primary method for them to distinguish themselves from their competitors, hospitals and physicians in competitive markets are quick to adopt new technology, raising their overall costs.[7] Providers, given a longer list of potential procedures that could be performed for a given condition, offer more intensive and more specialized care. The constraints on the demand for health insurance due to its increasing costs are reduced by tax policy.

COST MANAGEMENT STRATEGIES

Cost management strategies attempt to alter either patient or provider incentives, or both. There are four general cost management strategies: cost sharing, utilization review, packaging provider services, and selectively contracting with providers. Cost sharing includes the health plan's deductibles, coinsurance rates, and the limits on the insured's out of pocket expenses (stop-loss). Utilization review involves a number of strategies for intervening in the decision to purchase health care services, including second surgical opinion, pre-admission certification, concurrent review, case management, and retrospective review. Packaging provider services alters the reimbursement of providers from fee-for-service to some bundle of services ranging from an inpatient stay (as in Medicare's prospective payment system) to payment per enrollee (as in health maintenance organizations (HMOs)). Finally, selectively contracting with providers creates a panel of practitioners to perform necessary health care services. Cost sharing is often an element of this strategy, used to steer patients toward providers in the panel. Ideally, providers are selected on the basis of their cost-effective practice patterns, and agree to participate in utilization review and quality assurance processes.

Cost Sharing

Cost sharing is effective at reducing health care expenditures by reducing the utilization of health care services. For example, the Rand Health Insurance experiment found that individuals in plans with a 25 percent coinsurance rate had 15 percent lower per capita costs than individuals in plans with a zero coinsurance rate.[8] (It should be noted that the 15 percent may understate the response of individuals to increased coinsurance rates since the experiment compensated individuals who were in plans with greater cost sharing to induce them to accept these plans.)

Cost sharing is most effective at reducing the use of outpatient care. However, some of the care forgone may include preventive care, and forgoing preventive care might ultimately result in larger inpatient costs. The Rand study found that low-income individuals with lower coinsurance rates experienced specific health gains for three prevalent chronic problems—high blood pressure, myopia, and dental care—that are relatively inexpensive to diagnose and treat.

Some proponents of cost sharing have argued that it provides the patient with an incentive to shop for the most cost-effective provider. However, determining the cost-effectiveness of any provider requires information that may be prohibitively expensive to consumers, but that may be available to insurers.

Utilization Review

Utilization review (UR) includes a number of strategies for intervening in the decision to purchase health care. These may include pre-admission certification, in which care is reviewed before it is given; concurrent review (case management), in which care is monitored as it is provided; and retrospective review, which reviews care after it is given. In all cases care is reviewed against specific criteria to determine if it is (or was) necessary and appropriate. These criteria are either developed internally by utilization review firms, or are licensed from outside developers and then modified by the firms.

Three of the criteria sets that have been developed for licensing to UR firms were recently evaluated to assess their reliability and validity.[9] The reliability of the criteria was tested by comparing the conclusions of two different nurses who used the criteria to evaluate a hospital record and the validity of the criteria was evaluated by comparing the judgment of a nurse using the criteria to that of a panel of physicians for each hospital record. One of the criteria was found to have low reliability and validity; the other two were found to be moderately reliable and valid, although both scored better than individual physicians looking at the same record. These results indicate that not all utilization review criteria will be equally effective at reducing unnecessary or inappropriate care. They also suggest that utilization review that is used to determine eligibility for payment under a health plan should consist of several steps, perhaps beginning with a nurse review using predetermined criteria but including a panel of physicians as final decision makers.

In a survey of employers, UR was rated as the second most effective cost management measure, after cost sharing.[10] However, there have been few independent studies of the effectiveness of utilization review in controlling costs. One study examined the experience of 263 groups insured by a major insurer over 12 quarters, from 1984 to 1986. The authors of this study were unable to differentiate between the different types of utilization review programs such as pre-admission certification, concurrent review, or retrospective review in their comparisons. They found that UR reduced admissions by 13 percent, inpatient days by 11 percent, and total medical expenditures by 6 percent.[11] Another study performed a similar analysis on Blue Cross-Blue Shield data for the years 1980-1986, and did differentiate among the different types of UR. They found that neither pre-admission nor retrospective review had any significant effect on average plan cost. While concurrent review decreased inpatient payments, outpatient payments increased, yielding no significant differences in average costs.[12] An Employee Benefits Research Institute (EBRI)'s study of employers in the Houston area found that plans with utilization review had significantly lower inpatient charges. Outpatient charges however, were significantly greater in plans with UR, consistent with the hypothesis that UR shifts care from the hospital to an outpatient setting. In a separate EBRI study of employers in the Los Angeles area, UR was associated with lower total plan charges, but these savings were achieved not by lowering the admission rate but by decreasing total charges per admission. Utilization review in Los Angeles was also associated with lower outpatient charges.

Health Care Services Packaging

Another cost management strategy is to change provider reimbursement from fee-for-service or cost-plus to payment per diagnosis, by insured person, or by some other bundle of services. Providers are paid a set fee for each particular diagnosis or plan participant, for example, and provider profit is the difference between the costs of providing care for that diagnosis or participant, and the fee. Packaging services moves provider incentives away from the provision of more care toward the provision of cost-effective care. To be profitable, providers must weigh the costs of care in their medical decision making.

Health maintenance organizations, in some forms, are a type of provider service package. An HMO agrees to provide a prescribed set of benefits as needed by enrollees in return for a capitated payment—a fixed amount per enrollee—thus bearing the risks associated with the need and delivery of care. HMOs maybe the most studied of the cost management strategies. Depending upon the HMO, total costs for enrollees have been found to be between 10 and 40 percent lower than more traditional health insurance programs. These cost differences result from lower rates of service, especially lower hospital admission rates.[13] There are a number of HMO models, generally falling into two categories: group or staff models, and independent practice arrangements (IPAs) or network models. In group models, the physician is either an employee of, or receives a majority of his or her patients from, the HMO. In an IPA model, the HMO contracts with regular physicians or physician groups that also maintain a fee-for-service practice. Physicians in IPAs are typically reimbursed on a blended fee-for-service/capitation basis. Although IPAs have been the fastest growing type of HMO, the research literature has generally focused on the older, more established HMOs, which are more likely to be group or staff models. However, the few studies of IPAs that have been done suggest that these HMOs have more admissions per thousand members, and thus are less effective in constraining costs.[14]

There is some question as to whether HMO cost reductions stem from selection bias, a type of adverse selection. Some employers offering both an HMO option and a comprehensive plan have claimed that employees who represent lower risk choose the HMO and higher risk employees remain in the comprehensive plan, resulting in higher overall health care costs. Researchers investigating the impact of various benefit options on premiums found that a group health plan offering an HMO option had significantly higher premiums for its fee-for-service plan. They concluded that their findings "support the growing evidence that HMOs experience favorable selection when offered as an alternative to conventional coverage."[15]

In another study, the Rand health insurance experiment randomly assigned individuals to an HMO and found that these had lower utilization rates than individuals in the indemnity plans, although not as low as individuals who chose the HMO. They found no differences in health outcomes between individuals enrolled in HMOs and those in indemnity plans with no cost sharing, with the exception of low-income individuals who entered the experiment in poor health. The Rand researchers concluded the cost differences resulted mainly from cost-effective practice styles rather than differences in enrollees. Other researchers have found little or no evidence of selection bias. Some have found that, to the extent adverse selection exists, it is the HMO that attracts higher risk participants.[16] The relative numbers of employees enrolled in HMOs and indemnity plans could be determined in EBRI's study of employers in Rhode Island. In that study, increases in the ratio of employees enrolled in HMOs to employees enrolled in the indemnity plans were related to increases in total indemnity plan charges.

Finally, two major studies have found that the rate of cost inflation is the same for HMOs as it is for more traditional insurance plans.[17] The authors of one of these studies argue that this result indicates that HMOs adopt new technology at the same rate as the fee-for-service plans.[18] Another possible explanation is that the information necessary to evaluate the cost-effectiveness of a new procedure is simply not available, even to providers with a clear financial incentive to adopt cost reducing techniques. Another possibility is that maintaining the HMO's market share in competition with fee-for-service care requires the adoption of the same types of practices. Conversely, recent surveys of employers found that HMO premium increases have been about five percentage points less than indemnity plan premium increases.[19]

Selectively Contracted Networks

New health care plans have been developed that combine attributes of HMOs with utilization review and objective performance criteria for selecting providers. CIGNA, United Healthcare, Prudential, and others have created plans that are similar to HMOs but allow enrollees to receive covered care from providers not in the panel. This arrangement provides employees choice without increasing the number of plans the employer must contract with. Several large employers, among them Allied-Signal and Southwestern Bell, have contracted with insurers to create nationwide provider networks for their employee health care plans.

One of the most important features of the selectively contracted networks is the criteria used to identify providers for inclusion in the network. Most networks require that providers agree to accept utilization review procedures, refer patients only to other providers in the network, and accept the reimbursement procedures of the network. The network will also have quality standards, such as board certification, that the provider will need to meet in order to be considered for inclusion. Finally, a provider's practice patterns may be monitored while in the network in order to identify and remove providers with unjustifiably high costs.

Objective information on the quality of care is being used by some employer plans to identify providers for selective contracting. Employers are contracting with specific hospitals for high cost procedures such as open heart surgeries and transplants. These hospitals are selected on a number of criteria including mortality and morbidity rates. In selectively contracting on the basis of these criteria, employers are explicitly using outcome measures for determining reimbursement. However, the use of unadjusted outcome measures as a criteria for selection has been challenged by providers because providers with sicker patients will appear to be of poorer quality. Firms such as MedisQual, Iameter, and others have developed systems to analyze medical records adjusting for the severity of illness. The outcomes achieved by hospitals and physicians can then be objectively compared to assess the quality and cost-effectiveness of care.

Selectively contracting with providers using objective criteria represents the first viable method for directly rewarding providers for low-cost, high quality health care. Navistar International provides a good example of how information is being used to contract with selected providers. Using hospital discharge data adjusted by Iameter, Navistar is able to compare both the outcomes and cost-effectiveness of each hospital with those of its competitors and with a state norm. This information, along with site visits, is then used to select hospitals for contracting. The outcomes information is also offered to the winning hospital to use in marketing their services to other selectively contracting employers and insurers.

COST MANAGEMENT AND THE MARKET FOR HEALTH CARE SERVICES

Cost containment efforts have not been uniformly adopted in local markets. One survey found that while 79 percent of employers in the Pacific region (California, Oregon, and Washington) and 77 percent of employers in the Mid-Atlantic region offered employees an HMO option, only 44 percent of the employers in the South Central region and 51 percent in the Mountain region offered an HMO. Conversely, only 11 percent of the employers in the New England region and 14 percent of the employers in the South Atlantic offered a preferred provider option (PPO) compared with 56 percent in the Pacific region.[20]

Some of these differences in regional availability and utilization of cost containment may be reflected in differences in total plan charges. For instance, the differences in charges attributed to inpatient care in Los Angeles relative to Houston (as cited earlier) may be an important indication of the differences in the markets for health care services and their effects on practice patterns. During the period under study, Houston had low HMO penetration rates, no PPOs, and a relatively large number of for-profit hospitals; Los Angeles, on the other hand, had a much higher HMO penetration rate, a number of provider networks, a Medicaid program that selectively contracted for hospital services, and three years more experience in developing utilization review programs. The results of these studies are consistent with other research on the relationship of market characteristics on the effectiveness of utilization review.[20]

The Los Angeles health care services market might be characterized as a more mature health care services market with respect to cost management than Houston. Inpatient charges accounted for over two-thirds of total plan charges for the employers in the Houston study, but less than half of the total plan charges for the Los Angeles employers. For Los Angeles employers, the presence of a mandatory utilization review program did not shift inpatient care to outpatient settings. In fact, UR decreased both inpatient and outpatient charges per claim, but did not affect the number of admissions or claims. The market penetration of HMOs, coupled with earlier implementation of utilization review programs, may have moved the Los Angeles market beyond the stage in which the result of utilization review is the shifting of care.

The "maturity" of the Los Angeles health care services market may also be reflected in the relationship between the cost sharing variables and plan charges. Patients may rely on their physician less in an ambulatory setting—physicians may recommend care, but may play less of a role in actually procuring it than they would if the patient were hospitalized. In an outpatient setting, patient compliance may be reduced; patients may feel more in control and be more likely to consider the economic incentives of their insurance plan. Finally, providers may be more actively competing on the basis of costs in the Los Angeles area than in other markets. The association of utilization review with both lower costs per admission and lower outpatient charges in Los Angeles suggests that providers may alter their practice patterns to reflect changes in the way payers are purchasing health care services.

Taken together, this evidence suggests that health care service markets are evolving as payers develop new mechanisms for evaluating and purchasing health care services. This evolution is unlikely to take the same path in every health care service market. Moreover, this evolution may determine the effects of cost management strategies on plan costs. For example, in markets where the effect of utilization review is to shift care to the outpatient sector the net effect will be to increase costs unless there is also some mechanism to control outpatient costs.

PRIVATE COST MANAGEMENT STRATEGIES AND NATIONAL HEALTH CARE COST INFLATION

It has often been observed that a decade of cost management has not seemed to slow health care cost inflation, but that proposition ignores the fact that cost management strategies have not been universally adopted. Employers have been hesitant to implement cost management strategies for several reasons. First, employee benefits are provided to attract and retain a particular quality of work force. Changes that make the benefit package less desirable affect employee morale in the short term, and the employer's competitiveness in the labor market in the longer term. Second, implementing many of these strategies, such as utilization review, are administratively costly—even evaluating the effectiveness of cost management strategies increases administrative costs. Finally, as discussed above, local health care service markets and an employer's relative market power in that health care market vary widely; what works in one market may be ineffective in another.

The question remains as to whether these cost management strategies will ever restrain health care cost inflation. The aging population, labor costs within the market for health care services, and the continual introduction of new technology all continue to drive up health care costs. Schwartz and Mendelson argue that cost management reduces unnecessary and inappropriate care and can achieve one-time savings, but does nothing to affect the underlying causes of health care cost increases.[21] Although in its infancy, the development of objective measures for evaluating the quality of care and for comparing health outcomes with the cost of treatment is beginning to affect the health care services market. It is likely that these measures will continue to be developed and improved. If they become widely employed in both the marketing and purchasing of health care services, they would greatly mitigate the current health care delivery system's wide variation in treatment for similar diagnoses, degree of inappropriate and unnecessary care, and cost disparity between competing providers.

1. Foster Higgins, 1991.

2. EBRI Notes, June 1991.

3. WS Custer, "Hospital Attributes and Physician Prices," 1986 *Southern Economic Journal* 52 (April 1986): 1010-27

4. DR Cohodes and BM Kinkead, *Hospital Capital Formation in the 1980s*, Baltimore: Johns Hopkins University Press, 1984

5. For a good review of the evidence, see J Wennberg and A Gittelson, "Variations in Medical Care among Small Areas," 1982 *Scientific American* 246 pp 120-135

6. MV Pauly, "Taxation, Health Insurance, and Market Failure in the Medical Economy" 24 *The Journal of Economic Literature* 2 (June 1986) pp 629-75

7. H Luft, JC Robinson, DW Garnick, RG Hughes, SJ McPhee, SH, and J Showstack, "Hospital Behavior in a Local Market Context," 43 *Medical Care Review* 2 (Fall 1986)

8. WG Manning, JP Newhouse, N Duan, EB Keeler, A Leibowitz, and MS Marquis, "Health Insurance and the Demand for Medical Care," 77 *The American Economic Review* 3 (June 1987) pp 251-76

9. I Strumwasser, N Paranjpe, D Ronis, D Share, and L Sell, "Reliability and Validity of Utilization Review Criteria: Appropriateness Evaluation Protocol, Standardized Medreview Instrument, and Intensity-Severity-Discharge Criteria," 28 *Medical Care* 2 (February 1990) pp 95-111

10. MAPI-Economic Report, "Health Care Costs and Cost Containment—Getting Specific," Washington, DC (June 1988)

11. PJ Feldstein, TM Wickizer, and JRC Wheeler, "Private Cost Containment: The Effects of Utilization Review Programs on Health Care Use and Expenditures," 318 *The New England Journal of Medicine* 20 (May 19, 1988) pp 1310-1314

12. RM Scheffler, JO Gibbs, and DA Gurnick, "The Impact of Medicare's Prospective Payment System and Private Sector Initiatives: Blue Cross Experience, 1980-1986," monograph from Blue Cross and Blue Shield Association and the Research Program in Health Economics, University of California, Berkeley, July 1988

13.   HS Luft, *Health Maintenance Organizations: Dimensions of Performance*, New York: John Wiley, 1981

14.   KM Langwell and LM Nelson, "Physician Payment Systems: A Review of History, Alternatives, and Evidence," 43 *Medical Care Review* 1 (Spring 1986) pp 5-58

15.   GA Jensen and MA Morrisey, "The Premium Consequences of Group Health Insurance Provisions," paper presented at the American Public Health Association meetings, Boston, November 14, 1988.

16.   *See, e.g.*, WP Welch and RG Frank, "The Predictors of HMO Enrollee Populations: Results for a National Sample," 23 *Inquiry* 1 pp 16-22 (Spring 1986) and SA Garfinkel, WE Schlenger, KR McLerory, FA Bryan, BJB York, GH Dunteman, and AS Friedlob, "Choices of Payment Plan in the Medicare Capitation Demonstration," 24 *Medical Care* 7 pp 628-640 (July 1986)

17.   JP Newhouse, WB Schwartz, AP Williams, and Christina Witsberger, "Are Fee-for-Service Costs Increasing Faster Than HMO Costs?" 23 *Medical Care* 8 (August 1985) pp 960-6619; *see also supra* note 8.

18.   Foster Higgins and HIAA study (to be published)

19.   JRC Wheeler and TM Wickizer, "Relating Health Care Market Characteristics to the Effectiveness of Utilization Review Programs," 27 *Inquiry* 4 (Winter 1990) pp 344-51

20.   Foster Higgins, 1989.

21.   WB Schwartz and D Mendelson, "Hospital Cost Containment in the 1980's: Hard Lessons Learned and Prospects for the 1990s," 324 *New England Journal of Medicine* 15 (April 11, 1991) pp 1037-42. This article appears in this book at pp 3-14.

Part 1

HEALTH CARE COST CONTROL: THE NATIONAL SETTING

1. Hospital Cost Containment in the 1980s: Hard Lessons Learned and Prospects for the 1990s

William B. Schwartz   Daniel N. Mendelson

The era of easy reductions in the number of inpatient days, with the associated attenuation of rising costs, is largely over. If further reductions in inpatient days are accompanied by an increase in the amount of ambulatory care similar to that during the past few years, the net savings will probably be negligible. Once the potential savings due to reductions in the number of inappropriate inpatient days has been exhausted, real hospital costs can be expected to rise, unless other effective measures to contain costs are implemented.

Throughout the 1980s, both the private sector and the federal government energetically attempted to contain the continuing increase in the costs of hospital care. A key part of their strategy has been to eliminate unnecessary hospital days and to shift as much care as possible from inpatient to outpatient settings. As a result of these efforts, the annual number of days patients spent in the hospital (inpatient days) fell, and the rate of increase in costs was slowed. On the basis of these findings, many observers believe that further efforts to eliminate inappropriate inpatient days, particularly through the use of new practice guidelines, can solve the problem of rising costs.

Reprinted, with permission, from THE NEW ENGLAND JOURNAL OF MEDICINE, Vol 324, No 15, April 11, 1991, pp 1037–1042.

We are indebted to Joseph P. Newhouse, Ph.D., Harvard Medical School, and Peter W. Van Etten, University of Massachusetts Medical Center, for their helpful comments and criticisms and to Bernice M. Golder for valuable assistance in the preparation of the manuscript.

3

In the present study we used published and unpublished data from the American Hospital Association (AHA) and the Health Care Financing Administration (HCFA) to address these issues. First, we assessed the degree to which the total number of inpatient days per year was reduced during the 1980s and the effect of this reduction on the increase in hospital costs. Second, we estimated the rate of increase in costs that would have occurred had there been no reduction in the number of inpatient days. Third, we calculated the increase in hospital costs that could be attributed to the increased use of outpatient services. Fourth, we compared the changes over time in Medicare expenditures and all other (non-Medicare) expenditures for hospital care. Finally, we estimated the potential savings from a further reduction in the total number of inpatient days per year.

THE NUMBER OF INPATIENT DAYS SAVED

We first examined the cumulative percentage of inpatient days saved during the 1980s. To calculate the savings, we measured the cumulative reduction in the total number of inpatient days per year between 1981, when admissions peaked, and 1988, the most recent year for which data were available. The beginning of this period also marked the initiation of major cost-containment efforts, including prospective payment by Medicare and a variety of efforts in the private sector.

The reduction in the number of inpatient days in community hospitals between 1981 and 1988 was 18.6 percent (Table 1).[1] Although striking in itself, this percentage understates the actual reduction because it does not take into account the fact that the number of inpatient days in acute care hospitals had been increasing in previous years. Between 1976 and 1981, the total number of inpatient days in community hospitals rose at an annual rate of 1.3 percent.[1] About 1 percentage point per year of this increase can be attributed to the growth and aging of the population, with the small remainder accounted for by other factors, such as technological innovation. Because the most important forces responsible for the historical increase in the annual number of inpatient days were acting throughout the 1980s, it is reasonable to assume that without cost-containment efforts the number of inpatient days would have continued to grow at a rate close to the historical rate.

The total effect of cost-containment programs as a percentage of the number of inpatient days in 1981 could thus be calculated as the difference between the actual cumulative reduction in the number of inpatient days since 1981 and the estimated cumulative increase in inpatient days that would otherwise have occurred during this period. Our calculations indicated that 28.1 percent of inpatient days had been eliminated by 1988 (Table 1). We call this sum the "imputed reduction" in days.

Table 1. Cumulative Changes in the Number of Inpatient Days per Year and the Contribution of Changes in Admissions and Length of Stay, 1981 through 1988.*

Category Of Change	Admissions	Length of Stay	Inpatient Days
		percent change	
Observed	− 13.4	− 5.2	− 18.6
Estimated	10.2	− 0.6	9.5
Imputed	− 23.6	− 4.6	− 28.1

*"Estimated" percentages indicate the change in the number of inpatient days that we estimated would have occurred in the absence of cost-containment efforts. "Imputed" percentages are the deviation of the observed change in the number of days from the historical upward trend—i.e., the algebraic difference between "observed" and "estimated" numbers of days. The percentages listed for admissions and length of stay represent the change in total inpatient days attributable to each of these factors. Because of rounding, the percentages for inpatient days are not always exactly equal to the sum of those for admissions and length of stay.

The annual savings in inpatient days, both observed and imputed, is shown in Figure 1. Each year from 1982 through 1985, the percentage of 1981 days saved increased dramatically; the largest savings occurred in 1985, when the imputed savings was 9.1 percent. In each of the following two years, the rate of savings slowed markedly, and by 1988 the imputed reduction in the number of inpatient days was only 1.5 percent.

Contribution of Changes in the Number of Admissions

The total number of inpatient admissions fell by 13.4 percent between 1981 and 1988 but would have increased by 10.2 percent over this period if the historical trend had persisted (Table 1). The cumulative savings in the number of inpatient admissions during this period was thus 23.6 percent. To calculate the portion of the observed change in the number of inpatient days that was caused by the decrease in the number of inpatient admissions, we multiplied the cumulative change in admissions by the average length of stay over the period from 1981 through 1988 and divided the result by the number of inpatient days in 1981. The estimated reduction was calculated on the basis of the annualized change in the number of admissions from 1976 through 1981.

On an annual basis, the imputed savings in the number of inpatient days that was due to reductions in admissions peaked in 1985, with a reduction 6.3 percent, and diminished during each subsequent year. Annual figures on the savings in inpatient days attributable to reductions in the number of admissions and the average length of stay are available elsewhere.[2]

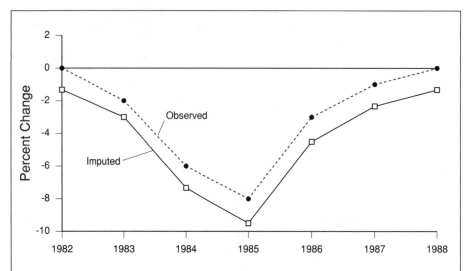

Figure 1. Observed and Imputed Reductions in the Number of Inpatient Days per Year, 1982 through 1988.

See the text for an explanation of the calculation of the imputed reduction in inpatient days. The solid circles indicate the observed reduction, and the open squares the imputed reduction.

Contribution of Changes in the Average Length of Stay

About 4.6 percentage points of the reduction in the number of inpatient days was due to reductions in the average length of hospital stays. The observed reduction was 5.2 percent, but on the basis of historical trends, the length of stay would have been expected to drop by 0.6 percentage point without cost-containment efforts (Table 1). To calculate the portion of the change in the number of inpatient days caused by reductions in length of stay, we multiplied the cumulative change in length of stay by the average number of admissions between 1981 and 1988 and divided the result by the average length of stay in 1981. Nearly all of these reductions were achieved in 1984 and 1985, and there were no reductions after 1985. In fact, during subsequent years the average length of stay increased slightly.

Savings in Inpatient Days According to Sector

There were considerable differences in the savings in inpatient days used by Medicare beneficiaries and patients not covered by Medicare (non-Medicare patients). To obtain the number of inpatient hospital days used by Medicare beneficiaries, we used unpublished figures on admissions to short-stay acute care hospitals from the HCFA[3] and published figures on the average length of stay for

Table 2. Aggregate Changes in the Number of Inpatient Days Used by Medicare and Non-Medicare Patients between 1982 and 1988.*

Category Of Change	Medicare	Non-Medicare
	percent change	
Observed	− 20.7	− 16.9
Estimated	20.4	− 1.5
Imputed	− 41.1	15.4

*"Estimated" percentages indicate the change in the number of inpatient days that would have occurred in the absence of cost-containment efforts. "Imputed" percentages indicated the deviation of the observed change in the number of days from the historical upward trend—i.e., the algebraic difference between "observed" and "estimated" numbers of days. "Non-Medicare" days are defined as the number of hospital days used by patients not covered by Medicare.

Medicare beneficiaries in short-stay acute care hospitals.[4] The number of inpatient days used by Medicare patients was subtracted from the total number of days used in the United States to obtain data for non-Medicare patients.

Between 1982 and 1988, the number of inpatient days used by Medicare patients was reduced by 20.7 percent from the levels in 1982, the year before cuts began in that sector (Table 2). When we calculated the deviation from the historical upward trend between 1976 and 1982, the cumulative imputed savings in the number of inpatient days for Medicare patients was 41.1 percent (Table 2). By contrast, the savings in the number of inpatient days used by non-Medicare patients between 1982 and 1988 was only 15.4 percent. Because there was no increase in the number of inpatient days used in the non-Medicare sector between 1976 and 1982, the imputed reduction in the number of days was close to the observed figure (Table 2).

THE OBSERVED AND UNDERLYING RATES OF INCREASE IN COSTS

The dramatic reductions in the number of inpatient days per year, documented above, raise a crucial question: Did these efforts have an effect on hospital costs? To answer this question, we first looked at what actually happened to hospital costs during the 1980s. We then estimated the increase in costs that would have occurred in the absence of reductions in the number of inpatient days.

The Observed Increase in Costs

The annual real increase in community-hospital costs is shown in Figure 2.[1, 5] During the five-year period immediately before 1982, the average annual increase in hospital costs was 6.1 percent. In 1982 costs rose by 8.7 percent, but by 1984

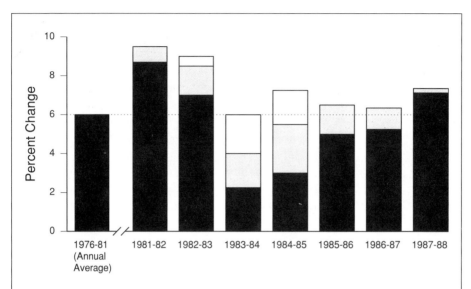

Figure 2. Observed and Underlying Annual Increases in Real Hospital Costs, 1976 through 1988.

The solid portion of each bar represents the observed rate of increase. The hatched and open portions represent the real savings due to the reduction in the number of inpatient days; the hatched portion shows the savings that resulted from a reduction in the number of admissions, and the open portion the savings that resulted from a reduction in the average length of stay. The full height of each bar indicates the underlying rate of increase in costs, as described in the text. The dotted line indicates the average annual increase from 1976 to 1981.

the annual increase in costs had fallen to a low of 2.2 percent. It then rose steadily, reaching 7.2 percent by 1988. All dollar figures reported here have been adjusted to eliminate the influence of economy-wide inflation.[5]

THE UNDERLYING RATE OF INCREASE IN COSTS

To what degree can the attenuation in the rate of increase in costs in the mid-1980s be attributed to reductions in the number of inpatient days per year? To answer this question, we estimated the increase in costs that would have occurred if there had been no reduction in inpatient days. We call this value the "underlying" rate of increase in costs. This value was calculated by adding the dollar savings due to the reduced number of inpatient days to the observed increase in costs (Figure 2).[1, 5]

The dollar savings due to reductions in the number of inpatient days was calculated by multiplying the percent reduction in the number of days by an estimate of how much costs are reduced when inpatient days are eliminated. To measure the reduction in days, we used the number of "adjusted patient days"—a figure calculated by the AHA to take into account both inpatient days and outpatient visits. As discussed earlier, we estimated the savings in adjusted patient days as the deviation from the increase between 1976 and 1981. To measure the reduction in costs that resulted from a decrease in the number of hospital days, we started with an estimate of what the typical hospital might expect to save, after adjusting to the new level of occupancy (typically called the "long-run marginal cost"). Pauly and Wilson have estimated that the long-run marginal cost of a hospital day is 90 percent of the average cost[6]; the difference between this value and the average cost is accounted for by fixed costs (such as those of administration, insurance, and heat), which persist in the face of small reductions in the occupancy rate. There are, however, two factors that probably caused the savings to hospitals to be lower during this period. First, it takes time for hospitals to adjust to operating efficiently after making reductions in the number of patient days. Second, it is possible that the cost of the patient days eliminated during this period was lower than that of the typical marginal hospital day, because the patients may have been less sick than average. For this reason, we assumed that the cost of the days saved was only 65 percent of the average patient day. We thus calculated the savings achieved by the reduction in the number of inpatient days by multiplying the percent reduction in adjusted patient days by 0.65.

The annual savings due to the reduced number of inpatient days is shown as the upper (hatched and open) portions of each bar in Figure 2 (the upper portion is divided into savings from reduced admissions and reduced length of stay). The total height of each bar represents the increase in costs that would have occurred if there had been no reduction in the number of adjusted patient days. In every year between 1982 and 1988, the underlying rate of increase exceeded 6 percent, the real increase in costs between 1976 and 1981. The attenuation of the rate of increase in costs in the mid-1980s can thus be attributed entirely to the reduction in the number of inpatient days.

The Effect of Outpatient Care within the Hospital

As the number of inpatient days has fallen, the number of outpatient visits to the hospital has risen. Figure 3 shows the effect of this phenomenon on costs; the reduction in costs due to fewer inpatient days is plotted downward, whereas the offsetting increase in costs from increased visits for ambulatory care is plotted upward. We used annual data from the AHA[1] to calculate the increase in outpatient costs and adjusted for economy-wide inflation as described above.[4] As shown in Figure 3, the increase in costs due to the increase in outpatient visits remained at about 1.2 percentage points per year between 1984 and 1988.

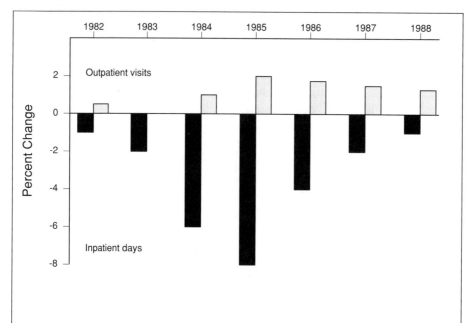

Figure 3. Impact on Hospital Costs of Reductions in the Number of Inpatient Days and Increases in the Number of Outpatient Visits, 1982 through 1988.

The solid bars show the reductions in costs due to fewer inpatient days, and the hatched bars the changes in costs due to increased outpatient visits.

The Increase in Medicare and Non-Medicare Costs

The pattern of increases in costs for the Medicare and non-Medicare sectors over time has changed remarkably. To assess Medicare spending on hospital care, we obtained unpublished data on actual disbursements to acute care hospitals for inpatient care under Medicare Part A[7, 8] and on spending for outpatient care for beneficiaries of Supplementary Medical Insurance (Medicare Part B).[9] We aggregated data on inpatient and outpatient care in order to make our figures compatible with the total expenditures for care at community hospitals reported by the AHA. We used actual disbursements to acute care hospitals rather than the standard time series on Medicare hospital spending published in the HCFA review, because the published data included spending on long-term care hospitals, home care, and other facilities not included in the AHA data.[10]

Table 3 shows the rates of increase in overall spending for hospital services by Medicare and by all payers other than Medicare. Between 1976 and 1982, Medicare expenditures rose by 9.2 percent per year, whereas non-Medicare expenditures rose by 4.6 percent per year. By 1987 and 1988, this pattern had been reversed; Medicare expenditures for hospital services rose by only 0.6 percent per year, whereas non-Medicare spending rose by about 9.0 percent per year.

Table 3. Observed Annual Increases in Real Hospital Costs in the Medicare and Non-Medicare Sectors, 1976 through 1988.*

Year†	Medicare	Non-Medicare
	percent change	
1976–1981	9.2	4.6
1982	10.0	8.2
1983	5.8	7.3
1984	5.0	0.8
1985	7.7	0.2
1986	3.0	5.8
1987	– 9.2	8.7
1988	3.5	8.9

*These figures include the costs of both inpatient and outpatient care, as explained in the text. Figures for non-Medicare costs were derived by subtracting Medicare costs from total costs.

†The 1976–1981 percentages are the annualized increases during this period. The percentages for 1982 through 1988 are the percent increases from the previous year.

DISCUSSION

Between 1981 and 1988, a period of intense cost-containment efforts, there was an observed decrease of 19 percent in the total number of inpatient hospital days. This figure understates the real savings, however, because inpatient days have historically been increasing by more than 1 percent annually and would have been expected to continue increasing in the absence of cost-containment efforts. In terms of the deviation from the historical upward trend, we estimated that inpatient days were reduced by more than 28 percent between 1981 and 1988.

The year-by-year pattern of reductions is perhaps of even greater relevance, since it suggests that further savings will be difficult to achieve. After a steady increase in the percentage of days saved through 1985, the fraction of days saved shrank each year, so that by 1988 there was virtually no further savings (Figure 1). This near-halt in the number of inpatient days saved merits particular attention, because it occurred in the face of continuous expansion of managed care and other initiatives designed to reduce the number of inpatient days overall.

Figure 2 shows the effect of the reduction in inpatient days on the increase in hospital costs. The solid bars, depicting the increase in real costs, indicate that the increase in costs slowed from a historical average of over 6 percent per year to about 2 percent per year by 1985. By 1988, the increase in costs had returned to a level above 6 percent.

A comparison with Figure 1 indicates that it was during the years in which the increase in costs was slowed that the bulk of the savings in the number of inpatient days was realized. The hatched bars quantify this observation by adding to the real increase the estimated additional increase in costs that would have occurred in the absence of reductions in the number of inpatient days.

The full height of each bar in Figure 2 thus represents our estimate of the increase in costs that would have occurred if there had been no reduction in the number of inpatient days. This value, which we call the "underlying" rate of increase in costs, exceeded 6 percent in each year throughout the 1980s. Because in the late 1980s this value was not appreciably different from that in the late 1970s and early 1980s, we conclude that efforts to contain costs did little to limit expenditures beyond decreasing the total number of inpatient days per year. Moreover, it seems likely that the upward pressure on costs will continue in the future, as a result of wage increases required to attract and hold personnel, a wave of expensive new forms of technology, a growing number of patients with the acquired immunodeficiency syndrome, and a new commitment to insurance coverage for the uninsured and underinsured.

Our calculations include only changes in expenditures for acute care in hospitals and do not indicate the overall effect of these changes on system-wide expenditures for health care. When care is transferred to free-standing ambulatory care facilities and physicians' offices, the resulting costs partially offset the savings accomplished in hospital-based care. Because there are no readily available measures of care shifted to settings outside the hospital, we have been unable to calculate the net savings to society.

Prospects for Future Savings in the Number of Inpatient Days

The sharp slowing in the number of inpatient days saved per year (Figure 1) suggests that a further substantial reduction in inpatient days will be hard to achieve unless new practice guidelines are successfully implemented. We also believe that the data indicate that whatever further reductions are likely to be achieved will have only a limited and transient effect on costs.

To illustrate this point, we estimated the effect on costs of saving a total of 20 percent more inpatient days between 1989 and 1995, for a total reduction of nearly 50 percent of inpatient days since 1981. Assuming that each day eliminated saves 65 percent of the cost of an average day of inpatient care, the increase in expenditures would be reduced by 2 percentage points annually. But because a decrease in the number of inpatient days would almost inevitably be accompanied by an increase in visits for ambulatory care (Figure 3), a reduction of this magnitude would probably not be observed. If the increase in the number of visits for ambulatory care were equal to that in 1987 and 1988, much or all of the savings from cutbacks in inpatient care would be offset.

Equally important, if by the mid-1990s we are successful in eliminating nearly all remaining inappropriate inpatient days, no further cutbacks will be available to mask the underlying rate of increase in costs. Only if other cost-containment measures are put in place will the control of costs be possible.

Differences between the Medicare and Non-Medicare Sectors

The aggregate figures just discussed conceal important differences between the rate of increase in Medicare and non-Medicare expenditures. Most notably, between 1982 and 1988 the number of inpatient days used by Medicare patients fell by 41 percent, whereas the number of days used by non-Medicare patients fell by only 15 percent (Table 2). This finding indicates either that most of whatever days remain to be saved are in the non-Medicare sector, or that the fraction of unnecessary days originally present in the Medicare sector was substantially larger than that in the non-Medicare sector.

The pattern of increase in costs in the two sectors was also remarkably different. Between 1976 and 1982, real costs to Medicare rose at about twice the rate in the non-Medicare sector; between 1982 and 1988 the situation was completely reversed. Medicare expenditures under the prospective payment system fell steadily, so that by 1987 and 1988 the increase averaged only 0.6 percent per year. By contrast, the increase in non-Medicare expenditures accelerated to almost 9 percent per year during this period. It is important to note that the large increases in Medicare costs that have been reported in the popular press have been driven to a considerable extent by Medicare payments to physicians, which rose by more than 11 percent annually in 1987 and 1988.[11]

These data clearly indicate that the private sector is carrying a steadily increasing share of the responsibility for maintaining the quality of care for both Medicare and non-Medicare patients in the hospital. How long this burden will be accepted by private payers remains uncertain.

1. Hospital statistics, 1976-1988 editions. Chicago: American Hospital Association, 1976-1988.

2. See NAPS document no. 04857 for two pages of supplementary material. Order from NAPS c/o Microfiche Publications, P.O. Box 3513, Grand Central Station, New York, NY 10163-3513. Remit in advance (in U.S. funds only) $7.75 for photocopies or $4 for microfiche. Outside the U.S. and Canada add postage of $4.50 ($1.50 for microfiche postage). There is an invoicing charge of $15 on orders not prepaid. This charge includes purchase orders.

3. Bureau of Data Management and Strategy. Table AN-3A: number of admission notices processed since 7/1/66 by state and calendar year as of August 1989. Baltimore, Md.: Health Care Financing Administration.

4. *Id*. The Medicare decision support system: Medicare short-stay hospital utilization trends. Health care financing data compendium, 1989 update. Baltimore, Md.: Health Care Financing Administration.

5. Department of Commerce, Bureau of Economic Analysis. Economic report of the President transmitted to the Congress, February 1990. Washington, D.C.: Government Printing Office, 1990:298.

6. MV Pauly, P Wilson Hospital output forecasts and the cost of empty hospital beds. Health Serv Res 1986; 21:403-28.

7. Bureau of Data Management and Strategy. Annual Medicare program statistics reimbursement tables. Baltimore, Md.: Health Care Financing Administration, 1986.

8. *Id*. Table AA4-TOTAL: hospital insurance, number of inpatient hospital bills, total and covered days of care, total and covered charges and amount reimbursed by period, expense incurred, and type of hospital as of August 25, 1989. Baltimore, Md.: Health Care Financing Administration.

9. *Id*. SMI-1 Medicare: estimated supplementary medical insurance disbursements, calendar years 1966-1988. Baltimore, Md.: Health Care Financing Administration, June 21, 1989.

10. Office of National Cost Estimates. National health expenditures, 1988. Health Care Financ Rev 1990; I1(4):20.

11. *Id*. National health expenditures, 1988. Health Care Financ Rev 1990; 11(4):33.

2. Making Health Insurance Available to Small Employees: Robert Wood Johnson Foundation Demonstration Projects

W. David Helms   Daniel M. Campion   Victoria D. Weisfeld

The main reason small firms don't offer health insurance is its cost. This program showed that attractive insurance products could be developed for the working uninsured. Both government subsidies and reforms of the small group market are needed in order to maximize the potential benefit of this approach. An incremental strategy, it falls short of the "universal coverage" ideal.

The Health Care for the Uninsured Program (HCUP) was launched by The Robert Wood Johnson Foundation in 1986 to support state and local projects intended to make health insurance more accessible and affordable. Through this five-year, $8.4 million national demonstration and its accompanying evaluation, the Foundation sought to encourage and assess a variety of public/private sector strategies that had the potential both to become self-sustaining and to be replicated in other locales. Fifteen such projects were funded, with seven of the grants going to states, one to a city, and seven to private organizations.

The program was co-sponsored by the National Governors' Association, the National Conference of State Legislatures, the U.S. Conference of Mayors, and the National Association of Counties. These groups promoted the program among their members and helped elicit proposals. Their representatives served on the

This article is excerpted from a SPECIAL REPORT based on the experience of the 15 projects in The Robert Wood Johnson Foundation's Health Care for the Uninsured Program, reports of its administrators and evaluators, interviews with participants and other key individuals, a series of interviews with federal policymakers, and reports in the published literature.

15

Foundation's National Advisory Committee, along with representatives from federal, state, and local government, the insurance industry, health care providers, and the health policy and research communities. This committee reviewed proposals and assisted in providing technical assistance to funded projects.

As intended, the 15 HCUP projects proposed varied strategies, but ultimately, they targeted one specific population group: the working uninsured and their families. All of the projects except Washington State's concentrated on the large number of uninsured people who are employees of small firms. Many projects dealt with very small firms (those having 10 or fewer workers), which account for nearly half of uninsured workers and dependents.

In this country, a person's employer is the usual source of health insurance. Many small businesses, which tend to be newer and less fiscally stable, with few or no administrative personnel, can't afford to offer coverage to their employees. In fact, 90 percent of firms that do not offer a health insurance benefit have fewer than 10 employees. Their employees, who tend to be lower-wage workers—two thirds of uninsured workers earn less than $10,000 per year—cannot afford to pay for coverage, either. Given the choice, such workers might well prefer higher wages to an insurance benefit that typically costs $4,000 per year.

Because of the dominance of employment-based health insurance in the U.S. health financing system, all 15 HCUP projects ultimately focused on improving insurance options for small employers or self-employed individuals. These efforts presaged the current state and federal push for reforms, noted above.

By the beginning of 1992, HCUP projects had enrolled more than 26,000 people, most of whom had no health insurance coverage in the previous six to 12 months. They were the employees—or the employees' dependents—of nearly 5,500 small businesses. In addition, the Washington Basic Health Plan, which received developmental funding under the HCUP, has reached its enrollment maximum, set by the state legislature, of 22,000. While these enrollment figures make the tiniest dent in the number of uninsured Americans, the projects' more significant contribution has been to the understanding of the insurance needs of small businesses and what it takes to reach them.

Among the program's key findings and lessons are the following:

- The main reason that small employers say they do not offer health insurance is its high cost
- Small firms that do not offer insurance are concentrated in certain industries and tend to employ women, low-wage, and part-time workers
- Public/private partnerships to expand health insurance for the small-employer market are difficult and time-consuming to develop
- Managed care systems like HMOs are generally more receptive to forming such partnerships and offer more appropriate coverages than indemnity insurers

- To keep premiums low for small employers, private insurers use various means to exclude individuals and groups they believe are high-risk (and, therefore, potentially costly)
- Extensive marketing is needed, not only to attract small business owners but also their uninsured workers and dependents
- Although low-cost, very limited benefit packages ("bare-bones" packages) can be developed, few small employers are interested in purchasing them—they want hospital coverage and outpatient benefits as generous as those that large employers can offer
- To extend insurance coverage to low-income workers, direct premium subsidies may be needed
- Premium costs also can be reduced through various indirect subsidies that defray the higher administrative and marketing costs of the small-group market
- Voluntary efforts alone appear unlikely to produce universal access to health insurance; the most successful HCUP projects believe they can reach only about 20 percent of working uninsured people in their market areas, even though their premiums are considerably below market rates
- Finally, projects have found that enrollees' utilization of health services so far is lower than anticipated and below national averages

THE PROGRAM

The Robert Wood Johnson Foundation's Health Care for the Uninsured Program was intended to help provide new public/private health care financing and service delivery arrangements in states and large urban areas. When the Foundation issued its call for proposals in January 1986, it did not require that applicants follow any specific strategy nor target any particular uninsured group. However, the Foundation did want to fund projects that would become self-sustaining—particularly ones that could achieve permanent financing—and that could be replicated elsewhere.

The strategies proposed by the applicants reflected the political realities that they faced. There was little federal support for expanding programs like Medicaid to cover low-income workers. Nor could state governments, many of which face severe budget shortfalls, invest in major new health insurance programs. HCUP projects therefore took an incremental approach, working within the constraints of the existing employer-based health insurance system.

In developing their public/private partnerships, the grantees had to analyze the problems of the small-employer insurance market, forge myriad new relationships with providers and insurers, and closely monitor their results. Their challenges included:

- Finding out why small employers in their market areas do not provide coverage to their employees and what kinds of insurance products and incentives would be appropriate and attractive
- Establishing networks of providers
- Negotiating payment arrangements and utilization control mechanisms
- Persuading an insurer or managed care partner to underwrite and sponsor their product or products
- Working out agreements with providers, insurers, and government agencies regarding benefits and premiums, as well as arrangements for cost-sharing, medical underwriting, and reinsurance,
- Developing marketing strategies aimed at both employers and employees.

Now, about five years since the program began, these projects have enrolled more than 48,000 people employed in some 5,500 firms, including 22,000 covered by the Washington Basic Health Plan.

Major Strategies

During the planning phase, HCUP projects surveyed small employers to find out more about the health insurance market in their locales. The cost of health insurance premiums was the number one reason business owners cited for not offering this employee benefit.

Projects also learned that many insurers are not interested in serving the very small business market because of higher administrative costs and fears that plans covering these groups attract a disproportionate share of high-cost users (adverse selection).

If the demonstration projects were going to expand coverage among small businesses, clearly they would have to figure out ways to keep premium costs and insurers' concerns at a minimum. To accomplish this, they developed a variety of key strategies:

- *Limited benefits.* Limited-benefit plans typically emphasize basic primary and preventive care and hospital inpatient services. A few plans, notably Alabama's, also have restrictions on the number of inpatient days or physician office visits covered. In addition, some plans exclude benefits for mental health and substance abuse services, as well as dental and vision care.
- *Major cost-sharing.* Although most of the plans keep copayments and deductibles low, in order to encourage employees to purchase coverage, two projects—Colorado's SCOPE and the Utah Community Health Plan—require major cost-sharing. They chose this approach in order to keep the total premium low and to encourage enrollees to seek the preventive and primary care services that may reduce the need for costly hospital and specialty care.
- *Limited provider networks.* The managed care arrangements developed with health maintenance organizations (HMOs) or preferred provider organiza-

tions (PPOs) typically use physician gatekeepers to provide primary care services, control hospital admissions, and refer patients to specialists. The Alabama and Utah projects further restrict enrollees' choices by relying on a limited group of low-cost providers, such as community health centers or public hospitals.

- *Direct premium subsidies.* In four state-sponsored projects (Maine, Michigan, Washington, and Wisconsin) the state government (augmented in Michigan's case by funds from the Charles Stewart Mott Foundation) subsidizes premiums for low-income enrollees using a sliding fee scale. The Florida program uses state funds to subsidize dependent coverage.

- *Indirect subsidies.* Three states (Arizona, Florida, and Maine) indirectly subsidize premiums by helping projects with administrative and marketing costs. Pooling small employees into a single organized buying cooperative, as is done in Florida, lowers insurers' overhead and gives employers greater bargaining power. All three states have helped projects purchase reinsurance or provided stop-loss protection to reduce the risk of adverse selection.

- *Provider discounts.* Projects negotiated discounts from providers, especially hospitals. In return, participating hospitals are assured of receiving at least partial payment for treating people who otherwise might be unable to pay anything at all.

- *Links to state high-risk pools.* Twenty-six states have established insurance pools to cover people deemed "uninsurable" due to various medical conditions. Several projects created mechanisms for referring eligible people to these high-risk pools and subsidizing the difference between the project's premium and the pool's higher one.

- *Insurance information and referral.* As an adjunct to their demonstration programs, some projects provide general information on insurance and refer interested businesses to insurance brokers. The San Francisco project is testing whether a health insurance brokering and information service alone, using available plans, will increase coverage in the small employer market.

Projects' success with these strategies varied, as measured by the number of enrollees and their ability to maintain the support of the parties subsidizing and underwriting their efforts.

PROJECT DESCRIPTIONS

Eleven of the 15 HCUP projects moved from planning and development to implementation. As described below, ten projects tested strategies to make health insurance more affordable and one developed a health insurance information and referral service. The remaining four projects were unable to implement their strategies, largely because of difficulties in securing an underwriter or in obtaining state support for the subsidy arrangements they proposed.

Limiting Benefits and Using Public Providers to Keep Premiums Low

Central Alabama Coalition: BasicCare

The Central Alabama Coalition for the Medically Uninsured markets a very limited benefit plan, called BasicCare, to uninsured small businesses with three or more employees in metropolitan Birmingham. The project offers one model for low-income communities where direct premium subsidies are unavailable and public assistance programs inadequate.

BasicCare does not restrict the types of services covered, but their quantity. The plan covers basic outpatient medical services (six physician office visits per year), hospital inpatient services (up to ten days per year), maternity and emergency care, and prescription drugs.

Employers can choose between a public and a private delivery network. The public network relies on five county-sponsored health clinics for primary care and the county and university hospitals for most acute care. Benefits and cost-sharing provisions are the same in both networks, but premiums are about 40 percent lower for the public option.

Complete Health, Inc., Alabama's largest commercial HMO, underwrites BasicCare and began enrolling employers in March 1990.

Subsidizing Administrative and Marketing Costs to Keep Premiums Low

Arizona: Health Care Group

Arizona's Health Care Group was created by Arizona's Medicaid program (AHCCCS) to provide affordable insurance to workers in small firms and their families through prepaid, managed-care health plans already under contract with the state to provide services to Medicaid beneficiaries. The model shows that a state can help reduce premiums by subsidizing administrative and marketing expenses and by facilitating the purchase of reinsurance. In this case, the state worked with the reinsurer that underwrites AHCCCS.

The project collects monthly premium payments, provides technical assistance to participating managed care organizations, conducts limited marketing, and tracks enrollment. It finances these activities through in-kind contributions from the state and an "administrative fee" included in employers' premiums.

Employers have a choice of four benefit packages, ranging from a traditional HMO plan, with a focus on preventive and primary care, to what amounts to a catastrophic-care only plan. The four plans differ substantially in copayments, deductibles, and premiums.

In January 1988, enrollment began in the Tucson area, expanding two years later to rural Cochise County and metropolitan Phoenix.

Referring Small Employers to Existing Insurance Plans

United Way of the Bay Area, San Francisco, California: Health Insurance Information and Referral Service
Rather than develop a new insurance product for the working uninsured, as other HCUP projects have done, San Francisco's Bay Area Health Task Force steers uninsured small employers toward existing health insurance plans through its education, information, and referral services.

The Task Force, a United Way-sponsored organization, has published a health insurance guidebook for small employers that includes general information on insurance and specific data on premiums, benefits, and underwriting criteria of selected plans. It also has cultivated a network of agents and brokers who will try to meet the health insurance needs of small employers. The project has passed on to brokers more than 1,000 leads generated by direct mail promotions to 40,000 small businesses in San Francisco and an additional 23,000 in San Mateo County.

In September 1989 the project opened an Employer Health Insurance Hotline for San Francisco, providing information about available health insurance options and participating brokers. After 20 months, the hotline had received some 3,000 calls. About 750 of these callers were referred to brokers; of these, 255 enrolled in new insurance plans covering 875 employees.

The project developed additional agent/broker referral networks in Marin County in September 1990, in San Mateo County in December 1990, and in Alameda and Contra Costa Counties in August 1991.

Reducing Premiums for a Comprehensive Insurance Plan Through Major Cost-Sharing

Colorado: SCOPE
Colorado's SCOPE (Shared Cost Option for Private Employers) project illustrates how major cost-sharing can reduce premiums substantially. Sponsored initially by the Denver Department of Health and Hospitals and underwritten by the United States Life Insurance Company, the project began marketing in the Denver area in August 1989. It had expanded to all of the state's major metropolitan areas by March 1990. SCOPE is a modified HMO product developed under the HCUP.

Premium rates for SCOPE are 50 to 60 percent of those of traditional policies available to small firms in the Denver area. Aware that the state would not be providing subsidies for premium costs, project planners had to keep premiums low by other means: high coinsurance and deductibles for inpatient care, discounts from providers, and hospital care coverage only if provided at more cost-efficient facilities.

SCOPE is a cross between a catastrophic plan and an HMO. Preventive services are covered in full, while most other physician visits require a $15 copayment. For inpatient care, enrollees pay a $250 deductible. For most services other than preventive care and physician visits, enrollees must pay 50-percent coinsurance on the first $5,000 in charges (after any deductibles). The state's indigent care fund subsidizes the cost-sharing obligations of low-income enrollees.

Using a State Buying Cooperative to Reduce Premiums for Small Firms

Florida Health Access Corporation: Florida Health Access

The Florida Health Access Corporation (FHAC) was established by the state legislature in 1987 to develop an affordable insurance program for the working uninsured. The project pools small employers into a single large buying group, which gives important negotiating leverage, and has reduced insurance costs 25 to 40 percent through various subsidies.

FHAC has taken over the administrative functions of providing insurance to the target market and shares the cooperating insurers' risks. It markets its plans through insurance agents, screens applications, underwrites premiums, bills employers, collects their payments, and services enrollees' accounts. It uses state funds to purchase reinsurance and partially subsidizes dependent coverage.

FHAC products are sold in 16 counties under the name Florida Health Access. In some locations, employers have a choice between a standard plan and a high-option plan, which has higher premiums but lower copayments. Av-Med Health Plans, Inc., a Florida-based nonprofit HMO, is the underwriter for Florida Health Access at its original site in Tampa (where enrollment began in May 1989), as well as in St. Petersburg, Clearwater, Gainesville, and Orlando. Capital Health Plan sponsors the plan in Tallahassee. Project staff hope eventually to make Florida Health Access available statewide.

Using Direct and Indirect Subsidies to Reduce Costs

Maine Managed Care Insurance Demonstration: MaineCare

MaineCare, developed by the Maine Department of Human Services and the University of Southern Maine's Human Services Development Institute, is a state-subsidized managed care program for small employers and the self-employed that uses both direct and indirect subsidies to make coverage more affordable. Healthsource Maine, Inc., a private, for-profit HMO, sponsors the insurance plan at two sites and provides health services to enrollees.

The project reduced Healthsource's usual premium rates indirectly through a variety of means: purchasing reinsurance, negotiating discounts and risk-sharing arrangements with providers, and assuming some administrative and marketing functions. For example, the state pays the salary of one marketing representative at each site who is responsible for selling MaineCare, enrolling new members, and servicing accounts.

Direct premium subsidies are available on a sliding scale for employees with household incomes between 100 and 200 percent of the federal poverty line. For workers at or below 100 percent of the poverty level, the state and the employer split the premium equally, and employees pay nothing. Part-time workers and self-employed individuals also may be eligible for subsidized premiums. In addition, certain low-profit small businesses may receive premium reductions if they hire people from state job training and placement programs.

The project minimizes medical underwriting, and most applicants with pre-existing conditions—including pregnant women—are accepted into the program. Those with catastrophic conditions are referred to the state high-risk pool. Depending on income and family size, such people may be eligible for premium reductions, and employers are expected to contribute to their premium payments.

After opening enrollment in December 1988 in the Bath/Brunswick area, in February 1991 the project began enrolling people in rural Skowhegan/Somerset County as well.

Covering Former Welfare Recipients and Low-Wage Workers

Michigan: One-Third Share Plan

The One-Third Share Plan, which operated from January 1988 until March 1991, was a state-subsidized health insurance program for uninsured former welfare recipients and other low-wage workers. It was one of six separate initiatives to improve and expand access to health care for these groups sponsored by the state Department of Social Services and the Michigan League for Human Services.

Under the One-Third Share Plan, employers hiring a former Medicaid or general assistance client could receive a subsidy from pooled public/private funds to help cover the insurance costs for all their low-income workers. Employers could choose among a number of indemnity and HMO plans approved by an oversight committee. The amount of the subsidy depended on the actual premium and the employee's income. For employees below 100 percent of the poverty line, the employer paid one-third of the premium, and the state paid two-thirds; for those between 101 and 200 percent of poverty, the employer, the state, and the employee each paid one-third; for those above 200 percent of poverty, employers paid one-third and employees two-thirds.

The state marketed the project to employers in the Flint area and in rural Marquette County. At its peak, more than 200 companies and 1,100 previously uninsured individuals participated. Because of the state's fiscal crisis, as of March 1991 the subsidies were no longer available; enrollees who could not afford their premiums have since lost coverage.

Substantial Hospital Discounts and Limited Benefits Reduce Premiums

Tennessee Primary Care Association: MedTrust

The Tennessee Primary Care Association, working with the Tennessee Primary Care Network—a private, nonprofit HMO serving Medicaid recipients—developed an affordable, comprehensive benefit plan, called MedTrust, for uninsured small businesses and self-employed individuals in the Memphis area. The project's primary strategy for reducing the cost of insurance was to negotiate deep discounts from hospitals already serving the uninsured.

The Regional Medical Center, a public hospital, provides inpatient services to MedTrust enrollees for about 80 percent less than normal charges, and two other hospitals provide discounted specialty services. The project has contracted with primary care physicians from a large, four-site private group practice, two non-profit health clinics, and four private practices to provide capitated primary care services.

The MedTrust benefit package covers most basic outpatient services, including maternity care, and requires a $5 copayment per office visit. Hospital inpatient services require a $200 copayment per admission; emergency room visits require $25. Enrollees may purchase supplemental coverage for substance abuse and mental health services. Enrollment began in March 1989.

Hospital Discounts And a Limited Provider Network Reduce Premiums

Intermountain Health Care Foundation: Utah Community Health Plan

The Utah Community Health Plan (UCHP) is a comprehensive, low-cost HMO available to previously uninsured small business employees and their dependents in the Salt Lake City area since September 1989. The plan was developed by Intermountain Health Care, a large private, nonprofit health care provider system. UCHP illustrates how such a large organization can develop products for small businesses by using a subsidized ambulatory care network (community health centers) and hospital discounts.

UCHP has negotiated substantial discounts from the limited provider network it developed. Enrollees choose a primary care provider from seven community health clinics and five private physicians, all of whom receive a monthly capitated fee. Specialty physicians and laboratories receiving referrals from these primary care providers are paid 65 percent of billed charges. UCHP also pays six participating hospitals 65 percent of billed charges for the first 30 inpatient days, with the hospitals' providing care free thereafter.

The project also keeps premiums low by controlling administrative and marketing costs. These costs account for only 16 percent of the project's premium, compared to around 30 percent for other HMOs serving the small group market.

Finally, in order to achieve premiums that are 40 percent lower than those of comparable plans, UCHP requires major cost-sharing, especially for inpatient services. For example, under its high-option plan, copayments for ambulatory care are modest ($10 for primary care office visits and $20 for specialists), but copayments for hospital care are $150 per day for the first four days, and for inpatient maternity care, $350 per day for the first three days. UCHP's low-option plan has less expensive premiums, but copayments are even higher.

Direct Subsidies Enable Coverage of Low-Income, Uninsured Individuals

Washington State: Basic Health Plan

In 1986 Seattle's Health Systems Resources received a two-year grant to organize existing HMOs or other area health care providers into new primary care networks at three test sites. Once formed, these managed care systems would be eligible to apply to the state to become providers under a proposed state-subsidized insurance program for the uninsured. In February 1987, the state legislature approved the program, called the Washington Basic Health Plan (BHP).

The state sets premiums after negotiating rates with various managed health care systems serving plan members. BHP members pay premiums according to a sliding fee schedule based on a family's size, age of its members, gross income, and area of residence.

BHP began enrollment in January 1989 in King (Seattle) and Spokane Counties and has now expanded to 11 service delivery areas. By March 1991, just 26 months after enrollment began, the BHP reached its legislatively set limit of 22,000 members.

Direct Premium Subsidies and Links to High-Risk Pool Reduce Premiums

Wisconsin: Small Employer Health Insurance Maximization Project

The Small Employer Health Insurance Maximization Project sponsored by the Wisconsin Department of Health and Social Services did not create new insurance products, but relied instead on existing indemnity or managed care products that met special criteria established by the state insurance commissioner. It provided direct premium subsidies to low-income employees of participating businesses. Any worker rejected from group coverage due to a pre-existing medical condition was referred to the state high-risk pool.

Employees whose gross family incomes were at or below 175 percent of the poverty level were eligible for a state subsidy of their premiums, but still had to contribute a set amount, depending on income and whether they chose individual or family coverage. Employers also contributed.

In February 1989, one pilot project was initiated in Outagamie (Appleton) County, and a second site began the following year in rural Portage County. Marketing and enrollment stopped at both sites by the end of 1990, after the governor vetoed legislation that would have continued state subsidies for current enrollees for two more years. The subsidy program ended in June 1991.

At the project's peak, 84 firms were participating, covering 320 people.

INSURANCE PRODUCTS DEVELOPED BY HCUP PROJECTS

Of the projects that reached the enrollment/operational stage, eight designed and marketed one or more new insurance products, and two—Michigan and Wisconsin—subsidized existing products.

Features

Overwhelmingly, the HCUP projects found managed care service delivery systems to be the most congenial potential partners because of their shared emphasis on preventive and primary care, their belief that managed care is cost-effective, and the greater willingness of managers in these systems to work with the projects. Some projects have contracted with existing HMOs or PPOs, while others have established their own provider networks by negotiating directly with hospitals and physicians. Three projects (Alabama, Tennessee, and Utah) have organized network-model HMOs that use community health centers or county-sponsored clinics to deliver primary care.

To protect enrollees from catastrophic expenses, 11 out of the 16 products marketed by the projects have set either an annual coinsurance cap or a maximum amount that an enrollee would have to pay out-of-pocket.

Eleven plans offer unlimited coverage for most physician and hospital services, not including mental health, substance abuse, or convalescent care. The remaining plans have annual maximum benefit limits of $20,000 to $25,000 per person, or lifetime ceilings of $1 million per person.

Nearly all of the projects limit coverage for pre-existing conditions. While not as extensive as the limits employed by the private insurance industry for the small group market, some medical underwriting was deemed necessary in order to protect projects from adverse selection and attract insurer partners.

Benefits

In creating attractive yet affordable insurance products, plan designers could limit the variety of services offered or the volume of services covered. Most did both.

All cover physician office visits (including prenatal care), outpatient radiology and laboratory tests, outpatient surgery, well-baby care, emergency care, ambulance services, and basic inpatient hospital services. Only Alabama's Basic-Care limits the number of visits—six doctor visits and ten hospital days per year.

In general, the projects emphasize preventive and primary care in managed care settings, believing that this will reduce the need (and costs) for inpatient care. Routine physical examinations and immunizations typically are covered. Most plans include home health visits, and about half offer convalescent care in skilled nursing facilities.

Mental health services, considered a high-cost benefit, are offered by about half of the plans, all of which impose some limitations such as copayments for inpatient care ($100 to $200 per day), maximums for outpatient counseling ($1,000 to $2,000 per year), or limits on the units of care (usually 20 outpatient visits and 30 inpatient days per year).

Premiums

Despite their considerable range, nearly all of the monthly premiums for projects still enrolling new members as of January 1, 1992, are below the national average for HMOs, and 25 to 50 percent lower than comparable locally available products. All but two projects require employers to pay a portion of employee premiums.

The Maine and Washington programs subsidize family coverage for those with incomes below 200 percent of the federal poverty level. (The Michigan and Wisconsin projects also offered direct premium subsidies, but are no longer enrolling new members.) At the high end of their sliding scale, these two comprehensive plans have been among the costliest offered by any project. Only Arizona's plan, which receives no major cash subsidy from the state, charges higher premiums.

KEY FINDINGS AND LESSONS

Although the projects have been in operation for only a few years, a number of important findings and lessons already are apparent. Early planning and research revealed a great deal about the small business market that projects used in developing their specific strategies. Project staff learned how to reduce premiums through the creative use of subsidies and benefit design and how to forge partnerships with state and local government, providers and insurers, and the business community. In the enrollment phase, they learned how to market and administer products for very small firms. Now they are learning the extent to which formerly uninsured people use health services.

Market Research Findings

Early on, most projects surveyed small businesses in their areas to understand more thoroughly the nature of this insurance market and the characteristics of small employers and their employees. They learned that:

Businesses with fewer than 25 employees, and especially those with fewer than five, account for a significant proportion of the uninsured. National data show that most uninsured families (77 percent) have at least one adult who is employed; 44 percent of these employed adults are in firms with fewer than ten workers, and well over half are in firms with fewer than 25 workers. Surveys conducted by HCUP confirm that the smaller the business, the less likely it is to offer health insurance. Only about half of employers with one to four employees do so.

Small employers have a variety of reasons for not offering health insurance, but the principal reason is its high cost. Many small firms have narrow profit margins, and their owners tend to avoid fixed-cost obligations like monthly insurance premiums. Because such businesses tend to employ lower wage workers, employees cannot usually afford to contribute to premiums either. The projects did find some employers, however, who said they were not interested in offering coverage even if employees paid the entire premium.

The second most frequently cited reason for not providing coverage is that employees are insured in other ways, usually through a spouse's plan. In the Michigan project, for example, 40 percent of employees in participating firms were insured dependents of people employed elsewhere. Other reasons employers can hire workers without offering health benefits include high employee turnover and employees' preference for larger paychecks.

Employers also cited problems with the insurance market. Many said they had been turned down because of the size or type of their business or their employees' pre-existing medical conditions. Some employers said that they could not find an "acceptable" plan or that they lacked enough information to find and evaluate health plans. Most non-insuring small businesses said they had no "regular source of information" about health insurance plans.

Small firms that do not offer insurance are concentrated in certain industries and employ higher proportions of female, low-wage, and part-time workers than do firms offering insurance. In HCUP communities, firms in the construction, retail trade, and service industries were least likely to offer insurance, whereas firms in the manufacturing, mining, and wholesale trade industries—where unions are more prevalent—tended to offer it.

Non-insuring small firms generally have higher proportions of women employees. For example, in both Alabama and Wisconsin, women constitute more than half of the workforce in non-insuring small firms, compared to around

30 percent in firms that offer insurance. The two biggest reasons for this difference probably are that health insurance usually costs more for women of child-bearing age than for men in the same age bracket, and employers often believe women can obtain coverage through their husbands' plans.

Non-insuring small firms hire more low-wage workers than do insuring small firms. In Wisconsin, approximately one-half of all workers in firms with fewer than 100 employees earned $3.35-$5.99 per hour, which at the time of the marketing survey (1987) was just above the minimum wage.

Few small firms offer health insurance to part-time workers, even if they do offer it to full-time employees. In Wisconsin, only 17 percent of employers provided insurance to both full-time and part-time employees. National data show that some 30 percent of uninsured workers are employed part-time.

Even when small employers do contribute to employees' health insurance, they often pay a relatively small percentage of the premium, or don't pay at all for dependent coverage.   While there was considerable variability across market areas, surprisingly few small employers in Tucson, Denver, or San Francisco paid the dependent portion of employee health insurance premiums. These data reflect a national decline in recent years in the number of employers, large and small, that pay for dependent coverage, a trend that has added many children to the ranks of the uninsured.

CONCLUSION

The projects clearly demonstrate that to increase coverage in the small group market health insurance must be both more available and more affordable. To increase availability, HCUP projects have tried to limit medical underwriting, marketed their products aggressively, and set up health insurance information and referral services for small employers and individuals. To make the product affordable for small firms and for their employees, projects offered fewer benefits or imposed high cost-sharing, or created direct and indirect subsidy programs.

To obtain a copy of the full Special Report on the Health Care for the Uninsured Program, write on your business letterhead to: Communications Office, The Robert Wood Johnson Foundation, P.O. Box 2316, Princeton, N.J. 08543-2316.

3. State High Risk Insurance Pools: Their Operating Experience and Policy Implications

James Studnicki

State high risk pools are providing a valuable service. But the operating experience of existing pools highlights the need to involve providers, purchasers and payers in developing an integrated approach to financing and managing health services. The cost-shifting strategies typical of the health care system today will provide little long-term comfort, because ultimately we will all pay.

One of the "conventional wisdoms" of national health policy experts is that the United States is facing a serious problem because of the number of people who do not have health insurance. The most recent data available suggest that nearly 50 million people lack coverage for at least part of the year, that approximately half that number remain uninsured throughout the entire year and that 36 million are uninsured on any given day during the year.[1] Uninsured persons are disproportionately poor, with one-third of all uninsured being in poor, near-poor or low income families. The uninsured also tend to be young (one-third under the age of 19), disproportionately Black and Hispanic and likely to reside in the South and West. One very small segment of the uninsured is those individuals who have such adverse health history that, even though they may be willing and able to buy health coverage, they cannot get private insurance at a

"State High Risk Insurance Pools: Their Operating Experience and Policy Implications," by James Studnicki, which appeared in the June 1991 issue, was reprinted with permission from the *Employee Benefits Journal*, published by the International Foundation of Employee Benefit Plans, Brookfield, WI. Statements or opinions expressed in this article are those of the author and do not necessarily represent the views or positions of the International Foundation, its officers, directors, or staff.

standard rate without specific exclusions. These are individuals with chronic conditions or disabilities who have been rejected for standard coverage by at least one private insurance carrier, but who are also not eligible for Medicaid benefits.[2] From a medical necessity perspective, these are the neediest, the "hard core" of the uninsured. It has been estimated that this group represents no more than 1 percent of the population under the age of 65.[3] While their numbers are relatively small, this category of the uninsured has stimulated the growth of comprehensive health associations, more commonly known as *high risk pools,* in a growing number of states. For the six oldest state pools, there is now sufficient history to describe their operating experience and to analyze the broader public policy implications of this unique initiative.

HISTORY AND BASIC DESIGN OF THE POOLS

State high risk pools were embraced as a solution to the problem of the uninsured largely because they were perceived to have very limited governmental participation. The assumption was that pool enrollees would be able to pay their own way and that any modest operating deficits would be made up by contributions from the insurance industry. Additionally, there appears to have been support from small business and agriculture groups, which often lack access to group style health insurance policies. These groups are known for their independence and fiscal conservatism and, at least in the beginning, there was no suggestion that the pools would be publicly supported in any substantial way. Minnesota and Connecticut were the first states to implement pools in 1976, followed by Wisconsin (1981), North Dakota (1981), Indiana (1982) and Florida (1983). Since 1985, an additional 18 states have implemented legislation to develop high risk pools: California (1989), Colorado (1990), Georgia (1989), Illinois (1989), Iowa (1987), Louisiana (1990), Maine (1988), Missouri (1990), Montana (1987), Nebraska (1986), New Mexico (1988), Oregon (1990), South Carolina (1990), Tennessee (1987), Texas (1989), Utah (1990), Washington (1988) and Wyoming (1990). The development of high risk pools is being actively considered in another 20 states.[4]

ORGANIZATION, COVERAGE AND PREMIUMS

While the pools differ substantially in some aspects of their operations, their composition follows a similar pattern. The state forms an association of all health insurance companies doing business in the state. The association is governed by a board (ranging in size from five to 15 members), with members typically representing the insurance companies, the state's insurance commissioner, hospitals, physicians, state legislators and the general public. The board develops a standard health insurance policy following the guidelines established in each state law regarding the composition of the benefit package and a financial plan. A plan administrator is selected. In the risk pools that are operational, the local Blue Cross and Blue Shield organization is most frequently chosen to administer the program. Commercial carriers are less often selected, although Mutual of Omaha has been the administrator of seven pools.

The benefit packages offered by the pools are quite extensive. Reflecting the philosophy represented by the title *comprehensive health insurance association,* the coverage follows the pattern of high style major medical approaches and usually includes inpatient hospital services, physician services, prescription drugs, diagnostic X-ray and laboratory tests, anesthetics, skilled nursing facility care, home health care, limited mental health care, durable medical equipment and physical therapy. The most typical maximum lifetime benefit is $500,000, although a few states have established both higher ($1 million) and lower ($250,000) maximums. There is usually a tier approach to the level of deductibles ranging in increments between $500 and $2,000. The pools generally require a 20 percent coinsurance payment by the policyholder for all covered expenses once the deductible has been satisfied. Most plans also provide for a stop-loss limitation that fixes the out-of-pocket expenses of the policyholder usually between $1,500 and $5,000. Plans contain a provision that excludes coverage for a period of time (usually six months or one year) from the effective date of coverage for preexisting conditions.

The insurance provided by the high risk pools is not inexpensive. Even though premium rates are usually capped by state law at no more than 150 percent of the average premium rates for individual standard risk policies, policy premiums range up to $7,000 annually. Existing plans usually calculate premiums based upon the age, sex, deductible selected and frequency of payment (annual, monthly, quarterly), and a few pools make an adjustment for residence within a particular, geographically defined rating area. Maternity benefits are provided as a plan option, and assigned premiums are priced separately. Since the pools, by definition, are composed of individuals with the highest levels of health care utilization, and since the premium levels are capped by state mandate, all of the operating pools have slipped very quickly into a deficit funding situation.

ENROLLMENT PATTERNS

Patterns of enrollment growth are emerging in the six oldest state pools (see Table I). Florida has shown the most accelerated increase in enrollees during the past three years, with the number of participants nearly doubling from 1987 to 1988 and then doubling again from 1988 to 1989. Wisconsin also experienced very large enrollment increases between 1987 and 1989. Even Minnesota, where the number of enrollees is three times that of the next largest state pool, had an

Table I

State High Risk Pools:
(I) Total Number of Enrollees; (II) Total Premiums Collected; and (III) Total Claims Paid by Calendar Year*

	1981	1982	1983	1984	1985	1986	1987	1988	1989
Connecticut									
I	3,441	3,853	4,399	3,579	3,388	2,531	2,239	2,014	2,200
II	$1,441,143	$2,182,388	$3,134,889	$3,473,145	$3,285,762	$3,532,941	$3,186,476	$3,460,377	$4,495,872
III	$1,289,025	$2,328,194	$3,442,223	$4,454,451	$4,579,461	$4,203,833	$6,663,081	$7,293,434	$10,438,000
Florida									
I			49	382	651	1,036	1,562	2,983	5,934
II			$23,759	$505,798	$1,107,581	$1,770,171	$2,858,173	$5,294,446	$12,443,960
III				$141,430	$774,174	$1,686,195	$3,963,710	$8,581,468	$17,425,025
Indiana									
I		41	2,288	3,510	3,276	2,998	2,610	2,668	3,132
II		$34,480	$2,352,179	$6,356,995	$7,505,144	$7,197,744	$6,301,707	$5,607,908	$6,210,701
III			$217,878	$6,843,691	$9,518,759	$11,552,494	$11,564,602	$9,640,579	$10,690,610
Minnesota									
I	2,918	4,250	6,669	9,158	10,139	11,784	12,300	14,386	18,797
II	$1,305,245	$2,325,060	$4,082,351	$6,413,829	$9,492,438	$10,772,454	$11,407,281	$14,197,219	$18,459,482
III	$2,852,845	$4,514,172	$6,981,967	$9,761,835	$13,324,992	$18,913,879	$21,893,358	$27,098,596	$38,373,578
N. Dakota									
I		78	245	615	1,017	1,279	1,463	1,551	1,646
II		$73,408	$138,666	$455,874	$894,701	$1,321,991	$1,626,970	$1,937,903	$2,261,638
III		$103,400	$345,918	$1,058,694	$1,704,988	$2,863,886	$3,389,229	$3,340,441	$3,691,487
Wisconsin									
I	309	977	1,798	1,918	1,919	2,075	2,476	3,760	6,077
II	$127,840	$618,216	$1,232,352	$2,079,996	$2,600,586	$2,856,286	$2,959,861	$4,056,671	$6,676,614
III	$37,165	$1,144,686	$2,463,703	$3,104,604	$3,265,492	$3,336,087	$3,956,056	$5,518,189	$9,754,103

*Table is derived from data appearing in A.K. Tripler, "Comprehensive Health Insurance for High Risk Individuals" in *Communicating for Agriculture*, 4th ed., 1990.

Table II

State High Risk Pools:

Percentage Difference Between Total Premiums Collected and Total Claims Paid by Calendar Year*

	1981	1982	1983	1984	1985	1986	1987	1988	1989
Connecticut	12	-6	-9	-22	-28	-16	-52	-53	-57
Florida				258	43	5	-28	-38	-29
Indiana			980	-7	-21	-38	-46	-42	-42
Minnesota	-54	-48	-42	-34	-29	-43	-48	-48	-52
N. Dakota		-29	-60	-57	-48	-54	-52	-42	-39
Wisconsin	244	-46	-50	-33	-20	-14	-25	-26	-32

*Table is derived from data appearing in A.K. Tripler, "Comprehensive Health Insurance for High Risk Individuals" in *Communicating for Agriculture*, 4th ed., 1990.

increase of more than 30 percent between 1988 and 1989. Indiana's pool did grow significantly between 1988 and 1989 as well, but its enrollment peaked in 1984 and still has not attained that previous high level. North Dakota has the smallest number of participants among the six oldest pools, and it has experienced consistent, if modest, growth. Connecticut's pattern of enrollment is unique among the pools. Since hitting a peak in 1983, the number of participants gradually declined each year through 1988. There was a very small increase between 1988 and 1989. Connecticut, however, has tried a different philosophy with its program, seeking to reduce adverse selection and keep premium increases low by achieving a broader pooling. This attempt to reach some of the "better risks" apparently has not been successfully reflected in increased numbers of participants.[5] Aggressively priced alternative insurance products are attracting younger and healthier people away from the Connecticut pool.

Enrollment patterns of the six oldest pools generally can be described as modest up until 1986. However, there is evidence that enrollment is climbing sharply in a few states during the past few years. There is no precise way to determine the potential size of this unusual population; i.e., individuals with chronic medical conditions who can afford the relatively expensive coverage made available by the high risk pools. Neither the insurance companies nor the states themselves exhibit much enthusiasm for advertising and promoting the existence of the pools.[6] Unless the pools can achieve a more favorable selection of lower risk patients and, at the same time, reduce the health care utilization of enrollees, they will continue to produce deficits. Therefore, at the moment there seems to be no serious interest in merely promoting enrollment growth.

THE OPERATING DEFICIT

After the initial years of operation, when limitations in coverage for preexisting conditions and the timing of claims processing keep payments depressed, the high risk pools very quickly develop operating deficits. Table II shows the annual percentage difference between total premiums collected and total claims paid for the six oldest pools between 1981 and 1989. The premium shortfalls are pervasive and consistent. While there is some variation from year to year due to the premium structure and utilization experiences, operating losses during the years 1987-1989 have averaged 54 percent in Connecticut, 32 percent in Florida, 43 percent in Indiana, 49 percent in Minnesota, 44 percent in North Dakota and 27 percent in Wisconsin.

While there is probably no realistic chance to make these pools self-funding, there appear to be a number of interventions that might at least stabilize the size of the operating deficits. Recently, a number of states have begun to implement serious cost containment features for the first time. In Florida, for example, mounting losses had caused the state legislature to end the program as of October 1990.

Subsequently, an extension of the program was passed into law, but with significant cost containment and utilization control elements included.7 The new Florida statute specifically requires that cost containment measures such as preadmission certification and individual case management be employed as well as preferred provider arrangements and the negotiated purchase of medical and pharmaceutical supplies.

On the revenue generation side, the Florida statute separates the premium structure into low, medium and high risk individuals and, further, raises the future limitation on premiums for the high risk group up to 300 percent of the standard risk rate. Expense reduction strategies, typified by various cost containment programs, are likely to be more effective than strategies to increase premium revenues. It is already clear that the high premiums required of pool enrollees are a major limitation in expanding participation.

SUBSIDIZING THE DEFICIT

Fundamentally, even though there are many minor variations, there are currently three basic approaches to funding the deficits that are inevitably experienced by the high risk pools.

Assessment to the Insurance Association Members With an Associated Tax Credit

This is the model originally established and still considered by many to be the fairest way to meet the pool's premium shortfalls. The insurance association members are assessed for the losses of the pool but permitted to offset the assessment against premium taxes or income taxes paid to the state. Those states with the "purest" version of this funding mechanism include: Florida, Indiana, Iowa, Missouri, Montana, Nebraska, Washington and Wyoming. In Minneosta, the tax offset was eliminated in 1987. In New Mexico, the tax credit is triggered when an insurance company's assessment reaches $75,000 and is limited to 30 percent. In North Dakota, only insurance companies doing more that $100,000 in accident and health insurance qualify for the assessment. In South Carolina, the tax offset has a $5 million ceiling, after which premiums must be raised. Louisiana probably fits loosely into this category because the subsidy does come from the participating insurance companies. However, the method of calculating the assessment is unique—a $2-per-day-of-hospital-stay fee. There is no tax offset.

General Fund Appropriations

In this model, the governmental subsidy is direct rather than indirect as in the case of tax credits. The legislature simply appropriates the funds to cover the losses associated with operation of the pool. In some states, there are limitations placed upon the amount of the appropriation. Georgia, Illinois and Utah are different versions of the general fund approach. In Illinois, there is a cap placed on the minimum number of pool enrollees in order to control the size of the deficit (and the state appropriation). In Utah, the appropriation currently has a $75,000 maximum. California has required a $30 million annual deposit to a major medical insurance fund. The money will come from three accounts in the Cigarette and Tobacco Products Surtax Fund. Oregon and Tennessee (after 1990) are interesting "hybrids" that combine a state general fund appropriation with assessments on the insurance association members. In Oregon, the general fund contribution is $2 million, and all losses beyond that amount are assessed to the association members. In Tennessee, the state appropriates $3 million, and another $3 million comes from the insurance companies and the state's HMOs and PPOs.

The method of funding in Colorado is quite unique; the pool deficit is tax supported through a surcharge on the state income tax for individuals.

Provider Subsidy

Only one state, Maine, currently uses a model that covers the premium shortfall of the pool by assessing the providers of care, in this case the hospitals. A reserve fund assesses all revenues from all hospitals with the amount calculated as a fraction of gross patient service revenues. There has been additional discussion, but no formal action, about extending this assessment to physician fees as well. While hospitals would strongly object to such a system, the major attraction of this model is that is takes advantage of a sizable revenue stream that should allow for ease of administration of the assessment. In reality, hospitals would merely pass the tax along to all the users of the health care system. Many experts feel that, ultimately, this may be the fairest system of all.

PUBLIC POLICY IMPLICATIONS

The experience of these comprehensive health insurance associations provides a number of important insights that may prove valuable as we develop new policy initiatives for health care.

In the End, We All Pay

Currently, the health care industry resembles the old children's game in which an object is passed from child to child while music is played. When the music stops, the child holding the object is "out." In our health care analogy, the object is the adverse risk population. All of the major health care players are busy developing strategies to see to it that they don't get stuck with the deficit producing population. Hospitals want full charge paying patients and admissions from profitable DRGs. HMOs want young and healthy people who don't utilize expensive services. Indemnity insurers are seeking ways to avoid coverage to potential high risk individuals, often seeking to identify them based upon certain characteristics (such as occupation) that presumably reflect lifestyles with negative health consequences. These cost shifting strategies will provide little long-term comfort because, as the experience of the high risk pools has demonstrated, eventually we will all pay. Directly or indirectly through taxes, higher prices on goods, rationing of selected health and medical services or loss of freedom of choice, society must ultimately pay the price. This reality argues for an integrated rather than a fragmented approach to financing, one that provides the same incentive for all of the major players to seek a joint solution to rising health care costs.

It is interesting to note that a number of states are using the pooling approach as a method for financing health care for the indigent. These state "pools for the indigent" are intended to be a solution to the problem of uncompensated care for hospitals, estimated to be $11.3 billion nationally in 1989. States like California, New York, South Carolina, Ohio, Virginia, Indiana and Kentucky are experimenting with a variety of funding mechanisms. Funding of these programs takes various forms: private health insurers, self-paying patients, Medicaid block grants, county funding, assessments on hospital charges and state appropriation.[8] What is remarkable is that both the high risk pools and indigent pools ultimately arrive at the same end point: deciding the mechanism for extracting the additional payment from society. Of course, in the end we all pay.

Uniform Information is Essential for Effective Policy

It is surprising and disappointing how very little is known about the characteristics and health care utilization experience of enrollees in the high risk pools. One would certainly like to have a better understanding about the sequence of life events and illness experience that bring individuals into a pool. What are the impacts of employment, marital status, age and other demographic factors on the pool composition? What do we know about the health care utilization of pool enrollees? What percentage of pool members make claims in a given year, and how does that pattern compare to other insured populations such as Medicare and Medicaid? It is time for a national information system that mandates a uniform data collection effort that reports utilization, financial and quality-of-care measures. A very good example is Pennsylvania's Health Care Cost Containment Council database, which is mandated by state law. The Pennsylvania system includes DRG-specific, hospital-specific information on volumes, average length of stay, a measure of patient severity, average charges, and observed and expected measures of mortality and morbidity (high degree of clinical instability after treatment). The exact data elements to be included in such a system will always be hotly debated, but the real power comes from being able to analyze and compare uniformly collected information representing the universe of care. Employers should throw their enthusiastic support behind the creation of such a system and then work with other major players to improve and refine it.

The Provision of Care Must be Managed

The pools have been operated very much as traditional insurance entities. Essentially, there have been only superficial attempts at utilization control, and the pools have tended merely to pay claims. That seems to be changing now in a number of states. Given the current health care environment, it makes absolutely no sense to ignore the management of health care utilization for any enrolled group — least of all those where high utilization levels are expected! If there is one clear lesson from the "managed care" experience in the United States in the last decade, it is that vigilance is rewarded. Monitoring does control health care expenditures and can enhance the quality of care delivered. Utilization control is a necessary, but not sufficient, requirement in making our health care system truly cost effective. As a nation, we seem to be building some momentum in bringing more science to the practice of medicine: identifying unnecessary and inappropriate care; identifying the most cost effective drugs, devices and procedures; and distinguishing between the conventional wisdoms of customary practice and those diagnostic and treatment methods that can deliver measurable improvement in patient outcomes. These systemic improvements will certainly enhance the viability of the state pools and could be the major factor in the continued existence of the pluralistic health care system in the United States.

CONCLUSION

State high risk insurance pools are providing a valuable service to a small segment of the "medically uninsurable." The operating experience of the existing pools highlights the need to involve providers, purchasers and payers in developing an integrated approach to both financing and managing health services. The tendency to separate and isolate high risk groups is contrary to sound insurance practices and, regrettably, tends to reinforce the adversarial nature of health care politics.

---

1. P Short, "Estimates of the Uninsured Population, Calendar Year 1987," (DHHS Publication No. PHS 90-3469, September 1990). *National Medical Expenditure Survey Data Summary 2, Agency for Health Care Policy and Research.* (Rockville, MD: Public Health Service).

2. Intergovernmental Health Policy Project, George Washington University, "The Risk Pool Strategy: Comprehensive Health Insurance Associations," *Focus On* No 20, February 1988, p 7.

3. R Bovbjerg and C Boller, "State Health Insurance Pools: Current Performance, Future Prospects," *Inquiry* 23 (Summer 1986), p 116.

4. AK Tripler, "Comprehensive Health Insurance for High Risk Individuals: A State by State Analysis," *Communicating for Agriculture,* 4th ed (Bloomington, MN (1990).

5. Blue Cross and Blue Shield Association, "Pooling Mechanisms for Uninsurables," *Legal Affairs Bulletin* No 513, March 19, 1984.

6. Employee Benefit Research Institute, "Employer Provided Health Benefits: Legislative Initiatives," *Issue Brief* No 62, January 1987.

7. Florida State Comprehensive Health Association Act, HB 3489.

8. American Hospital Association, "States Devise Methods of Financing Health Care for the Indigent," *AHA News,* January 7, 1991.A

4. Health Care Reform Legislation and the 102nd Congress: Pluralism and Politics

Ellen Goldstein

Writing about the array of legislation to reform the U.S. health care system several months before the end of this Congressional session and before the 1992 elections is sort of like trying to read the numbers off the side of a speeding train—a train that has no clear destination and that, even as the end of the line gets closer, has more passengers climbing on board. What can we make of this varied and often slap-dash swarm of legislative proposals? Here's a look at what's on the table, how the proposals would offset the national health care scene, and what their chances are of success.

The U.S. health care system has often been described as a pluralistic system—multiple payors in a no "one-size-fits-all" universe. Some observers from other nations that utilize a single payor system might take the "pluralism" of the U.S. system to mean disorganized and untidy, and definitely not universal. No matter, pluralism would also justly describe the array of legislative proposals now being considered in some fashion by Congress. On the table is everything from adopting a Canadian-style health system to a free market, consumer-choice system based on vouchers, tax credits, or individual spending accounts resembling IRAs.

Politics of course has played a major role in the number and types of health care legislation being proposed. This highly political year was ushered in by an upset Senate victory last fall in Pennsylvania, where the underdog victor, Sen.

41

Harris Wofford (D-PA), promised sweeping health system reform. Since then, introducing health reform legislation has become the policy equivalent of kissing babies. Stacked one atop the other, health system reform proposals introduced in this Congress would dwarf the works of Leo Tolstoy and perhaps several other long-winded Russian novelists. In this case however, quantity is no indicator of quality.

In reviewing the key proposals, it is important to separate the "press release" proposals (the ones for whom the primary audience is potential voters, not Congressional colleagues) from the more serious proposals (the ones introduced by members of relevant committees, often in coalitions, who have studied the health care system longer than an afternoon). This article will attempt to categorize and provide an overview of the more serious legislative proposals.

A BROAD CONTINUUM OF PROPOSALS

In mid-summer 1992, Democrats in the U.S. House of Representatives were trying very hard to cobble together a consensus document to send to the Senate for consideration before the November election. This is interesting for several reasons. First, the House Democrats, as a group, have lagged behind the Bush Administration and other "coalition" or "leadership" groups that have managed to develop consensus proposals. Second, the House Democrats seem to be interested in every form of reform idea except play-or-pay, the chief reform vehicle of the Senate Democratic leadership. In fact, House Democrats seem to favor the single payor approach above all. Finally, this late-in-the-game action is interesting because the proposal getting the most attention at this time is one that has the endorsement of both Rep. Pete Stark (D-CA), chairman of the House Ways & Means Subcommittee on Health, and House Majority Leader Richard Gephardt (D-MO) and would focus first and foremost on cost containment, rather than universal coverage. Mr. Stark in particular has concentrated first and foremost on universal coverage. It is hard to say in early July how this new effort to bring one consensus proposal to the floor of the House might fare (not to mention what the Senate Democrats might do), or what it would resemble by the time three House committees get done marking it up. What is becoming clear is that a focus on costs rather than coverage is foremost in the minds of Democrats— they have realized the impact of rising health care costs on the deficit and the political unreality of proposing new taxes to pay for universal coverage.

The breadth of legislative proposals, including those of major coalitions outside the government, can be viewed as on a continuum where the status quo (everyone's second favorite option, according to Brandeis University Professor Stuart Altman) is in the middle. To the left would be "play-or-pay" and other mandate proposals that build upon the employer-based system but remove its voluntary nature, as well as (farther to the left) single-payor proposals that would provide universal coverage with the government as main payor and regulator of health services.

To the right of the status quo is that amorphous category known as "incremental" reform. Perhaps the greatest number of legislative proposals fall within this category. These bills would make slight to significant changes to the current system, but without eliminating the employer role or the role of private insurance, and without imposing strict coverage mandates. The hallmark of most incremental bills are provisions that would reform the small group health insurance market; many would also include malpractice reform (not an idea strongly favored by many Democrats), increase the deductible for the self-employed to 100 percent, and offer tax credits or other tax incentives to expand coverage. Incremental reform bills do not set out to achieve 100 percent coverage, whereas comprehensive proposals such as single payor and play-or-pay do.

There is also the so-called "free market" approach which, like the single payor, effectively bypasses the employer-based system and instead envisions individuals getting subsidized insurance on their own. There are not many proposals in Congress that would implement such a system.

Managed competition—a set of ideas developed by Stanford University Professor Alain Enthoven, Dr. Paul Ellwood of InterStudy, and other academic colleagues known collectively as the Jackson Hole Group (JHG)—has recently worked its way into the legislative vocabulary, with thanks to the valiant efforts of *The New York Times* editorial page. While no member of Congress has of this date introduced a pure JHG-style proposal, elements of managed competition are finding their way into a variety of proposals on Capitol Hill. In fact, a proposal still being developed by a group of conservative Democrats known as the Conservative Democratic Forum (CDF) incorporates much of the JHG proposal and may, some day, become the coalition-building reform vehicle that brings together enough disparate elements from both political parties, within both Congress and the administration, to carry the day.

Almost all proposals, whether left or right of the spectrum, include such cost containment features as expanded outcomes research, development of practice standards, malpractice reform, administrative simplification and uniform electronic claims filings, and "quality" enhancement elements (everyone favors quality).

Here then is a brief overview of extant legislative proposals:

Single Payor Reform Proposals

H.R. 1300, The Universal Health Act of 1992, introduced by Rep. Marty Russo (D-IL), has sixty-six co-sponsors, and broad support among House Democrats. A companion measure, S. 2320, has been introduced in the Senate by Sen. Paul Wellstone (D-MN). Although Rep. Russo has lost his electoral bid to return to

Congress next year, there no lack of enthusiastic co-sponsors of this measure to fill his leadership role in promoting this bill. H.R. 1300 would impose a Canadian-style health system in the U.S. Basic benefits would include all "medically necessary physician and hospital care," including mental, dental, prescription drugs, preventive services, and home care. Like Canada, H.R. 1300 would require no deductibles or coinsurance. Financing would come from a new 6 percent employer payroll tax and increased corporate and personal income taxes, as well as other sources. A National Health Trust Fund, administered by the states, would collect funds and allocate spending by state. National "global budgeting"—setting national spending limits for all health care categories—and negotiated provider reimbursements, executed by special federal/state commissions, would keep spending under control. Savings, the sponsors claim, would be realized through the administrative simplicity of a single payor system. This plan obviously bypasses the employer-based system, although in Canada employers can provide supplemental benefits to the government's basic plan. One may wish to question the efficacy of the administrative savings, the estimate of the necessary payroll tax (paid by all employers), and the true cost of covering millions of new beneficiaries. Also debatable is the impact of global budgeting on the availability of and speedy access to quality health care, and the effects on medical research and development. The private health insurance industry would be eliminated except for possible government contracting for administrative functions and perhaps supplemental benefits. The clearest winner in this proposal would be the bureaucracy.

S. 2513, The American Health Security Plan, was introduced by Sen. Harris Wofford (D-PA) and Sen. Tom Daschle (D-SD). Part of the significance of this plan is that its chief sponsor, Sen. Wofford, was the come-from-behind winner in last year's special election in Pennsylvania. Analysis of the Pennsylvania election indicates, however, that those who voted for Mr. Wofford were most concerned about the state of the economy and had general dissatisfaction with the current health care system, but were less concerned about any particular health reform proposal. Although essentially a single payor proposal, S. 2513 would preserve a voluntary role for employers who could pay all or part of an employee's individual premium. An employer could deduct contributions, provided that the plan was approved by a state board. The federal and state governments would contribute 80 percent/20 percent, repectively, of the program's costs; individuals would pay a premium to a new Federal Health Trust Fund, charged with financing the program. Benefits promised by S. 2513 would include hospital and hospice care, preventive services, prescription drugs, substance abuse treatment, mental health care, "approved" experimental treatment, and long-term care. Cost savings would be achieved through global budgeting, (see above); other federal boards would set co-payment and out-of-pocket limitations and other cost sharing requirements. Negotiated provider reimbursement rates are also included. This plan, operated through separate state programs, is overly complicated by several government boards charged with a variety of overlapping functions. S. 2513 would also include long-term care.

H.R. 5514, Health Choice, introduced by Reps. John Dingell (D-MI) and Henry Waxman (D-CA), with the explicit support of Majority Leader Gephardt, entered the fray just as the House Democrats were pressing for a consensus measure in the Ways & Means Committee. Unlike the Senate, major health reform legislation would have to pass through three House committees—Ways & Means, Education & Labor, and Energy & Commerce—not two as in the Senate. Energy and Commerce, chaired by Rep. Dingell (and whose Subcommittee on Health is chaired by Rep. Waxman) has jurisdiction over a host of health policy and insurance programs. Health Choice, a $400 billion single-payor plan, would cover all Americans and put the federal government in the position of tax collector and reimburser of health care, with global budgeting and provider rate-setting. The program would be financed by an employer payroll tax, and to prove that no good deed goes unpunished, H.R. 5514 would tax employers who provide health benefits at a higher rate than those employers who do not. A 5 percent value-added tax (VAT) would also be included to finance the program. Universal coverage would be phased in over four years, starting with children and pregnant women. The payroll tax would also be phased in; employers providing employees with health benefits would be taxed 3 percent initially, and later 9 percent; employers not providing benefits would pay a 1 to 5 percent over four years. By the turn of the century all employers would pay a five percent payroll tax. Employers and union plans could voluntarily provide health plans but they would not be mandated to do so. Health Choice is similar to a plan offered every year for the last two decades or so by Chairman Dingell. Its introduction in the summer of 1992 may be more a signal to the Ways & Means Committee to get moving on reform than anything else.

Employer Mandates and Play-or-Pay

The Bush administration describes these proposals as "pay and pay." The theory behind play-or-pay is simple and consistent with other government policies in the era of deficits: let the private sector do it. Play-or-pay builds upon the current employer system but mandates that those employers who offer no health insurance must either offer an approved minimum package or pay a tax to the federal government, which would sponsor a new, huge public health plan that, depending on the proposals, might incorporate Medicaid as well. Employer plans would have to meet minimum standards established by a new federal commission and complex mechanisms would be established to determine the appropriate level of payroll tax "non-playing" employers would have to pay to cover their workers in the new public plan. Critics assail play-or-pay in two key areas: the complexity of determining the proper payroll tax, national spending limits (most include similar schemes as single payor global budgets described above), and provider reimbursement schedules; and second, they argue that play-or-pay would lead inevitably to a one-payor public plan since according to them, there is little likelihood that the payroll tax would ever be set high enough to pay the actual costs of the public health plan, and thus employers would drop their private plans and pay the lower rate for public plan coverage of their employees.

According to a recent study released by the Department of Labor and conducted by The Urban Institute, around 50 percent of all workers would eventually be covered by the new public plan in a play-or-pay environment. The study also showed that the higher the payroll tax, the lower the enrollment in the public plan. All in all, according to the study, the private system would still finance the bulk of nonelderly coverage. Under play-or-pay, the study says, employers' costs would climb 23 to 30 percent over 1989 costs, depending on whether the payroll tax was 7 percent or 9 percent. Because premium costs for small employers would soar over 80 percent according to this study, the administration and other critics maintain that play-or-pay would result in hundreds of thousands of lost jobs.

The chief play-or-pay proposal is S. 1227, The Affordable Health Care for All Americans Act, sponsored jointly by four key Democrats in the Senate: Majority Leader George Mitchell (D-ME); Jay Rockefeller (D-WV), Finance Subcommittee member who chaired the Pepper Commission which also recommended a version of play-or-pay; Don Riegle (D-MI), chairman of the Finance Subcommittee on Health for Families and the Uninsured; and Edward M. Kennedy (D-MA), chairman of the Labor and Human Resources Committee and a long-time supporter of health system reform. S. 1227's new AmeriCare public plan, which would incorporate Medicaid, would provide a wide array of benefits including mental health and preventive care; employers would be required to offer an actuarial equivalent or pay the payroll tax. Cost-sharing would be required for almost all beneficiaries. S. 1227 includes standard small market reforms and its mandate would be phased in for small employers, who would also receive tax credits. S. 1227 would have an estimated first year cost of "only" $6 billion. Bureaucracy is a big winner here. The four chief sponsors of this measure have campaigned hard for its passage and it still stands as the chief consensus measure of the majority party in the Senate.

A companion measure of sorts, H.R. 3205, The Health Insurance Coverage and Cost Containment Act of 1991, was introduced by House Ways & Means Committee Chairman Dan Rostenkowski (who has also introduced a major incremental reform measure, see below). Rep. Rostenkowski's measure is very similar to S. 1227, but includes these chief differences: Medicaid would be retained as a separate program, the Medicare eligibility age would be lowered to 60 (a FASB cushion for active plan sponsors), and firms with fewer than 100 workers would be barred from self-insuring. Chairman Rostenkowski seemed under pressure from labor to introduce this measure and, unlike the four horsemen of the Senate, has shown very little interest in play-or-pay since the day he introduced H.R. 3205. In fact, most of his energy has been spent trying to figure out a winning coalition measure to move out from his committee to the House floor and hopefully to the President's desk before the November election. So far that objective has remained elusive.

Also in the House, Education and Labor Committee chairman Bill Ford (D-MI) introduced H.R. 5050, the Universal Medical Care (UNIMED) Act of 1992. Mr. Ford's bill is an across-the-board mandate for employers to cover all full-time workers only; other programs would be established to cover children and everyone else not covered by the mandate. Most importantly, H.R. 5050 would establish a whole new ERISA title that would essentially "ERISA-fy" health benefits, a prospect that should concern plan sponsors everywhere. Mr. Ford deliberately chose a path that combined expanded private and public coverage; however, despite his important chairmanship in the House, his bill has thus far received little attention.

Play-or-pay has the strong support of some labor unions and even some corporations. The National Leadership Coalition proposal, also referred to as the Simmons Commission after its leader Dr. Henry Simmons, struggled to develop its play-or-pay proposal without losing too many of its initial corporate members. While not true in all cases, there is of course some self-interest on the part of certain companies who support play-or-pay; they are generally companies that offer their workers generous or reasonable health care plans and that believe they are also paying the costs of workers and dependents in other companies where health care is not covered.

Also of interest is the new reform proposal advocated by the Blue Cross and Blue Shield Association, which includes a requirement that large employers contribute toward a minimum benefit plan for their workers. Small employers would be assessed a tax of around 40 percent to pay for similar coverage. The Blues' plan would be paid for by limiting the tax exclusion for benefits. Managed competition finds its way into this plan as well—Community Care Partnerships, or managed competition networks, would eventually come to cover all Americans.

Play-or-pay got its biggest policy boost back in the early 1970s when a Republican president, Richard Nixon, offered up his Comprehensive Health Insurance Program (CHIP) employer mandate proposal. As has been true throughout the history of health care reform, labor and Democrats defeated CHIP because it did not go far enough. Today there are a wide variety of mandate proposals floating around Washington; some would apply only to children or pregnant women. Play-or-pay, including long-term care, has been endorsed by Gov. Bill Clinton (D-AR), the Democratic nominee for president. Unlike the two major Congressional proposals, Mr. Clinton, who has policy ties to the conservative Democrats who are pushing managed competition, stresses cost containment (via global budgeting) and suggests changing tax incentives to bring about a managed competition environment. He has also indicated a more deliberate phase-in of the mandate until cost savings are achieved.

Incremental Plans

As described above, incremental plans cover a wide range of proposals that have more limited scope when it comes to the two major objectives of health reform: universal coverage and strict cost containment. The most limited of these proposals focus on small market reform and are authored by the chairmen of the two tax committees.

S. 1872, The Better Access to Affordable Health Care Act of 1992, sponsored by Finance Committee Chairman Lloyd Bentsen (D-TX), almost became law earlier this year as a part of a much bigger tax bill sent to President Bush who promptly vetoed it. Like its House counterpart, H.R. 3626 (introduced by Ways & Means Chairman Rostenkowski), S. 1872 focusses on the reform of the small group market and includes provisions that would limit underwriting practices and premium increases for firms with 50 or fewer employees. Benefit packages that would be offered must include benefits similar to those offered by Medicare, plus well-child and preventive care. A federal cost containment commission would be established to study and advise on ways to limit costs (H.R. 3626 would use Medicare DRG and RBRVS rates as basis for provider reimbursements). State mandates and anti-managed care laws would be pre-empted for qualified benefit plans.

Although almost everyone supports small market reforms, even its supporters contend that by itself, small market reform may actually exacerbate health care inflation while not adding significantly (if at all) to improving access statistics. However, it is still possible that in the waning days of this Congress, should no other consensus vehicle for reform seem viable, a limited reform measure like this could pass—especially if Democrats and Republicans see themselves more in the mold of the "incumbent party" needing to pass health reform before election day. It would also be possible to graft onto this measure other "pet" ideas of key Congressional factions—such as ERISA changes, spending targets, and MediServe tax-qualified spending accounts.

Republicans in both chambers—and at the other end of Pennsylvania Avenue— have sponsored more far-reaching incremental proposals. A leadership group of House Republicans led by Minority Leader Robert Michel (R-IL) introduced H.R. 5325, the Action Now Health Reform Act. A consensus document that is also drawing additional support from President Bush, H.R. 5325 contains the usual suspects of incrementalism—small market reforms (including a provision that would require all employers, regardless of size, to bar pre-existing condition requirements), administrative simplification, malpractice reform, expansion of practice guidelines, insurance purchasing pools for small groups, and dissemination of information about provider cost-effectiveness. H.R. 5325 is a more limited incremental bill than one introduced by two members of this coalition, Reps. Nancy Johnson (R-CT) and Rod Chandler (R-WA), last year. Their bill, H.R. 1565, the Health Equity and Access Reform Today Act (HEART), included an employer mandate to offer a "MediAccess" minimum benefit plan and tax disincentives for plans lacking managed care features. Nothing like a limited mandate or even tax code changes are included, however, in the House leadership proposal.

A similar leadership consensus proposal, S. 1936, had been introduced in the Senate last year under the auspices of Minority Leader Bob Dole (R-KS) and Sen. John Chafee (R-RI). However, the Health Equity and Access Improvement Act of 1991, unlike the House leadership proposal, includes tax credits and subsidies to expand access for low income individuals and families, earmarks increased funding for expanding health care programs in underserved areas, provides a new Basicare program for working poor, and requires development of federal managed care standards. Given their minority status, the House and Senate Republican proposals aren't viewed as the chief vehicles of reform.

The Bush Hybrid

Two years after he declared health care a right of all Americans, President Bush announced his own sweeping proposal to reform the health system last February. His plan is a hybrid—incrementalism in approach (e.g., standard small market reforms) grafted onto the concept of managed competition. At the heart of the Bush proposal, however, is a complex system of transferable tax credits for the uninsured, including middle class families, to pay for coverage. Also included is another complex system of risk adjustment and purchasing pools (here called HINs, or Health Insurance Networks), to help provide that coverage in a more cost-effective way. The President's plan includes the promise that reasonable health packages will be developed in each area that will match the available tax credits; his Democratic critics disagree and contend that the Bush plan is an empty promise. In any event, the Administration has so far sent to the Hill specific legislative proposals to implement his proposals on small market reform, the HINs, the increased tax deduction for health insurance for the self-employed, and malpractice reform. Other aspects of his proposals will wait until next year. While critics of play-or-pay contend that it is a slippery slope to a government-sponsored one-payor system, some have argued that the President's plan is a slippery slope to what is called the "free market approach" to health reform, whereby individuals are provided income-based tax credits and/or vouchers to go out and purchase their own coverage. The President has endorsed the House Republican bill while some of his staffers indicate interest and support in the CDF proposal, discussed below.

Free Market

The idea that individuals properly financed, incented, and informed can go into the health marketplace, and wisely purchase appropriate insurance plans, thus driving down the costs of insurance and health care generally, is what is behind the so-called "free market" approach, advocated largely by the conservative Heritage Foundation and Professor Mark Pauly of the Wharton School in association with the American Enterprise Institute. These proposals would reconfigure the tax code so as to provide everyone with an appropriate level of tax subsidy to purchase health plans, and would largely by-pass the current employer-based system, although some modest, optional role is reserved for employers. There is no significant legislative proposal under consideration on Capitol Hill that would achieve a true free market approach, although interest is gathering around "MediServe Accounts," IRA-like spending accounts for health care that could be established to supplement current health benefits, or eventually substitute for group plans and incorporate the assumptions of the free market approach. Rep. Rick Santorum (R-PA) has introduced MediServe legislation (H.R. 4130) and Sen. John Breaux (D-LA) has indicated his interest in such an approach.

Managed Competition

Swirling above the scramble of health proposals is the CDF approach, based on the Jackson Hole Group proposal of managed competition. Elements of the JHG concept have found their way into a variety of proposals, but the CDF initiative—not yet drafted in legislative language—is the strongest version. A managed competition approach builds on the employer-based system but uses the tax code to re-shape the health care marketplace so that the opportunities for real competition are maximized, and the opportunities for wasteful and inappropriate care are minimized. The CDF proposal would require all employers to *offer* (not contribute to) coverage either through an approved corporate plan, or through an Accountable Health Plan (AHP)—a complex, vertically integrated network of providers, many of which could exist within communities. (Sometimes referred to as a "Super HMO.") AHPs would offer a standard package of coverage (to be determined by an independent federal board) offered on a capitated basis and would compete with other AHPs on the basis of their outcomes and cost effectiveness. AHPs could not discriminate against any applicants and would be protected from high risks through cross-subsidies from throughout the health care system. Part of these subsidies would be funded by employers. Corporate plans with 1,000 or more employees could become "closed AHPs" once qualified under the new system. Employers could only deduct health expenses equal to the least costly AHP providing qualified coverage in an area; the employee exclusion would not be affected. Those not covered by employer plans would shop various

AHPs for coverage. Small firms would be assisted by a pooled purchasing agent to handle their administrative functions. The federal government would assume from the states full responsibility for Medicaid coverage for individuals at or below 100 percent of poverty; the states would assume responsibility of Medicaid-eligible long-term care.

There are still many questions to be answered about the CDF proposal, most especially its funding mechanism as the CDF members have promised that their managed competition legislation would include financing. The risk adjustment operation and how it would be paid, as well as the accommodation and reform of ERISA in a new health care environment, are also unclear as of this writing.

However, the components of the CDF proposal together promise the most exciting venture in the current health reform game. Political support is building from all quarters—from the White House, both Democrats and Republicans in the Congress, provider and employer groups, etc. Many pet reforms of different advocates could easily be grafted onto the CDF vehicle as it moves toward statutory reality.

HOUSE DEMOCRATS STRUGGLE ON

Meanwhile, the House Democrats, powered by Majority Leader Gephardt and Rep. Stark, will struggle for the rest of the summer to wrest a compromise consensus proposal for a possible floor vote. The Gephardt/Stark measure, H.R. 5502, attempts to bludgeon medical cost inflation through a global budget and a scheme that would limit increased annual health care spending (public and private) so that in four years after enactment, spending increases would equal the annual increase in nominal gross domestic product. Access improvements would begin with all low-income pregnant women and children. Insurance reforms for the large and small group market are included (i.e., community rating, guaranteed issue, and premium increase limitations) and would apply to self-insured as well as fully-insured plans. MEWAs and firms with fewer than 100 workers would be barred from self-insuring. Cost savings would be realized through uniform electronic billing procedures and a strong anti-fraud program. Financing sources aren't indicated as yet.

In the push to move this new compromise bill through the House (and it has three committees to pass through before getting to the floor), proponents of any and all alternative approaches and measures will be permitted to introduce their pet proposal as substitutes or additions. Despite the new turn by the Democrats to focus mostly on cost containment rather than access, there aren't at this time enough votes in the House chamber to carry the day for any single measure. Ultimately all health reform proposals much be judged against these measures. But in keeping our eyes on the large movements to reform our health system, we may not be watching closely enough the more serious yet narrow reform efforts.

Frustrated with the policy vacuum in Washington, burdened by extensive federal health mandates and huge health care budgets of their own, closer to their constituents demanding greater protection and access to health coverage, and faced in many places with constitutional requirements to live within balanced budgets, the nation's governors are pressing Congress for freedom and flexibility from federal statutes—most notably ERISA and Medicaid—to design plans of their own. Some of these states—Minnesota, Vermont, and Florida (several other key states are watching closely)—are demanding that Congress provide them with ERISA waivers so that they can set mandates on and/or tax self-insured plans. Their pleas are not falling on deaf ears. Senators David Pryor (D-AR), Patrick Leahy (D-VT), and Dave Durenberger (R-MN) are readying legislative proposals that would give the governors what they want. The specter of sending large employers to a pre-ERISA world may chill enthusiasm for such changes at this time, but the administration has called upon the states to take the initiative on health reform, and while clearly opposed to weakening ERISA preemption in the Pilot Life legislative debate, there are supporters of the governors' demands within the Administration.

The question as we head toward year's end then is not whether major reform is on line for 1992—it isn't—but whether some combination of incremental reforms will be approved by the incumbent party. Such a limited program could include small market reform, malpractice reform, some ERISA changes, attempts to cap spending, and maybe even a modest form of MediServe accounts. Together they might form a viable legislative melange to be served up just in time for election day.

5. Managed Competition

Alain C. Enthoven   Richard Kronick

Roughly 35 million Americans have no health care coverage. Health care expenditures are out of control. The problems of access and cost are inextricably related. Important correctable causes include cost-unconscious demand, a system not organized for quality and economy, market failure, and public funds not distributed equitably or effectively to motivate widespread coverage. We propose Public Sponsor agencies to offer subsidized coverage to those otherwise uninsured, mandated employer-provided health insurance, premium contributions from all employers and employees, a limit on tax-free employer contributions to employee health insurance, and "managed competition." Our proposed new government revenues equal proposed new outlays. We believe our proposal will work because efficient managed care does exist and can provide satisfactory care for a cost far below that of the traditional fee-for-service third-party payment system. Presented with an opportunity to make an economically responsible choice, people choose value for money; the dynamic created by these individual choices will give providers strong incentives to render high-quality, economical care. We believe that providers will respond to these incentives.

Reprinted from Jama, *The Journal of the American Medical Association*, May 15, 1991, Volume 265, c 1991, American Medical Association. The authors gratefully acknowledge support from the Robert Wood Johnson Foundation, Princeton, NJ, and the Henry J. Kaiser Family Foundation, Menlo Park, Calif.

THE PARADOX OF EXCESS AND DEPRIVATION

American national health expenditures are now about 13 percent of the gross national product, up from 9.1 percent in 1980, and they are projected to reach 15 percent by 2000, far more than in any other country.[1-3] These expenditures are straining public finances at all levels of government. At the same time, roughly 35 million Americans have no health care coverage at all, public or private, and the number appears to be rising.[4-7] Millions more have inadequate insurance that leaves them vulnerable to large expenses, that excludes care of preexisting conditions, or that may be lost if they become seriously ill. The American health care financing and delivery system is becoming increasingly unsatisfactory and cannot be sustained. Comprehensive reform is urgently needed.

DIAGNOSIS

The etiology of this worsening paradox is extremely complex; many factors enter in. Some factors we would not change if we could (e.g., advancing medical technology, people living longer). We emphasize factors that are important and correctable.

First, our health care financing and delivery system contains more incentives to spend than to not spend. It is based on *cost-unconscious demand*. Key decision makers have little or no incentive to seek value for money in health care purchases. The dominant open-ended fee-for-service (FFS) system pays providers more for doing more, whether or not more is appropriate. ("Open ended" means that no budget is set in advance within which the job must be done.) Once insured, consumers are not cost conscious. Deductibles and coinsurance at the point of service have little or no effect on most spending, which is on sick people who have exceeded their out-of-pocket spending limits. "Free choice of provider insurance" blocks cost consciousness on the demand side by depriving the insurer of bargaining power. This approach is rapidly yielding in the marketplace to preferred provider insurance. In its present forms, preferred provider insurance helps to regulate price but is not yet very effective in controlling the volume of services. Medicare, Medicaid, and the subsidies to employer-provided health care coverage built into the income and payroll tax laws are all open ended and encourage decisions in favor of more costly care. These incentives are reinforced by a medical culture that esteems use of the most advanced technology, high patient expectations, and the threat of malpractice litigation if these expectations are not met.

Contrary to a widespread impression, America has not yet tried *competition* of alternative health care financing and delivery plans, using the term in the normal economic sense, i.e., *price* competition to serve cost-conscious purchasers. When there is price competition, the purchaser who chooses the more expensive product pays the full difference in price and is thus motivated to seek value for money. However, in offering health care coverage to employees, most employers provide a larger subsidy to the FFS system than to health maintenance organizations (HMOs), thereby destroying the incentive for consumers and providers to choose the economical alternative. Many employers offer no choice but FFS coverage.[8,9] Others offer choices but pay the whole premium, whichever choice the employee makes. In such a case, the HMO has no incentive to hold down its premium; it is better off to charge more and use the money to improve service. In many other cases, employers offer a choice of plan, but the employer pays 80 or 90 percent of the premium or all but some fixed amount, whichever plan the employee chooses. In all these cases, the effect is that the employer pays more on behalf of the more costly system and deprives the efficient alternatives of the opportunity to attract more customers by cutting cost and price.

The rational policy from an economic point of view would be for employers to structure health plan offerings to employees so that those who choose the less costly plans get to keep the full savings. Several factors discourage them from doing this. Employers became committed to paying the price of the FFS plan in the 1960s and 1970s, when costs were much lower and HMOs were few. Now this commitment is hard to break. When an employment group considers more costly and less costly health plans, it knows that government will pay about one third of the extra cost of the more costly plan through tax remission. Labor unions see management commitment to full payment of costs of the open-ended system as a precious bargaining prize. There is a need for collective action. If one employer attempts to convert to cost-conscious employee choice while other employers remain with the employer-pay-all system, the employer will get disgruntled employees in the short run but no reformed, cost-effective health care system in the long run. For the latter to happen, most employers in a geographic area must convert to cost-conscious choice.

The second major problem is that our present health care financing and delivery system is not organized for quality and economy. One of the main drives in the present system is for each specialist to exercise his or her specialty, not to produce desired outcomes at reasonable cost. In a system designed for quality and economy, managed care organizations would attract the responsible participation of physicians who would understand that, ultimately, their patients bear the costs of care, and they would accept the need for an economical practice style. Data would be gathered on outcomes, treatments, and resource use, and providers would base clinical decisions on such data. We have few outcome data today. The FFS system often pays more to poor performers who have high rates of complications than to good performers who solve patients' medical problems quickly and economically. High-quality performers are not rewarded, because of the payment system and because employers and consumers do not have the data to identify them.

There are too many beds and too many specialists in relation to the number of primary care physicians. A high-quality cost-effective system would carefully match the numbers and types of physicians retained and other resources to the needs of the population served so that each specialist and sub-specialist would be busy seeing just the type of patient she or he was trained to treat. We have a proliferation of costly specialized services that are underutilized. For example, in 1986, more than one third of the hospitals in California doing open-heart surgery performed fewer than 150 operations, the minimum annual volume recommended by the American College of Surgeons (*Los Angeles Times,* December 27, 1988:3).

The third major problem area is "market failure." The market for health insurance does not naturally produce results that are fair or efficient. It is plagued by problems of biased risk selection, market segmentation, inadequate information, "free riders," and the like.[10] Insurers profit most by avoiding coverage of those who need it most. The insurance market for small employment groups is breaking down as small employers find insurance unavailable or unaffordable, especially if a group member has a costly medical condition. Most employment groups are too small for risk spreading or economical purchase of health insurance. Systematic action by large collective purchasers is needed to manage competition to reward providers of high-quality economical care and to make affordable coverage available to individuals and small groups.

Fourth, public funds are not distributed equitably or effectively to motivate widespread coverage. The unlimited exclusion of employer health benefit contributions from the taxable incomes of employees is the second-largest federal government health care "expenditure," trailing only expenditures for the Medicare program. While providing incentives for the well-covered well-to-do to choose even more generous coverage, this provision does little or nothing for those (mainly lower-income) people without employer-provided coverage. Most of the $46 billion the federal budget lost to this tax break in 1990 went to households with above-average incomes, many of whom would have bought at least catastrophic expense protection without the tax subsidy, while little went to households with below-average incomes, people whose decisions to insure could be substantially affected by such subsidies. The system works backwards: the most powerful incentives to insure go to those in the highest income tax brackets. From a tax effectiveness point of view, it should be the reverse. Government-provided subsidies should give everyone strong incentives to purchase coverage and to choose economically.

OUR PROPOSAL

We propose a set of public policies and institutions designed to give everyone access to a subsidized but responsible choice of efficient, managed care (HMO, preferred provider insurance plans, etc).[11, 12] We propose *comprehensive reform of the economic incentives* that drive the system. We propose cost-conscious informed consumer and employer (or other sponsor) choice of managed care so that plans competing to serve such purchasers will have strong incentives to give value for money. We also propose a strategy of *managed competition* to be executed by large employers and public sponsors (explained below), designed to reward with more subscribers those health care financing and delivery plans that offer high-quality care at relatively low cost. The goal of these policies would be the gradual transformation of the health care financing and delivery system, through voluntary private action, into an array of managed care plans, each competing to attract providers and subscribers by finding ways to improve the quality of care and service while cutting costs. We propose restructuring the tax subsidies to create incentives to cover the uninsured and to encourage the insured to be cost conscious in their choice of plan. We propose the creation of public institutions to broker and market subsidized coverage for all who do not obtain it through large employers. We favor substantial public investments in outcomes and effectiveness research to improve the information base for medical practice and consumer/employer choice.

Public Sponsor Agencies

The Public Sponsor, a quasi-public agency (like the Federal Reserve) in each state, would contract with a number of private-sector health care financing and delivery plans typical of those offered to the employee population and would offer subsidized enrollment to all those who do not have employment-based coverage. Except in the case of the poor, the Public Sponsor would contribute a fixed amount equal to 80 percent of the cost of the average plan that just meets federal standards. The enrollee would pay the rest. (The 80 percent level was chosen to balance two incentives. First, we wanted the subsidy level to be low enough so that there would be room for efficient plans to compete by lowering prices and taking subscribers away from inefficient plans. Second, we wanted the subsidy to be high enough so that the purchase of health insurance would appear very attractive even to those who expect to have no medical expenses.) To the enrollee, the Public Sponsor would look like the employee benefits office.

In the case of the poor, we propose additional subsidies. People at or below the poverty line would be able to choose any health plan with a premium at or below the average and have it fully paid. For people with incomes between 100 and 150 percent of the poverty line, we propose public sharing of the premium contribution on a sliding scale related to income.

Public Sponsors would also act as collective purchasing agents for small employers who wished to take advantage of economies of scale and the ability of Public Sponsors to spread and manage risk. Small employers could obtain coverage for their groups by payment of a maximum of 8 percent of their payroll.

Today, a substantial part of the money required to pay for care of the uninsured comes from more or less broadly based state and local sources, including employers' payments to private hospitals for bad debt or free care and direct appropriations from state and local governments to acute-care hospitals. In our proposal, federal funds (the sources of which are described below) would be the main source of support for the Public Sponsors. These funds would be supplemented by funds from state and local sources.

Mandated Employer-Provided Health Insurance

For better or worse, we have an employment-based system of health insurance for most people under age 65 year. It can be modified gradually but not replaced overnight. Most employers and employees agree that health care will be included in the compensation package. This is responsible behavior; if one of the group gets sick, the group pays the cost. Some employers and employees do not include health care in the package. The effect is irresponsible behavior; if an employee becomes seriously ill, these employers and employees count on someone else to pay. They are taking a "free ride." It is hard to justify raising taxes on the insured to pay for coverage for the employed uninsured unless those uninsured are required to contribute their fair share.

The existence of Public Sponsors would give all employers access to large-scale efficient health care coverage arrangements. However, in the absence of corrective action, the availability of subsidized coverage for uninsured individuals would create an incentive for employers to drop coverage of their employees. This would create additional expense for the Public Sponsor without compensating revenue. To prevent this, our proposal requires employers to cover their full-time employees (employers would make a defined contribution equal to 80 percent of the cost of an average plan meeting federal standards and would offer a choice of health plans meeting federal standards).

Premium Contributions From All Employers and Employees

Many people who are self-employed, who have part-time or seasonal work, or who are retired and under age 65 years do not have enough attachment to one employer to justify requiring the employer to provide coverage. Thus, an employer mandate for full-time employees would leave out millions of people. Moreover, in the absence of corrective action, a requirement that employers cover full-time employees creates a powerful incentive to use part-time employees.

We propose that employers be required to pay an 8 percent payroll tax on the first $22,500 of the wages and salaries of part-time and seasonal employees, unless the employer covered the employee with a health insurance plan meeting federal standards. Self-employed persons, early retirees, and everyone else not covered through employment would be required to contribute through the income tax system. An 8 percent tax would apply to adjusted gross income up to an income ceiling related to the size of the household. The ceiling would be calculated to ensure that households with sufficient income paid for approximately the total subsidy that would be made available to them through the Public Sponsor.

The proceeds of these taxes would be paid by the federal government to the states, on a per-person-covered basis, for use by Public Sponsors in offering subsidized coverage to persons without employment-based coverage.

This tax would be at the federal level because individual states might be deterred from levying such a tax by employer threats to move to a state without the tax.

Limit on Tax-Free Employer Contributions

We propose that Congress change the income and payroll tax laws to limit the tax-free employer contribution to 80 percent of the average price of a comprehensive plan meeting federal standards. The average price of a qualified health plan in 1991 might be roughly $290 per family per month. As a condition of tax exemption, employer health plans would be required to use fixed-dollar defined contributions, independent of employee choice of plan, not to exceed the limit, so that people who choose more costly health care plans must do so with their *own* money, not with that of the taxpayer or employer.

The purposes of this measure are two-fold. First, it would save the federal budget some $11.2 billion in 1988 dollars. This money could be used to help finance subsidies for the uninsured comparable to those received by the employed insured. Second, making people cost conscious would help enlist all employed Americans in a search for value for money in health care, would stimulate the development of cost-effective care, and would create a market for cost-effective managed care. Thus, this tax reform is defensible on grounds of both equity and efficiency.

Budget Neutrality

The Congressional Budget Office has estimated the effects of our proposal on coverage, costs, and the federal budget and has found that our proposed new revenues would equal the added outlays.[13] We have not done a state-by-state analysis, but, in the aggregate, required state and local contributions appear to approximately equal outlays for care of the uninsured.

Managed Competition

The market for health insurance does not naturally produce results that are fair or efficient. It is plagued by problems of biased risk selection, market segmentation, inadequate information, etc. In fact, the market for health insurance cannot work at the individual level. To counteract these problems, large employers and Public Sponsors must structure and manage the demand side of this market.[10] They must act as intelligent, active, collective purchasing agents and manage a process of informed cost-conscious consumer choice of "managed care" plans to reward providers of high-quality economical care. Tools of effectively managed competition include the annual open-enrollment process; full employee consciousness of premium differences; a standardized benefit package within each sponsored group; risk-adjusted sponsor contributions, so that a plan that attracts predictably sicker people is compensated; monitoring disenrollments; surveillance; ongoing quality measurement; and improved consumer information.

Outcomes Management and Effectiveness Research

As Ellwood[14] and Roper et al[15] have pointed out, there is a poverty of relevant data linking outcomes, treatments, and resource use. Although such data are costly to gather, they constitute a public good, and their production ought to be publicly mandated and supported. Combined with the incentives built into our proposal, such data could be of great value to providers and patients seeking more effective and less costly treatments. Without incentives for efficiency, such data are likely to have little impact on health care costs.

Mutually Supportive Components

Some components of our proposal have been proposed individually. However, they would be much more effective as parts of an integrated, comprehensive reform program than they would be alone. Consider, for example, a law that employers must cover their full-time employees. Alone, this law would leave out people who are not employed on a full-time basis and their dependents—12 million people. Without a payroll tax on uninsured employees, employers would have a strong incentive to escape the mandate by using part-time employees. Without Public Sponsors, the law would not address the problem of availability of affordable coverage for small employers. Without the limit on tax-free employer contributions, the law would not address the need for a cost-containment strategy.

We recognize the propensity of the American political system to seek minimal, incremental change. Some components of our proposal would be viable and helpful on their own. However, we believe that effective solution of the problems of access and cost requires a comprehensive strategy, and the merits of the combined package exceed the merits of the individual components.

WILL IT WORK?

Our confidence that a reasonably well-managed comprehensive reform plan along these lines can be made to work rests on two propositions.

First, efficiently managed care does exist. It is possible to improve economic performance substantially over the non-selective FFS, solo practice, third-party intermediary model. The best documented example was a randomized comparison of per capita resource use between Group Health Cooperative of Puget Sound and traditional third-party insurance and FFS providers in Seattle, Wash, in the Health Insurance Experiment of the RAND Corp.[16] Group Health Cooperative of Puget Sound cared for its assigned patients at a cost about 28 percent lower than that in the FFS sector, resulting in essentially equal health outcomes and overall patient satisfaction about 95 percent as high. Satisfaction with interpersonal aspects of care and technical quality was 98 percent as high as in the FFS sector.[17, 18] Group Health Cooperative of Puget Sound accomplished this without much cost-conscious demand and without any significant competing organized system. One wonders how much better they might have done if there had been several such organizations competing to serve cost-conscious consumers. Other nonrandomized studies have produced similar results.[19]

Many physicians and patients may prefer practice styles other than prepaid group practice. We do not have similar experimental evidence on the economic performance of independent practice associations and preferred provider insurance plans. However, we have observed wide variation in the performance of providers. For example, in Los Angeles, Calif, in 1986, one hospital performed 44 coronary artery bypass grafts with an 11.4 percent death rate and median charges of $59,000, while another hospital performed 770 coronary artery bypass grafts with a 3.8 percent death rate and median charges of $16,000 (*Los Angeles Times,* July 24, 1988:3). Some managed care plans would find ways of selecting economical providers of high quality and would channel business to them, improving quality and cutting costs substantially.

Second, people do choose value for money. Our limited experience with even attenuated price competition in employment groups such as federal employees, California state employees, and Stanford University suggests that, over time, people do migrate to cost-effective systems. A recent study of health plan choice in the Twin Cities, Minnesota, area found that employees' decisions are quite sensitive to health plan prices.[20, 21] This accords with generally accepted principles of economic behavior.

We have been asked, "Why, if nonprofit HMOs are so much more efficient and desirable, have they failed to grow except very modestly?" In times past, legal and professional barriers were important, including illegal restraints of trade.[22] In recent years, the main inhibitor of the growth of HMOs has been the employer contribution policies we have discussed; that is, most employers do not structure their health plan offerings in such a way that the employee who chooses the most economical plan gets to keep the savings. Nevertheless, some nonprofit HMOs have been growing rapidly; through the 1980s, Harvard Community Health Plan averaged membership growth of more than 11 percent per year, and the Kaiser-Permanente Medical Care Program averaged 5.2 percent growth on a much larger base. However, the success of our proposal does not depend only on nonprofit HMOs. Other forms of cost-effective managed care may do the job. What we propose is a restructured market system in which the efficient prosper and the inefficient must improve or fail.

COMPREHENSIVE REFORM THAT RELIES ON INCENTIVES IS PREFERABLE TO DIRECT GOVERNMENT CONTROLS

One alternative to the system we have proposed is a system like Canada's, in which the government is the sole payer for physician and hospital services. While Canada's system has evident strengths, there would be major difficulties in successfully adopting or implementing it in the United States. First, it would require a political sea change to adopt such a system here. A tax increase of approximately $250 billion per year would be required, the intense opposition of insurers and many provider groups would need to be overcome, and the concerns of many employers and citizens about the effects of such a system on access and quality would need to be allayed. In the era in which the Berlin wall has been torn down, one must be cautious about branding any proposal as politically infeasible, but it is difficult to imagine a politician winning election on a platform including an extremely large tax increase. Second, government regulatory processes tend to freeze industries and often penalize efficiency. The Canadian system is not as frozen as it might be because proximity to the United States exposes Canadians to our innovations. If American medical care were also entirely financed and regulated by the government, the negative effects of regulation would likely loom larger.

A second alternative would be to leave the financing of health insurance for the employed population in the private sector but to have the government regulate physician and hospital prices for all-payers. It is possible to imagine a political compromise in which such a system could be adopted—in the midst of a recession, providers might agree to accept all payer price controls in exchange for an employer mandate, and employers might acquiesce to a mandate in exchange for price controls—but it is hard to imagine that such a regulatory structure could be effective over time in promoting quality or economy. Such price controls would be met by continuing provider efforts to circumvent and modify them. Providers would lobby for adjustments and exceptions deemed to enhance equity, increasing the complexity of the regulations and the incentives for those who were not favored to seek favor. Congress would have created a rich new barrel of pork to reward electoral supporters and contributors—an especially attractive source, because price increases for private sector rates could be granted without requiring a tax increase.

Furthermore, such a system does not contain incentives to shift medical care resources from less productive to more productive uses. The current mantra in cost containment is the development of practice guidelines and the application of these guidelines to eliminate the ineffective practices that exist in our medical care system today. While we strongly support the development of better outcomes data and practice guidelines, in the absence of change in the financial incentives created by the FFS system, such guidelines will do little either to control costs or to lead to improvements in efficiency. For guideline development to succeed, medical care would have to be much more of a science and much less of an art than it is likely to be at any time in the foreseeable future.

Finally, administrative costs in the present system are high and increasing.[23] These costs arise from many causes: the multiplicity of payers, each with its own forms, processes, and data requirements; the high marketing costs associated with the coverage of individuals and small groups; the costs of determining eligibility for coverage in a system in which millions have no coverage; the costs of billing patients for covered services; the costs of payers attempting to determine whether services were actually provided and were appropriate; and others. We believe administrative costs would be greatly reduced under our proposal. After a competitive shakedown, there would be relatively few managed care organizations in each geographic area. Everyone would get coverage through large group arrangements. Eligibility determination would be simple in a system of universal coverage. Today, the best managed care organizations do not bill patients for services. Providers are paid by health plans in simplified ways using prospective payments for global units of care. In a system with relatively few managed care organizations competing to serve competent sponsors and cost-conscious consumers, payers would not have to attempt to micromanage the delivery of care because providers would be at risk. Administrative costs and the "hassle factor" would be much lower than they are today. However, the most important economies would be in the effective organization of the process of care itself.

Over time, we would expect slowed growth in the price of the average health plan and continuing improvements in efficiency comparable to those in other competitive industries.

1. Office of the Actuary, Health Care Financing Administration. National health expenditures, 1986-2000. *Health Care Financ Rev.* Summer 1987;8:1-36.

2. GJ Schiedber and JP Poullier, Recent trends in international health care spending. *Health Aff* Fall 1987;6:105-112.

3. *1991 US Industrial Outlook.* Washington, DC: US Dept of Commerce: 1991.

4. R Kronick, *The Slippery Slope of Health Care Finance: Business, Hospitals, and Health Care for the Poor in Massachusetts.* Rochester, NY: University of Rochester; 1990. Thesis.

5. FR Wilensky, Filling the gaps in health insurance: impact on competition. *Health Aff* Summer 1988;7:133-149.

6. P Ries, Health care coverage by age, sex, race, and family income: United States, 1986. In *Advance Data From Vital and Health Statistics of the National Center for Health Statistics: No. 139.* Hyattsville, Md: Public Health Service; 1987. US Dept of Health and Human Services publication PHS 87-1250.

7. *Health Insurance and the Uninsured: Background Data and Analysis.* Washington, DC: Congressional Research Service, Library of Congress; 1988.

8. GA Jensen, MA Morrisey and JW Marcus, Cost sharing and the changing pattern of employer-sponsored health benefits. *Milbank Q* 1987;65:521-542.

9. Foster Higgins Health Care Benefits Survey. *Managed Care Plans.* New York, NY: Foster Higgins; 1989.

10. A Enthoven, *Theory and Practice of Managed Competition in Health Care Finance.* Amsterdam, the Netherlands: Elsevier Science Publishers; 1988.

11. A Enthoven, and R Kronick R, A consumer choice health plan for the 1990s: universal health insurance in a system designed to promote quality and economy, I. *N Engl J Med* 1989;320:29-37.

12. A Enthoven and R Kronick, A consumer choice health plan for the 1990s: universal health insurance in a system designed to promote quality and economy, II. *N Engl J Med* 1989;320:94-101.

13. S Long and J Rodgers, *Enthoven-Kronick Plan for Universal Health Insurance.* Washington, DC: Congressional Budget Office; 1988.

14. PM Ellwood, Outcomes management: a technology of patient experience. *N Engl J Med* 1988;318:1549-1556.

15. Wl Roper, W Winkenwerder, GM Hackbarth and H Krakauer, Effectiveness in health care. *N Engl J Med* 1988;318:1549-1556.

16. WG Manning, A Leibowitz, GA Goldberg, WH Rogers, and JP Newhouse, A controlled trial of the effect of a prepaid group practice on use of services. *N Engl J Med* 1984;310:1505-1510.

17. AR Davies, JE Ware, RH Brook, JR Petersona and JP Newhouse, Consumer acceptance of prepaid and fee-for-service medical care: results from a randomized controlled trial. *Health Serv Res* 1986;23:429-452.

18. EM Sloss, EB Keeler, RH Brook, BH Operskalski, GA Goldberg and JP Newhouse, Effect of a health maintenance organization on physiologic health. *Ann Intern Med* 1987;106:130-138.

19. HS Luft, How do health-maintenance organizations achieve their 'savings'? Rhetoric and evidence. *N Engl J Med.* 1978;298:1336-1343.

20. R Feldman, B Dowd, M Finch and S Cassou, *Employee-Based Health Insurance.* Rockville, Md: National Center for Health Services Research: 1989. US Dept of Health and Human Services publication PHS 89-3434.

21. R Feldman, M Finch, B Dowd and S Cassou, The demand for employment-based health insurance plans. *J Hum Res* 1989;24:115-142.

22. CD Weller, 'Free choice' as a restraint of trade in American health care delivery and insurance plans. *J Hum Res* 1989;69:1351-1392.

23. DU Himmelstein and S Woolhandler, Cost without benefit: administrative waste in US health care. *N Engl J Med* 1986;314:441-445.

Part 2

COST-EFFECTIVE PLAN DESIGN

6. Understanding Your Company's Health Care Costs

Virginia M. Gibson

The U.S. healthcare crisis stems from a multitude of factors that adversely impact corporate costs of providing benefits to employees. Businesses have implemented increasingly more sophisticated and diverse methods in an attempt to predict and moderate rising healthcare expenditures. Most methods, however, do not succeed in curtailing cost over the long-term because they fail to look at all the benefits areas that contribute to ongoing cost increases.

By trying to identify contributing factors to spiraling increases in medical care, companies often single out the practice patterns of physicians and other healthcare professionals as the most significant factors that fuel cost increases. As a result, corporate America has witnessed a phenomenal increase in employee benefits programs that place restrictions on providers, encourage access to the healthcare delivery system through gatekeepers, and offer incentives for participants to use preferred providers. More employers than ever before also have turned to self-insurance and self-administration arrangements because they believe these systems offer more flexibility and control. Insurance companies, third-party administrators and consulting firms today routinely conduct complex data analysis and utilization reviews. But with all these cost-control measures in place, a majority of companies, even ones that report successes, remain unsure if these interventions will have any long-term impact on healthcare cost management.

TWO COMMON PERSPECTIVES

Employers traditionally look at the cost of providing benefits from two perspectives: by plan and by participant. Looking at costs by plan involves analyzing healthcare expenses independently of other benefits, including workers' compensation, sick leave and disability programs. Analysis by participant focuses on costs per employee or employee dependent. Most benefits analysis systems provided by insurers and consultants measure the average cost by various categories, such as diagnosis, treatment codes, inpatient hospitalizations, outpatient procedures and managed care program utilization. Data then can be reported generally by various classifications, including employees, dependents, retirees, COBRA and long-term disability beneficiaries.

Although the responsibility for these programs may fall within the human resources department, the management, design and analysis for each one usually is conducted independently by specialists in benefits, occupational safety and risk management, and the corporate medical department. To further complicate matters, professionals from each division often do not exchange information freely because they do not see such communication as critical to controlling costs. These types of aggregate analyses eventually provide a distorted view of what's really causing cost increases.

Nevertheless, employers armed with volumes of data from these reports have tried to reduce costs by implementing blanket utilization reviews and managed care programs. Many companies now require precertification of hospital admissions, mandate second opinions for elective surgical procedures, encourage use of outpatient facilities, promote the purchase of generic prescription drugs and require high-risk/high-cost beneficiaries to submit to hands-on-management by specially trained professionals.

LIMITED IMPACT

Theoretically, a plan design that reduces or eliminates benefits for noncompliance would provoke employees to adhere to these requirements. Many employers agree that these approaches often produce positive results initially, but their impact diminishes as providers and beneficiaries adapt to the new requirements.

This limited impact often occurs because the utilization review is designed to look at aggregate costs by plan. Initial changes in the types of medical expenses and a reduction in bottom-line costs are attributed improperly to managed care interventions. But a more realistic explanation for the changes is that the costs have migrated or shifted to a more readily accessible plan, such as long-term disability or workers' compensation. Only by analyzing all programs in aggregate and by participant can HR professionals gain an accurate picture.

To develop a benefits program that allocates available resources efficiently and appropriately, HR must be able to accurately access the following:

- For which services are corporate dollars being spent?
- Where are these services being used?
- Who is spending these dollars?
- What incentives inherent in the program design encourage overutilization?

Without the answer to these questions, it is impossible to design programs that both effectively manage costs and meet the needs of employees.

Harold H. Gardner, M.D., president of Options & Choices Inc., a Cheyenne, Wyo.-based research company that provides preventative health services and participant-focused benefits financial systems, explained that traditional utilization review programs only exacerbate the cycle of increasing costs.

"Based upon extensive data analysis of our clients, we generally have found that less than 20 percent of an employee population incurs 80 percent of all expenses," Gardner said. "This is known as the 80/20 Law or the Pareto Rule. Therefore, unless employers begin to understand just who is in their Pareto Group, they will continue to see dramatic increases in all benefits costs including workers' compensation, sick days and disability programs, as well as group health."

WHERE DOLLARS ARE SPENT

Employers that look at benefits costs separately will not gain a true sense of what affects their costs. On average, the costs for employee medical expenditures represent only 52 percent of total dollars spent, with an additional 3 percent going toward dental, vision and life insurance benefits. Workers' compensation medical costs account for another 18 percent, and administrative expenses take up 10 percent. The real surprise is that employees on disability account for 17 percent of the total cost of medical benefits. This area traditionally has not been questioned and therefore left unmanaged.

As medical costs for disabled employees increase, overall program costs increase proportionally. The picture becomes clearer when sick leave and disability programs are viewed as compensation rather than benefits, and serious consideration is given to the incentives provided to employees to access this compensation. If restrictions are placed on access to healthcare benefits using managed care principles that are not integrated into the design of disability, sick leave and workers' compensation programs, employees will access the system that requires the least amount of effort.

AVOIDING MIGRATIONS

An employer, when reviewing changes to its health plan following implementation of managed care programs, may misinterpret the outcomes of the effort if workers' compensation and disability programs are not reviewed at the same time. Since these programs also require employees to interface with the healthcare community in order to access benefits, an increase in healthcare costs may result for typical claims under disability plans, such as low back injuries, cardiovascular disease and pregnancy complications.

If restrictions are placed on access to care in only one area, the natural migration will be to other, more accessible areas. For example, a participant may have a problem with lower back pain that occasionally flares up. When this situation occurs, the person will attempt to get medical treatment and reimbursement for care under the employer's healthcare plan. If too many obstacles to receiving care exist in the medical plan, and fewer and less onerous obstacles exist in an alternative system, such as disability or workers' compensation, the incentive will be to enter those systems.

From another perspective, employees on disability are not affected by layoffs, performance expectations or changes in management. When job security becomes less certain, claims for workers' compensation and disability often will rise. This artificially inflates the employer's healthcare costs because medical treatment is required to access these forms of compensation.

WHO SPENDS THE DOLLARS

Only by preparing an aggregate analysis by participant will employers ever begin to get a handle on rising costs. An understanding of who spends the benefit dollars will help employers take a more aggressive, proactive approach to improve the health status of its employees and educate managers and workers about the risks that could directly affect their health.

Employers, however, should not take this identification to an extreme, such as sending a letter home to all of its overweight employees that encourages them to join a weight reduction program. Rather, the analysis establishes the Pareto Group for each plan. These groups then are overlaid to establish the subsets of the Pareto Group—the distribution of high-risk people and costs. The first statistic identifies the Pareto Group: 16.3 percent of the total employee population consumes 80 percent of the company's healthcare dollars. The second statistic shows the Pareto Group subset — of the 16.3 percent that consumes 80 percent of the dollars, 1 percent spends 26 percent of those dollars.

If companies can identify who spends the most money and offer appropriate health education programs, they can manage current treatments more effectively in terms of medical costs and lost productivity. In addition, they will begin to prevent or reduce the severity of future episodes of illness among employees.

This model requires employers to shift away from looking at medical treatment to the broader issues of people and jobs. There should be less concern about hospital care, diagnosis or treatment and more focus on the issue of people, health and productivity. The first step is to determine what people need. Once this is determined, then appropriate programs and plans can be developed.

7. First Chicago's Integrated Health Data Management Computer System

Wayne N. Burton   Donald A. Hoy

During the past two decades, there have been enormous improvements in infor-mation processing systems—today a mini-computer system, such as the one discussed in this article can perform tasks that were possible only on the largest mainframe computers. At the same time, a parallel evolution has been taking place in the manner in which employers provide access to health care for their employees. These separate developments came together at First Chicago/The First National Bank of Chicago (First Chicago) within the last few years to revolutionize the management of health care delivery for its 15,000 employees, retirees, and dependents.

Not too many years ago, the role of an employer like First Chicago was largely to design medical benefits sufficiently attractive to assist in obtaining and retaining qualified personnel, and to finance the costs of providing the covered health care services. In the early 1980s after a decade in which First Chicago's health care costs increased 25-35 percent annually, First Chicago made a decision to fundamentally change its role with respect to health care purchasing. Along with changes in plan design, funding and administration came two other strategic directions: the implementation of a hands-on wellness program, and the focus on where the corporation's health care dollars were being spent.

For First Chicago to gain any degree of control over the escalation of its health care costs, the company's benefits and medical units agreed that a detailed understanding of the sources of expense was required. Several areas in particular were identified for analysis: the highest cost patients; the largest dollar volume areas; the highest claims volume areas; the areas with the largest year-to-year growth; utilization outside of the regional norms; and especially the areas most susceptible to preventive intervention or early detection and therapy. Data analysis by the claims payor was virtually non-existent during the 1970s, although in the early 1980s substantial improvement was realized through cooperative efforts with the claims administrator. However, the information available was still lacking in specificity, and could not be coordinated with the data regarding short- and long-term disabilities, health screening exams, participation in the wellness program, nursing records, etc. Equally important, almost one-half of First Chicago's employees are participants in one of the health maintenance organizations (HMOs) made available to them, and data from the HMOs was very limited and difficult to obtain.

Accordingly, First Chicago determined in the mid 1980s that it would be necessary to commence in-house data management. This entailed developing and enhancing outside software and allowed longitudinal studies and statistical analysis capabilities that could be applied to both data from the indemnity claims and the HMO plans (which can supply such information). The objective was to develop a system that could provide general health care cost utilization analysis information as well as *ad hoc* analysis of almost any specific health care issue, demographic group, or geographic area. The result was the Occupational Medical and Nursing Information (OMNI) system, an integrated health data management computer system. OMNI was installed at First Chicago in 1987 for the purpose of better managing health care and disability costs and to evaluate the effectiveness of medical intervention efforts. This innovative system integrates all of the employee, dependent, and retiree data available from a number of different sources including:

- Inpatient medical claims
- Outpatient medical claims
- HMO encounter data
- Disability/absence records
- Wellness Program
- Laboratory test results (e.g., cholesterol)
- Health risks (e.g., blood pressure, alcohol intake, etc.)
- Medical department records
- Employee Assistance Program records
- Physical examinations
- Disability designations
- Demographics (age, sex, location, medical coverage, job, etc.)

First Chicago's medical and benefits units have worked in unison for the past decade to design health care cost management strategies. Our basic strategy was twofold: (1) to implement changes in a very liberal medical benefits plan to

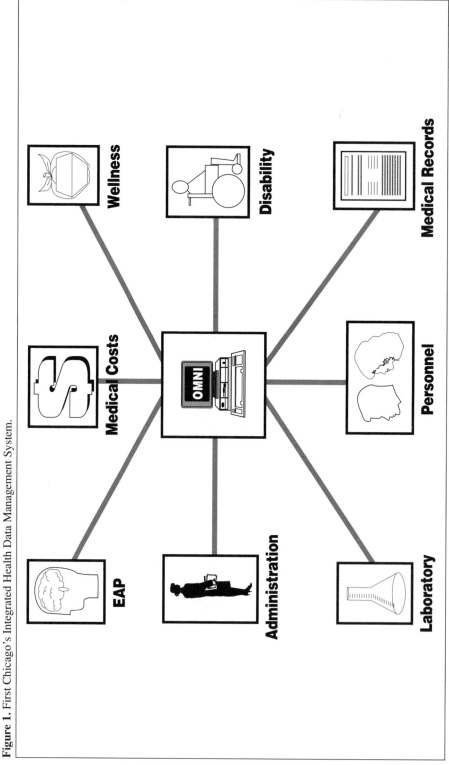

Figure 1. First Chicago's Integrated Health Data Management System.

effect an immediate impact on health care costs, and (2) to implement comprehensive health promotion programs (wellness and on-site preventive medical services) for medium and long-term impact on health care costs.

In the 1990s, health care cost management is an information business. Information technology will be the engine that drives health care cost and quality management efforts. Most major companies have access to health care costs and utilization data, but few have access to health care *information*; the distinction between the two is essential. Health care data are a stack of computer sheets, while health care information provides insight into the drivers of health costs. An integrated health data management system is a powerful tool to provide a company with information that can result in health care cost avoidance and improvements in the quality of health care. Such systems can identify the problems, point to potential solutions, and evaluate the results of your strategies.

Health care costs are interrelated, a fact often overlooked and difficult to track. For example, a reduction in mental health benefits may be counterproductive in containing costs—it may result in employees or family members not seeking prompt or proper treatment for these problems. Untreated or inadequately treated mental health problems may lead to both increased medical costs for non-psychiatric health problems and increased short- and long-term disability costs (because an employee may be unable to work without appropriate treatment).

BACKGROUND

In 1986, First Chicago's medical and benefits units began conceptualizing a computer system for day-to-day medical unit services that would analyze a multitude of factors that affect health care costs. After extensive evaluations, we selected two computer consultants to divide the work of acquiring and analyzing insurance claims into two stages. Health Decisions, Inc. (Minneapolis) would collect, verify, and organize claims data for employees and dependents into an event-based computer file encompassing both inpatient and outpatient information. Stephens Systems Services, Inc. (New York) would then merge this file into the medical unit's integrated medical records systems, thus allowing for comparisons and correlations among various elements of both insurance claims and medical information.

THE OMNI SYSTEM

OMNI is an on-line, multinumerical system that allows numerous users to access and update information simultaneously. Immediate access for authorized users is provided to the records of more than 35,000 individuals, including present and former employees. The OMNI data base is constantly changing and growing as a result of regular updates of personnel information and the daily recording of new in-house medical services.

The OMNI system runs on a Digital MicroVax II minicomputer. Presently there are a total of 18 work stations linked to the computer, which is potentially expandable to serve 64 work stations. The minicomputer is located in the medical unit and is totally separate from First Chicago's general purpose computers to ensure the security and confidentiality of medical records. The internal scrambling of staff names, three levels of passwords, date stamping of input information, and transaction logs capable of reporting who is entering information as well as who is viewing it provide further levels of security.

As a repository of integrated records, OMNI accepts information from a number of external services, including First Chicago's personnel system, a commercial laboratory (i.e., results of blood tests), and an IBM PC–based data collection subsystem (i.e., a computerized health risk appraisal system).

Personnel Data Base

OMNI's personnel data base is updated monthly on-line from First Chicago's central personnel data base. Employee information includes date of birth, gender, ethnicity, marital status, home address, home and work telephone numbers, full-time or part-time work status, disability designation, hire date, job location, job group, employee level, and type of medical insurance coverage (i.e., HMO or indemnity plan).

Medical Claims Data

Inpatient and outpatient medical claims data are supplied by the indemnity claims administrator and are reviewed and aggregated into event files by Health Decisions, Inc. All costs related to individual hospitalization (including physician fees, pre-admission laboratory tests, room and board charges, surgical fees, and other ancillary charges) are combined and grouped as part of the hospital event. Outpatient charges are similarly combined for an individual visit. Data fields include: encounter date, claimant gender, provider name, relationship of claimant (i.e., employee, spouse, or dependent), ICD-9 diagnostic code, CPT-4 procedure code, length of hospital stay, room and board costs, ancillary treatment costs, secondary procedure costs, other billed amounts, post-admission costs, primary procedure costs, other procedure costs, ancillary diagnostic costs, and total cost.

Figure 2. First Chicago Medical Plan Mental Health Costs (% of Total Medical Plan Costs)

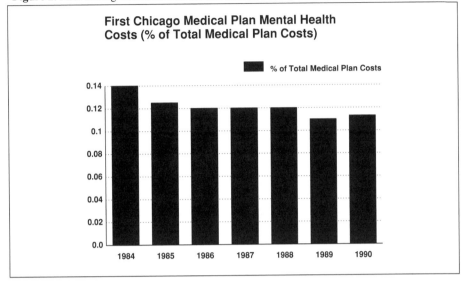

CLAIM DATA ANALYSIS

Using OMNI, medical claim analysis can be done on a timely basis. Detailed claims analyses based on gender, ethnicity, job location, job level, home location, and a multitude of other variables can be performed. Health insurance data from the OMNI system has been utilized to develop and evaluate the effectiveness of specific intervention strategies—for example, in the area of mental health.

Information from the claims administrator for the self-insured medical plan showed that mental health/substance abuse was the most costly category of health costs. The quality of mental health care, especially for adolescents, was of particular concern. As a result, a strategically designed program was developed and implemented in 1984 to address mental health/substance abuse costs for employees, dependents, and retirees. The four major components of the program are:

1. An Employee Assistance Program (EAP)/Wellness Program;
2. Psychiatric hospitalization utilization review;
3. Consulting psychiatrists for major case management; and
4. Benefit plan design changes.

As a result of the program, mental health/substance abuse costs actually declined during a period when overall medical costs for the bank substantially increased. Mental health benefits were enhanced to cover such services as partial and day hospitalization. Figure 2 summarizes mental health/substance abuse costs for employees and dependents for the period 1984 to 1990. During this period, mental health costs fell from 13.9 percent of total costs to 11.4 percent, while mental health benefit coverage was actually enhanced.

QUALITY OF CARE ANALYSIS

OMNI is able to identify health trends, evaluate the quality of health services, evaluate individual providers of health care, and facilitate and evaluate employee compliance with health and life-style interventions. For example, Cesarean section information is available from short-term disability forms submitted by an employee's doctor. The personnel database contains the type of the medical plan that the employee has selected (i.e., HMO, indemnity plan, or waived coverage). The results for the percentage of Cesarean sections by type of medical plans for employees were:

HMO A	19.4 percent
HMO B	22.6 percent
HMO C	26.7 percent
Indemnity Plan	30.1 percent

As a result of this analysis, a variety of programs were developed and implemented to address the high Cesarean section rate, which was affecting both health and disability costs. Employees having a Cesarean section delivery will generally require two weeks more of disability absence. The cost of a Cesarean section delivery is several thousand dollars more because of surgical fees and longer hospitalization. Greater than 40 percent of disability absence at First Chicago is attributable to pregnancy.

The intervention programs for Cesarean section deliveries initially included a mandatory second surgical opinion for elective Cesarean sections, a worksite prenatal health education program with financial incentives for participation, and employee education on the issues of unnecessary Cesarean sections. Recently we revised the program to make a second opinion for elective Cesarean sections voluntary and now offer prenatal obstetrical services on-site, with delivery at a nearby major teaching hospital. Preliminary data analysis is very encouraging; employees who have participated in the worksite prenatal health education program have significantly lower costs for a delivery and a much lower Cesarean section rate than those who haven't.

WELLNESS PROGRAM COST-BENEFIT ANALYSIS

Since 1985, First Chicago has offered a variety of women's health programs, including the bringing in of part-time, on-site gynecologists who perform annual women's health examinations. Since 1987, in cooperation with the March of

Dimes, a worksite prenatal health education program has been available to employees and their spouses. The goal of the prenatal education program is to encourage appropriate prenatal care. The noontime seminar topics include "Early Prenatal Care," "Healthy Life-Styles," "Nutrition and Exercise During Pregnancy," and "Pregnancy over 30." To encourage participation, employees or spouses who complete the classes by the fourth month of pregnancy are eligible to have the $300 deductible waived for the newborn.

OMNI is also used to track the potential benefits of the prenatal education program, as well as a variety of other wellness programs offered by First Chicago. The results to date, summarized below, support the findings of research that indicates that proper prenatal care will result in cost avoidance rather than cost shifting to the employee. Participants in the prenatal education program in the Chicago area had average inpatient hospital costs for delivery of about $3200 less than individuals who did not participate in the program.

	Did not attend a prenatal class	*Attended a prenatal class*
Number	61	60
Age (mean)	32.4 years	32.8 years
Total Inpatient Costs	$598,715	$394,849
Average Inpatient Costs	$9,815	$6,581

CONCLUSION

First Chicago's OMNI system has resulted in true cost reduction by cost avoidance rather than cost-shifting. These savings have been demonstrated consistently over several years in the areas of mental health/substance abuse and women's health. The system integrates all available data from several data bases, including inpatient and outpatient health claims, disability, health promotion program participation, personnel, and a computerized medical record. OMNI provides information that is being used to more accurately predict health care and disability costs and design intervention strategies for health care costs avoidance. Clearly, OMNI is providing information to manage the increasingly complex issues of health care cost versus quality.

Integrated health data management systems have the potential to assist in the selection of the highest quality and most cost-effective health care providers and to establish benchmarks for quality improvement. The OMNI system is critical to the ongoing analysis of the effectiveness of new intervention strategies, such as a managed mental health program. First Chicago is increasingly moving away from the role of financing health care services to managing—and delivering—those services.

Burton, W.N., Hoy, D.A., Stephens, M. "A Computer-Assisted Health Care Cost Management System." *Journal of Occupational Medicine*. 33(3) 268-271. 1991.

"Putting the Pieces Together: A Guide to the Implementation of Integrated Health Data Management Systems." Prevention Leadership Forum. Washington Business Group on Health (To be published in early 1992.)*

"Integrated Health Data Management Systems: A Tool for Avoiding Health Care Costs." Prevention Leadership Forum. Washington Business Group on Health. 1990.*

"Integrated Health Data Management Systems." Prevention Leadership Forum. Washington Business Group on Health. 1988.*

Yenney, Sharon L. "Solving the Health Data Management Puzzle." *Business and Health*. September, 1990. p. 25-31

Crowell, J., Carroll, M. "Company's Integrated Data Base Cuts Health Care Costs." *Group Practice Journal*, September/October, 1991 p. 27-31

---

* May be purchased from: Washington Business Group on Health, 777 N. Capital Street, NE, Suite 800, Washington, DC 20002. (202) 408-9320.

8. A New Wrinkle
in Cost Sharing

Basing a medical indemnity plan's deductible on enrollers' salaries may help achieve a variety of objectives.

A bank teller receives a benefit confirmation statement, which indicates that his medical plan deductible for the coming year will be $156. Upstairs, an assistant vice president enrolled in the same health coverage but earning three times as much learns that her annual deductible will be $468.

At a communications company, a $35,000 a year manager is subject to a $250 annual deductible while an executive earning $75,000 is assigned a $350 deductible for the same coverage.

In both situations, the employer relates deductibles to compensation. The bank applies a straight percentage of pay formula while the communications company's deductibles correspond to salary brackets.

Although salary-driven deductible schemes have been implemented in a variety of forms and settings, for the most part they remain outside the indemnity plan mainstream. Many employers have shied away from this strategy because of concerns about administrative complexity, the communications challenge and how certain segments of the population would be affected.

Currently, employer acceptance of salary-based deductibles, while not widespread, is conspicuously higher than it was a few years ago. "It's something we are running into more and more," reports Ken Sperling, a benefit consultant in Hewitt Associates' Rowayton, Connecticut office. In 1985, 7 percent of 560 large employers surveyed by Hewitt Associates utilized pay-based deductibles. By 1990, 11 percent fell into this category.

Why are more employers considering the installation of a salary-based deductible structure? The answer, Sperling suggests, is that "it accomplishes a number of objectives."

KEEPING DEDUCTIBLES UP TO DATE

Typically, when employers tinker with their medical plan's deductibles, the direction is upward and the goal is to make sure the copayment level is sufficient to help contain costs and to serve as a barrier to unnecessary utilization of the benefit. In this regard, many organizations have decided that the $100 individual deductible, which was virtually the standard in indemnity plans a few years ago, had become irrelevant because of inflation.

There also is a widespread perception that a higher deductible may affect plan costs. In a recent survey, Foster Higgins found that per employee medical costs averaged $246 less among employers with a $200 deductible than those with a $100 deductible.

Another factor prompting some employers to raise deductibles is that they perceive this to offer a relatively easy way to shift more costs to those people who use the benefit.

However, many employers also are concerned that in attempting to keep up with inflation they could end up increasing the deductible almost annually. And, as one benefit executive maintains, some companies would rather not deliver bad news to employees that often.

In this environment, a salary-based deductible can become increasingly attractive as a mechanism to automatically adjust the copayment upward without a lot of fanfare. Or as a benefits manager at a Fortune 500 company suggests, this tactic offers a long-term fix.

For example, a design which incorporates a percentage of pay formula can effectively suppress the overall rate of cost increases, Sperling advises. "It takes whatever the pay increase rate is and removes this component from the trend equation."

Another factor that has influenced some employers to adopt salary-related deductibles is that it represents a benefit change which a majority of the employee population is likely to perceive as fair and equitable. Usually there is a reasonable correlation between the deductible level in a salary-based plan and the ability to pay. "That seems to make a lot of sense when you step back and think about it." Sperling states.

Among those who share this perspective is the director of compensation and benefits at a Connecticut-based manufacturing concern where salary-related deductibles were installed in 1984. "I don't think we would put the highest level of deductible on the lowest paid person by any means, but that is what would happen if you use a single deductible," he maintains.

The manufacturing company bases its medical deductible on three annual earnings brackets: under $20,000, $20,000 to $40,000, and over $40,000.

A STEERING MECHANISM

In the mid-1980s, when only Xerox and a few other employers had installed salary-based medical deductibles, this move typically was portrayed as a hedge against inflation and as a way to assure employees who were being asked to pick up a larger share of plan costs that the burden was being distributed equitably based on the ability to pay.

Today, another objective frequently plays a major role in how the deductible is set up. Having led open-ended managed care programs, some employers want to underscore the financial incentive for employees, particularly the highly compensated, to seek care through network providers where prearranged fees apply rather than through the indemnity option which allows them to select a non-participating physician, but requires higher copayments.

"If you offer an indemnity plan where the deductible typically is $150 or $200, the higher-paid people are going to say 'I can afford that,'" explains Brenda Ballard Pflaum, an associate with consultants William M. Mercer, Inc., in Chicago. "But if they start to look at something that may be a percent of income on a $75,000 salary, there clearly is a much more distinct economic choice to make."

At Allied-Signal Inc. employees who use the managed care network pay set fees, such as $10 per office visit. Those who go to non-network providers encounter a 1 percent of pay annual deductible (3 percent for a family) and then are subject to co-insurance on an 80-20 basis. Their out-of-pocket maximum is 4 percent (12 percent for a family) of pay. "I don't think there is any question that this is a motivator for people to seek care in network, particularly the higher paid," observes Ron McGurn, vice president, group insurance and labor relations.

Allied-Signal's network currently covers more than two-thirds of the New Jersey-based company's 70,000 U.S. employees. In areas where the network is not yet available, the company has developed other arrangements, often with pay-related copayments. "It is not unusual in 1991 (in non-network areas) to have a one percent uncapped deductible with an out-of-pocket at two or three times this," McGurn reports.

THE BETTER FIT

Several factors can determine whether an employer is a good candidate for a pay-based deductible program. Generally, the fit is better when the salary range is broad, Sperling notes. Otherwise, if a large number of people have low salaries and a few are highly paid, this strategy may not accomplish much, he observes. "You are really only affecting a small group of people."

Also, the concept of benefits as pay versus benefits as entitlements can tip off whether an organization will be comfortable with salary-based co-payments. The further along an organization has moved on the road toward the compensation perspective the more likely it is to adopt this approach, Pflaum suggests, "because it does have this equity aspect to it."

For example, The Equitable Financial Companies installed salary-based co-payments for two health care options when flexible benefits were introduced January 1, 1991. "What is starting to evolve is that benefits are treated as a form of pay," explains Robert Sjogren, vice president.

Within both health plans at The Equitable the deductible and stop-loss limits are the same for single and family coverage. One option offers a 1 percent of pay deductible and 3 percent stop-loss. However, for a lower premium the employee can elect a plan with a 2-percent deductible and 6-percent stop-loss.

The Equitable designed the higher deductible option to keep costs at a minimum and to provide a greater benefit for lower-paid people, Sjogren explains. The premium is substantially lower than for the one-percent plan, and for many the stop-loss is an improvement since, in their previous coverage, the family limit had been $2,000.

How an employer views the issue of who will be affected also can influence its comfort level with a pay-based design. "A salary-based contribution to the cost of the benefit affects everyone," Sperling says, "but a salary-based deductible or benefit schedule only hits those who get sick." In addition, the consultant observes, "you are asking the higher paid people to pay more for the same benefits that everyone else gets."

What's more, when an employer moves to pay-related deductibles it is not unusual for co-payments to increase at almost all levels. "Even at one percent of a $25,000 salary you are up to $250 a year, and for a lot of companies that would be a fairly large net shift to employees," Pflaum explains.

An organization with numerous lower-paid employees might not want to go this route, the Mercer consultant suggests. But where a company has a lot of different pay levels and job classifications, she adds, salary-based deductibles can become a way to spread the resources of the plan.

THE BIGGEST OBSTACLE

Another key issue for many employers looking at pay-related deductibles is whether this approach is workable in its administrative environment. A company that has a good level of electronic interface and does personalized communications is not going to see this as a big jump, Sperling notes. "But a company without a whole lot of automation, one that might have multiple independent payroll vendors, or is not accustomed to doing a lot of reporting with its carrier, might find it a little bit cumbersome."

Some industry specialists consider the administrative issue to be the biggest hurdle that must be cleared before a salary-based methodology is adopted. "You have to get your pay information into the claims payment system," Pflaum says, "and for some organizations this is a real onerous sort of thing because they don't have good transmittal capabilities, and they just don't want to capture and move that stuff around."

The claims-processing entity, whether it is a carrier or third-party administrator, also has to be prepared to work with pay-based deductibles. At least among the major insurance companies, this may not appear to be a big problem. "They've done it before," Sperling notes.

Essentially, what the employer and administrator need to work out are the details of what information will be transmitted and in what form. Is the company going to transmit all the deductible information, or is it going to transmit salary information and the insurance company will figure out the deductibles?

Usually employers don't have problems doing it either way, Sperling reports. However, some carriers prefer to have the salaries because they can use that for life insurance, and they will write a front-end program to calculate the deductible. Some carriers, however, prefer that the employer provide the deductibles which they then download directly into the eligibility file, he notes.

At the Connecticut manufacturing company all claims are certified by the divisional human resources offices before they are submitted to a major commercial carrier for administration. "The certification indicates to the claims processor the level of deductible that applies to that particular claim," explains the benefits manager.

DIFFERENT APPROACHES

A common salary-based design is for the employer to set the deductible at some percentage of earnings, such as 1 percent of pay, and then have the out-of-pocket maximum at a higher percentage, perhaps four or five percent. "They kind of move in tandem," Pflaum says.

However, some companies elect to do some relative grading at higher salary levels when they relate deductibles to pay brackets. For example, at Ameritech where health care delivered outside a managed care network is subject to salary-driven co-payments, the individual deductible is $250 and the out-of-pocket maximum is $1,000 for an employee earning less than $50,000. However, when the salary exceeds $85,000, the deductible is $450 and the stop-loss caps at $1,500.

The University of Chicago offers another variation. It offers employees an indemnity plan where the deductible is zero but out-of-pocket limits are tied to income brackets.

BRACKETED VS. PERCENTAGE OF PAY

Some companies have elected the bracketed approach because they felt this would be easier to administer. "When you get into an exact deductible, one percent or 1.5 percent of pay, that data needs to be downloaded into a claims payer's eligibility system," Sperling observes.

Also, a percentage a pay formula can generate some odd amounts, and the company may want to have rounding-off rules, Pflaum suggests. On the other hand, use of a flat percentage may be a little bit easier for employees to understand.

In assigning deductibles to pay brackets, an employer must decide how many levels to use and what the break points will be. Most companies use three or four levels. "You want to keep it fairly simple," Sperling advises. But even a sizable array of deductibles can be handled depending on the level of automation, he adds.

In attaching set deductibles to pay levels, an employer may find that "bracket creep" prompts some complaints. "There is always going to be someone at the edge," Sperling notes. For example, a benefits executive for an employer in the Midwest reports that there has been some feedback from employees whose pay puts them just inside a higher bracket.

Still, many employers feel that the pluses of the pay-based system outweigh an occasional gripe. For example, at the University of Chicago, where the out-of-pockets are bracketed, "the break for the lower paid people has gone over extremely well," reports Hank Webber, assistant vice president for human resources.

IN THE FLEX ENVIRONMENT

Several employers have incorporated salary-related deductibles into flexible benefit plans. "Depending on the level of options, deductible and out-of-pocket amounts are different percentages so they can ratchet up in the same way as set deductible or out-of-pocket amounts would," Pflaum explains. For example, the employer might make a half-percent of pay deductible its high option, set one percent as the middle choice and use 2 percent for the low option.

The deductibles in a flex plan also can correspond to pay brackets, but a company taking this approach may run the risk of confusing employees. However, if the employer has a sophisticated enrollment set-up that includes examples, communications may not be that difficult, Pflaum advises.

For example, American Savings Bank in White Plains, New York, has found automation to be a big help in communicating a bracketed, pay-graded deductible program that was introduced when the bank first implemented flexible benefits in 1990. The bank established nine deductible levels for each of the applicable health coverages. These salary grades start with pay up to $15,000 and increase by $5,000 increments, until the top level, over $50,000, is reached.

At the annual enrollment, the bank provides each employee with an individualized form that has been generated by the bank's flexible benefits system. The form indicates the specific deductible based on that person's salary for each indemnity option and the core plan.

Moreover, the bank's experience, in regard to the actual administration of the health plan, is that the use of pay-related deductibles has not posed any problems. "We send the option and the salary range for each person to our carrier and they take care of it," reports Lori Staats, assistant vice president.

SETTING CAPS

Frequently, the impact of pay-based copayments on the higher paid will be allayed through the use of deductible and co-payment limits or by capping the salary base. At Marsh & McLennen Inc., there is a 1 percent of pay deductible, but the most anyone is required to pay is $1,000.

The Equitable has established a $100,000 ceiling on pay used to calculate the deductible in 1991, but the cap will be adjusted annually based on the consumer price index.

Where the cap is relatively low or there are not enough brackets at the high end, benefit specialists warn that the employer might encounter questions about fairness. "We've heard complaints from people earning $50,000 that they are paying the same deductible as someone at $75,000," reports one benefit manager.

Also, by setting the salary cap too low, an employer can dilute the value of the whole approach, benefit specialists suggest. However, if the cap rises to something like $75,000 or $100,000, the use of a salary-based formula can force the highly paid to make some more discrete economic choices, Pflaum suggests.

Allied Signal's decision to leave its deductibles uncapped was consistent with its overall benefit strategy. "We clearly don't want our people using out-of-network providers," McGurn states.

SOME BASIC CHORES

Before an employer rolls out a salary-based deductible scheme there usually is some examination of what the definition of pay is going to be. "For people who have a commissioned sales force, sometimes that decision can get a little tricky," Sperling says.

A related question concerns when pay is going to be measured. Usually, a company will pick a date, such as pay as of January 1 or September 30 of the prior year, and that will be used throughout the plan year. It also can be the prior year's W-2, Sperling notes.

In addition, an employer may need to devote some attention to making sure that employees understand that their deductible could change every year. Yet, many employees already are accustomed to salary-based arrangements in life insurance, 401(k) matching formulas and long-term disability benefits, Sperling states. "So it is not a new concept, but rather it extends an existing concept into a new benefit area."

DIFFERENT REACTIONS

The ultimate hurdle for some employers considering pay-based deductibles is that this is something that usually has to be approved by the people who it will hurt the most, senior management. And the highest paid people frequently are the most vocal in an organization. "A company that puts in a salary-based system is likely to hear more than one reaction," Sperling advises.

There are several reasons that a salary-related deductible may strike a sour note with higher paid employees. For one thing there are tax issues. "What you are doing is really shifting part of their total income away from a tax-preferred vehicle into a taxable one," Pflaum says.

"If the company has a $150 deductible and the premium is set at a certain amount, the company contribution is not taxable to the employee and is tax deductible to the company," she explains. "If they go to a much higher deductible, let's say $750, then that $750 has to be paid in after-tax dollars, plus the tax rate is at the high end."

Being up front about the plan's objectives may help deflect some objections from higher-paid employees. A bank, for example, was able to mollify critics by pointing out that its medical costs were skyrocketing and that it needed some protection against inflation.

OTHER ISSUES

In some organizations, getting middle managers to buy into a pay-based deductible scheme can be critical for a smooth implementation. At least one employer has scuttled a salary-related scheme because of a problem getting these influential people to appreciate and understand what was being done. The bottom line was that the supervisors did not like this approach, Pflaum notes, "and if the company could not sell it to them, it would not be able to sell it on down."

Another reason some employers are uncomfortable with a tie-in the pay is that it may be perceived as a surrogate for an age-driven scheme because people who are at the higher salary levels generally tend to be older. "There has been some thinking that there is a bit of a discriminatory issue with asking those people to pay more," Pflaum notes.

On the other hand, she observes, there is some presumption that highly paid employees somewhat disproportionately use the health plan. So, if the company wants to shift costs in a focused way to those employees who are more likely to use the benefit, it may decide that a pay-based deductible is a good approach to take, she adds.

The biggest advantage of a salary-driven deductible program, depending on the demographics of the workforce, Pflaum suggests, "is the ability to shift more costs to employees in a way that is perceived as equitable."

9. Coordination of Benefits: How and Why It Works

Jack B. Helitzer

Coordination of benefits (COB) is the method used to deal with duplicate health care coverage. Its purpose is to prevent a person from profiting from excess health care coverage. Although it was not designed to serve as a cost-saving device, its operation results in important cost savings to plans by eliminating duplicate payments and the ability to profit from over-utilization of health care services.

Each element of COB is simple, but when the elements are put together, COB becomes quite complex. In fact, many people who work with health care plans do not fully understand COB. This article explores the basic principles of COB, examines the order of benefit determination rules (which are the critical heart of COB), and demonstrates why an "always secondary" position is unacceptable. The article then analyzes several issues dealing with what the secondary plan pays, and looks at the interrelation of COB and ERISA.

Two-wage-earner families are common in our modern society. So is the availability of medical and other health insurance or coverage. Often, when an employer pays the full cost of health coverage or when employee contributions are relatively small (and sometimes regardless of how much employee contributions are), both wage earners will have coverage not only for themselves but for their families. This results in duplicate group health coverage.

Long ago we learned that when excess insurance coverage exists, the chance that a claim would be made increases dramatically. This problem is heightened when a person can profit financially by incurring a loss. Therefore, it becomes very important to have a mechanism in place that precludes such profit. In the field of health insurance (or uninsured health coverage), the mechanism is *coordination of benefits.*

COB is interesting in several respects. First of all, it is at the same time deceptively simple and deceptively complex. Each rule or element of COB is quite simple. However, when these simple rules come together, the package is amazingly complex. Second, COB is widely misunderstood, especially by those who work with it day by day, and it cannot be understood at all by virtually anyone who comes upon it for the first time (such as a claimant).

When more than one plan provides coverage, there are only two ways in which to coordinate their benefit payments: (1) have each plan pay a "fair share" of the total claim: or (2) establish a sequence, or order of benefit determination, and let one plan pay first and the other plan "top off" any unpaid amount determined to be due. COB works sequentially.

In this article, we shall first focus on the basic principles of COB in order to understand what it does and why it is structured sequentially. Next, we will discuss the sequence or order of benefit determination rules of COB and just what is wrong with trying to be always secondary. Then we shall consider several issues that must be faced by the plan that pays second in determining how much it must pay. Finally, we shall look at how COB is affected by ERISA.

BASIC PRINCIPLES OF COB

Perhaps the most important point to make is that COB is not a cost containment device. It is the mechanism by which we eliminate the opportunity for a person to profit from duplicate health care coverage when that person incurs health care expenses. When it works, it has a cost containment *effect.* Almost every major problem we have with COB is caused by employers that distort the mechanism by attempting to use it for the main purpose of reducing the plan's expenditures. There is a second major point: COB may not be perfect, but it is better than any other mechanism that could be created.

Essentially COB is a sequential system. When two or more plans cover a person:

- First, the sequence in which the plans pay benefits or provide services must be determined. Obviously, there must be uniform rules to determine the order of benefits. This uniformity is absolutely essential. Without it, there can be no satisfactory way to deal with duplicate coverage. The validity of the COB rules is established not by law or regulation, but rather by the fact that there will be chaos without uniform rules to determine the order of benefit payment.
- Once the order of benefits is determined, the *primary* plan (the plan that pays benefits or provides services first) pays its benefits or provides its services as

it would in the absence of duplicate coverage. It never pays more. It never pays less.

- Finally, the *secondary* plan (the plan that pays benefits or provides services second) pays the difference between some maximum amount (which is never more than the total expenses actually incurred, but which can be less) and whatever the primary plan paid. Under no circumstances does the secondary plan ever pay more in the aggregate than it would have paid had it been the primary plan.

Building on this basic foundation of a sequential system, COB was designed with five principles in mind:

- *Optional.* Use of COB is *not* mandatory. Any employer may elect to have its group health plan be always primary simply by not adopting a system to coordinate benefits. However, any employer that elects to have its group health plan deal with the problem of duplicate coverage may do so simply by incorporating the COB rules into the plan.
- *Universal.* There is only one way to deal with the problem of duplication of coverage, and that is by having everyone follow the same rules with respect to the order of benefit determination. The alternative is chaos. In other words, there is no "better" way to determine the order of benefits. If anyone tries to "improve" on the universally accepted rules, the results always end up worse.
- *Simple.* The rules must be simple to administer. This means that everyone involved—employers, claimants, health care providers, and plan administrators (be they insurers, service plans, HMOs, or others who administer uninsured plans)—must be able to instantly know which plan pays first. Once this sequence is determined, the rule applicable to what the primary plan pays is simplicity itself. The rules that apply to what the secondary plan pays must also be simple, easy to understand, and easy to administer.
- *Reliable.* The rules must be free from manipulation by any party: employer, claimant, or plan administrator. If some plans can easily cheat or manipulate the COB system, other plans will be discouraged from participating unless they too can cheat or manipulate the same way. If everyone can cheat or manipulate, we do not have a system to deal with duplication of benefits; we have only chaos.
- *Certain.* Especially with respect to order of benefit determination rules, there can be no conflicts that would produce a standoff. In other words, the mechanism must always produce a plan that pays first and another that pays second. Both plans cannot end up being primary, and both plans cannot end up being secondary. Thus, if order of benefit determination rules are changed for any reason, there must be some built-in resolution that avoids such results.

The need for formal rules dealing with duplication of coverage developed in the 1950s as employer-provided medical care plans became prevalent along with two-wage-earner families. Because in those days virtually all plans were insured, during the 1960s the group insurance industry developed COB rules. In December 1970 they were adopted by the National Association of Insurance Commissioners (NAIC). Since then, thirty-nine states have formally adopted those rules either in whole or in substantial part. Insurance departments of the other states will not approve group insurance policy forms that substantially depart from those rules.

During the 1980s there was concern that the COB rules did not satisfactorily resolve some social problems, so the NAIC rules were changed several times, both before and after June 1985, when the NAIC approved its completely revised and updated model COB regulations. At all times, the structure of COB was built on the basic principles described above.

Because the NAIC rules are followed by all responsible plans regardless of whether they are insured or self-insured and regardless of whether they have been adopted by a state, we can now examine the most critical part of COB: the order of benefit determination rules.

ORDER OF BENEFIT DETERMINATION RULES

COB is sequential system in more than one way. COB operates by determining the sequence under which one plan pays first and the other plan pays second. COB does this by applying order of benefit determination rules in a specified sequence. In other words, the rules are applied in a specific sequential order until you determine that one plan pays first and the other plan pays second. If the first rule does not result in a sequence, you move on to the next rule, and so on until you get a sequence. Interestingly, with about forty years of experience with COB, we know of no case where the rules have failed to result in a sequential order of benefit determination.

If plans use order of benefit determination rules that differ from the accepted standards or provide that such plans are always secondary, there can be the result that both plans are secondary. When this happens, it is clear that the fault lies with the nonconforming plan.

RULE 1: NON-DEPENDENT/DEPENDENT

The benefits of the plan which covers the person as an employee, member or subscriber (that is, other than as a dependent) are determined before those of the plan which covers the person as a dependent; except that: if the person is also a Medicare beneficiary, and as a result of the rule established by Title XVIII of the Social Security Act and implementing regulations, Medicare is

    (a)   Secondary to the plan covering the person as a dependent, and

    (b)   Primary to the plan covering the person as other than a dependent (e.g., a retired employee),

then the benefits of the plan covering the person as a dependent are determined before those of the plan covering that person as other than a dependent.[1]

In the employee welfare benefits situation, this rule applies when both husband and wife cover each other as dependents under their respective plans. The plan covering the person as an employee pays benefits first. The plan covering the same person as a dependent pays benefits second.

The exception, which was adopted by the NAIC in December 1990, modifies the rule in the unique situation where a retired worker is covered by Medicare, by a retiree plan, and as a dependent of a spouse who is an active employee. In that situation, we end up with a vicious circle under which Medicare is secondary to the dependent plan (because of federal law making Medicare secondary in such cases), the dependent plan is secondary to the retiree plan (because of the COB rule), and the retiree plan is secondary to Medicare (because of plan design). To help break this vicious circle, the COB rule was recently modified to make the dependent plan primary.

If you think about it, this is the only intelligent and workable way to break the vicious circle. Most plans have operated this way in the absence of a COB rule because there is no real or practical alternative.[2] The COB rule just makes it official.

RULE 2: DEPENDENT CHILD/PARENTS NOT SEPARATED OR DIVORCED

The rules for the order of benefits for a dependent child when the parents are not separated or divorced are as follows:

    (a)   The benefits of the plan of the parent whose birthday falls earlier in a year are determined before those of the plan of the parent whose birthday falls later in that year;

    (b)   If both parents have the same birthday, the benefits of the plan which covered the parent longer are determined before those of the plan which covered the other parent for a shorter period of time;

    (c)   The word "birthday" refers only to the month and day in a calendar year, not the year in which the person was born;

    (d)   A group contract which includes COB and which is issued or renewed, or which has an anniversary date on or after sixty days after the effective date of [the COB rule or regulation] shall include the substance of the provision in [paragraphs] (a), (b) and (c) above. Until that provision becomes effective, the group contract may instead contain wording such as: "Except as stated in [the rule relating to dependent children whose parents are separated or divorced] below, the benefits of a plan which covers a person as a dependent of a male are determined before those of a plan which covers the person as a dependent of a female."

(e)   If the other plan does not have the rule described in paragraphs (a), (b), and (c) above, but instead has a rule based upon the gender of the parent; and if, as a result the plans do not agree on the order of benefits, the rule based upon the gender of the parent will determine the order of benefits.[3]

When the plans cover a child, the applicable rule depends on whether or not the parents are separated or divorced. If they are *not* separated or divorced, the plan covering the person whose birthday falls earlier in the year pays benefits first. If both parents have the same birthday (which appears to have the mathematical likelihood of occurring once every 365 times, but which probably occurs far less frequently than that), the plan that covered a parent longer pays first, and the plan that covered the other parent pays second.

This rule, adopted by the NAIC in 1985 and incorporated by all thirty-nine states that use the NAIC model, replaced a gender (or sex-based) rule under which the father's plan paid benefits first and the mother's plan paid benefits second. This gender rule had the advantage of being very easy to follow. There was pressure to find another rule, however, because many people thought a gender rule was unlawfully discriminatory when applied to employee welfare benefits. The birthday rule is the next best thing insofar as simplicity of operation is concerned.

The final paragraph of the rule recognized that some plans would be able to lawfully retain the gender rule, at least for some transitional period of time. The paragraph meets the criterion of certainty by allowing the gender rule to prevail if the coordinating plans have different rules. The reason for this is simple. If a plan following the birthday rule is secondary and its rule prevails under a state law or regulation, the plan that pays second by lawfully using the gender rule would not have its order of benefit rule reversed, as neither a law nor a contract provision can modify someone else's otherwise valid contract provision. At best, there would be prolonged litigation to determine whether the gender rule was unlawful sex discrimination.

Because certainty is one of the basic principles of COB rules, it is best to have the newer birthday rule give way to the older gender rule. If a plan that would be secondary under the birthday rule ends up being primary under another plan's gender rule, it would have to pay benefits first, but it might be able to recover damages from the plan with the gender rule if it could successfully argue that the gender rule as used by the other plan is indeed unlawful sex discrimination.

RULE 3: DEPENDENT CHILD/SEPARATED OR DIVORCED PARENTS

If two or more plans cover a person as a dependent child of divorced or separated parents, benefits for the child are determined in this order:

(a) First, the plan of the parent with custody of the child;

(b) Then, the plan of the spouse of the parent with custody of the child; and

(c) Finally, the plan of the parent not having custody of the child.

(d) If the specific terms of a court decree state that one of the parents is responsible for the health care expenses of the child, and the entity obligated to pay or provide the benefits of the plan of that parent has actual knowledge of those terms, the benefits of that plan are determined first. The plan of the other parent shall be the Secondary Plan. This paragraph does not apply with respect to any Claim Determination Period or Plan Year during which any benefits are actually paid or provided before the entity has that actual knowledge.

(e) If the specific terms of the court decree state that the parent shall share joint custody, without stating that one of the parents is responsible for the health care expenses of the child, the plans covering the child shall follow the order of benefit determination rules outlined in [Rule 2], Dependent Child/Parents Not Separated or Divorced.[4]

When the claim is for a child whose parents are separated or divorced, use of either the birthday or gender rule can cause serious problems, since the primary plan can turn out to be the one covering the noncustodial parent. Then, if the parents fail to cooperate, or if the noncustodial parent has disappeared or cannot be reached by the custodial parent (which happens all too often) the custodial parent usually ends up with the medical bill and secondary benefits (which often are the rough equivalent of no coverage at all). In these cases, the health care provider is often unpaid.

When this problem started to arise with frequency, the custodial parent was almost always the mother. Her employer's plan became vulnerable to charges of sex discrimination. As a result, no one was happy with the outcome: the custodial parent had big expenses and no benefits, the employer had an unhappy employee and the threat of sex discrimination charges, the health care provider was not paid, and the sick or injured child faced the prospect of being denied further health care. A solution had to be found.

This COB rule, adopted by the NAIC in June 1980, generally presents an excellent workable solution. The plan covering the custodial parent pays first. This plan covers the parent who is exercising responsibility and control over the child's health care. In most cases, it is obvious to both plans who this parent is.

The plan of the custodial parent's spouse (the child's stepparent) pays second. Once again, it is easy to identify this person. If the stepparent covered the stepchild as a dependent, then he or she has taken sufficient steps to acknowledge and accept that level of financial responsibility.

Finally, the plan of the noncustodial parent pays last. This is often for the best, because that parent may be either hostile to the custodial parent (and thus uncooperative) or missing (and thus simply unavailable).

Today some divorced parents share joint custody of the child. When this happens, it is reasonable to assume that the parents are cooperating with respect to the child's welfare, just as parents who are not separated or divorced do. In these cases, the birthday (or gender) rule can apply.

There is an exception to the custody rules, however. If a court decree imposes responsibility for the child's health care on one of the parents, the provisions of that court decree (rather than custody) determine the order of benefits. This exception is unfortunate because it compromises the principles of reliability, simplicity, and certainty. It is unreliable because it permits the parents to manipulate the COB rules by allowing them to decide which plan will pay first. It is not simple, because court decrees are usually not written with COB principles in mind and thus are hard for lawyers to interpret, much less the people who process claims. It is not certain, because if the parent with financial responsibility under a court decree disappears (as has been known to happen), the custodial parent either is stuck with secondary payments or has to go through the expense of retaining a lawyer to get the court decree modified.

As a practical matter, most insurers and plan administrators avoid inquiries into the existence of court decrees. When parents are separated or divorced, plans usually pay benefits based on custody. If it is subsequently learned that a court decree exists, the rule requires the plans to stay with the custody rule at least to the end of the current plan year. It would be quite costly and complex for the plans to reverse the transactions and change the order of benefit payments if they discover a court decree after benefit payments have started. Changing the order of benefit payments at the start of the next plan year, however, would be relatively easy to do as long as both plans have adequate advance notice of the facts.

RULE 4: ACTIVE/INACTIVE EMPLOYEE

> The benefits of a plan which covers a person as an employee who is neither laid off nor retired (or as that employee's dependent) are determined before those of a plan which covers that person as a laid-off or retired employee (or as that employee's dependent). If the other plan does not have this rule; and, if, as a result, the plans do not agree on the order of benefits, this rule is ignored.[5]

This rule does *not* supersede the first (nondependent/dependent) rule. The active/inactive employee rule covers the situation in which a person is covered directly under one plan as an active worker and directly under another plan as a retiree or a laid-off-worker. Thus, if Plan A directly covers a person who is laid off or retired (that is, not as a dependent), and Plan B covers that person as a dependent of an actively employed spouse, the first COB (the nondependent/dependent rule) applies, and Plan A is primary for that person. On the other hand, if a laid-off or retired worker has family coverage both under the former employer's plan and a current employer's plan, this rule applies, making the current employer's plan primary and the former employer's plan secondary, regardless of whether the claim is for the employee or a family member.

The NAIC adopted this rule in December 1982 in response to concerns by employers that had large numbers of early retirees and laid off employees who were allowed to retain health care coverage and who had found other full-time employment with health coverage. The rule recognizes the principle that the employer that has the advantage of the individual's active employment should bear the primary cost of that individual's health care expenses.

Because this was a new rule that changed the order of benefit determination rules then in effect, it was drafted with a built-in self-destruct mechanism, so that if the other plan with which it was coordinating did not have the same rule, the order of benefits would be determined by ignoring this rule.

Unless the rule is viewed in the context just described, its name (the active/inactive employee rule) can be misleading. The rule applies only to individuals who are "inactive" due to layoff or retirement. Obviously, a person can become "inactive" due to many other reasons (such as being fired, quitting, taking a leave of absence, etc.). As a result, this rule did not take care of people who were no longer active and who retained coverage with the former employer under COBRA, state mandated continuation of coverage laws, or the employer's own voluntary continuation of coverage program.

This situation caused the NAIC to develop a new rule to deal with most of those situations.

RULE 5: CONTINUATION COVERAGE

> If a person whose coverage is provided under a right of continuation pursuant to federal or state law is also covered under another plan, the following shall be the order of benefit determination:
>
> **(a)**   First, the benefits of a plan covering the person as an employee, member or subscriber (or as that person's dependent);
>
> **(b)**   Second, the benefits under the continuation coverage. If the other plan does not have the rule described above, and if, as a result, the plans do not agree on the order of benefits, this rule is ignored.[6]

This rule is similar in its operation and effect to the active/inactive employee rule. That is, it has the effect of relegating continuation coverage under the Consolidated Omnibus Budget Reconciliation Act of 1985 (COBRA) or a state-mandated continuation of coverage to a secondary position when the same individual is covered (either directly or as a dependent of a covered person) both through active employment and government-mandated continuation coverage.

In 1989, when COBRA was amended to allow individuals to retain COBRA continuation coverage along with other group health coverage in certain situations, there was a strong preference to have the COBRA continuation coverage secondary to coverage through active employment in as many situations as possible. The amendment to COBRA did not deal with the coordination of benefits issue primarily because Congress, congressional staff, and insurance-industry experts could not find a workable way of doing this in all cases. As a result, Congress left the COB issues to the states, which have generally dealt with it properly and effectively.

It would be very costly (to say nothing of causing significant delays in payment of all claims) to operate under a rule by which COBRA continuation coverage would always be secondary.[7] When an individual with COBRA continuation coverage acquires other coverage through active employment, however, there is no reason why a "COBRA secondary" rule could not work easily and effectively. The new rule, which was adopted by the NAIC in December 1990, does just this. Once again, because it is a new rule that could disrupt the currently operating rules, it has the self-destruct mechanism.

RULE 6: LONGER/SHORTER LENGTH OF COVERAGE

If none of the above rules determines the order of benefits, the benefits of the plan which covered an employee, member, or subscriber longer are determined before those of the plan which covered that person for the shorter term.

(a) To determine the length of time a person has been covered under a plan, two plans shall be treated as one if the claimant was eligible under the second within twenty-four hours after the first ended.

(b) The start of a new plan does not include:

(i) A change in the amount of scope of a plan's benefits;

(ii) A change in the entity which pays, provides or administers the plan's benefits; or

(iii) A change from one type of plan to another (such as from a single employer plan to that of a multiple employer plan).

(c) The claimant's length of time covered under a plan is measured from the claimant's first date of coverage under that plan. If that date is not readily available, the date the claimant first became a member of the group shall be used as the date from which to determine the length of time the claimant's coverage under the present plan has been in force.[8]

This rule takes over when all other rules (applied in the sequence shown here) do not determine an order of benefits. A plan covering a person longer pays first, and the plan covering that same person for less time pays second.

The subparagraphs of the rule explain how to determine how long a plan has covered an individual. These details provide fair, practical, and simple guidelines as to what is or is not a new plan, when it starts, and what to do if it cannot be determined exactly when coverage became effective.

We know of no instance in the more than forty-year history of COB in which the correct application of these rules has failed to determine the order of benefits. Difficulties can arise only if and when a plan fails to use these order of benefit determination rules. In those cases, both plans can end up being secondary. This is a result that cannot and should not be acceptable to anyone.

THE PROBLEM OF "ALWAYS SECONDARY"

In some isolated instances, uninsured plans write their contracts so that they are excess or always secondary to all other plans. The stated intent is to save money, or "contain cost."

Plan sponsors or administrators who try to use this technique argue that such a provision enables a plan to focus its health care benefits on employees (and/or their dependents) who do not or cannot have health care coverage from other sources. These sponsors or administrators argue that in the absence of such a provision, the plan would have to eliminate or greatly reduce the benefits available to the employees who have no other health care coverage because the cost of providing benefits to everyone would be greater than the plan (or the sponsoring employer) can afford. In some instances when such plans are sponsored by nonprofit institutions (such as schools or churches) there is an added argument that the institution is somehow different because of the unique services it provides.

Although it is easy to understand why the plan sponsor or administrator tries to take an always-secondary position, it must be recognized that this approach simply is irresponsible regardless of the motive or rationale for its adoption. If any plan can be free to set its own rules to determine the order of benefits, every other similarly situated plan should also be free to do the same. When other plans are affected by such a cost shift, they would have to encouraged to adopt similar, always-secondary approaches, causing large-scale chaos.

The argument that some employers are more worthy or important than others has no merit. That argument entails social, moral, and/or religious values. Even though those values are real the fact is that every employer, however meritorious, has the same obligation to treat its employees fairly. It must be remembered that if Employer A has the right to be always-secondary, so does Employer B. In addition, Employer C has the right to use the NAIC model. The fact that A chose the always-secondary approach should not, does not, and cannot change whatever B or C chooses to do. If each plan can operate independently in setting its own order of benefit determination rules, then it is inevitable that significant numbers of people will find themselves covered by two or more plans, each of which is secondary and none of which is primary.

Whatever "good" reasons employers might have for wanting to be always secondary, they cannot escape the fact that the effort to do so will doom at least some of their employees to a double-secondary situation, in which the individual has double coverage and neither plan has the obligation to pay anything substantial. Responsibility for the resulting problem lies with the employer or plan that adopts a unique order of benefit determination rule, and not with the one who follows accepted practices.

Some (but not all) courts that have considered this problem have held that the always-secondary position cannot prevail.[9] We believe that if the issue is presented properly, virtually all courts will reach this conclusion.

Some plans maintain an always-secondary position and offer to settle any dispute with any other plan following the NAIC model by splitting the covered expenses fifty-fifty. Although this may be a practical way to resolve the problem in order to prevent an innocent employee from being caught in the middle of a dispute between sophisticated insurers or plan administrators over an arcane and complex coordination of benefits provision, it has the disadvantage of rewarding a renegade plan for using a nonconforming provision.

The NAIC Model COB Regulation adopts a strategy that provides a reasonable protection against an always-secondary plan.

(1) Some plans have order of benefit determination rules not consistent with this regulation which declare that the plan's coverage is "excess" to all others, or "always secondary." This occurs because certain plans may not be subject to insurance regulation, or because some group contracts have not yet been conformed with this regulation.

(2) A plan with order of benefit determination rules which comply with this regulation (Complying Plan) may coordinate its benefits with a plan which is "excess" or "always secondary" or which uses order of benefit determination rules which are inconsistent with those contained in this regulation (Noncomplying Plan) on the following basis:

(a) If the Complying Plan is the Primary Plan, it shall pay or provide benefits on a primary basis;

(b) If the Complying Plan is the Secondary Plan, it shall, nevertheless, pay or provide its benefits first, but the amount of the benefits payable shall be determined as if the Complying Plan were the Secondary Plan. In such a situation, such payment shall be the limit of the Complying Plan's liability; and

(c) If the Noncomplying Plan does not provide the information needed by the Complying Plan to determine its benefits within a reasonable time after it is requested to do so, the Complying Plan shall assume that the benefits of the Noncomplying Plan are identical to its own, and shall pay its benefits accordingly. However, the Complying Plan must adjust any payments it makes based on such assumption whenever information becomes available as to the actual benefits of the Noncomplying Plan.

(3) If the Noncomplying Plan reduces its benefits so that the employee, subscriber, or member receives less in benefits than he or she would have received had the Complying Plan paid or provided its benefits as the Secondary Plan and the Noncomplying Plan paid or provided its benefits as the Primary Plan, and governing State law allows the right of subrogation set forth below, then the Complying Plan shall advance to or on behalf of the employee, subscriber or member an amount equal to such difference. However, in no event shall the Complying Plan advance more than the Complying Plan would have paid had it been the Primary Plan less any amount it previously paid. In consideration of such advance, the Complying Plan shall be subrogated to all rights of the employee, subscriber or member against the Noncomplying Plan. Such advance by the Complying Plan shall also be without prejudice to any claim it may have against the Noncomplying Plan in the absence of such subrogation.[10]

This technique permits the so-called complying plan to make the employee whole and then seek recovery from the so-called noncomplying plan. Thus, any plan willing to bear the cost of litigation should be able to recover the amounts it advances in excess of its proper secondary liability.

WHAT THE SECONDARY PLAN PAYS

It is always very easy to determine what the primary plan pays: It pays whatever it would pay in the absence of duplicate coverage. The existence or nonexistence of duplicate coverage is irrelevant to a plan when it is primary. It is harder to determine what the secondary plan pays.

Standard COB and *Total Allowable Expenses*

Under COB in its standard form, the secondary plan pays the difference between *total allowable expenses* (which generally are the total expenses actually incurred) and whatever the primary plan actually paid. There is a limit on what the secondary plan must pay: It never need pay more than it would have paid had it been the primary plan. This limit is usually determined not on a claim-by-claim basis, however, but over a *claim determination period* that is usually a calendar or plan year.

To make this approach work, the secondary plan has to determine how much it would have paid on each claim had it been primary, how much it actually paid in its secondary position, and (on a cumulative basis over the year) how much it has saved. As the year goes on, it may have to dip into those savings in order to top off what the primary plan paid to meet it obligations under the COB rules.

These savings are sometimes called the *benefits bank,* which is a rather unfortunate term because it implies that there is actually some kind of savings account that exists as an asset. This simply is not the case. The plan should not think of the benefits bank as an asset that may be used in any way. The so-called benefits bank only reflects the fact that the secondary plan's remaining potential liability in the applicable period is cumulative and not determined claim by claim.

As indicated, the claim determination period is usually a calendar or plan year. At the end of the year, the account is wiped clean, and a new claim determination period starts with a zero balance in the so-called benefits bank.

These concepts lead to results that often confuse and alarm plan or claim administrators who are not fully familiar with COB. An *allowable expense* is defined as "the necessary, reasonable and customary item of expense for health care when the item of expense is covered at least in part under any of the plans involved, except where a statute requires a different definition."[11]

Under this definition, an expense covered by the primary plan but excluded by the secondary plan must be considered in determining the secondary plan's liability. As a result, the secondary plan may have to pay benefits toward items of expenses that it does not cover.

This determination should not be as troublesome as it sounds at first. Remember that the secondary plan's overall total liability is never more than it would have paid had it been primary. The amount it pays toward excluded items is limited to the total dollars it would have paid on a primary basis. In other words, the amounts paid toward excluded items come out of COB savings.

The reason for this can be found in the political history of COB. As a group, the NAIC feels strongly that an individual who has duplicate coverage should never incur out-of-pocket expenses. Accordingly, the concepts of the allowable expense and claim-determination period were developed to assure that over a plan's operational year an individual with duplicate coverage generally would not have to pay deductibles, copayments, and (to a large extent) exclusions.

Private Room Differential and Cost Containment Programs

Not all expenses actually incurred by an individual are allowable expenses.

> The difference between the cost of a private hospital room and the cost of a semi-private hospital room is not considered an Allowable Expense

under the above definition unless the patient's stay in a private hospital room is medically necessary in terms of generally accepted medical practice.[12]

Second, when benefits are reduced under a Primary Plan because a covered person does not comply with the plan provisions, the amount of such reduction will not be considered an Allowable Expense. Examples of such provisions are those related to second surgical opinions, precertification of admissions or services, and preferred provider arrangements.

(a)   Only benefit reductions based upon provisions similar in purpose to those described above and which are contained in the Primary Plan may be excluded from Allowable Expenses.

(b)   This provision shall not be used by a Secondary Plan to refuse to pay benefits because an HMO member has elected to have health care services provided by a non-HMO provider and the HMO pursuant to its contract, is not obligated to pay for providing those services.[13]

Under the first exception, the so-called private room differential (that is, the difference between the cost of a private and semiprivate hospital room) in *not* automatically an allowable expense.

Under the second exception, if an individual fails to comply with the cost containment requirements of the primary plan, and under those requirements the benefits available are reduced, that individual cannot look to the secondary plan to make them up.

For example, assume the primary plan pays 80 percent of covered expenses of $1,000 if the cost containment requirements (such as second surgical opinion) are met, but pays only 70 percent if they are not met. In the absence of this exception, an individual with duplicate coverage could ignore the cost containment requirement, collect the reduced $700 benefit from the primary plan, and recover the remaining $300 of cost from the secondary plan. Under this provision, it would appear that the allowable expense becomes only $700, thereby relieving the secondary plan from further liability.

On the other hand, it should be noted that if the primary plan has no cost containment requirements but the secondary plan does, the provision does *not* preserve those cost containment requirements of the secondary plan. In other words, in our illustration, the primary plan would pay its $800. Whereas the secondary plan would have paid only $700 (the reduced benefit for failure to comply) had it been primary, it now has to pay $200 out of the $700 it saved under COB. Thus, the full $1,000 would be an allowable expense.

Obviously, the approach of the NAIC Model COB Regulation goes only part way toward preserving the cost containment features of both plans. This half-step reflects the intention of the regulators to permit 100-percent recovery whenever possible if a person has duplicate coverage.

It should be noted that this cost containment provision is *not* applicable when the primary plan is a Health Maintenance Organization (HMO) and the covered member elects to have health care services provided outside the HMO. This difference raises the next issue: How does COB apply to HMOs?

COB AND HMOs

In 1985 when the NAIC modernized its Model COB Regulation, the HMO industry joined the insurance companies and Blue Cross/Blue Shield on its industry advisory committee. The HMO industry recognized that there were major social and economic advantages in having HMOs participate in COB. The Model COB Regulation applies exactly the same way to both HMOs (or any other capitated plan) and indemnity plans (whether they are insured or uninsured).

In general, HMOs and indemnity plans can and should participate in COB on the same basis. Whereas an indemnity plan pays cash benefits that indemnify a covered person for expenses incurred, many HMOs provide health care services directly. The Model COB Regulation covers this by providing, "When a plan provides benefits in the form of service, the reasonable cash value of each service will be considered as both an Allowable Expense and a benefit paid."[14]

Using this concept, indemnity plans and HMOs can easily coordinate their benefits. When the HMO is primary and simply provides the services, the indemnity plan should simply pay the plan participant any out-of-pocket copayment that may exist. If the HMO is secondary but provides the services anyway, the HMO should simply bill the indemnity plan for the reasonable cash value of the services provided, and the indemnity plan will generally pay to the HMO the amount the indemnity plan would have paid had it paid other providers. However, the coordination of benefits between indemnity plans and HMOs is not without its troubles from both viewpoints.

The first problem is the one referred to in the rule regarding allowable expenses. It arises when the HMO is the primary plan, but the HMO member elects to have health care services provided by a non-HMO provider. Usually under these circumstances, the HMO properly excludes coverage and pays no benefits. As primary payer, the HMO only considers its *covered* expenses — not *allowable* expenses. This leaves the secondary indemnity plan in the same practical position that it would have been in had it been the primary plan.

Indemnity plans that end up stuck with the equivalent of primary liability when the HMO member obtains health care services outside the HMO (a process called *self-referral*) properly feel that there has been an unintended and inappropriate cost shift of responsibility to them. This violates the basic COB principle of reliability, or being free from manipulation by the claimant. Unfortunately, no one has determined how to combat this result without violating other socially important principles.

There would be great public outcry against a rule that would deny the choice of health care provider to a person with duplicate coverage by an HMO and indemnity plan. Most people, including virtually all members of the NAIC, would be extremely uncomfortable with a rule that would permit the indemnity plan to escape liability in such a case. As a society, we do not appear to be ready to have our government impose rules that would limit the choice of health care provider.

So far, this situation has not developed into a major problem. Although individual cases occur with some moderate frequency, they do not occur on such a widespread basis as to cause major continuing dislocations or cost shifts. Yet sooner or later, this problem will have to be addressed.

The second problem arises in the same way but is perceived as an imposition by the HMOs. In this scenario, the indemnity plan is primary, the HMO is secondary, and the claimant again self-refers to obtain care outside the HMO. Because the indemnity plan is primary, it pays its benefits without concern as to the nature of the provider (as long as the provider is licensed to provide the services, does so at reasonable and customary cost, and the services are covered by the primary plan). This turns the *incurred* expenses *covered* by the primary plan into *allowable* expenses, so the HMO, as the secondary plan, must pay amounts equal to the deductibles and/or copayments not covered by the indemnity plan.

This compromises the HMO's ability to control health care costs and services. Maintaining this control over health care is why HMOs do not cover expenses based on self-referral. Because excluded services become allowable expenses, however, HMOs must use any COB savings achieved earlier in the year (for example, if the HMO provided services and was reimbursed by the indemnity plan based on the reasonable cash value of those services) to pay the deductibles and/or copayments even though the services that gave rise to those deductibles and/or copayments were not covered by the HMO plan.

In this regard, the HMO is no worse off than an indemnity plan that excludes coverage of a particular service in a similar secondary position to another indemnity plan that does not have such an exclusion. When the primary plan covers a service not otherwise covered by the secondary plan, the reasonable and customary cost of that service becomes an allowable expense, and to the extent the secondary plan has cumulative COB savings over the calendar year (or other claim determination period), it must use those saving to cover that allowable expense.

If any other rule applied, a person with duplicate coverage would incur out-of-pocket expenses. The NAIC Model COB Regulation in its present form is based on the premise that this is an unacceptable result. Plans subject to the COB regulation (as most HMO plans currently are) must live with the rule.

It is best to think of this rule as the price of admission a plan must pay to get the benefits of COB. It is a reasonable price to pay. Some studies have indicated that overall savings from the use of COB are reduced no more than 1 percent or

2 percent overall as a result of its application. In the next section we shall discuss alternative approaches under which some plans may preserve their deductibles, copayments, and/or exclusions.

Whereas both HMOs and indemnity plans may have some difficulty with some aspects of the rule relating to allowable expenses, some HMO, Preferred Provider Organization (PPO), and/or point-of-service health care providers may have other difficulties with the application of COB rules when they agree to provide services at a discounted fee.

Assume that a doctor provides a patient services with a reasonable and customary value of $100. Under a primary indemnity program, the doctor would bill $100 and receive $80 from the plan and $20 from the patient. If the secondary plan were a PPO that contracted with the same doctor to provide that service for only $75, there would be a problem. Part of the PPO arrangement is that the patient will have no out-of-pocket payments (or perhaps a $5 or $10 copayment). In this case, the patient would be aggrieved, and the doctor would probably not be too happy, either.

Actually, the issue should not really come to light in a COB environment. Rather, it should be resolved at the time the HMO, PPO, or point-of-service network contracts with the doctor or health care provider. This situation arises frequently enough that it might be best if it were faced at the outset, when the contract with the health care provider is negotiated, and resolved up front. If this resolution were done, it would reduce claim payment complexities and would eliminate (or at least greatly reduce) subsequent discontent between the health care provider and the plan.

Unfortunately, at the time of contracting, both the health care provider and the plan may focus on other issues that appear to be more important, so this rather arcane issue can be overlooked, only to raise hackles later on when it arises as claim payments are administered.

PRESERVATION OF DEDUCTIBLES, COPAYMENTS, AND EXCLUSIONS

There is an absolute need for all plans to follow the same order of benefit determination rules. Unless they do, there is chaos. The NAIC has determined that when duplicate coverage exists, it is more important for the individual to be free of out-of-pocket costs than it is to allow plans to preserve their deductibles, copayments, and exclusions. However, while the rule on order of benefit determinations is essential to avoid chaos, the rule on out-of-pocket costs is a political decision.

A rule that would allow plans to preserve their deductibles, copayments, and exclusions would *not* result in chaos. As a matter of fact, in 1985 the NAIC approved such a rule, which was subsequently adopted by eight states,[15] but in 1988 the rule was repealed by the NAIC and soon after that by two of the states.[16]

Some self-insured plans that were never subject to state regulation still use this technique to preserve deductibles, copayments, and/or exclusions.

The major argument against the preservation of deductibles, copayments, and exclusions is that a person who pays two premiums (either in cash or in exchange for their labor) for duplicate coverage should not have to incur deductibles, copayments, or exclusions to the extent that one of the two plans ends up with savings. The major argument in favor of the preservation of deductibles, copayments, and exclusions is that a person who has no economic stake in the cost of health care tends to overutilize the health care system or to accept excessive cost without any question.

When deductibles, copayments, and exclusions are preserved, the covered person usually must bear some manageable or affordable liability for health care costs. When the technique is used properly, it affords the covered person with the equivalent of the coverage provided by the richer of the two coordinating plans. This is a relatively benign problem (if it is indeed a problem at all), compared to the serious problem when both plans are secondary and a person who has duplicate coverage ends up with virtually no benefits.

There are, however, good, practical reasons for plans that provide rather generous benefits at little or no contributory cost to the employee to avoid the preservation of deductibles, copayments, and exclusions. An employee covered by such a plan is likely to perceive that when a spouse incurs medical expenses, the overall benefits paid by both plans do not exceed what the employee's own plan would pay. This employee can rapidly conclude that there is no reason for the family to pay contributions for the spouse's health care coverage. This is especially clear when the spouse's program is a cafeteria plan and the spouse can trade health care coverage for some other benefit or for cash.

As more and more employees and their families reach this conclusion and drop the spouse's coverage, the additional COB savings can be rapidly undermined. Suppose that employee Brown's wife incurs a $10,000 medical expense and receives $8,000 from her primary plan (covering her as an employee). If Mr. Brown's own plan would have paid only the same $8,000, he ends up with a $2,000 out-of-pocket payment instead of no out-of-pocket cost. If Mr. and Mrs. Brown decide to drop her coverage (because it requires significant contributions toward the cost of coverage with no compensating advantages) and rely on Brown's own coverage (which requires little or no contributions), consider what happens on the next $10,000 claim Mrs. Brown incurs.

Because there is no other plan that can be primary, Mr. Brown's plan pays $8,000. In the first claim, the plan saved $2,000 (which it would have paid under a standard COB approach). It now pays $8,000, thereby ending the year with a $6,000 loss. One need not be an actuary to see that if relatively few employees make this kind of decision, the preservation of deductibles, copayment, and exclusions can actually end up costing a plan considerable money.

Once an employer starts down this path, it becomes very difficult to reverse, as employees whose spouses have elected to drop their own coverages probably will be unable to get back into their employers' plans. Anyone who drops coverage under a group plan is unlikely to be able to reinstate the coverage without establishing evidence of good health. A person who incurs significant medical expenses will probably find this impossible to do.

COB AND COST SHIFTING

When a person is covered by two plans and when the system operates sequentially so that one of the plans pays first and the other pays second, someone will always have an incentive to design a plan that will shift the primary cost to the other plan. The most obvious technique is to provide that the plan is always secondary. As we previously indicated, such a design is both irresponsible and unacceptable.

Other techniques can be valid and effective. For example, an employer may offer employees a choice of plans so that a richer plan is available for the worker whose spouse does not work and a more modest plan (such as one with larger deductibles or more coinsurance) is available for the worker who is also covered under a spouse's employer's plan. Or the plan may be structured to be noncontributory for employee coverage and contributory for dependent coverage (perhaps employee-pay-all for spousal coverage). These techniques have nothing to do with COB. Instead, they are designed to encourage employees to limit or forgo coverage when they can obtain it elsewhere at lower out-of-pocket cost.

These techniques have two major advantages. First, they do not distort COB. Second, and even more important, they play to the employee's own interests rather than against them.

Another technique is to limit eligibility for coverage of spouses to situations in which the employee provides a major portion of the family's income (such as one-half or more). This approach is used by one major employer, and so far the courts have not found it to be invalid.[17] A difficulty with this technique, however, is that it requires skill and care by the employer in managing and policing enrollment.

Coordination With a "Phantom Plan"

One apparent but illusory technique would be to attempt to coordinate benefits with a plan for which a person is eligible even if that person is not covered under that plan. We call such an arrangement coordination with a "phantom plan" because the plan for which a person is eligible does not actually cover the person.

Coordination with a phantom plan is difficult, if not impossible, to administer. First of all, it is not always possible to determine that a working spouse
was eligible for and could have been covered by the spouse's employer's plan.
Administration of COB works well mainly because people voluntarily report
duplicate coverage. It usually is not against their interests to do so. Considering
the devastating consequences to a family if the existence of such a plan were
uncovered, there would be powerful incentives for employees to conceal the
existence of the spouse's employment. It is best to avoid programs that encourage
people to lie or commit fraud.

Second, assuming we knew that the spouse was eligible for coverage, we would
have to know important details of the plan's design to determine what it would have
paid had it been in effect. This is very difficult to learn. Neither the spouse's employer,
insurer, or plan administrator would be likely to be very helpful in furnishing plan
information. Even if it were possible to get a summary plan description or certificate
of insurance, someone would have to read it very carefully to find out what it would
pay. Then, benefits would have to be determined manually by an experienced claim
approver rather than by a computerized claim payment program. This is extremely
costly, time-consuming, and difficult to do.

Finally, when coordination against a phantom plan is put into effect, the
result is draconian. A person essentially receives no benefits for expenses arising
from an illness or injury. It is very difficult to justify such a result unless there is
clear and unambiguous notice up front so that affected employees and their
spouses have been given fair warning. Though it may be argued that such notice
can be given when the plan first takes this approach, it is not reasonable to argue
that such notice remains clear and effective as time goes on.

For example, suppose that Smith's wife is not working when the plan
announces that it will coordinate against the plan for which a working spouse
is eligible even if the spouse elects not to accept the coverage. If Smith is an
average worker, such an announcement will be meaningless and easy to
ignore. Suppose that four years later, Mrs. Smith takes a job and is eligible to
participate in her employer's health care plan if she pays a significant contribution toward her coverage. It is not likely that the Smiths will actually
remember this provision, or that they will be inclined to check Mr. Smith's
summary plan description. Ordinary people do not have these issues in mind
under these circumstances.

Suppose Mrs. Smith does not elect coverage. When Mr. Smith's employer's
plan tries to enforce the coordination against her phantom plan, it will have to
argue that the availability of the summary plan description gave the Smiths
constructive notice of the consequences of her failure to elect coverage under her
employer's plan. Because the problem will arise when Mrs. Smith has a claim
for medical expenses, the Smiths will be effectively without coverage if this
argument succeeds. A court may not be willing to reach this result.

COB AND ERISA

As we have indicated throughout, coordination of benefits works mainly for practical reasons. Although it is not perfect, it is the best mechanism available for dealing with duplicate coverage. It works primarily because everyone follows it voluntarily. After all, it is, the best game in town.

Its formal structure is set forth in a model regulation developed by the NAIC, which is a voluntary association of insurance commissioners whose model regulations have no legal weight. Because its membership does have a tremendous amount of expertise in regulation of group health insurance, however, and it receives a great deal of technical assistance from insurers and HMOs, its models are worthy of very serious attention.

The NAIC Model COB Regulation has been adopted in most of its essential parts by thirty-nine states.

It seems quite clear that ERISA preempts the application of state laws or regulations to uninsured employee welfare benefit plans that are subject to ERISA.[18] This does not mean that uninsured welfare benefit plans subject to ERISA should be or are free to adopt any rules they want to deal with duplication of coverage. We believe that plan sponsors or fiduciaries who adopt provisions that attempt to be always secondary are likely to be sued and that these organizations are likely to find the courts unsympathetic, particularly if application of such a provision would deny the employee substantial coverage, or when both plans claim to be always secondary.[19]

We do not believe that most efforts to preserve deductibles, copayments, and exclusions would be found to violate ERISA fiduciary responsibilities. However, employers who try to preserve them may run the risk of having the technique backfire as employees and their families elect to rely on those plans as the sole (as distinguished from primary or secondary) health care plan available. They may accomplish the very opposite result from the one intended.

Plan sponsors or fiduciaries who attempt to coordinate with plans that do not actually provide coverage but for which an employee's dependent is (or was) eligible may at best find the provision impossible to enforce.

CONCLUSIONS

The day-to-day administration of COB is not difficult. Insurers and experienced claim administrators have been remarkably successful in handling it. The administration of COB works somewhat the same way our tax system operates — mainly because claimants voluntarily report the existence of duplicate coverage. Insurers and experienced claim administrators who have installed effective electronic reminders, prompts, and information into their claim payment systems have not found any significant fraud or misreporting of duplicate coverage. In other words, the COB mechanism works pretty well.

COB is not easy to understand. It does not solve every problem (such as all the problems of coordination between indemnity plans and HMOs). It is not totally immune to individual manipulation (such as by divorced or separated parents who can get a court order to determine which insurer will pay first). There is no better method to deal with duplication of coverage, however.

It is important to understand that COB is not a cost-saving technique, but rather a useful device to prevent the evils of overinsurance that could arise when a person has coverage under more than one health care plan. When it works, it has a major cost-saving effect. This understanding should lead plan sponsors and plan administrators away from efforts to distort COB. Such efforts only weaken the effectiveness of COB to do what it was designed to do and in the long run will fail to achieve the intended cost savings.

Finally, plan sponsors and administrators should understand that COB is valid because it really works and not because it is backed by the legal authority of state law or regulation. Such an understanding would go far to eliminate efforts by a minority of sponsors and administrators to distort COB by using provisions that make a plan always secondary. This understanding would go far to eliminate attempts to do the impossible by coordinating with phantom plans. It would go far to dissuade sponsors and administrators from adopting techniques such as preservation of deductibles and copayment in situations in which these techniques might backfire and end up costing the plan far more than these techniques can save.

An understanding of COB is not easy to achieve, but once it is reached COB can be seen for what is really is: an effective device to preclude the possibility that a claimant will profit from incurring health care costs. The use of COB results in the very important by-product of saving a plan a great deal of money by concentrating benefits where they count

COB has one very important thing going for it: It works.

1.   NAIC Group Coordination of Benefits Model Regulation, Section 5 B (1).

2.   For a more detailed discussion of the problem of the vicious circle, see J.B Helitzer, "Medicare Secondary: The Status and Impact of Cost Shifting," 2 *Benefits Law Journal* 197, at 209-212 (Summer 1989).

3.   NAIC Group Coordination of Benefits Model Regulation, Section 5 B (2).

4.   *Id.*, Section 5 B (3).

5.   *Id.*, Section 5 B (4).

6.   *Id,,* Section 5 B (5).

7.   For a more detailed explanation of why this is so, see J. B. Helitzer, "Coordination of Benefits Rules vs. COBRA," 2 *Benefits Law Journal* 401 (Autumn 1989).

8.   NAIC Group Coordination of Benefits Model Regulation, Section 5 B (6).

9. See, e.g., Northeast Dep't ILGWU Health and Welfare Fund v Teamsters Local Union No. 229 Welfare Fund, 764 F 2d 147 (3d Cir 1985).

10. NAIC Group Coordination of Benefits Model Regulation, Section 7 B.

11. *Id,,* Section 3 A (1).

12. *Id.,* Section 3 A (4).

13. *Id.,* Section 3 A (6)

14. *Id.,* Section 3 A (3).

15. Indiana, Kentucky, Minnesota, New Hampshire, New York, Tennessee, Utah, and Wisconsin.

16. Indiana (effective March 16, 1990) and Utah (effective July 1, 1989).

17. Colby v JC Penney Co., Inc., 926 F 2d 645 (7th Cir 1991).

18. FMC Corp v Holliday, 111 S Ct 403 (1990).

19. Winstead v Ind Ins Co 855 F 2d 430 (7th Cir 1988); Northeast Dep't ILGWU Health and Welfare Fund v Teamsters Local Union No 229 Welfare Fund, 764 F 2d 147 (3d Dir 1985).

10. The Challenge of Reducing Workers' Compensation Medical Costs

Joseph C. H. Smith

Workers' compensation is becoming more and more of a cost problem all across the country, and medical costs are becoming a more significant part of the total workers' compensation bill. The purpose of this article is to provide an overview of some specific approaches that we believe will enable you to get control of those costs. This article is designed as a practical guide to how to approach the problem and make good decisions relative health care cost containment. It will not offer a prescription for how to solve the problem once and for all.

UNDERSTANDING THE WORKERS' COMPENSATION PROBLEM

The workers' compensation health care cost containment problem is different from the health benefit cost containment problem. It is important to understand how they are different so that you can recognize the limitations of simply applying solutions designed for health benefits to the workers' compensation problem. This section will briefly point out the major differences.

Wage Replacement Costs and Health Care Objectives

Perhaps the most fundamental difference between the workers' compensation problem and the health benefit problem is that the WC costs include the wage replacement costs. Currently, medical costs are only about 40% of total WC costs, so the objective for WC cannot be to reduce just medical costs, but rather, it must be to reduce total costs. This translates to the medical outcome objective: Cure the injured workers and get them back to work. The objectives for most health benefit plans focus on cost reduction and include other aspects such as quality of care, access to care, and patient satisfaction. While all of these may be important, return to work must be the guiding principle for a WC program.

This difference in objectives makes a difference in the way you buy services and the types of services you buy. For example, many utilization review systems get paid based upon the amount of money their data shows that they saved. These savings may accumulate from reduced lengths of stay, reduced frequency of outpatient visits, and other such elimination of non-essential care. These reductions may be very appropriate in the health benefit environment. For example, it may be perfectly fine to discharge a patient to the home. However, in the WC environment, that discharge must include the discharge planning and follow-up activity to assure a continued recovery. If the patient can stay in the hospital another week and then be discharged back to work, it may be much better than letting him or her sit at home to recover. The wage replacement benefits can outweigh the medical costs.

The need for prompt return to work adds to the importance of good quality of care. Unnecessary surgery (particularly back surgery) can cost incredible amounts of money. People can be out of work for years or forever, rather than for a few weeks or months. Good physical therapy can work wonders and get people back to work quickly. Poor physical therapy can cost a lot of money and have no effect whatsoever.

Physician Roles

We expect and need more from the physician when they are dealing with a WC case. In the health benefit arena, the physician's function is healer and patient advocate. In WC we need for the physician to also determine when the patient can return to work, (s)he may have to determine the degree of patient disability, and (s)he may even have to testify if the case is disputed. These are roles that many physicians are unwilling or unable to play.

Most physicians have no knowledge of the requirements of the jobs in your workplace. It would be good if your WC physician knew your workplace and job environment. Occasional visits to the workplace could improve their ability to make tough return-to-work decisions. Good relations between the physicians and the company enable them to have a dialogue to discuss possible light duty or work alternatives.

Physicians are oriented toward helping the patient. They want to be in an advocacy role. They do not want to be in an adversarial position with the patient.

Getting a physician to fill this role can be a problem. The problem can be particularly complicated if the WC physician is also the worker's family physician. The family physician may not be able to afford to make tough return-to-work decisions because (s)he also provides care to the worker's family and has a continuing relationship with them. If the worker does not want to return to work, it is difficult for the physician to sign the release.

These special demands on physicians suggest that the choice of physician is a critical issue—much more critical than the choice of physician in the health benefit arena. Many major health benefit programs have developed large networks of providers that agree to discounted fees and adherence to utilization standards. It is probable that these same networks will not work very well for WC. The physician it the key to quality of health care and early return to work. Considering that it may be worth more to get the best physicians to care for your patients.

Patient Incentives

Most WC patients are the victims of unfortunate workplace accidents, and they are highly motivated to get well and return to work; however, there are many aspects of the WC system that create perverse incentives that can adversely affect outcomes. The WC patient has little or no incentive to conserve on health care utilization since, for all practical purposes, WC must pay 100% of all medical costs. What is worst, in a workers' compensation case, the injured worker may have incentives to use more health care than is necessary.

- Wage replacement benefits can, in some situations, give the injured worker more take-home pay than was being received before the injury. This is particularly true if you consider factors such as child care and commuting costs.
- If the injured worker is seeking a settlement of a case (a lump sum payment), the amount of the settlement may be higher if the patient looks sicker. The more health care that is being used, the higher the potential settlement.
- An injured worker may purposely run up costs in an effort to "get even" with the employer.

Another area of concern in WC is fraud and abuse. Data show that the number of WC claims increases during hard economic times. When faced with possible lay-offs, injuries increase. A recent television news investigation in California documented numerous WC scams.[1] One case showed that recruiters for physicians and lawyers were soliciting WC cases from the unemployment lines and running up excessive medical bills at the initial visit. In another case, a major lay-off at a security company resulted in a large number of WC claims filed by laid-off workers. While fraud and abuse may represent a small portion of total cases in WC, a medical cost containment program needs to include a component to try to identify and deal with such cases.

Small Purchaser

Another area of concern for cost-containment in WC is that for the most part, WC is a small purchaser of health care. This has important ramifications for the ability of WC to negotiate favorable conditions, and in the number of cases that share administrative costs.

WC medical costs represent only about 2% of the total health care costs. Because of this, WC is not in a good bargaining position to get favorable rates or influence practice patterns. Even though WC is a small purchaser in the global sense, for certain categories of providers (e.g., physical therapists), WC may represent a large portion of total work. The key to negotiation is to deal with entities that have a significant amount of WC business, or work to piggy-back on other programs.

Another important consequence of the small volume of cases is that the administrative costs per case increase significantly. If a particular company has only ten WC cases per year, it is very difficult for the company to do all of the design work and contracting necessary to implement a comprehensive cost containment system. This small volume is even a problem for major insurers because the massive costs of computer systems, setting up provider networks, and creating specialized utilization review and case management systems tends to be high relative to the number of cases. The conclusion here is that cost containment programs for WC may have to be more efficient than similar programs for health benefits.

Legal and Regulatory Issues

Workers' compensation is an entitlement program that is governed by complex rules and regulations. Each state has unique rules that govern the WC system.[2] These rules include such things as provider choice, physician fee schedules, compensability criteria, provider authorization, and a myriad of reporting and disability determination issues. Any cost containment program that is implemented must be in compliance with these rules.

A fallout from the complex legal environment is that it often leads to lawyer involvement in medical cost-containment issues such as choice of provider, level of services provided, and release for return to work.

In addition to the complex legal environment, unionized environments can create special issues for workers' compensation. Union contracts often have provisions that limit the ability of a company to arrange for limited duty return to work or offer a partially disabled worker alternative employment. Further, union advisors may become involved in choice of provider and other such decisions.

The important point here is that there are complex rules and regulations that are outside the direct control of the company or the insurer. It is worth some effort on the part of the insurers and companies to collect and analyze the data that are necessary to inform the political debates that surround efforts to change and improve the legal environment.

DEVELOPING A MEDICAL COST CONTAINMENT PROGRAM FOR WORKERS' COMPENSATION

There are clearly approaches that can be used to reduce the cost of WC. The methods are not necessarily easy to implement, nor is it easy to be sure in the end whether or not you really saved any money. Further, we are confident that no matter how effective the approach you implement today, you will have to continually monitor activities and adjust the process or its effectiveness will wane. The conclusion here is that to save money in WC, you must get control of the costs and manage them just like you would manage inventory costs or raw materials costs. It simply will not work just to implement some program such as bill review and assume that the problem is solved.

This section discusses a number of different issues that influence medical cost containment for WC, and briefly introduces a number of possible cost containment strategies. For the most part, medical cost-containment methods for WC mimic those that have been used to try to reduce health benefit costs. All of these techniques can work to reduce costs, and all of them can fail. The important message we want to get across is that it is important to have a cost containment program, and it is important to measure how the program is working and modify it as necessary to keep it effective.

Prerequisites

Before you can have an effective medical cost containment program for WC, there are certain requirements that must be met. These include:

- The company must have reasonably good employee relationships and a general sense of trust between the employees and management. If the relationship is adversarial from the beginning, it is very difficult to implement effective medical cost containment programs.
- The company must want injured workers to come back to work, and must be willing to work with the physicians and other health care providers to enable

early return to work. WC is not a good mechanism for eliminating poor employees from the work force.

- The company needs a process in place to identify and report workplace injuries. Being aware of the injury at the point of injury is critical be satisfactory management of the case. Once the injured worker has started receiving care, it is much more difficult to influence the service delivery process.[3]

Setting up a Program and a Plan

If you are serious about medical cost containment for WC, the first step has to be to make a commitment, assign responsibilities, and develop a plan. One of the major sources of failure for cost containment efforts is that companies will buy isolated services provided by insurers, third party administrators or other vendors without having a clear picture of the problem or the potential effect of the service. The plan must include stated objectives for the program, and some approach to measuring progress toward meeting those goals.

One important aspect of this plan is to determine how the savings from the program are going to accrue to the company. If the company is self insured, the savings are returned to the company in a fairly straight forward manner. However, if you are purchasing WC from an insurer, or if you are part of the risk pool in your state (a frequent problem for small companies or company with bad historical experience) it may be very difficult to get the benefits of the cost containment effort to be returned to the company.

Part of the task of putting together a plan and trying to design a cost containment program is to determine whether or not there really is a cost problem and if so, where costs are excessive. Doing this analysis requires data, and data on medical costs for WC is very difficult to get. Data is required to develop the plan, and data is also necessary to measure the success of the program. We discuss the data issue and how to use it in a separate section below.

Once the objectives for the program are established, the next step is to determine what cost containment approaches will work best to achieve those objectives. A number of possibilities are discussed below.

Channelling Patients to Good Providers

As mentioned above, the physician is a key part of any effective medical cost containment program for WC. Getting injured workers to high quality providers that understand the work requirements and the objective of getting the patient back to work can be the key factor in any cost containment program. This sounds simple, but it is not. There are many obstacles to achieving this goal,

One of the major difficulties is that there is very little information available to enable you to identify the good providers. If you already have providers that you work with and are happy with, that is a good starting point, but even then, it is difficult to know how good they really are. The difficulty with identifying the good providers points to the need to monitor performance and eliminate poor performers from the program. Another potential problem area is that many states give the injured workers the right to choose their own provider. These laws limit the ability of the employer to force injured workers to use particular physicians. However, this may not be a major problem. If you have reasonably good relationships with your employees they are very likely to go to the provider recommended by the employer. Even if an injured worker chooses a different provider, if you are aware of the selection, it may be worthwhile to establish a relationship with the provider so that you can influence return-to-work decisions.

There are many different approaches to channelling patients to good providers. One approach is to identify a provider network and require the injured workers to use the network providers. If this approach is selected, the network should have specific providers designated for your WC cases, and there needs to be an opportunity for those physicians to understand your workplace. Another approach is to simply identify one or more providers in your area that you want to use, and post numbers and instructions for access in the event of an injury. This approach can be implemented relatively easily and inexpensively for small companies.

Utilization Review

Another important set of tools for cost control includes review of service delivery by an external review firm. The two distinctly different types of review are retrospective review and concurrent review. Retrospective review takes place after care is provided while concurrent review takes place at the time care is provided or before. There are many different approaches to review: telephone versus on-site, inpatient cases only versus both inpatient and outpatient cases, specialty review such as mental health or orthopedic cases only, etc. However, most systems rely upon some sort of screens or criteria that are used to determine whether or not the care recommended by the physician is appropriate for the patient based upon the patient's diagnosis and condition. For the most part, all of these programs work to negotiate alternative treatment strategies with the provider if the proposed treatment in deemed not appropriate.

Generally, the only enforcement tool available to utilization review programs is to recommend that payment for services be denied if they are deemed inappropriate. With a retrospective review program, since services have already been provided before the review, whenever the review firm finds that care was not appropriate, it results in non-payment for services that have already been delivered. Either the physician loses the income from that case, or the patient becomes liable for payment. In either case, there is high potential for an appeal of the decision, particularly if a significant amount of money is involved. Even with concurrent review, if the provider goes ahead with the treatment despite the denial of authorization, there is a possibility that the case will be appealed and the insurer will have to pay for the services.

Case Management

In a case management program, a case manager or case management team is assigned to the patient and given the responsibility to coordinate all the care for that patient. This approach is different from the other forms of review discussed above in that the case manager usually works directly with the patient and may recommend changing from one type of provider to another or making use of available community services. The other types of review generally just assess the appropriateness of care being recommended by the provider.

Case management programs vary a great deal depending on the types of cases being managed and the specific role of the case manager. Many workers' compensation programs have been using case management concepts for years for special cases such as burns and amputations. Further, the structure of many claims adjustment offices is similar to the structure of a case management program. Cases are assigned to an individual claims adjuster who has the responsibility for all aspects of the case. It may be possible to implement a workers' compensation case management system by just redefining the role of the claims adjuster, upgrading qualifications to include medical case management skills, and making appropriate changes in workload.

The key to cost-effective case management is program design: the types of cases managed, workloads for case managers, capabilities of specialized case management teams, the point at which cases are turned over to the case manager, and resources available to the case manager. For certain cases such as back injuries or burns, it may be important to have a designated center of excellence with the expertise to deal with the case. The case manager must have the flexibility and the authority to arrange transportation so the patient can get to the center.

There are many case management programs have proved their effectiveness over the years (e.g., HCX in Washington, DC and Kemper National Services, Ft. Lauderdale, FL), and I believe that this area may best overall opportunity for significant cost savings in WC. The primary reason for this belief is that the case manager becomes a party to patient care decisions and facilitates communications among all parties concerned. Since the case managers work directly with the patients, they can facilitate communications between the worker and the employer. Also, the case manager, as a party to the return-to-work decision, can protect the provider from the patient's potential hostility.

Proper Payment Systems

An area of concern in WC is the area of proper payment for services. While health benefit programs have been using sophisticated medical bill payment systems for years, many workers' compensation programs still use relatively simple, often manual, systems for paying medical bills. Fairly straight forward checks (e.g., checks to prevent duplicate payments, checks to assure that the payment level is in accordance with the fee schedule or usual and reasonable charges, checks to prevent unbundling of services, and auditing of hospital bills to assure that services billed were actually provided) can reap significant benefits in the workers' compensation arena.

Summary

This section has briefly discussed the approach to developing a medical cost containment program for workers' compensation. In setting up such a program, it is important to keep in mind that medical costs are only 40% of the total WC bill and thus WC patients probably need an approach that is different from the approach applied to health benefit costs. There is little information to tell us what works best and what doesn't. However, we are confident that all of the possible cost containment strategies can work if implemented properly, and they can fail if implemented poorly. This leads us to stress the importance of starting the cost containment program by collecting and analyzing data relevant to your particular situation, and then monitoring the data to assure that the methods you select are working for your program.

Another important issue is that regardless of the approach taken, if it works, some segments of the health service delivery system will see their revenues falling. That segment will react to falling revenues by implementing special programs to increase revenues and thus increase your costs. If you do not counter these new programs your costs will increase and again be out of control. Whatever strategy you take, it must be continually be revitalized to remain effective. In the next section we briefly discuss the need for data and how it can be used to monitor program effectiveness.

THE IMPORTANCE OF DATA

Good information is an essential requirement if you hope to develop and maintain a medical cost containment program of any sort. Unfortunately, the availability of good medical information in WC is very limited. Even when there is good current information, there is very limited historical data. This section briefly discusses data that would be useful for managing and evaluating medical cost-containment programs for WC. If these data are available, that's all the better. Even if the data are not available, the model points to a general approach for collecting and analyzing data to measure the progress of the cost containment programs.

A Model for Total Costs

The first step in being able to use the data is to develop a model that guides the way you propose to use the data. Our proposed model focuses on the employees and the injured workers as the unifying principle that guides our analysis efforts and data aggregation. The basic model is as follows:

$$Total\ Cost = Employees \times \frac{Injuries}{Employee} \times \frac{Medical\ Costs + Other\ Costs}{Injury}$$

The equation above shows our essential view of WC costs as the product of the number of employees, the injury rate, and the total cost (both medical and non-medical) per injury. This view is different from the usual approach to charging premiums for WC coverage. Most premiums are computed as a percent of total wages paid and they do not even consider the actual number of employees. While this approach may work for determining premiums, we don't believe that it provides a reasonable approach to the design or evaluation of a cost containment program. Wages are an important factor for determining wage replacement benefits, and wages can affect the incentives of the injured worker and thereby affect medical costs. However, our view is that the number of employees is a better starting point for analysis. If one is able to get the information to calculate the values for Total Cost for a number of time periods (say quarters), it is then possible to identify the major trends for the factors influencing your WC costs: work force size, injury rate, medical costs, and other costs.

If the data used to compute total WC costs are collected by case, then it will be possible to make the same computations for various subgroups that are of interest. For example, you may be interested in separating costs by category of labor (e.g., office staff versus assembly line workers). It may be useful to analyze those injuries that involve other costs separated from those that involve only medical costs. Or it may be interesting to examine cases in which there is lawyer involvement separately. There are many different forms the analysis could take; however, the goal is the same: identify if there is a cost problem, and if there is, where is it. If the problem is non-medical costs, then it may not make sense to expend a lot of effort on controlling medical costs.

A Model for Medical Costs

Once it has been determined that medical costs are a problem, additional information is necessary to determine where the major problems exist. The medical costs can be computed using the equation below:

$$\frac{Medical\ Costs}{Injury} = \frac{Number\ of\ Services}{Injury} \times \frac{Cost}{Service}$$

This equation shows that the medical costs are the product of the average number of units of service provided and the cost per unit of service. Calculation of the factors of this equation over time will show whether the medical cost problem is one of increasing use of services, or rising cost per service. Again, it will probably be useful to stratify the information by type of service (inpatient or outpatient, surgery, etc.), types of provider, individual provider, or type of injury. For example, it may be useful to examine back injuries, compute the surgery rate, and the cost per surgery. This sort of analysis could tell you what percent of your total medical costs are for back injuries, and it could tell you if the rate of surgery is growing. With some external information, you would be able to tell whether or not the surgery rate is excessive. Once you are armed with this information, you are in a position the bargain effectively with a group that specializes in case management of back cases. You can set target surgery rates and measure progress toward meeting those targets. You can also estimate what the estimated savings will be so that you have an idea of what the case management services are worth.

The primary limitation on what you will be able to do is the lack of data. It may be very difficult to get basic information such as whether or not surgery was performed on a particular patient or how many days the injured worker was in the hospital. Other information such as the diagnostic codes, procedure codes, service dates, provider name, and provider type are even harder to get. These types of data are important for the design and evaluation of medical costs containment programs, but it is expensive to collect the data, and because of the volume of data involved, it can be expensive to process and store the information. Until the major insurers and third party administrators begin collecting these data, it will be difficult to control medical costs.

CONCLUSION

This paper has presented a general discussion of requirements for an effective medical cost containment program for workers' compensation. The key points are:

- Workers' compensation is different from a health benefit and cost containment strategies must be designed specifically for WC or adapted for WC.

Otherwise, they will probably will not be effective. Further, because of the complex legal and regulatory environment, they may not be legal.

- It may be difficult for the employer to reap the rewards of an effective cost containment program in WC. WC rates are generally regulated, and employers, particularly small employers, may not see any change in rates even though their own costs drop significantly.
- There are many different techniques that are available to control WC medical costs. Most of the techniques will be effective if they are properly implemented and managed. The key to an effective program is the development of a cost containment plan and measure of progress toward achieving the plan.
- Medical data in WC are very limited and are just beginning to be collected by the major insurers and third party administrators. Availability of data is critical for the design and maintenance of effective cost containment programs.
- Our costs are revenues for the health care industry. A decrease in our costs will be a decrease in the health care industries revenues and it will change behavior to recoup the loses. Thus, effective cost containment strategies must be dynamic and adapt to system changes. Static strategies simply will not work.

The message here is that there are many obstacles to effective medical cost containment; however, it is possible to design effective programs, and the potential cost savings are significant.

1. Special investigative report by Harvey Levin, Channel 2 News, Southern Califoria.

2. The laws in 30 of the 51 jurisdictions covered give the employee the right to choose the initial provider. v for additional details, see *Medical Cost Containment in Workers' Compensation: A National Inventory, 1991–1992,* Workers Compensation Research Institute, 245 First Street, Suite 1402, Cambridge, MA 02142.

3. For example, the patient may leave the hospital and receive home health care services.

11. Controlling Long-Term Disability Costs

Jim Mishizen

Disability costs are a big line item in the health benefits budget—in some cases, almost 10 percent of payroll.

Nancy, a 37-year-old assistant professor of information science at the University of Pittsburgh, loved teaching. But in January 1986, she became disabled with chronic fatigue syndrome. Within a year, Nancy could work only a few hours a day and could not keep up with her full-time responsibilities.

Because of her love for teaching, Nancy refused to give up. She worked with her employer and her disability insurer's rehabilitation specialist to redesign her job around her disability by using a "remote" teaching approach.

Today, Nancy teaches her classes using written and videotaped lectures. Her students contact her directly through prearranged telephone office hours. Using innovative technology and teamwork, Nancy and her employer have redesigned her job to fulfill both her needs and the university's needs.

While the specifics of Nancy's situation are unique, her case illustrates how well the concept of disability management can be put into action using a well-executed strategy. In the past, people like Nancy may have remained on full disability benefits. Today, disability management programs encourage solutions that help employees return to productive lives while reducing the employer's disability costs.

Reprinted with permission from HR MAGAZINE (formerly PERSONNEL ADMINISTRATOR) published by the Society for Human Resources Management, Alexandria, VA.

For example, in Nancy's case, the disability management strategy saved her employer $63,000 in disability benefits. In addition, Nancy remains an active member of the university faculty and is on track for tenure.

If this approach doesn't sound familiar, it's because it has been the exception, not the rule.

During the 1980s, employee benefit managers focused much of their efforts fighting turbulent health-care costs. They often overlooked the quiet "eye of the storm"—the costs that disabilities add to an employer's benefit tab. Total disability costs run an estimated $160 billion a year, according to the Washington Business Group on Health's Institute for Rehabilitation and Disability Management (IRDM). Short-term disability (STD) costs frequently run 2 to 4 percent of payroll. Long-term disability (LTD) costs add another 0.5 to 1 percent, boosting disability plan costs to as much as 5 percent of payroll. When a company adds the indirect costs for labor replacement, administration and lost productivity, IRDM estimates that total disatility costs could reach almost 10 percent of payroll.

Employee benefit managers are taking notice of these mounting disability costs. In the 1980s, the prevailing winds on the health-care front led to the creation of managed-care strategies. The same pressure to reduce benefit expenses and monitor the value of service to employees has inspired the disability management movement today.

An effective disability management program includes four basic strategies:

- Integration
- Cost reduction
- Prevention
- Management information

INTEGRATION

Until recently, employers and benefits advisors viewed disability insurance as a specialty line purchased from a specialty carrier. Companies often split short- and long-term disability plans between separate carriers. Often, large employers have even self-insured and self-administered their short-term programs.

Today, benefits experts appreciate the important interrelationship among short- and long-term disability plans and the other benefit programs. An employee's disability starts a "ripple" that flows across an employer's benefit and human resource operations. This single event may influence health and life insurance, workers' compensation and funding for pension and savings programs. A company's staffing and productivity also feel the repercussions.

An integrated, disability-management approach unites all the elements in the benefits package. This unity helps simplify the administration of programs, streamline unnecessary paperwork, reduce costs and sometimes eliminate important coverage gaps.

The Sherwood Co., a valve and regulator manufacturer in Lockport, N.Y., took its first step toward integration by combining short-term and long-term disability plans into a single program. The company had used two separate carriers for their short- and long-term coverage.

"Separate plans increased the time we spent working with two different carriers and two different claims procedures. Whenever a claim extended into a long-term disability, we had to file a separate claim with the LTD carrier," said John Daigler, human resource manager at Sherwood.

"For our employees, the lack of coordination meant a lag before the LTD benefit began," he added. "The integrated STD/LTD plan gives our employees a smooth flow of service and benefits," said Daigler.

In addition to a smooth benefits flow, the STD/LTD plan provides the one point of service, one case manager and one claim filing. This means better claims handling for the claimant.

Soon after converting to the integrated STD/LTD, Daigler encountered a case that demonstrated the value of the unified approach. Mark, a 32-year-old assembler, had hurt his neck in two off-the-job accidents. The injuries gradually left him numb along his left side. He soon reached the point where he could not perform his routine duties.

In August 1990, doctors diagnosed a herniated disk and told him he would need surgery to correct the problem. He went on short-term disability for the operation. Mark's biggest concern was having a steady source of income to meet his financial obligations while he was out of work. Because of the integrated STD/LTD, his LTD payment began immediately at the six-month mark.

More importantly, physical therapy and rehabilitation began right after his operation while he was on short-term disability, which reduced the length of his long-term disability. Mark returned after 10 months. His doctors had originally predicted he would be on disability for a year or longer.

Besides STD/LTD plans, employers also are beginning to look for ways to link the claims and disability management processes for LTD and workers' compensation plans. This reduces the potential for double-dipping and helps speed up LTD payments. A work-related disability claim will usually trigger workers' compensation benefits well before LTD benefits begin. With an integrated program, the LTD benefits analyst can use medical and payment information gathered by the workers' compensation claims office to help evaluate the LTD claim. The LTD benefits analyst also can coordinate early intervention and rehabilitation service with the workers' compensation claims team.

Integrated disability plans also can fill important gaps in coverage. For instance, retirement contributions often cease when a disability occurs, though a disabled employee's retirement needs continue to grow. Integrated LTD plans, however, can be designed to pay additional benefits to continue saving for retirement.

COST REDUCTION

For many employers, controlling claims expenses remains the most important part of a disability-management program. Employers want to know that benefits are paid to people who qualify as disabled for as long as they are disabled but not longer.

Most cost reductions in disability management come from applying the right strategies at the right time. Disability management from day one can begin by applying diagnostic-specific duration guidelines to a short-term disability. These guidelines allow claims professionals to work with physicians, patients, rehabilitation specialists and employers to answer the difficult question of how long a short-term disability will last.

Rehabilitation was one of the first disability management strategies. It is also the most rewarding way of saving money, since it helps people return to useful and productive lives. In some cases, rehabilitation helps the worker return to work with the same employer.

Maria, a 37-year-old facilities engineer who worked for Texas Instruments, became disabled after a stroke. After more than a year of diagnostic, educational and career counseling, Maria returned to work full-time with the help of a rehabilitation therapist. Her employer helped by providing a specialized computer-aided design (CAD) station that was reprogrammed to favor her good hand.

In other cases, rehabilitation helps injured workers find new occupations. Gregory, a 32-year-old offshore instrument technician, became disabled when he injured his back on the job.

When it was clear Gregory could not continue in his present job, his disability insurer invited Gregory to meet with a vocational counselor. Gregory soon discovered he had other talents through a series of educational and career counseling sessions. He returned to school for two years and obtained an associate's degree in electronics technology. With financial and relocation assistance from his disability insurer, Gregory launched a new career as a biomedical electronics technician following his graduation.

Because of this successful rehabilitation, Gregory now leads a productive life and his former employer's disability plan was able to reduce reserves for the claim by $160,000.

Other cost reductions come from helping claimants secure their Social Security disability benefits. These efforts not only help reduce employer liability, they ensure that an employee's entitlement to Social Security benefits are protected.

David, a 57-year-old accounting supervisor at Martin Marietta Manned Space Systems in New Orleans, was diagnosed with a nonfusion, degenerative disk problem in May 1988. David, a long-term employee at Martin Marietta, was told his condition was irreversible. He took a six-month leave of absence.

Once his case became a long-term disability, David filed for Social Security benefits. Like many others before him, David's claim for Social Security disability benefits was denied.

Martin Marietta's disability provider stepped in to help David appeal the decision. The insurer helped provide David legal assistance in preparing the appeal and helped gather the information necessary to document that David's condition was long-term and irreversible. David's appeal was finally granted for the Social Security disability benefits he was due.

Approval of David's claim, which included retroactive benefits, recovered $24,000 in disability benefits that had already been paid to the employee and reduced reserves by $165,000.

These cost savings, however, are not the only reason the Social Security benefits are important. Social Security disability benefits include yearly cost-of-living increases that are not subject to offset by disability benefits.

"This translates into a much better income situation for the employee," said Ray Regan, chief of employee benefits at Martin Marietta Manned Space Systems in New Orleans. "When an insurance company helps people get the Social Security disability benefits they justly deserve, everybody wins."

These cost-reduction programs—duration guidelines, early and aggressive rehabilitation and Social Security appeal assistance—illustrate how disability management works to benefit both the employee and the employer.

PREVENTION

The simplest way to reduce disability costs is to prevent disabilities before they happen. Employers and benefit advisors alike agree that health promotion and injury prevention programs can yield significant payoffs.

A special committee of the Institute of Medicine recently concluded that 35 million Americans suffer from physical or mental disabilities. One researcher who led that study estimated that two-thirds of those disabilities could be prevented. His committee recommended establishing a broad national program that includes more research into prevention and an analysis of the causes and costs of disabilities.

An array of programs and services already exists to prevent and limit disabilities. For example, EAPs can reduce the incidence of mental health and substance abuse disabilities. Wellness programs that emphasize injury prevention and health promotion also reduce the number of physical disabilities. Workplace safety reengineering helps avoid accidental and occupational disabilities.

MANAGEMENT INFORMATION

Disability management requires a keen understanding of the forces at work. Employers need access to information about how their benefit dollars are spent.

A disability management system can help consolidate STD, LTD and worker' compensation claims information. Reports must go beyond a simple statement of payments. They should provide a cost/benefit and trend analysis as well as claims frequency and duration studies.

For employers such as Craig Foster, corporate human resource director at FHP Inc. in Fountain Valley, Calif., the biggest advantage of an integrated STD/LTD program is the managment information.

"We get reports showing us exactly what benefits have been paid so we know exactly where each claim stands. We had an inefficient method of tracking STD before. The integrated plan will give us a realistic idea so that we can plan better."

John Dailer, human resource manager at Sherwood added, "We now get biweekly reports so we are aware of who is on disability; how much they are getting; and when they are paid. We can track our costs and the insurer's performance to see that the employee is getting what they're due."

A strong disability management system makes sure all disability payments meet withholding, depositing and reporting requirements of the federal and state regulations. Solid management information enables benefit managers and their advisors to "close the loop." The data help employers develop new integrated programs, identify opportunities for further cost reductions and design programs that help prevent future disabilities.

It may be a long time before the health-care storm passes. In the meantime, employers will look more to disability insurers for help in conserving their benefit dollars.

The four basic principles of disability management—integration, cost reduction, prevention and management information—offer havens of hope in the eye of the storm. Applied together in a concerted disability-management program, they promise to rescue employers from excess paperwork and administrative costs in their disability programs.

More importantly, a disability management program ensures that employees receive fair, coordinated and compassionate care to help them weather their disabilities.

12. Health Care: Mothers, Infants and the Workplace
Irene McKirgan

Today, about 33 percent of the work force is of childbearing age. That figure is expected to rise to as high as 65 percent by the year 2000. The implications for the business community are clear. More employers need to take a proactive approach to prenatal health care issues. In doing so, they could both cut costs and play a leading role in sharply reducing the incidence of low birthweight, birth defects, and infant death in the United States.

Employers are recognizing the importance and urgency of promoting maternal and infant health issues today more than ever before. Demographic and economic trends, coupled with our nation's poor infant mortality rate, have been responsible for this increased attention within the private sector. Today's work force includes millions of women of childbearing age, many of whom remain on the job throughout pregnancy and return to the workplace shortly after delivery.

For an employer, the impact of unhealthy births will be of even greater significance during the decade ahead. With a shrinking labor force, the need to recruit and retain healthy, productive and skilled workers will increase. The potential for our nation to do so, however, begins with the healthy birth of each baby.

Fortunately, much can be done to increase a woman's chances of delivering a healthy baby. Positive lifestyle behaviors such as good nutrition and avoiding alcohol, tobacco and drugs, all play a major role in improving the outcome of pregnancy. In addition, adequate and early prenatal care is one of the most effective ways to increase a woman's chance of delivering a healthy baby.

Many employers have experienced cases in which health care costs for a single unhealthy baby have totaled over $1 million. In addition, the problems surrounding these unhealthy babies have a significant impact on employee absenteeism, productivity and ultimately, company profits.

OUR CHANGING WORK FORCE

The United States work force of several decades ago contrasts sharply with today's. Then, employees were predominantly male. Before the 1970s, most female employees were between the ages of 20 to 24 and 45 to 54. Women between 24 and 45 usually stayed at home to raise families.[1] By the end of the 1980s, 57 percent of all employees in the nation's work force were women. More than 38 million of these women are of childbearing age (18–44) and give birth to one million babies each year.[2] Many of them continue to work during pregnancy and fewer leave the work force after having a baby. In 1985, of all women with children one year or younger, close to 50 percent were working. This statistic is up from 30 percent as recently as 1980.[3]

Many women in the work force start their families at a later age than women did a generation ago, with the most dramatic increase in first pregnancies among 35- to 39-year-olds.[4] While these women have a good chance of delivering a healthy baby with proper prenatal care, they are also at greater risk. They are more likely than younger women to miscarry in the first trimester and to have difficult labors and deliveries. Moreover, first-time deliveries among this age group are more likely to be Cesarean sections, and the newborn is more likely to have a genetic birth defect, Down syndrome being the most common.[5]

Still another difference that affects the work force is the composition of the family itself. In 1970, 11.4 percent of all households with children under age 18 were headed by a single parent. In 1988, that figure rose to 24.3 percent.[6] The single parent in most such households is a working woman.

These demographic changes have increased significance for employers when coupled with our nation's high infant mortality rate. According to the Department of Health and Human Services, the U.S. ranks 24th in the world in infant survival—lagging far behind Japan and Western European nations. Birth defects, prematurity, and Sudden Infant Death Syndrome are the leading causes of infant mortality and are responsible for more than half of all infant deaths each year. Nearly 40,000 infants die every year, and more than 8,000 babies with a serious birth defect do not survive to their first birthday.[7]

The Report of the White House Task Force on Infant Mortality found that each infant death represents $380,000 in lost productivity. If the United States could achieve the year-2000 objective set forth by the Surgeon General's office of seven infant deaths per 1,000 live births (the 1989 infant mortality rate was 9.8), it would realize an increase in U.S. productivity of $2.3 billion.[8]

UNHEALTHY BIRTHS AND THEIR IMPACT ON EMPLOYERS

The Bureau of National Affairs reports that for most employers, childbirth-related expenses are the largest single component of health care costs.[9] Each unhealthy birth means higher employer health care costs, especially if neonatal intensive care is required. According to the Health Insurance Association of America, 10 percent of all newborns will spend time in a neonatal intensive care unit at an average cost per day that ranges from $1,000 to $2,500.

A study released in 1992 by the CIGNA corporation found that unhealthy births cost American businesses and their employees $5.6 billion in health care costs in 1990. This represents about 3 percent of aggregate after-tax corporate profits that year.[10] The study was based on an analysis of 59,000 pairs of mother and infant claims processed by Cigna over a two-year period (1989-1991). One out of four of the women delivered a baby with some type of health problem. These infants and their mothers represented 40 percent of all charges, or approximately $304 million.

The study also showed that if the rate of poor birth outcomes had been about half of the 25 percent it was over the two-year period of the studies, the total cost of infant and maternal care would have dropped 10 percent, for a savings of $2.9 billion per year.

A second CIGNA study found that employers paid $3 billion in 1989 to cover uncompensated health care costs for mothers and infants who were uninsured, underinsured, or on Medicaid. Both of these new studies clearly demonstrate that the infant mortality problem is affecting employers and that it is clearly an expensive issue.

Compounding the problem is the fact that many employers simply are not aware of their companies' expenditures for maternal and infant health care. The March of Dimes Birth Defects Foundation surveyed 48 worksites that were implementing the Foundation's Babies and You prenatal health promotion program. The study showed that participants had difficulty answering questions such as their ratio of pregnancy-related claims to total yearly claims, the number of pregnancy and delivery claims per year that exceed the average cost of delivery, and the amount spent per year on neonatal intensive care.

Employers who fail to consider the pregnancies of employees and their dependents in their overall benefits and health care planning also risk costs other than financial. When women employees have problem pregnancies or their babies are unhealthy, costs to a company in absenteeism, productivity, and morale can be high. If the employee is male, similar costs may be incurred if his spouse has a difficult pregnancy, gives birth prematurely, or has a low-birthweight infant.

While these costs have an immediate impact on an employer, there are other costs that have a delayed impact. Demographic studies show that in the coming decade, a smaller pool of workers will be available, but the demands of the workplace will require higher levels of education. Fifty percent of all new jobs will require education beyond high school, and 30 percent will require a college degree.[11] Each birth of an unhealthy baby has the potential to deprive tomorrow's work force of a productive and skillful employee.

PREVENTING THE PROBLEM

Fortunately, many of the infant deaths today can be prevented. In fact, the White House Task Force on Infant Mortality estimates that one-quarter of the total number of infant deaths could be prevented with the knowledge and technology now available.[12] For example, it is well established that early and regular prenatal care is one of the most effective ways to improve pregnancy outcome. Yet, in 1990, 8.4 million women of childbearing age did not have health insurance coverage to allow them access to prenatal care. And 6 million of these women were working women.[13] In addition, 5 million women with private insurance have policies that do not include maternity care. The majority of these women also are employed.[14]

Besides the lack of cost-effective prenatal care, there are other factors that place a woman at risk for delivering a baby prematurely or with a birth defect. Medical problems and some environmental influences can cause birth defects. Examples include: Rubella, certain drugs (both prescribed and illegal), X-rays, heavy alcohol use, and certain sexually transmitted diseases. Deliveries of premature babies, the majority of whom are low birthweight (weighing less than 5 pounds, 8 ounces at birth) can also result from such maternal factors as smoking, inadequate weight gain, alcohol consumption, certain drugs, hypertension, diabetes during pregnancy, and age (less than 17 or more than 35 years).

Through the promotion of prenatal care and education, risks such as these can be identified and either eliminated or modified with the appropriate intervention. For example, maternal smoking doubles a woman's chances of having a low-birthweight baby.[15] According to the Centers for Disease Control, 25 percent of pregnant women in the U.S. smoke throughout pregnancy. The CDC estimates that the elimination of maternal smoking could decrease the infant mortality rate by approximately 10 percent.[16] Worksite-based prenatal education programs could be the vehicle to either provide or refer women to smoking cessation programs.

THE BENEFITS OF PRENATAL CARE AND EDUCATION

Increasingly, as companies find that promoting healthy pregnancies is beneficial for employers as well as employees, they are offering incentives for early prenatal care, redesigning benefit plans, and providing on-site medical care and case management. They are finding that such approaches can lead to significant health care savings, increased employee productivity, fewer absences, higher morale, and an earlier return to work after the delivery.[17]

An Illinois insurance carrier saw absences decrease an average of 4.5 days per pregnant employee 18 months after initiating its prenatal program. The company also reported that employees worked closer to their due dates and returned to the job earlier.[18] Another company found that, after establishing a comprehensive prenatal education program, its average cost per maternity case dropped from $27,242 to $2,893. At one time, this company paid $500,000 in medical costs for four premature infants.[19]

Finally, according to the Committee for Economic Development, babies who are properly cared for are less likely to become burdens on our health care, welfare, and educational systems.[20] The birth of healthy babies helps to fulfill the potential for healthy, productive, and skilled workers, thus ensuring that the requirements for future job markets will be met.

WHAT EMPLOYERS CAN DO

Clearly, employers cannot afford to ignore these issues. Forward-thinking companies are already offering maternal and infant health services that support healthy pregnancy outcomes and reduce their associated costs. These services include:

- Health benefit plans that emphasize prevention;
- Risk assessment and rescreening;
- Case management;
- Prenatal health promotion; and
- Information and referral services.

Additional programs and benefits for working parents include parental leave of absence, alternative work schedules, and alternative job arrangements. The following section will describe some of these elements in more detail.

Maternal and Infant Health Benefits

Worksite maternity benefits vary, depending on such factors as company size, the state in which the woman is employed, and individual decisions made by the employer. The typical plan covers usual and customary physician fees for prenatal care services, delivery, and postnatal care. Charges for high-risk mothers and deliveries are often accommodated under other aspects of the plan. Hospitalization or birthing center fees are covered for a standard number of days, usually two to three days for a normal delivery and healthy baby. In addition, many companies give full or partial disability benefits, as well as job-protected leave of absence, continued participation in other benefit plans, and ongoing job or company seniority.

Although 38 million women of reproductive age have employment-based health insurance (their own or through a spouse or parent), as stated earlier, significant gaps exist in maternal and infant health. In addition to uninsured and underinsured women, another 20 million women belong to employment-based plans that require a waiting period before coverage begins. Of these, more than half impose waiting periods of three months or more, thereby precluding prenatal care during the critical first trimester of pregnancy.[21]

Even when coverage by an employer is available, there are significant differences among policies. Most do not cover the full bill or provide all essential preventive services[22]:

Only 26 percent of women are fully insured for physician charges for maternity care.

Only 7-8 percent of those in group plans are fully insured for hospital room and board and other charges, such as anesthesia.

Only 50 percent of the policies cover routine physician care of the newborn in the hospital.

Fourteen percent of insurers do not cover Rh immune globulin injections, which are essential to prevent miscarriage or stillbirth for a pregnant woman with the Rh-negative blood factor.

The Pregnancy Discrimination Act of 1978 addresses the issue of maternity benefits, but only in a limited way. The act requires employers to treat pregnancy and childbirth in the same way as other disabilities or medical conditions. That is, an employer cannot deny health insurance for pregnancy if there is insurance available for other medical conditions, or deny disability benefits if available for other individuals. There are several factors that limit its effectiveness, however, including the following:

- It does not apply to firms with 15 or fewer employees.
- It does not apply to an employee's non-spouse dependent.
- There is no national mandate that requires employers to offer short-term disability. Currently, only five states require disability insurance: California, New York, New Jersey, Rhode Island and Hawaii.

What makes a good maternal and infant health benefit plan?
A good plan should emphasize prevention and include, but not be limited to, the following elements:

- Prenatal care (includes provider fees, prenatal tests, and postpartum visits);
- Labor and delivery at a hospital or birthing center;
- Genetic counseling and testing (if indicated);
- Hospital room and board;
- Normal newborn nursery care;
- Neonatal intensive care; and

- Well-baby care (birth to one year, including immunizations and well-baby checkups).

Perhaps the single largest gap in private indemnity insurance plans is well-baby care. Currently, only 50 percent of conventional plans offer any well-baby care; yet, the American Academy of Pediatrics recommends two exams before the baby leaves the hospital and six well-baby visits during the first year of life.

In addition, a preconception health care visit for women planning pregnancy should also be included as part of prenatal care. According to a report of the Public Health Service Expert Panel on the Content of Prenatal Care, released in 1989: "The preconception visit may be the single most important health care visit when viewed in the context of its effect on pregnancy."[23] The purpose of preconception care is to ensure that women enter pregnancy healthy. It allows an opportunity to identify and treat risks prior to pregnancy. The Expert Panel recommends that preconception care be part of prenatal care with reimbursement and coverage provided in health insurance plans.

Preconception care makes good sense, given that the developing fetus is most vulnerable 17-56 days after conception (from the third through the eighth week). By the end of the eighth week, structural anomalies that may affect the fetus are already determined. At this point, a woman may not even know she is pregnant or have been to a health care provider unless she has made a preconception visit.

Prenatal Education

Because of the importance of healthy lifestyle to the birth of a healthy infant, the March of Dimes Birth Defects Foundation developed Babies and You, a worksite prenatal health promotion program to be included among a company's maternal and infant health strategies. Developed in partnership with leading maternal health content specialists throughout the country, Babies and You was extensively field-tested at March of Dimes chapters and worksites prior to its release in 1982. It is continuously updated and enhanced to ensure that the program content and methodology reflect current worksite needs as well as new knowledge about maternal and infant health.

This comprehensive and nationally recognized program seeks to promote healthy birth outcomes through an educational approach. The March of Dimes works in partnership with an employer to tailor the program around that company's particular work force. Because employers are at different stages in their health promotion activities, Babies and You offers three levels of implementation:

1. A company-wide employee information campaign, using low-cost print and audiovisual materials provided by the March of Dimes;

2. Educational seminars on topics such as preconception care, nutrition, substance use, and prenatal care, led by health care professionals provided free by the March of Dimes; and

3. Training of company health professionals to facilitate Babies and You seminars and free technical assistance in program implementation.

The Babies and You program design is adaptable to the unique needs of any work force or segment of a work force. The March of Dimes works closely with employers to help them reach worksite employees, spouses, and family members. Consideration is given to the education level, ethnicity, culture, and language of prospective participants, as well as to worksite restrictions and available resources in the local community. This approach makes it possible to convey clear and meaningful information that can be easily translated into practical steps for better prenatal health.

TIPS ON DEVELOPING MATERNAL AND INFANT HEALTH INITIATIVES

Regardless of what comprises a company's maternal and infant health strategies, there are two important factors to keep in mind during program planning and implementation: the need to be sensitive to changing employee demographics and the need to develop a strong communication component.

As we move toward the year 2000, it is expected that more women will enter the work force (although this rate will taper off), minorities will represent a larger share of the work force, and immigrants will represent the largest share of increase since World War I.[24] Given this evolution, employers need to continually monitor their programs to ensure that they are responsive to the changing needs and characteristics of their employees and their cultural differences, language barriers, and varied educational levels.

Employers also must develop strong communication campaigns so that employees know about and use their programs fully. Formal information campaigns might include sending materials about the program directly to each employee's home or the development of a special company prenatal health education booklet or video library. Less formal means might include lobby displays, pay envelope stuffers, and articles in employee newsletters. Even the best and most carefully developed maternal and infant health program will be meaningless if employees don't use it in a timely fashion.

EVALUATING THE EFFORT

Program evaluation is an integral component of worksite health promotion that should not be overlooked. The type and extent of program evaluation will vary, depending on program objectives. Some employers may initiate a health promotion program to lower risk factors, while others may be concerned with containing health care costs. Still others may want to improve employee health and morale. No matter what the objectives, evaluation starts at the program-planning stage. It will show whether the program is effective and worth the investment and indicate any areas that need strengthening.

Measuring the effectiveness of prenatal services and programs is still in its pioneering stages. As yet, few companies have developed reliable measurements. But some of the worksites surveyed by the March of Dimes Birth Defects Foundation reported better health and pregnancy outcomes. Ameritrust Bank, for instance, found that its rate of premature babies had decreased in less than a year. Other survey respondents reported cost savings they attributed to their maternity services and programs. American Express, for example, realized a 16 percent decrease in pregnancy-related and neonatal intensive care claims in the first quarter of 1990. Burlington Industries saved over $150,000 in these same two areas in fiscal year 1989 alone, and Health Management Corporation saved $531,076 in pregnancy-related claims from August 1989 to July 1990.

In fact, based on actuarial study and research, Blue Cross/ Blue Shield of Virginia came to the conclusion that it was a wise business investment to implement its benefits plan for all its "fully insured" groups at no cost to those subscribers. Other self-funded employers are also implementing prenatal education and risk assessment programs. Ohio State University reported two cost savings: first, the monthly benefits cost per member has stabilized over the past three years; second, the university has saved approximately $50,000 a year in hospital fees because mothers have opted for early hospital dismissal after delivery, using fully paid home-nursing services instead.

EVERYBODY WINS

The director of health and safety services of one of the surveyed companies summed up the benefits of promoting prenatal health care: "We view this as a win-win situation. Our employees see that we care about them and their families. We see a more productive work force. The physicians are happy; they like having better educated patients. Everybody wins . . . most important, the babies."

1. I McKirgan, *Promoting Prenatal Health in the Workplace*, Washington, DC: Washington Business Group on Health, Worksite Wellness Series, November 1986, p 7.

2. *Fertility of American Woman*, Washington, DC: Bureau of the Census, June 1988.

3. *Monthly Labor Review*, Washington, DC: US Department of Labor Statistics, February 1986.

4. *Trends and Variations in First Births to Older Women 1970–1986*, Washington, DC: US Department of Health and Human Services, National Center for Health Statistics, Vital and Health Statistics Series 21, No. 47, June 1989.

5. "Managing Pregnancy in Patients Over 35," *Contemporary OB/GYN*, May 1987.

6. *Child Health USA '89*, Washington, DC: US Department of Health and Human Services, Office of Maternal and Child Health, October 1989, p. 11.

7. K Johnson, *Birth Defects and Infant Mortality,* White Plains, NY: March of Dimes Birth Defects Foundation, 1991.

8. *Infant Mortality in the United States*, White House Task Force on Infant Mortality, unpublished report, Nov 30, 1989.

9. "Cost of Cesarean Deliveries, Focus on . . . Report," 1988 *Benefits Today* 5.

10. *Infant Health in America: Everybody's Business,* Columbia, MD: CIGNA Corporation, conducted by The Center for Risk Management and Insurance Research—Georgia State University and The Center for Health Policy Studies, 1992.

11. Clendenin and Kolberge, "The Road Ahead," *The New York Times*, September 1987.

12. White House Task Force, *supra* note 8.

13. J Foley, *Uninsured in the United States: The Nonelderly Population Without Health Insurance,* Employee Benefit Research Institute, 1991.

14. RB Gold, et al, *Blessed Events and the Bottom Line: Financing Maternity Care in the United States,* New York: Alan Guttmacher Institute, 1987.

15. *The Health Consequences of Smoking*, Washington, DC: US Department of Health, Education, and Welfare, Public Health Service, 1973.

16. *Reducing the Health Consequences of Smoking: 25 Years of Progress—A Report of the Surgeon General*, Rockville, MD: US Department of Health and Human Services, Centers for Disease Control, 1989.

17. McKirgan, Michaels, Davis, and Klerman, "Promoting Maternal and Infant Health in the Workplace," 7 *Journal of Compensation and Benefits Management* 1, Fall 1990.

18. Hopkins, "Report on Cost Containment Benefits," Wellness in the Workplace Conference, Pittsburgh, PA, April 29, 1986.

19. *Corporate Prenatal Programs: Healthier Babies, Healthier Bottom Line,* Washington, DC: Bureau of National Affairs, Inc, 1991.

20. McKirgan, *supra* note 15.

21. Gold, *supra* note 14.

22. *Id.*

23. *Caring for Our Future: The Content of Prenatal Care*, Washington, DC: US Department of Health and Human Services, Public Health Service, National Institutes of Health, 1989.

22. WB Johnston and AE Parker, *Workforce 2000: Work and Workers for the Twenty-First Century*, Indianapolis: Hudson Institute, Inc, 1987.

Part 3

SELF-INSURANCE

13. Self-funding Health Care Plans

Dale H. Yamamoto

Although self-funding of health care programs is usually thought of as an option available only to large companies, the last two decades have seen an increasing number of smaller companies—those with 1,000 or fewer employees—choosing to self-insure. The smaller companies choose this option for the same reasons as large companies: Self-insuring provides an employer with much greater flexibility and much more control over costs than is allowed by traditional insurance company coverage. The tradeoff, of course, is in foregoinog the insurance company's umbrella of protection from unexpected costs.

The decision to self-insure is not one to be made lightly. Employers must carefully assess the issues involved—particularly the costs and potential risks—and consider the various alternatives, including premium delay, retrospective premium, and minimum premium options. Exhibit 1 shows the percentage, by size, of employers who self-fund.

THE COMPONENTS OF THE PREMIUM

Before looking at the issues of self-funding health care plans, it is important to understand where each penny of your group insurance premium dollar goes. Premiums consist of four major components: claims, retention (insurance company jargon for expenses), claim reserves, and dividend margins. The first component (claims) is controlled by various cost management measures and is

Exhibit 1. Percentage, by Size of Employer, with Self-Funded Plans

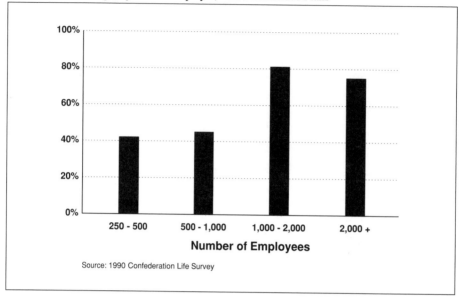

Number of Employees

Source: 1990 Confederation Life Survey

beyond the scope of this article; alternative funding methods, including self-funding, have been developed to control the last three components.

Retention Charges

Retention charges reflect the insurance company's costs of doing business. They include general administration and claims processing costs, state premium taxes, risk charges, and profit. Exhibit 2 shows a typical allocation of these charges as a percentage of expected premium.

Claims processing includes the cost of investigating, calculating, and processing the claims submitted to be paid under the plan. The general administration charge includes the insurer's underwriting costs, production of communication materials (brochures and letters), statistical reporting, and periodic reporting of claims experience. Most of these costs will be incurred under any type of funding method; some insurers or third-party administrators (TPAs), however, may be in a better position than others to provide these services efficiently.

The risk charge premiums accounts for potential claim fluctuations. The more predictable the claims, the smaller the risk charge.

In almost all states, insurance companies must pay taxes on premiums received from employers for insured plans, although some states exempt Blue Cross and Blue Shield and health maintenance organizations (HMOs). Each state has different rules on the level of premium paid, and taxes may be calculated

Exhibit 2. Allocation of Premiums

Expense Type	Percent of Premium
Claims processing	4.50%
General administration	2.00%
Premium tax	2.50%
Risk and profit charge	2.50%
Commissions	1.00%
Conversion charge	0.50%
Total expenses	13.00%

based on the state where the employees, employer, and insurance company are located.

The commissions paid to brokers by insurance companies represent payment for the broker's assistance to the employer. In many cases, these services are paid for on a fee basis and would not be included in the premium calculation.

For an insured plan, most states require a group insurance plan to provide individual coverage for employees who terminate from employment. Most insurers will charge the employer for this conversion privilege. The additional charge covers the additional cost of persons who elect this conversion coverage because they have higher costs than the average employee. This charge may be a flat amount for each conversion or included as a percentage of premium charge.

Claim Reserves

Claim reserves are funds held by insurers to account for costs in the period in which services were provided. Due to the time between the date services are provided and the date a check is cashed, a reserve or claim liability needs to be established to maintain proper accounting. After adjusting paid claims during the year for these reserves, the insurer will have an estimate of incurred claims for the year. The idea of paid and incurred claims is analogous to the accountant's cash and accrual accounting systems. The incurred claim amount allocates the costs to the appropriate period.

At the end of each policy period, the insurer will estimate the amount of claims that have been incurred, but not paid, during the period. This reserve has commonly been called the "incurred but not reported" liability (IBNR) or "incurred but unpaid" liability (IBU). This liability may be determined based on the actual experience of the employer or by general factors established for similar plans.

Dividend Margins

A dividend margin is another premium component. It is intended to:

1. Account for potential claim fluctuations;
2. Reduce the risk of understating the health care trend in the premium calculation; and
3. Recoup losses from earlier plan years.

The amount of this component depends on the level of risk the employer shares with the insurer. The more risk the employer assumes, the lower the margin.

WHY DO EMPLOYERS SELF-FUND?

A 1987 survey by the Self Insurance Institute of America (SIIA) showed that 77 percent of employers that are self-funding are doing so to control costs. Flexibility in plan design was a distant second, with only 13 percent citing this as the main reason. Exhibit 3 summarizes all of the responses to the survey.

Exhibit 3. Main Reason for Self-Funding

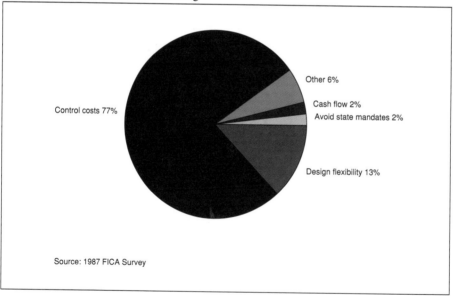

Control costs 77%

Other 6%

Cash flow 2%
Avoid state mandates 2%

Design flexibility 13%

Source: 1987 FICA Survey

Cost Control

Self-insuring increases health care plan cost control several different ways, including the following:

- **Reduction or elimination of state premium taxes.** Taxes range from less than 1 percent to as high as 4 percent; the most common rate is around 2.5

percent. Alternative funding methods can reduce or completely eliminate these taxes.

- **Reduction of general administration costs.** The insurance company's administrative expenses (retention) may include some services that are not needed by the employer. These charges might include reports that are not used and elaborate utilization control programs that do not yield savings to the employer. Some services may be needed but are available from other sources (e.g., legal, actuarial, claim audit services). It may be possible to save money by streamlining some processes and only purchasing needed services. General administrative costs are generally around 2 percent to 4 percent of the typical premium.

- **Reduction of risk charges.** If an employer is willing to assume more of the risk for potential claim fluctuations, the risk charge can be decreased. These charges can range between 1 percent and 5 percent of the total premium.

- **Elimination or reduction of dividend margins.** This additional charge above the risk charge minimizes the insurer's losses from unfavorable claim experience. This charge can be either reduced or eliminated by negotiations with the insurer or through self-funding. Typical dividend margins are 5 percent to 15 percent of the premium.

- **Reduction of insurer's profit margin.** Insurance companies need to make a profit on providing health care insurance, but employers do not. Employers eliminate this charge by self-funding. However, companies providing other types of services (e.g., claim administrators) need to make a profit too. Typical profit loads are 1 percent to 3 percent of the premium.

- **Cutback of contingency reserves.** These are reserves generally held by the insurer to help reduce the effect of claim fluctuations on the premium rates. In years with good experience, all or a portion of the surplus is put into the contingency reserve. In years when the premiums do not pay for the claims and expenses, the deficit is taken out of the contingency reserve. This is a negotiated reserve, but having one reduces the risk charge. These types of reserves vary greatly, but are usually limited to between 25 percent and 50 percent of the premium.

- **Reduction or redetermination of conversion charge.** Since this is a state-mandated provision for insured plans, a self-funded plan can eliminate the benefit. Typical conversion charges will run from zero to 1 percent of premium. It may be possible to change the method of paying for the conversion charge to reduce the cost.

Plan Design Flexibility

Employers gain unlimited flexibility in plan design by self-funding. Many insurers provide a fixed number of plan provisions that do not leave a great deal of leeway for change. The self-insured employer has the freedom to design a plan with specific benefit formulas, limitations, exclusions, and provider definitions that meet its philosophy and objectives.

Avoidance of State-Mandated Benefits

Nearly all 50 states have passed laws requiring insurance companies to cover specific illnesses in group health plans. Examples include minimum benefits for treatment of alcoholism, mental illness, and drug dependencies. Although under constant scrutiny, employee benefit plans are generally exempt from state regulations under the Employee Retirement Income Security Act (ERISA) of 1974. An employer may avoid providing these state-mandated benefits by self-insuring since the mandated benefits arise only under state insurance laws and apply only to traditionally insured plans.

Cash Flow

Improved cash flow is achieved by delaying the point at which cash is actually paid from the employer's general assets. Under a group insurance program, this can be accomplished in two ways:

1. Reduce or eliminate reserves held by insurers for future claim payments. These incurred and unpaid claim liabilities are usually between 20 and 30 percent of annual paid claims.
2. Reduce the time delay between paying cash from general assets and the point when the employee actually cashes the check (the "float").

Other Reasons

Some employers have adopted self-funded plans for other reasons. An employer's general management approach may be to do as much internally as possible. Employers may desire to assume as much risk as possible as long as it will benefit them in the long term.

Some employers believe that they can get better overall service by contracting out the various functions needed to provide benefits. This can be particularly true in the area of claim administration. Many local claim administrators (TPAs) are more effective because they are more familiar with the local medical markets than larger insurance companies.

IS SELF-FUNDING THE DIRECTION TO GO?

Interestingly, with the exception of avoiding state-mandated benefits, most of the advantages of self-funding can be realized without self-insuring. An employer can reduce or eliminate some expense charges, improve administrative services, increase the interest earned on reserves, reduce state premium taxes, and change many benefit design features simply by negotiating its current insured contracts.

Over the years, several different financing alternatives to self-insurance have evolved. Each alternative has its own specific target for cost control, along with its own degrees of risk and flexibility. Exhibit 4 shows these different funding methods as a series of steps going from traditional, prospectively rated

Exhibit 4. Alternative Financing Methods

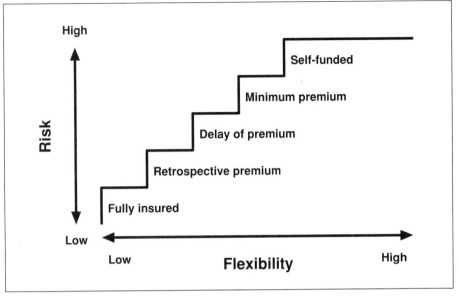

insurance to full self-insurance. Each alternative enhances the employer's cash flow by minimizing reserve accumulations and reducing the insurer's risk. In exchange for these financial "favors," the employer assumes more of the in-surance "risk;" with each step in Exhibit 4, the amount of risk assumed by the employer increases. Along with this higher risk, however, the employer gains increased control over cash flow and plan design features. Following is a discussion of each of the alternatives.

Fully Insured

Fully Insured (prospective premium) is the traditional, fully insured financing arrangement. The insurance company determines a premium rate per covered person and, in return, pays benefits and provides other services (e.g., actuarial, legal, communication, and underwriting). The rates are determined before the beginning of the plan year and hence the term prospective premium. These rates may be determined based on the employer's own claim experience, the insurer's "book of business," or a combination of the two.

The plan may also be "experience rated." This is a cost-sharing arrange-ment where the insurance company will refund premiums that exceed the claims and expenses for the year (a surplus). Alternatively, the insurer may hold the surplus in a reserve (claim stabilization reserve) to help pay for future years when claims and expenses are higher than premiums. If a deficit occurs at the end of the year, a portion of it may be included in future premium rates until it is recouped.

The insurance company carries most of the risk on its shoulders with this type of funding arrangement. Insurers will, therefore, be the most conservative when they determine premium rates under this method.

Retrospective Premium

A "retro" contract will eliminate most of the dividend margins included in a prospective premium calculation. These margins are replaced with a retrospective or additional premium agreement that allows the insurer to receive additional payments after the end of the plan year if premiums are less than claims and expenses (a deficit), but only up to an agreed limit. For example, the insurer may charge $2,000 per year per covered person, but if, at the end of the year, $2,200 per person was spent, the employer will pay the extra $200. If they agreed that the employer will only be responsible for an extra $150 per person, that is all the employer will pay in additional premiums; the additional $50 will be carried forward to future years. This additional amount is generally amortized over more than one year. The primary component eliminated under this approach is the dividend margin.

Delayed Premium

This is a special agreement in the insurance contract that allows the employer to pay premiums later than the standard 30-day grace period. The typical extension is 90 days. For example, instead of paying the January premium at the end of January, the employer will delay payment until the end of March. This allows a float of three months so the cash can be used within the company. The employer effectively borrows all or a portion of the claim reserves that the insurer has established. Under this funding method, the insurer will include an interest charge on the delayed premium in the premium calculation. This interest charge is typically less than most companies' cost of capital.

This method, in effect, reduces the actual cash held by the insurance company for claim reserves. Both the retrospective premium and delayed premium methods may be used together to eliminate two of the major components of the premium—claim reserves and dividend margin.

Minimum Premium

Many employers use this method, also called split funding, as a first step into self-funding. It reduces many elements found in the retention component of the premium. Instead of paying the insurance company the full premium, the employer pays a "minimum" premium each month. This monthly premium is generally equal to the retention component. The employer also opens a bank account that the insurer uses to pay claims; each time a benefit payment is paid, the employer funds the account for the amount of the payment. In a variation of this method, the employer may negotiate with the insurer so that the reserves will be held as employer assets rather than remain with the insurer.

Because the money used to pay claims never goes through the insurance company's accounts, premium taxes do not have to be paid on claim amounts. This eliminates about 90 percent of the premium tax payable. For example, if the state premium tax is 2 percent of premium, this approach will save about 1.8 percent of the total premium. (Note: California considers the total claims plus minimum premium in calculating premium tax.)

A minimum premium contract is still an insured plan, and therefore, all state-mandated benefits still apply. The insurer continues to provide the same services that it provides a fully insured policyholder. If actual claims exceed the projected amount, the insurer pays for this excess. If the insurer does pay for an excess, they will carry forward the payment to future years just like any other conventionally insured funding method.

Full Self-Funding

Under full self-funding, the employer has full responsibility for all costs—claims and expenses. The insurance company has no claim liability, holds no reserves, and does not pay premium taxes. Since the insurance company no longer has any liability, all risk charges and dividend margins are eliminated.

The employer can limit its risk of annual claim fluctuations by buying "stop-loss" insurance. There are two general types of stop-loss insurance. Specific, or individual stop-loss insurance pays for claims in excess of a specified dollar amount for an individual. Aggregate stop-loss insurance pays for claims greater than a specified target (or "attachment point") for the whole group. For example, a specific stop-loss policy may pay for claims higher than $75,000 for any one insured person, while an aggregate stop-loss policy might pay for all claims over 125 percent of expected claims for the year.

Under this method, the claim reserves and dividend margins are generally eliminated, and the retention component is reduced. If the employer purchases stop-loss insurance, claims are slightly reduced, but the stop-loss premium adds back in their expected cost plus the cost of a risk margin element.

Exhibit 5 summarizes the general characteristics of the methods discussed above. The three conventional methods—prospective, retrospective, and delayed premium methods—are summarized under one heading.

Exhibit 6 provides a summary of advantages and disadvantages of each method.

The most appropriate funding method for an employer will depend on the company's willingness to assume greater risk in exchange for more flexibility in plan design, expense control, and cash flow. A key question that employers must answer as they consider the various options is: "How much risk can the company assume?"

Exhibit 5. Funding Method Comparisons.

Method	Accounting	Funding	Documents/ Communication
Conventional	Rates set prospectively	31-day grace period	Insurance contract issued by company
	Retention and deficit recovery set retrospectively	Other financing arrangements can be made (e.g., retrospective and delayed premium)	Insurer may provide communication material for employees
Minimum premium	Administrative costs estimated prospectively	Claims funded as needed up to predetermined amount	Insurance contract issued by company
	Monthly claim fluctuations up to predetermined limits funded by employer	Claim reserves generally held by employer	Insurer may provide communication material for employees
	In most cases, retention and deficit recovery set retrospectively	Insurer dictates the level of reserves	
Self-funded	Expense fees set prospectively	Claims funded as needed	Plan documents and employee communication controlled by employer
	Claim costs estimated by employer	Claim reserves retained by employer	
	Stop-loss insurance provides budget limit		

WHAT IS RISK?

Defined simply, risk is the chance of loss in a particular situation. A company that self-insures exposes itself to two obvious kinds of risk:

1. Significant loss from individual catastrophic claims and overall claim fluctuation; and
2. Additional fiduciary responsibility.

Exhibit 6. Funding Method Advantages and Disadvantages

Method	Advantages	Disadvantages
Conventional	Budget set in advance Claim fluctuation borne by insurance company Insurer guarantees claim payments	Expenses are higher than other methods Potential cash advantage to insurer Insurance company controls documents, communication, and budgeting Deficits are carried forward
Minimum premium	Cash flow advantage may be to employer Most state premium taxes eliminated Reserves may be held by employer	Deficits carried forward Daily claim fluctuation borne by employer Possible taxation of employer reserve amounts Insurer controls documents and communication
Self-insured	Fixed costs are low and set prospectively Employer controls administration and communication Budget and reserve levels set by employer	Monthly claim fluctuations and other adverse experience borne by employer (minimized with stop loss insurance) Budgeting is not pre-established Possible increased fiduciary responsibility

Claim Fluctuation Risk

The possibility of a catastrophic claim will always exist for both large and small employers. The more employees covered under the plan, the easier it is to absorb these high costs.

Exhibit 7 shows the variability to be expected in any one year for employers of different sizes, as well as the probability a plan will have claims at various levels of their expected costs. A result of 100 indicates that the actual

Exhibit 7. Claim Fluctuations Per Year by Number of Employees

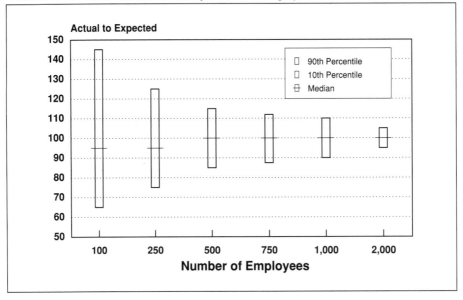

costs are exactly equal to the expected costs. For example, the 90th percentile for a 100-employee plan is 145. That means there is a 10 percent chance that the plan will have claims more than 145 percent of the expected claims in any one year.

On average, over time, these ratios should all move closer to 100. Exhibit 8 shows the same ratios of actual to expected claims over a ten-year period for a 100-employee company. Actual claims for all ten years are compared to expected claims for the same period. The ratios move closer to 100, but there are still significant fluctuations even after this extended period.

Fiduciary Risk

In a traditionally insured plan, the insurance company and the sponsoring employer share the liability for any lawsuit brought against the plan. A company that self-insures its plan, however, will typically lose the protection of the insurance company and assume full fiduciary responsibility. For a fee, some insurance companies will agree to accept a portion of this risk as part of the general services provided in their administrative contract.

Hidden Risks

External factors may create some hidden risks to self-insuring. Many state legislatures have tried to control self-funded benefit plans, and some have actually tried to treat self-funded plans the same as insured plans. In most cases, employers have prevailed on the premise that ERISA exempts employee benefit plans from state laws. Recently, states have tried to regulate the various managed care

Exhibit 8. Claim Fluctuations for a 100-Employee Company Over Ten Years

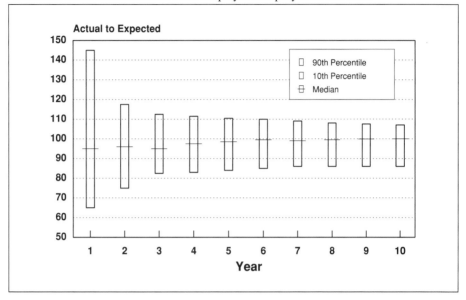

programs that attempt to pass more risk back to insurance companies. These managed care programs may include insurer guarantees of savings in claims and administration over a period of years. This risk shifting may mean that these plans have now become subject to state insurance laws and therefore subject to mandated benefits.

Self-insured plans, however, are subject to the ERISA nondiscrimination rules, while conventionally insured plans are not. These rules are usually easy for employers to follow, although a minor problem may occur if a significant number of employees enrolls in an HMO. Today, there are many employers with a high proportion of HMO enrollees that sponsor self-funded plans.

CONCLUSION

Is self-insurance the best option for your company? The only way to answer that question is by carefully considering all of the issues discussed in this article and weighing the advantages against the disadvantages; use the following list of steps to help guide your decision making process:

1. Formulate why you want to change the current financial arrangement. Is it to control costs or to gain plan design flexibility?

2. Decide which plans to review. Remember, plans that are good candidates for self-funding are those that have very predictable benefits from year to year.

Dental and medical plans, for example, are better choices for self-funding than disability or life insurance plans.

3. Review your current financial arrangement. Identify whether your objective can be met by renegotiating the current contract.

4. Review the financial implications of making any changes. Remember to factor in the cost of services that replace those currently provided by the insurance company.

14. Managing Risks and Claims
Ellis Simon

Many entities that turned to self-funding as a way of gaining control over their insurance premiums have come in for a rude awakening. While they eliminated their insurers' overhead from the cost of financing risk, their expenses were nearly as great as they had been prior to self-insuring.

The actual delivery [cost] of the insurance product is about 15 cents of the premium dollar with claims making up the reminding 85 cents. Do you focus on the 85 or the 15?" asks Eric Ewing, president of E.F. Ewing Insurance, a consulting firm in Mars, Pa.

"You can hone delivery of the insurance product to razor sharpness, but if you're not focused on loss prevention and post-loss issues, you're missing the point."

The point is that the leverage in self-funding comes from coupling it with loss prevention and claims management. "Ten years ago, employers were looking for a free lunch. They looked to self-insurance as the salvation of cost control. Then they learned that the salvation of cost control is claims control," asserts James Kinder, executive vice president of the Self-Insurance Institute of America Inc., in Santa Ana, Calif.

"Most companies that self-insured in the 1980s looked only at the price of coverage," notes David Tweedy, senior consultant with Betterley Risk Consultants in Worcester, Mass. "People are getting more sophisticated by necessity. In the 1990s there's more cost consciousness, and less rash decisions are being made."

When an entity self-funds, whether by taking a large deductible, using a captive or becoming a self-insurer and purchasing excess coverage above its self-insured retention, it decides, in effect, that it will pay losses that it can afford and transfer away that risk which is too great to bear.

As a result, losses that fall within the entity's retention or working layer can now be readily charged back to individual profit or cost centers. Line managers who previously saw insurance as an overhead expense that they had little control over now see that non-catastrophic losses have a direct impact on their profitability and, ultimately, their bonuses.

"The change in attitude is immediate," says Michael Murphy of Denver-based Risk Consultants Inc. Companies that previously maintained their insurers had responsibility for controlling losses expenses are now putting the onus on their line managers through internal premium allocation schemes.

When a company chooses to self-fund, loss prevention and claims management become paramount, Murphy adds. "Once you come to that step, you're at the court of last resort. There's no other place to go for better leverage."

MAKING MANAGERS ACCOUNTABLE

The impact can be dramatic. Dan Dillen, risk manager for Ward Trucking, an interstate common carrier based in Altoona, Pa., reports a 27 percent improvement in claims costs for the 12-month period ended June 30. He attributes the result to increased accountability for losses by line managers following the company's decision to raise deductibles via its captive to $250,000.

"Before, we were looking at just paying bills. Now we have an accounting system whereby we charge each profit center for a portion of the loss experience they have," Dillen reports. "Terminal managers see the losses come to the bottom line and it comes off their bonuses."

The change in awareness has resulted in local managers setting up incentive programs for their employees and management showing a willingness to "spend a few bucks to save a few thousand on a worker's comp claim," he says.

In addition, management has been seeking input from employees on how to make their jobs safer and acting quickly on their suggestions. For instance, at a safety meeting last January, drivers identified the lack of a grab bar on older trailers as a hazard. The problem was presented to the company's mechanics. By the end of the day they had presented a diagram for attaching a nylon handle to the vehicles.

While such changes may not be revolutionary, Dillen points out that "it's the little things that nickel and dime you to death."

Effective loss prevention means "getting back to basics," according to Wayne Johnson, vice president of risk management for another self-insurer, Ryder Systems Inc., the Miami-based truck leasing and specialty carrier firm.

"It's not rocket science. It's just good basic employee management and changing the culture of the company to think about safety first." Stricter enforcement of rules requiring shop employees to wear safety glasses, for example, has reduced the severity of injuries in several cases, Johnson reports.

Ryder redoubled its emphasis on loss prevention about two years ago as a result of rising worker's comp costs. A key component of that effort was the formation of a safety and accident-prevention task force, headed by senior vice president James Herron. The group, which includes Johnson and senior operating managers, meets quarterly to review current safety programs and establish new ones. Responsibility for implementing the programs falls to line managers. "With over 700 locations, we can't have a big safety staff walking around the shop," Johnson explains. "It takes the involvement and attention of supervisors and lead men to make it happen."

To get management's attention, Ryder raised its deductible—the portion of loss costs charged to individual profit centers—from $5,000 to $25,000 per occurrence last year, and Johnson says the company is considering going to full allocation. "The $25,000 deductible certainly got people's attention. It's one reason we've had an improvement this year."

PROMPT CLAIMS HANDLING

At the Southern California Rapid Transit District (SCRTD), a rash of accidents followed by public alarm prompted an emphasis on loss prevention and claims management. That, in turn, has lowered the accident rate by 27 percent since 1984 and reduced the number of outstanding claims by 33 percent since 1987.

Although the agency, which provides bus and rail transit in metropolitan Los Angeles, was self-insured, the decision to self-fund was made solely for financial reasons without consideration of operating issues, recalls Barbara Anderson, SCRTD's director of risk management. Consequently, there had been no emphasis on formalized accident prevention and claims management.

That began to change after Anderson arrived five and one-half years ago. After a two-year study, a traffic accident-reduction program was put into effect using the statistical information the agency had been compiling on its accidents, but did not know how to apply.

The program was developed by the operating department, which is solely responsible for its implementation and success. "Often organizations believe safety is the responsibility of the safety department, but it's the people on the line who are responsible," states Anderson. "Safety people are advisers. They are highly trained people who can develop a program, but they are not the watchdogs."

Under the program, a traffic engineer sets accident-reduction objectives for each route and addresses the unique characteristics of each line, such as whether there are a lot of left turns or a lot of elderly passengers. This is followed up with a campaign that has begun to make drivers aware of these "hot spots." The public has also gotten into the act with pedestrian and rider safety programs developed for schools and libraries. The result: SCRTD's accident frequency rate fell to 3.75 per 100,000 hub miles in 1984.

At the same time, SCRTD tightened its claims-management procedures. Working with its third-party administrator (TPA), Hertz Claim Management of Park Ridge, N.J., it established a special investigation unit that has uncovered approximately $2 million in fraudulent claims and has helped convict and incarcerate 10 perpetrators, including a doctor and an attorney.

The agency furthermore saved $6 million in worker's comp costs by cleaning up its database and closing "hundreds" of open claims, Anderson says. "The reliability and accuracy of reports often were taken for granted. The closure program increased case closures by 300 percent.

Anderson draws on the image of a triangle to explain how the TPA, risk management department and field managers work together in a special analysis group to handle unusual claims or those involving a high number of fatalities. Operating people prepare the first report on the accident, while risk management and the TPA work with police officers, lawyers and an occasional accident-reconstruction specialist to gather additional information. Within five days, the team meets to hammer out a claims strategy and an action plan.

This system "gets the triangle working early on the accident," Anderson explains. "The information has to go back and forth. With the traditional approach of letting the TPA handle it, nothing happens. Operation can't handle it alone and risk management can only take care of the insurance."

These and other programs have helped SCRTD reduce its loss reserves to $57.3 million from $72.5 million in 1987, while the number of outstanding claims has fallen to 5,332 from 7,949, according to Anderson.

Prompt reporting is also a key element of Ryder's claims-management strategy. "In workers' comp, if you don't get on top from day one you lose," declares Tad D'Orio, the firm's director of workers' compensation . Those initial efforts at Ryder focus on determining the nature and extent of an injury, making sure the employee is getting appropriate treatment and encouraging the employee to return to work as quickly as possible.

Within 48 hours, a manager has contacted the employee and his or her doctor, while the claims representative begins an investigation at the accident location. Supervisors are encouraged to stay in touch with injured employees to support their morale and encourage their early return to work. Often this prevents the malingering that results from people feeling alienated and lost in the process.

Company nurses and outside medical consultants play an important role in evaluating medical treatment and looking for questionable practices. "If they [doctors] are questioned by someone who's knowledgeable, they will back off,"

D'Orio contends. "If you don't use a medical professional, you're wasting everyone's time."

The approach works, D'Orio stresses. In one instance, a person who was expected to stay out for a year returned to light duty after six months and to full duty after another two months. "If you take a guy with an injury who becomes permanently disabled, you can be on the hook for life," he says. "A 40-year-old driver who becomes seriously injured can cost between $500,000 and $1 million. If you can bring that guy back to work, you cut off a lot of that."

SHARING PHILOSOPHIES

Leprino Foods, a privately held food manufacturer and wholesaler based in Denver, which has self-insured its workers'comp exposure since 1982, also uses light-duty assignments to help people return to work quickly. In addition, it has taken a hard line against fraudulent claims and has gone out of its way to find a TPA that shares its philosophy; in this case it's Sedgwick James' Irvine, Calif.-based office.

Risk manager Jim Kreger maintains that it is imperative that TPAs look at claims the same way the client would, and he constantly reminds administrators of what his company's position is. As a result, Leprino's workers' comp costs run about 20 percent below industry norms.

SCRTD's Barbara Anderson shares Kreger's view that TPAs need to heed the client philosophy on claims management. To get that point across, she went through files on a case-by-case basis to show Hertz Claims Management where that philosophy was not being applied. As a result, the TPA agreed and changed its practices to comply with her wished.

Like other self-insurers, Leprino practices claims-cost allocation to get profit center managers committed to loss prevention and claims control. Operating people are involved in the claims process from the beginning, getting medical attention for the injured party and following up with doctors on the employee's condition and prognosis for returning to work. "We look at a comp claim as a human resources issue that needs to be addressed," Kreger says. "You have an individual who has an injury and you have to provide the best medical care possible and return the person to a productive position as soon as possible."

Leprino's corporate risk management staff is in daily contact with its TPA to review claims status and prognosis for return to work. Quarterly meeting are held with the TPA and field managers to review open claims and map out future strategies. "Without a direction to a claim, the claims administrator has a whole file full of claims," Kreger remarks. "You cannot expect them to go through the drawer on a constant basis without a review and setting a course on when you expect things to happen."

Even though self-funding does not by itself achieve the kind of cost savings that many risk managers hope for, it spawns an awareness that losses directly impact the bottom line and can, to a great extent, be controlled. Only when companies implement effective loss-prevention and claims-management programs do they reap the full benefits of their decision to self-insure.

15. Auditing Medical Bills

As the movement toward expanded employee incentive programs grows, employ-ers are continually exploring new areas of wellness and health care in which employees can be motivated to participate in behavior that will ultimately benefit the corporate bottom line. At the same time, wellness programs are being linked and integrated with some areas of the corporate culture to which they tradition-ally may not have been related.

In a fully integrated core incentive program, a company's wellness program and its benefits package become inextricably linked. A new wrinkle in the benefits area that could well become part of such corporate core incentive programs are incentives geared at uncovering errors in hospital billing.

Frustrated by hospital overcharges that have gotten lost in the administrative paper shuffle, some companies have turned to their employees for auditing assistance. In return, they are sharing the refunds they receive with the employees who uncover the billing errors. At one mobile home manufacturing company in California, the system employed has thus far saved an average of $600 for each employee who has opted to participate in the checking system.

"We had read and been told that hospitals make a great number of mistakes," says Lee Shealy, CPCU, ARM, risk manager with Fleetwood Enterprises Inc., in Riverside, CA. A self-insured company, Fleetwood hired an administrator to audit hospital bills, but it was not economically feasible to audit every single bill. "What ended up happening was that they picked a threshold of, say, $15,000 to $20,000, and audited every bill above that amount," explains Shealy. "This meant, of

Reprinted with permission from *Employee Health & Fitness*, American Health consultants, Inc., Atlanta, Georgia.

course, that a lot of bills were not being audited but were simply being paid blindly." Shealy says such "blind" bill paying is rampant in corporate America.

In an attempt to eliminate (or at least minimize) non-audited bills, Fleetwood decided to try the Double-Check program, the management program offered by Garner Consulting of Pasadena, CA. The program works like this: For every dollar saved, the employee receiving the care who spots the error gets a specified percentage, Garner gets a specified percentage, and the rest of the savings is retained by the employer. Garner's standard fee (and total compensation) is one-third of gross employer savings, while the employer/employee ratio is determined by the employer. Fleetwood splits the remaining savings evenly with its employees.

The system made a lot of sense to Shealy. "Who better to look at the bill than the person who was there, and who knew what had been done?" he asks. "We decided to use our employees to do our auditing for us; it's a win-win situation."

The system grew out of a project Garner Consulting undertook for the Health Care Finance Administration a couple of years ago. "We audited 2,500 hospital bills, and during the course of the project, we really got an idea of the kind of mistakes that can occur on these bills," recalls John C. Garner, president of the consulting firm. "We also read up on companies who were using their employees to audit hospital bills. But most of them were not getting much employee response to the program."

Garner concluded that they key to successful implementation of such a program was communication or, in his words, "getting the right message to the right people at the right time." Those people, of course, are the employees who will soon be getting a bill.

Garner Consulting arranges for the utilization review firm to notify the company when an employee is precertified for admission to a hospital. At that time, Garner sends the employee an audit log to track the services performed in the hospital and a checklist of the most common reasons for hospital overcharges. If employees find an overcharge, it's their responsibility to get the hospital to correct the bill. If they do, they submit a Double-Check claim form to Garner Consulting, which verifies the savings and notifies the employer. The employer in turn awards the employee the designated percentage of the savings.

It's important that the employees know what to look for, notes Garner, and one of the largest sources of overbilling is central supply. "This often is the result of a well-meaning but overworked nursing staff," he explains. Every time supplies are ordered, says Garner, the nurses are supposed to put an appropriate sticker on the patient's chart. This is a wonderful system in theory, but in reality, he says, busy nurses often "temporarily" place the sticker on their name badges. At the end of a shift a nurse could have as many as 50 stickers on the badge and has to put them somewhere. "That's how a teenage boy can end up getting charged for sanitary napkins," he muses.

Finding most errors does not require great medical knowledge, just common sense. "For example, if you haven't had surgery, you have good cause for questioning recovery room charges," Garner concludes.

The system has been in place at Fleetwood for a little more than a year, and while both Shealy and Garner are pleased with the average per-employee savings figure, both would like to see much greater participation. Of all the employees who received the Double-Check packet, only 2.5 percent filed a claim using the system.

While this is a relatively high return for a direct mail campaign, Shealy had hoped for even more activity. "If we could have saved $600 on every one of those employees, that would really have been great," he admits.

Garner says the system itself is still evolving. "We originally thought a massive announcement in the company newsletter would be enough, but apparently it primarily fell on deaf ears."

In the future, he plans to use payroll stuffers and strategically placed posters to get the message out at Fleetwood.

"We will do more in-house advertising," adds Shealy. "I believe it will produce better results."

One of the limitations of systems like Double-Check is that they are far more practical and easily implemented for companies that are self-insured, and thus have total control over the disposition of funds saved by the discovery of billing errors.

In fact, one client of Garner Consulting, Bourns Inc., has dropped Double-Check because it is no longer self-insured. "It's a good program," says Bonnie L. Hopkins, corporate benefits manager for the Riverside, California-based electronics subassembly firm. "Employees need someone to jog their memory, and it reminded them which items to look for. We had a lot of people find errors, and it definitely paid for itself."

Hopkins says there was no reason, other than the firm's change in status, for dropping the program. In fact, she notes, there is no reason not to implement the program with its new insurance carrier.

The roadblock is presented by the carrier itself. "They would have to buy off on the system as well," she explains. "The carrier would have to be willing to share the savings with us."

16. Should Employers Make Physicians Account for Costs?

Joyce Frieden

Economic credentialing is a growing trend among health care buyers seeking to make doctors more accountable.

Physicians have in the past been told to give good care no matter what the cost. But today, cost conscious employers and hospitals are using a variety of techniques, ranging from threatening the loss of hospital privileges to choosing managed care plan physicians based on their economic proficiency, to make physicians more cost efficient.

Take Southern New England Telephone Co. as an example. The telecommunications company, based in New Haven, Conn., will audit the practices of the physicians in its preferred provider network when physicians appear to be overusing services or otherwise providing inefficient care, says Gerry Martens, SNET's manager for benefits planning. Although the tactic is rarely used, the fact that the program exists has a sentinel effect, Martens says. Unlike most companies with PPOs, SNET contracts directly with the doctors in its PPOs. A self-insured company with operations throughout Connecticut, SNET has 12,000 employees.

Such scrutiny, dubbed economic credentialing, is part of a growing trend among health care payers to make physicians more accountable—in terms of economics or patient outcomes—for the work they do.

Just how widespread is economic credentialing? The answers vary

Just how popular is economic credentialing? The answer depends on who is asked. The results of a survey of 3,348 hospitals last year by the American Hospital Association show that only 1.4 percent of respondents requested that applicants for hospital privileges provide evidence of cost effective care, down from 7 percent in 1985.

"The decrease may be a result of hospitals adjusting to the DRG system of reimbursement, a recognition of the problems encountered when comparing economic data from different institutions, and the fact that physicians immediately out of their residencies have not had an opportunity to develop a record of cost-effectiveness," the study says. DRGs, or diagnosis-related groups, are used by Medicare to control health care costs.

Anecdotal evidence suggests an increase in credentialing. "I see a lot of economic profiling by everybody," says Kenneth Smithson, M.D., the medical director for Blue Cross and Blue Shield of Arizona. "There's not anybody in business here who isn't looking at economics at some level."

A Big Movement

"This is a big movement," says Paul Pietzsch, president of the Health Policy Corp. of Iowa, a coalition of employers, in Des Moines. "I see employers moving from being payers of health care to being purchasers, and certifying health care suppliers using the same techniques as they would for other suppliers who are supposed to meet certain expectations," he adds.

For employers trying to cut health care costs, putting pressure on hospitals—not physicians—should be sufficient, says Paul Pietzsch, president of the Health Policy Corporation of Iowa, a coalition of employers, in Des Moines. "Employers don't need to know how hospitals hold the physicians accountable," he says. "Of course, employers want accountability from hospitals in terms of outcomes data. Once that is done, the dynamics start changing. Suddenly, the hospital administrator says, 'Hey, my customers are telling me what they want.' He is then empowered to say to the physician, 'Do you care about keeping half of our business? If you do, you need to be my partner and see that you do the best job you can.'"

FACTORING IN EXCELLENCE

Navistar, a truck and bus manufacturer in Chicago, had good reason to develop a process for working with providers and making them more accountable for their services. Last year, it spent $184.2 million on health care for its 13,000 employees and their families. That amounted to an average of $4,715 per household, says Sylvia Grant Morrison, Navistar's director of corporate health care.

Self-insured Navistar found that its highest cost expenditures had been for cardiac care. "Cardiac procedures are high volume and high cost, and there is potential for quality problems," Morrison says. A medical audit done for Navistar in August 1990 showed that 15 percent of 202 coronary bypass procedures and 22 percent of 268 coronary angiographies were inappropriate.

Concerned about the number of inappropriate surgeries, Navistar developed a program to contract with five cardiac centers of excellence in Ohio, Illinois, and Indiana. The hospitals are being evaluated on many factors—outcomes, resource utilization, existing and future cardiac program content, and the desire of the hospital and physicians to work with Navistar over the long term, Morrison says. "Data show that providers that perform significant volumes of procedures and that have good outcomes use resources efficiently and end up being high-quality, lower cost providers," she says.

Morrison is concerned as much with the practicing habits of particular physicians as with a facility's overall outcomes. She adds that "if the hospital has outliers, it's up to them to do something about it." She finds that hospitals and physicians are justifiably afraid that outcomes data could be misused. "We're using physician profiling as a tool to ask questions, not as a tool for punishment." Two of the centers will be named within several months and the others should be named by year-end, Morrison says. Employees' use of the centers will be voluntary.

ACCOUNTABILITY

Most employers prefer to persuade errant providers to change their ways rather than penalize them for spending too much money. "The issue is: How do we get accountability from the health care provider?" says Charlene Rothkopf, director of benefit operations for the Marriott Corp., a hotel and restaurant chain based in Bethesda, Md. "I believe that physicians, given the proper feedback and information, would want to provide good service."

While employers may not be concerned with physicians directly, hospitals are. At the Upper Chesapeake Health System, a two-hospital corporation about 25 miles north of Baltimore, for example, physicians are being monitored under a program started in 1985. The hospitals review each doctor's performance in five areas:

- Average number of patient days;
- Above-average hospital charges;
- Denials from utilization review programs;
- Uncollectible percentage of hospital bills; and
- Number of malpractice cases.

Physicians who fall outside the statewide norms in two of the categories are given a more detailed review by management and asked to adjust their practice patterns. If no results are forthcoming, the physician is warned to make his practice more cost efficient or lose his hospital privileges. He is also informed that his appointment is probationary for a year. So far, the hospital has warned nine doctors. None has lost privileges.

Some hospitals are more subtle in their approach. Nazareth Hospital, in Philadelphia, shares information with physicians on how cost efficient they are, but it has no current plans to expand into formal economic credentialing, says Carl Hoffman, M.D., Nazareth's director of medical affairs.

SCRUTINY BY INSURERS

In addition to hospitals and HMOs, insurers are also examining doctors' expenditures. Blue Cross and Blue Shield of Arizona, for example, began reviewing physicians' costs when it was establishing PPOs in the early 1980s, says Kenneth Smithson, M.D., the plan's medical director. "As with most PPOs at that time, we lost our shirt in the first few years," he says. The Arizona Blue Cross/Blue Shield PPO, among others, features what's called a withhold system, in which the plan withholds a certain amount of physicians' fees until year-end to make doctors operate more efficiently. If the plan's costs are lower than, or equal to, expectations, the physicians get money back. If not, the plan keeps that withhold. The result, however, was that the move cost the plan more than the amount being withheld. "Doctors saw the withhold system as a volume discount arrangement, so we ended up with massive volume that ate up the withhold, plus a lot more," says Smithson.

At the time, Arizona Blue Cross/Blue Shield contracted with an outside group of physicians to monitor utilization, which also failed to stop the physicians from increasing the volume of services. "Since that didn't succeed, we had to do it ourselves," Smithson explains. The plan became more selective about which physicians it would include in its PPO. "We decided we would only have so many doctors and so many locations, and we would add additional patients to the doctor's practice," says Smithson. Each physician would have so many patients and would not be as concerned about building volume to make up for any discount.

Under one of the criteria used in choosing PPO physicians, the doctor's economic performance was compared with that of his peers. Smithson says, the plan decided to "find out where we were paying out dollars and see how many patients were being taken care of for that amount."

But while Arizona Blue Cross/Blue Shield has had this economic data on each physician, it did not often use the information when deciding whether to use certain doctors, Smithson say. "Economic profiling is most useful as an analytical tool," he explains. "As a criterion for panel selection, it is only one of many deciding factors, such as whether the physicians have hospital privileges or whether they are board certified." After the physician is added to the panel, the plan continues to collect the economic data. "If we find someone is an outlier on costs, we will ask for the reason," Smithson says.

By using the economic data, and by removing physicians who used services excessively, the plan reduced its physician costs by 10 percent in 1986. Although Smithson says figures are unavailable for succeeding years, the plan has kept its cost increases about 33 percent lower than its competitors and has expanded the number of lives it covers from 250,000 to 425,000. "That's the ultimate test—what happens to your business," he says.

Then, Arizona Blue Cross/Blue Shield focused on its HMO. "We got detailed reports on the gatekeepers and looked at their practices compared with their peers—how many patients were admitted to the hospital, for example. We gave the outliers their reports," Smithson says.

Richard Fox, M.D., a family physician in Phoenix who has been profiled by Blue Cross/Blue Shied of Arizona, says most of his colleagues have come to accept the program. "Everyone's reaction initially was that it was too much scrutiny," he says. "But the reviewers have been very fair," he says, and once the doctors have seen the results, they haven't had any complaints.

OTHERS COMPLAIN

But physicians aren't always happy with the scrutiny. "We do agree there's an important role for physicians to play in decreasing utilization," says Jill Silverman, director of medical staff activities and quality assurance at the California Medical Association (CMA) in San Francisco. "But it needs to be evaluated in clinical determinations, not in cost-based decisions."

The economic pressures on hospitals are causing them to look twice at physicians who don't have profitable practices. "There have been cases where physicians were pressured because they had too many MediCal patients," Silverman says of the state's health insurance program for poor residents.

"A lot of physicians don't want to see any MediCal patients, so the doctors who agree to see them, see a lot of them. The next thing you know, the physician has a huge MediCal practice, and the hospital is saying, 'Gee, we're losing a lot of money.' We want to make sure physicians are not rewarded for treating patients profitably, but are free to remain committed to taking care of sick people." Worries that economic credentialing will interfere with the practice of medicine are causing the CMA to consider proposing legislation restricting economic credentialing, she adds.

Some physicians may be wary of economic credentialing, but others say the practice might become more appropriate under certain circumstances. "Until we get good measures to distinguish levels of severity of illness and to consistently adjust for case mix, the unsophisticated or superficial use of economic credentialing will do more harm than good," says Clifford Guy, M.D., medical director of the Winston-Salem Health Plan in Winston-Salem, N.C. "But with good tools, such as accurate case mix, this is a characterization of practice that is sorely needed."

To make economic credentialing a useful tool, it should be combined with measures of appropriateness, Guy continued. "The key to all of this is not cost, but appropriateness, which ties together concepts of quality and cost. If people complain that doctors are driven financially, and then they turn around and drive them financially, it becomes a self-fulfilling prophecy. But there is a great need for accountability, and if economic credentialing addresses accountability and appropriateness, then it will be a good tool."

Making physicians accountable requires working with them as partners instead of using credentialing in a punitive way, says Spencer Borden, M.D., medical director for the purchaser services division of MediQual, a medical software company in Westboro, Mass. "Hospitals will get more physician cooperation with a carrot than with a stick," he says. "The issue of economic credentialing of physicians is overblown because there's too much fear associated with it, and not enough emphasis on learning."

If hospitals want to improve physicians' practice styles, says Borden, "they have to measure them, compare them with other doctors, coach them, and then keep measuring to see if the intervention had any impact. And that should be done behind closed doors, not through the mail or through newspapers. If that collegial approach is used, some of the physicians' sensitivities will diminish."

One situation that dramatically demonstrated physician dissatisfaction with increased financial accountability occurred recently at Harvard Community Health Plan (HCHP) when former CEO Thomas Pyle was forced to resign after plan physicians rebelled against his efforts to increase physician accountability. Pyle wanted to make physicians account for the number of patients they saw during their working hours and to tie efficiency to additional pay.

Even though the amount of additional pay tied to efficiency was small, many physicians were uncomfortable with making it a permanent part of a compensation program, says John Ludden, HCHP medical director. Furthermore, under such a system, HCHP doctors might end up being judged partly on factors they could not control. For instance, physicians would have been grouped together for comparison, even though the size of each group may have differed. And yet, under the proposed system, "If you saw a few more patients, you'd get a little more money," thus skewing results in favor of larger groups, he says.

Ludden sympathizes with the physicians, noting that it's not always easy for the plan to determine which behaviors should be rewarded. In other words, "If an HMO decides it wants to increase visit rates and pay physicians for seeing more patients, you have to ask yourself, 'Why are these patients being seen?'"

In the wake of the controversy, HCHP is seeking a new CEO and has postponed implementing the accountability program.

PARTNERING WITH AN HMO

Bull HN Information systems, Billerica, Mass., followed the HCHP controversey with interest. A software company with 6,500 employees, Bull has about 600 workers enrolled in HCHP, says Suzanne Mercure, Bull's manager for benefits planning. The situation at HCHP, which includes both staff- and group-model settings, made Mercure wonder whether patients seeing staff physicians were treated differently from those in the group practice. "For me, it said, 'If you do this for the staff model, how do you deal with it in your group model?'" she said.

Mercure is working with Thomas Hawkins, M.D., chief of HCHP's clinical support development group, to get answers to her questions and to improve the quality of the health care her employees receive. She is also doing similar work with InterGroup, a group-model HMO in Phoenix. "We're asking what data they have to show how the medical groups perform in the fee-for-service sector versus the HMO," Mercure explains. "From this, we want to develop standards for our managed care organization."

Part 4

FLEXIBLE BENEFITS

17. Are Flexible Benefit Plans Right for Your Company?

Arthur G. Dobbelaere   Kathleen H. Goeppinger

Flexible benefit plans provide benefit specialists with an excellent opportunity to meet the challenge of a diverse workforce. Innovative, non-traditional benefits can be introduced in a cost effective manner while providing options that meet individual needs. Are they right for every employer? Only if the objectives are clear and measurable and meet the corporate and employee needs, are they right for any employer.

Is your benefit plan meeting the needs of your employees? Are you containing benefit costs? Do your benefits exceed 40 percent of your payroll costs? How is your organization addressing the growing demands for child care programs, elder care options, vision care, wellness, dental plans, and 401K plans while maintaining sound pension and health care plans? The answers to these questions are forcing many benefit professionals to strategically redesign the foundations of their programs. No longer can the plan address the one wage earner family member who supports a homemaker spouse and 2.5 children, only one in five workers fits that description today.[1] Benefit specialists are finding that they can no longer design one benefit program that meets the needs of every employee. The workplace is rapidly changing and the benefit programs need to reflect these changes. In response, many organizations are implementing flexible benefit plans but these may not be the answer for all organizations.

During the late 1980s, benefit managers saw the erosion of the concept of one health care plan for all employees. As health care costs increased, many employers determined that different levels of health care plans provided employees with options. They could take the good, better, or best plan, each of which had a rate structure reflecting the level of coverage. In many organizations, this was the first step toward flexible benefits. Few managers realized that it was the onset of a change to their overall benefit structure.

WHAT IS A FLEXIBLE BENEFIT PLAN?

Today, many employers are rapidly turning to flexible benefit programs. Broadly defined, a flexible benefit plan (often referred to as a cafeteria plan) is a program under Section 125 of the Internal Revenue Code that offers employees the choice between taxable benefits such as vacation pay, and non-taxable benefits, such as health life insurance. Not all flexible benefit plans are alike. Some employers have instituted plans called flexible spending accounts. These plans allow the employee a choice of taking cash or health care coverage. By using the Section 125 provision, an employee can pay their share of the cost of their group insurance benefits with pre-tax dollars. Under this provision, employees' paychecks are reduced by the amount they contribute toward the cost of their health care benefits. That money is removed from the company's salary structure before federal income, Social Security, and (usually) state income taxes are calculated. For employees, this results in lower taxable income and higher take-home pay. For the employer, it means a tax savings because payroll taxes are also reduced.[2]

Other employers have instituted a second form of flexible benefits, referred to as stand-alone health care spending accounts. Also known as medical reimbursement accounts, these plans allow an employee to set aside part of their income, pre-tax, to cover expenses that are not eligible for coverage under the traditional health care plan. These plans have been modified, under the "insurance risk rule" to allow for the entire annual salary reduction amount to be available for reimbursement throughout the year. Employee claims for medical expenses up to the annual maximum must be reimbursed, even if the claim is in excess of the salary reduction to date. When these rules were first issued in 1989, many employers voiced concern about an employee terminating after receiving a flexible spending account reimbursement in excess of their salary reductions to date. To avoid substantial loss, many employers have implemented a service related participation requirement and restricted the annual employee contribution to their plans. The average contribution is $2,900, down from a 1989 high of $3,700 per employee. Consequently, the insurance rule has not been detrimental to employers.[3]

The third type of cafeteria plan is a full flexible benefit program allowing employees to have a set dollar amount from which they purchase the benefits that meet their own personal needs. Under the full flexible benefit program employees can purchase additional weeks of vacation, place additional dollars in their family dental plans to cover orthodontia expenses for children, or invest additional dollars in their savings plans. When employers institute full flexible benefit plans they often maintain a "core" plan of basic health care coverage, life insurance, and pension coverage. A core plan provides minimal coverage for all employees while allowing them the opportunity to spend the remainder of the employer's contribution in the most effective manner. In a survey of 444 organizations conducted by Hewitt Associates in 1991, 72 percent of the flexible benefit programs included both benefit choice-making and spending accounts.[4] This preference for full flexible plans is extending to unionized employees; Hewitt Associates found that 45 percent of employers with union-represented employees are currently offering flexible benefits to some or all of their bargaining hourly employees. An additional 15 percent plan to include bargaining hourly employees within the next three years.[5]

THE GROWTH OF FLEXIBLE BENEFIT PROGRAMS

A research study conducted by the authors in the fall of 1991 and sponsored by Marion Merrell Dow Inc. found that approximately 49.4 percent of Fortune 2000 participants claim to have already instituted a flexible benefit program. This study also found that 83.3 percent of the corporations surveyed plan to have a full flexible program in place within the next five years.[6] The growth of flexible benefits has been rapid. According to a 1988 employee benefits survey, only 5 percent of all full-time employees were eligible for flexible benefits, and 12 percent were eligible for reimbursement accounts. These plans were originally more common among white collar workers than among blue collar workers but today this is changing.[7]

This rapid growth can be attributed to a number of factors. The implementation of a flexible benefit plan can unify and equalize the dollars spent on benefits between employee groups and company divisions. While some employers have used flexible benefits as a means to stabilize their benefit program after a merger or acquisition, the concept is being expanded to establish a set dollar amount between employee groups. Three major factors are driving the need to provide flexible benefits workplace diversity, recruitment and retention of employees, and costs.

The primary factor driving employers to add flexible benefits is the diversity of their workforce. They see this type of plan as "a one-size-fits-all benefit plan used to satisfy employees. Today . . . more women work, more families have two wage earners, and more single people are in the labor pool."[8] Diversity in the workplace has resulted in diversity in benefit needs, and in response, many employers are turning to the concept of flexible benefit plans, allowing employees to select the kinds of benefits that are most meaningful to their own personal circumstances. However, many employers have not linked their changing demographics, or even a shortage of workers, with their benefit planning. Diversity in the workplace has resulted in diversity in benefit needs.

A second factor is the ability to attract and retain employees in a tightening labor market. The Hewitt Associates study found that 42 percent of the 444 companies studied implemented flexible benefits in response to competition.[9] Although some companies are already plagued with a shortage of workers, a recent survey by the Hudson Institute and the consulting firm of Towers Perrin found that few employers are addressing their current shortage or preparing for future demographic changes.[10] Although the Workforce 2000 study is under considerable debate by employers today, its basic premise revolves around the need to assess future workforce requirements. The Hudson study of 645 companies found that some employers have implemented innovative benefit programs and family assistance plans, such as child and elder care programs, flexible hours, new training plans, and long-term care benefits, to attract and retain employees, but that many other employers still do not perceive a need for such new benefit programs. Both the popular and academic press continue to report on employee needs for family assistance plans, relating the implementation of these to greater productivity, higher attendance levels, and less stress-related illnesses. Some employers believe non-traditional benefit programs will help manage the high costs of absent, unhealthy, and unproductive employees in the future.[11] Today, for example, approximately one third of all families are caring for an older relative. The primary care givers are women. By the year 2000, it is projected that 75 percent of all women between the ages of 45 and 60 will be employed, and this group will still be the primary care givers for the aged.[12] Employers may find decreased productivity, absenteeism, tardiness, excessive phone use, and lower work quality as elder care responsibilities increase for their employees. By providing a flexible benefit program that allows an employee options to purchase pre-tax elder day care programs, in-home nursing care, and even shopping services, the employee's productivity and general satisfaction may increase dramatically. A complete elder care program can be a heavy expense to an organization. IBM currently maintains a nationwide elder care referral service for its 270,000 employees and retirees, and has committed over 3 million dollars to enhance in-home elder care for their employees. Hallmark, headquartered in Kansas City, Missouri, provides a pre-tax reserve account for hearing aids, eyeglasses, and health care related travel expenses for elderly parents.[13] These programs may have great appeal, but it may only be so for a limited portion of the entire workforce since not every employee needs an elder care benefit plan. But, by providing this plan as part of the flexible benefit program, an employee is given the freedom of choice while the employer's costs are contained. Limiting an elder care option to only the flexible benefit plan may be the only way in which a small employer can afford such a benefit.

Employees can be attracted and retained to both large and small organizations through these non-traditional benefit plans. Until this time, implementation of flexible benefit programs has been common in larger organizations. However, smaller employers need to start more active consideration of cafeteria plans in order to compete for employees. "Employees who are lured to small firms from large ones may come with the expectation of having choices in benefits."[14] A study conducted for UNUM Life Insurance Company by the Life Insurance Market Research Association found that the number of small firms with flex plans grew from 2,900 in 1986 to 8,300 by 1988. An additional 45 percent will put in a flex plan by 1994.[15] Nevertheless, the flex plan approach is still not the preference for all employers or employees.

A third major reason for implementing a flexible benefit program is to reduce overall benefit costs. Employers implement flexible benefit programs to save benefit dollars by designing the programs under the "defined contribution" approach to benefit spending. By establishing a set dollar amount to be allocated to an employee's account each year, the employer caps its total dollar expenditure. A study by Deloitte & Touche of 78 New England firms found that 42 percent of the firms believe that flexible benefits can reduce their overall benefit costs. While 40 percent were unsure, only 18 percent did not think that their costs would be reduced.[16] The Hewitt study found that flexible benefit plans have successfully contained the medical costs of 76 percent of the 444 employers surveyed. In addition, they found that 78 percent of the employers were able to control other benefit costs while increasing the number of new benefits available to employees.[17]

While the first year of a flexible benefit program can be expensive due to increased administration costs, new information management system installation and design, and additional employee communication, long-term savings can be achieved by limiting the amount of additional dollars placed in the employee's flexible benefit account over the next few years. Employers often cap new monies available to employees, regardless of benefit inflation. For example, a health care plan may cost an additional 16 percent, and the employer's contribution to the flexible benefit plan is limited to only an 8 percent overall increase. By doing this, they have effectively shifted half the cost of the health care increase to the employee participating in the health care plan.

STRATEGIC IMPLEMENTATION ISSUES

There are a number of issues that must be addressed prior to implementation of a flexible benefit program. The first key factor is the reason for the plan. Converting a benefit program from a traditional plan to a flexible benefit plan represents a major philosophical shift for many employers. By establishing a sound basis for the plan, an employer can better establish both short- and long-term measurable objectives. A benefit manager, along with top management, needs to consider the following reasons for implementation:

- Unifying the entire benefit program
- Meeting competitive pressures
- Increasing employee understanding of their benefits
- Educating employees as to the value of each benefit and the overall cost to the employer
- Teaching employees to be smart consumers of benefits
- Increasing employee involvement in the selection of plans
- Containing overall benefits costs
- Containing health care costs
- Allowing cost variations by geographic locations
- Reducing compensation inequities resulting from life circumstances, such as age and the need for dependent coverage
- Providing a framework for adding new benefit plans or features
- Providing a total compensation perspective to the benefit program
- Varying benefit contributions based on business performance

Once the reasons for the plan are defined, it is important to determine how the plans will be measured. By having defined objectives, it is easier to assess whether the flexible benefit program has been successful. These objectives need to be viewed as both short- and long-term goals. Benefit managers need to be cautious not to overestimate their ability to measure the effectiveness of specific benefit plans such as child care. While management needs to assess the value of benefits, it is usually difficult to place a specific dollar value on specific benefit programs. The issues regarding the measurement of socially orientated benefits vary, and many employers find that the measurement incidence is very low.[18]

A second key factor is the selection of meaningful benefits based on the employee population. The benefit program needs to provide a wide range of options that not only offer cost-effective choices for the employer, but also are aligned with the needs of the employees. It is critical that the employer consider employee demographics and employee needs in the design of the benefit program. Various levels of coverage and benefit choices may be required in order to meet the demands of company demographics. For example, Abbott Laboratories, a hospital supply and pharmaceutical corporation with 36,000 employees, found that they had to convert their traditional health care plan into six medical options and four dental options, including a "no coverage" option under each benefit, in order to meet the needs of their work force.[19]

By conducting an employee benefit survey, an employer can assess which benefits are meeting employee needs today while looking at future plans. It is important that the survey be conducted as part of the overall strategic design of new plans. While there is always concern that such a survey may raise employees' expectations with regard to improved benefits, it is a critical step in the development of a flexible benefit program. Any concerns regarding employee perceptions need to be dealt with openly and honestly with each of the employee groups.

A third key factor is effective employee communication. While flexible benefits can be the most successful way to get employees involved in the value of their benefit plan, it will not be successful unless the plan is well communicated. It is common for an employer to incorporate medical coverage, dental plans, life insurance, and disability income plans into their cafeteria plan, with two or more options in each category. These options must be understandable—the individual will be making a choice that has many personal and family ramifications. The task of successfully communicating these benefits is a serious challenge to an employer.

Communication of the plans begins in the design stages. An employee involvement process that allows the employees to participate in the design and communicates the options to them and their peers is an important first step in employee understanding. As the plans are designed, employee groups need to be a part of the review system. Bringing employees together to read the proposed announcement letters, encouraging them to be a part of the communication program, and seeking their assistance in talking with their peers can lead to an effective and more credible communication program.

When establishing the communication program a number of issues should be considered. It must be well designed with specific objectives. A critical step will be the involvement of family members in benefit choices. While the more traditional methods of regular benefit communications are directed toward the employee, family involvement is important in flexible benefit selection. Often there are family options to be selected that need careful consideration of other coverages; the needs of different family members greatly influences the determination of specific benefit selections. Contact with the family should be part of the design of the communication program. Different factors include the type of media that will be used, the timetable, and a budget. The cost of communicating a flexible benefit program can be high depending on the overall plan design.

When Not to Implement Flexible Benefit Plans

Employee benefit managers should carefully weigh the support of top management in making a switch from a traditional benefit plan to a flexible benefit plan. The initial objectives of the plan may be to offer employees choices, but if choice translates to additional corporate cost, you may not be meeting business needs and may not receive the support of top management. The benefits specialist should not underestimate the need for this support. In some organizations, the top management may not be ready to make a philosophical shift from a paternalistic benefit plan to one where the employee makes decisions and has the right to opt out of plans that were previously provided for everyone. As an example, some benefit managers claim that their chief executives consider it a corporate responsibility to offer everyone the same health care plan, regardless of their own needs.

A benefit department must use caution in not overselling the opportunity for cost savings with flexible benefits. While there can be a savings over the long term, the initial implementation of a flexible benefits plan will almost certainly result in higher costs due to increased communication and administration. If the only objective is to save benefit dollars, then a plan design other than a flexible benefit plan should be utilized.

Benefit administration increases with a flexible benefit plan. Small employers may find the increased administrative cost prohibitive, especially if additional computer support is required. Although there are outside administrators, many benefit departments find that they want to maintain the control, and ultimate cost, in-house.

Employers that have not previously invested in employee communication and participation may find that flexible benefit programs require an entirely new communication plan. These plans are costly in terms of both dollars and time. Should an employer not be willing to make the investment, they should not implement flexible benefits.

Finally, employee education is required. If an organization converts their benefit plan to a flex plan, they are making a decision to educate employees. With benefit options come choices. These choices have to be weighed against personal financial goals, family circumstances, spouse benefits, and adequate benefit coverage. If a benefits department is going to implement flex plans, they also need to commit to helping an employees to make educated decisions.

1. Carol Bialkowski, "Flexible Benefits: More Options or More Headaches? *Black Enterprise*, October, 1991. pp. 106-110.

2. Barry Carron, CLU, "Group Insurance Planning for Small and Mid-size Companies," *LAN*, February 15, 1991, pp. 86-89.

3. "Strategies in Section 125 Plan Design Discussed," *Employee Benefit Plan Review*, December, 1990, pp. 15-16.

4. "Flexible Compensation Programs and Practices," Hewitt Associates, 1990-1991.

5. Ibid.

6. Arthur G. Dobbelaere, Ph.D., and Kathleen H. Goeppinger, Ph.D., *The Future of Corporate Health Care: A National Study*. Publication scheduled for release August 30, 1992, by The Business Word.

7. Joseph R. Meisenheimer II and William J. Wiatrowski, "Flexible Benefit Plans: Employees Who Have a Choice," *Monthy Labor Review*, December, 1989, pp. 17-23.

8. Robert O'Brien, "Freedom of Choice," *Small Business Reports*, January, 1992, pp.49-58.

9. "Flexible Compensation Programs and Practices," Hewitt Associates, 1990-1991.

10. "Workforce 2000: Competing in a Seller's Market," survey report published by Hudson Institute and Towers Perrin, 1991.

11.   Arthur G. Dobbelaere Ph.D., and Kathleen H. Goeppinger Ph.D., "Demographic Challenges", *Employee Benefits Journal*, International Foundation of Employee Benefit Plans, August, 1992, pp. 7-10 & 13.

12.   Bette Ann Stead, "Eldercare: Personal Triumph! Professional Downfall?", *Business Horizons*, May/June, 1991, pp. 72-76.

13.   Ibid.

14.   O'Brien, "Freedom of Choice," p. 50.

15.   "Data Watch: Flex Plans On the Rise," *Business & Health*, March, 1991, pp. 8-9.

16.   Ibid.

17.   "Flexible Compensation Programs and Practices," p. 7.

18.   Janet Norwood, "Measuring the Cost and Incidence of Employee Benefits," *Monthly Labor Review*, Vol. III, No. 8, August, 1988, pp. 3-8.

19.   "Flex Plan Choice Used As Cost Control Device," *Employee Benefit Plan Review*, December, 1989, p. 54.

18. Flexible Benefits
for Smaller Companies
Roger Thompson

Susan Herman gave her boss a suggestion he couldn't ignore: Offer employees new health and child-care benefits and, by doing so, save the company money. "He thought it sounded too good to be true," Herman recalls. But it wasn't.

Since last October, ChromatoChem, Inc., a biotechnology firm in Missoula, Mont., has enabled employees to set aside a portion of their salaries in untaxed reimbursement accounts to pay for certain health-care and day-care expenses. Every dollar that goes into an employee's reimbursement account lowers both the employee's and the company's tax bills. Four of ChromatoChem's six employees are taking part, and every body is happy, says Herman, the firm's controller.

Welcome to the new era of flexible benefits, where the combination of employee choice and tax breaks is reshaping the delivery of company benefit costs.

The technique adopted by ChromatoChem—the use of reimbursement accounts—is one of three basic flexible-benefits approaches that can be used individually or in combination.

Reimbursement accounts are particularly appealing because of the tax breaks they offer. For every $1,000 put into a reimbursement account rather than the employee's paycheck, an employee in the 28 percent federal tax bracket saves $280, while one in the 15 percent bracket saves $150. In every state except New Jersey and Pennsylvania, employees also save on state taxes, which typically are 5 to 7 percent. In addition, both the employer and the employee save an additional 7.65 percent, or $76.50 per $1,000, on Social Security taxes. In many cases, the

Reprinted by permission, *Nation's Business*, © July 1991, US Chamber of Commerce employer's payroll tax savings offset the added administrative costs of flexible reimbursement accounts.

The program at ChromatoChem was easy to set up and is a snap to administer, says Herman. She does all the record keeping on a personal computer with the aid of specially designed software. Moreover, employees got two new benefits that the company could not have offered otherwise. And the tax savings made the option attractive for everyone involved.

For employers, reimbursement accounts also create a mechanism for shifting a greater share of rising health-care costs to employees, but on a tax-favored basis that cushions the financial impact for the employees.

Although tax incentives drive reimbursement accounts, choice itself is the dominant factor in another type of flexible benefits plan—the cafeteria plan. Cafeteria plans offer employees a full range of choices among different *types* of benefits and *levels* of coverage, in addition to reimbursement-account tax savings.

Cafeteria plans once were the exclusive domain of large companies, but they are now being implemented by smaller companies as well, such as Image Express, a Southfield, Mich., firm that edits, television commercials and has 22 employees.

Says Pearl C. Lipner, a consultant with Image Express: "We have a formula based on seniority and salary that determines how much money goes into each employee's benefit package. They can take those dollars and spend them however they want."

By necessity, small companies once stood on the sidelines and watched as corporate giants pioneered the "flex" concept. The barriers to entry were just too high: Start-up and administrative costs made flex prohibitively expensive; insurance companies showed little interest in developing flex products for the small-business market; and companies too small to have a full-time benefits administrator couldn't find affordable advice about flex.

Now, most of those barriers have begun to fall, and small companies are moving from the sidelines onto the flex playing field, proving they can compete on a benefits level with their much larger counterparts. Image Express, for example, pays an administrative firm $5 per employee per month to handle the paperwork for its cafeteria plan.

Although benefits experts expect an explosion of flex plans among small companies during the 1990s, few small firms now offer flex. J.R. Chipman, the Missoula consultant who guided the development of ChromatoChem's reimbursement plan, estimates that less than 5 percent of all firms with fewer than 50 workers have flexible benefits.

Yet the demand is there. Given the choice between two identical jobs—one that provides employees with some flexibility in choosing benefits and one that does not—90 percent of American workers would select the job with benefit choices, according to a recent Gallup Poll. Nearly half of the respondents said they have special needs that could be met with flexible benefit plans, including child care, dental and eye care, additional health insurance, and retirement savings.

Employers, it seems, are listening to their workers. "I'd say that interest in flex among small employers recently has risen dramatically," says William Bennett, president of BenefitAmerica, a Columbia, S.C., consulting and administrative firm specializing in flex for small companies.

As employers seek advice about flex, professionals who advise small companies—such as accountants, lawyers, and insurance brokers—are making it their business to learn more about it. For example, Nelson Rutherford, a partner in the Portland, Ore., accounting firm of Alten Sakai, says that his small-business clients' curiosity about flex spurred the firm to give reimbursement accounts a try. "We wanted to see just how difficult [flex] is to operate and whether we could recommend it," says Rutherford. "Clearly, it is something I would recommend."

What is flex? "It's not a benefit per se," says Kenneth Feltman, executive director of the Employers Council on Flexible Compensation, a Washington, D.C., lobbying organization that promotes flex on Capitol Hill. "Flex is a delivery system for existing benefits."

As such, flex comes in three basic forms: Two are built on the employees' ability to set aside untaxed dollars to purchase benefits that are not otherwise provided by the employer, and one is built on choice itself, enhanced by tax breaks.

PREMIUM-CONVERSION ACCOUNT

The first and simplest form of flex, the premium-conversion account, allows employees to pay their share of premiums for health insurance, group term life insurance, or disability insurance with pretax dollars. Since employees know the amount of these premiums they will pay over a year, they simply direct their employer to deduct the money in equal amounts from their paychecks.

Many companies can handle the payroll adjustments in-house with their current accounting systems. Others may need to add special software. Or a company can contract with one of the numerous payroll accounting or insurance companies that handle the paperwork as part of their service to employers.

Among small and midsized employers, premium-conversion accounts are by far the most common flex-benefit offering. Nineteen percent of companies with 50 to 1,000 workers had implemented premium-conversion accounts by the end of 1988, according to the latest survey on the subject, commissioned by UNUM Life Insurance Co. of Portland, Maine.

REIMBURSEMENT ACCOUNTS

The second form of flex, known variously as flexible spending accounts, salary-reduction plans, or reimbursement accounts, allows employees to use untaxed dollars to pay for health-care expenses not covered by company insurance or for dependent-care expenses. There is no statutory dollar limit on medical reimbursement accounts, although few employers allow sums greater than $3,000 a year. By law, dependent-care accounts may not exceed $5,000 a year.

Reimbursement accounts may stand alone, but typically they are set up to work alongside premium-conversion accounts, since the latter also offer tax advantages for life and disability insurance. In effect, reimbursement plans give employees a benefits checking account. And they do not require a company to redesign its existing benefits plan.

Here's how reimbursement accounts work: Before the start of the company's benefit plan year, employees must estimate their medical and dependent-care (child-care or elder-care) expenses for the coming year. They may set up either or both types of reimbursement accounts. Then the amount they designate is deducted from their paychecks in equal installments over the year and never reported to the Internal Revenue Service as taxable income.

When employees incur dependent-care expenses or medical expenses not covered by the insurance plan, they pay for them out of pocket, then submit a request for reimbursement.

Medical reimbursement accounts make up "the real key to flex for small employers," Chipman says. "If all you offer is one health plan, each employee can use the medical reimbursement account to cover deductibles and even uninsured dental and vision care. That gives employees a range of choice formerly available only with large companies."

Medical reimbursement accounts can be used to provide employee benefits that a company otherwise cannot afford. For example, some health insurers now sell small-employer medical plans that give employees the option to purchase dental, vision, or prescription-drug coverage. Because there is no minimum participation requirement, the additional coverage can be offered to as few employees as choose to purchase it. They pay the premiums themselves with the tax-advantaged reimbursement account.

Some employers boost their workers' purchasing power by contributing to their medical reimbursement accounts. This is accomplished with either lump-sum contributions, for example, $1,000 per worker, or by establishing a percentage match for each dollar of employee set-aside, for example, 50 cents from the employer for every dollar set aside by the employee.

Medical reimbursement accounts aren't solely for companies that already have health insurance, however. Even companies without health insurance still can offer these accounts, permitting employees to pay deductibles—but not premiums—and other unreimbursed expenses incurred under a spouse's health plan with another employer.

About 25 percent of all large companies already offer both reimbursement accounts and premium-conversion accounts, according to a 1990 survey by Hewitt Associates, a consulting firm based in Lincolnshire, Ill. Among the companies surveyed by Hewitt, an average of 18 percent of all eligible employees signed up for medical reimbursement accounts and 3 percent for dependent-care accounts. Medical reimbursement account contributions averaged $594 per worker, and dependent-care contributions averaged $2696.

Significantly higher percentages of employees tend to sign up for reimbursement accounts among small companies, says Chipman. He estimates that 35 to 40 percent of all eligible employees pick medical reimbursement accounts, and 5 to 10 percent pick dependent-care accounts.

Although size is an issue with cafeteria plans, it poses no barrier to implementing either a premium-conversion or reimbursement plan. "I would recommend premium-conversion and reimbursement accounts all the way down to one employee, as long as the company is a corporation," says Bennett, of Benefit-America. Under current law, flex plans must benefit "employees" solely. Thus, partners and proprietors of a firm may not participate in their company's plan. In addition, S-corporation owners are treated as partners or proprietors and are excluded from participation.

CAFETERIA PLANS

The third type of flex plan, called full flex or cafeteria plan, gives employees a fixed amount of benefit dollars to spend on a variety of types and levels of benefits. If the cost of the benefits selected exceeds the amount of employer contribution, employees may fund the remainder with tax-free dollars through both their premium-conversion account and reimbursement account. Thus, employees have wide latitude in tailoring benefits to fit their individual needs.

The cafeteria menu typically includes health, life, and disability insurance, 401(k) retirement savings plan, dental and vision care, and vacation time. Employees have the option of selecting different levels of insurance. For example, health plans may offer deductibles set at $100, $500, and $1,000. The higher the deductible, the less expensive the plan. Employees also may be able to choose several different multiples of annual salary for group term life insurance, paid with after-tax dollars or different levels of long-term or short-term disability insurance. For disability insurance, employees could use untaxed dollars to pay the difference between the employer contribution and their own selection.

The larger the company, the more likely it will offer a cafeteria plan. While relatively few small firms have implemented cafeteria plans, 27 percent of all firms with more than 1,000 workers had done so by 1990, according to a survey by Foster Higgins, a New York-based consulting firm.

Nonetheless, cafeteria plans aren't out of reach for small firms. "One of the big myths about cafeteria plans is that you have to have 1,000 employees to implement one," says Gary Kushner, president of Kushner & Company, Inc., a Kalamazoo, Mich,. consulting and administration firm specializing in small-business flex. "With groups of 50 or above, we look at full flex," unless employees' ages, health, or other characteristics militate against it, says Kushner. Insurers still balk at offering coverage to small groups with unusually high numbers of unhealthy employees.

"We administer cafeteria plans for companies with as few as 50 or 60 employees, and if you compared their plans to those offered in big companies, you couldn't tell the difference." says Kushner. He has helped even smaller companies, like Image Express with 22 employees, set up cafeteria plans.

Because cafeteria plans require considerable attention to details of design, communication, and administration, small companies usually hire an outside administrator to handle the job. Lipner, of Image Express advises: "Get yourself the best administrator you can find, and move all the paper work outside the company." Buying special flex computer software to mange the job in-house becomes practical for companies with more than 300 employees, says Bennett, of BenefitAmerica.

Lipner cites two other convincing reasons to hire an outside administrator.

First, she says, "if you have someone in-house who tells an employee he can do something under the plan, and if the advice turns out to be wrong, that opens up a liability issue for the employer. I want a professional handling that kind of problem."

Second, an outside administrator takes the heat off the employer when somebody has a problem or complaint concerning the plan, Lipner says. An outside administrator takes the problem out of the workplace.

Regardless of the type of flex plan offered, from the simplest to the most elaborate, employee education is the key to its success. "I can design the best flex plan in the world, and if the employees don't understand it, it's going to die," say Kushner. He recommends that details of the plan be presented to small groups of employees and their spouses.

"A lot of employees today may not be able to read all the written materials an employer hands out about the plan," adds Kushner. "When there is good communication during implementation of a plan, [followed by] ongoing communications, employers will be pleasantly surprised by the level of employee understanding and appreciation of the benefits."

Flex plans are not without certain drawbacks, however, and these should be considered carefully in advance of implementation. Regardless of the company's size, flex poses two important risks, one for the employer and the other for the employee.

Under the IRS rule issued in 1989, the full yearly amount of a medical reimbursement account must be available to an employee at any time during the account. Thus, large claims early in the year may require some advance funding by the employer.

An employee who quits and has received reimbursements in excess of contributions causes the company to take a loss, unless the company has structured the plan to permit the employer to deduct the remaining contribution from the final paycheck.

While this 1989 rule caused much initial concern among employers, it had no serious adverse financial impact on companies during its first year of implementation, according to a Hewitt Associates survey of large companies.

One effective way for employers to limit exposure under the rule is to cap the size of medical reimbursement accounts. Small employers might set a limit of $1,000. The Hewitt survey found that after the rule was issued, large employers reduced their limits from an average of $3,800 to $2,900.

The risk for employees under flex is the use-it-or-lose-it feature of medical and dependent-care reimbursement accounts. Any money remaining in an employee's account at the end of the year is forfeited to the employer.

Benefits experts say this rule has stunted the growth of reimbursement accounts because employees are afraid of losing unspent funds. Those who do use the accounts tend to keep their contribution levels low. As a result, employee forfeitures also are low, ranging on average about $33 for both medical and dependent-care accounts, according to Hewitt research.

Flex plans require nondiscrimination testing to ensure that highly compensated employees don't receive a disproportionate share of the benefits. Although the tests are not difficult, compliance is essential. Failure to pass the tests may mean that all benefits under the plan are taxable to plan participants.

Flexible benefits plans aren't a new idea. Congress gave its blessing to the concept when it enacted Section 125 of the Tax Code in 1978, permitting employees to choose between nontaxable benefits—such as health insurance and life insurance up to $50,000—and taxable benefits—such as vacation days or cash. Section 125 also established the legal basis for premium-conversion and reimbursement accounts.

Although Section 125 has been refined through regulations, it still governs the entire range of flex plans offered by employers today.

Throughout the 1980s, major corporations perfected the flex concept. The initial push came from the desire to create benefit plans that would meet the needs of an increasingly diverse work force, experts say. The traditional one-size-fits-all benefits plan has become as outdated as the Ozzie and Harriet era. Gone are the days when the typical worker was a middle-aged white male with a spouse at home taking care of two children. Just one in five employees now fits that description.

But concern for work-force diversity is no longer the leading issue for employers pursuing flex plans. Diversity now takes a back seat to rising health care costs. During the past two years alone, average health-insurance premiums have jumped more than 40 percent, according to Foster Higgins. For many small companies, increases of that magnitude have come annually.

"Cost control is now the No. 1 reason that small employers are looking to flex," says Kushner. "If rising costs have created a health-care crisis for large employers, they have had a catastrophic effect on small employers. Many are looking to flex to help control benefit costs in the future as opposed to cutting benefits now."

One way employers use flex to control costs is to shift some of the increase in health-care expenditures to employees. At the same time that most companies introduce flex, they also raise health-plan deductibles, increase dependent-care costs, and/or require a higher percentage of employee contribution after the deductible is met. However, premium-conversion and reimbursement accounts soften the financial blow by allowing employees to pay their higher share of costs with untaxed dollars.

Cafeteria-style benefit plans also give employers the ability to implement a "defined-contribution" approach to benefits. As health and other benefit costs continue to rise, employers can determine what portion of the added costs to absorb and what portion to pass on to employees, thus gaining a new measure of control over the future costs.

Costs shifting with flex is a delicate issue and one that employers handle in various ways.

"The amount of cost shifting that takes place is completely dependent upon the employer's objectives behind the flex design," says Karen Graves, a flex consultant in Boston with the Wyatt Co., a benefits consulting firm. "Some employers have no intention of having any shift to employees. They just want to make sure the employees get the range of choices that they need. And some say they want to shift, say, 10 percent of any future cost increases to employees."

Adds Graves: "There has been some bad feeling when employers have tried to gloss over the issue of cost shifting. We urge employers to be up-front about the realities of benefit costs."

Even when flex means a larger financial burden for employees, most still prefer the new plan to the old one because they value the ability to choose that accompanies the introduction of flex, says Feltman, of the Employers Council on Flexible Compensation. "We found that 93 percent of all women who had been in flex for at least one year didn't want to go back to traditional benefits. Among men, almost 80 percent didn't want to go back."

In Kushner's experience, most companies are more interested in long-term cost containment than quick-fix cost shifting. "It's rare to have clients go into flex primarily looking to shift costs to employees," he says. "By far, most want to control utilization of the health plan to prevent use where it is inappropriate."

Flex helps to eliminate unnecessary medical services—not just shift costs— in three ways, says Kushner.

First, flex tends to eliminate expensive duplication of coverage, where both an employee and spouse have health insurance. Health insurers have mechanisms to prevent duplicate reimbursements when claims are filed with two companies for the same expense; when spouses are covered by each other's insurers, however, the second insurer generally must pay the portion of the expense not reimbursed by the first company. Most employers find that health claims for a spouse or children are 2 to 2.5 times higher than average claims made by employees. When given the option under flex to spend benefit dollars in another area, many employees drop their duplicate health coverage. As a result, claims for dependent coverage also decline.

Second, "by educating employees about health costs, you reduce utilization of health care," says Kushner. "The employer is helping move the employee from being a passive recipient of health benefits to a knowledgeable consumer."

Third, flex also helps small companies save money be forcing them for the first time to get involved in health-plan design and financing, says Kushner. "Small employers are used to buying medical plans off the shelf. But flex allow them to tailor-make their plans."

These factors can add up to real savings on health expenditures, says Kushner, citing his own research. Over a nine-year period, some 200 of Kushner's small-business clients with cafeteria plans have experienced average annual health-care cost increases of 8.5 percent. Without flex, those same companies would have received average annual increases of 15.5 percent, based on price quotes from insurers, says Kushner. Among his clients, the average per-employee cost for health insurance under flex last year was $2,706, compared with a projected cost of $4,463 without flex. That amounts to a 39 percent cost advantage for flex over the nine-year period.

Results like that are hard to ignore. And as long-standing barriers continue to fall, experts predict that thousands more small companies will make the move to flex in the years ahead. Says Feltman: "By the middle of the decade, probably over half of all employers will have flex. By the end of the decade, I would think it would be almost a rarity for an employer not to have flex."

19. Flexible Benefits and Managed Care: Making It Work

Kenneth L. Sperling

The concept of integrating flexible benefits and managed care may seem contradictory. Flexible benefits seek to maximize choice, while managed care attempts to restrict choice. Can these two disciplines be intertwined without delivering conflicting messages to employees? The answer is definitely yes. By following some basic ground rules in design, flexible benefits and managed care can be combined effectively in a way that is attractive to both employers and employees. This article presents some general guidelines for designing a successful "managed flex" program and raises other issues as well, including financial, administrative and communication concerns.

Dealing with flex or managed care can add layers of complexity to administering a health plan. In an area growing more confusing with each passing regulation, why would a company take on the burden of incorporating both flex and managed care in its indemnity arrangements?

There are several reasons. The combination of flexibility and choice has proven to be an extremely positive way to offer a benefits package. It can provide an employer with *defined contribution* rather than *defined benefit* structure through the use of flexible prices and credits instead of a specific benefit level. Flexible programs also facilitate the introduction of new, employee-sponsored benefits like long term care. For the employer, flex can control utilization by providing incentives to employees to elect lower cost options with greater cost sharing. So, by itself, flex offers a number of advantages.

What flex cannot accomplish is to monitor the utilization and quality of services delivered once benefit choices have been made. An effective managed care program can accomplish this very well, but managed care alone is not appealing to many employees due to a perceived lack of choice. While flex allows choice once per year, managed care networks can be structured to allow choice whenever health services are required.

The combination of these two disciplines, therefore, can incorporate the best of both. Employees still can have the freedom to tailor the benefit program most appropriate for them, but the employer has the comfort of offering a system with enough control mechanisms to keep costs in check.

BEFORE YOU BEGIN

Prior to embarking on the flex and managed care journey, there are a number of things any company should do to ensure that the program will meet with broad management and employee support.

Set Objectives

Take the time to look at your business, human resource and benefits environments. Are cost concerns driving benefit decisions? If so, this will impact the ultimate design of the program. How does industry or regional competition affect benefits planning? What messages have employees received in the past about the company's position on benefits? Understanding where you are coming from and where you want to go will simplify the process later.

Perform Data and Cost Analysis

In order for managed care to work, there has to be something to manage. Many companies receive detailed utilization reports indicating the source of their benefit dollars, but few use this data for planning purposes. Interpreting what could be a mountain of paper is by no means an easy task, but the results could save a lot of energy in trying to fix something that might not be broken.

Look at Geographic Dispersion

Health care has been and always will be delivered locally. Managed care networks have been built by individual contracting with hospitals, doctors and ancillary facilities. Since network development activities for many managed care organizations have been only a recent phenomenon, many networks may not yet be fully formed. Both depth and breadth of services are still expanding. As such, it is important to measure employees' ability to access network providers prior to committing resources to managed care activities. This can be accomplished through zip code matching to employee residences or comparing currently utilized providers with network directories.

Choose a Model Type

Incorporating managed care into flexible benefits will often involve one or more options with a point-of-service choice. The term *point-of-service* means that individuals selecting this option will have the choice, every time treatment is needed, of whether to utilize network or non-network providers. To encourage network use, benefit levels in the network are substantially higher than out of the network.

Two types of point-of-service networks are generally available today: preferred provider organizations (PPOs) and open-ended health maintenance organizations (OEHMOs). The most significant difference between PPOs and OEHMOs is the use of a *gatekeeper* physician. In the OEHMO, each participant must choose a *primary care gatekeeper* (internal medicine, family practice, pediatrics and sometimes OB/GYN) who will handle all specialist referrals and hospital admissions. The PPO has no such requirement. Employees in the PPO are free to seek treatment from any network provider and receive the higher network benefit. Specific variations of these rules exist in the marketplace, but the vast majority of networks operate as described above.

The two models have different cost implications. Most managed care network sponsors project that cost savings will accrue from two sources: discounted provider fees and cost effective provider utilization patterns. Provider utilization savings will emerge primarily from OEHMOs through the controlling effect of the gatekeeper physician. Therefore, the OEHMO rather than the PPO is more likely to reduce the rate of increase in costs relative to a nonmanaged indemnity plan. The "price" of this additional management is potential intervention between the patient and his or her physician, since OEHMO participants must select and use a gatekeeper. Some companies choose not to intervene in this process. Others see it as a necessary step to control long term costs.

Each model has distinct design characteristics. PPO provider reimbursements are made based on fee-for-service charges. Since claim forms are required to receive payment, incorporating upfront deductibles in a PPO is quite easy. OEHMOs, in contrast, do not generally require claim forms. This difference drives OEHMO design toward office visit *copayments* instead of deductibles.

Having been in existence longer than OEHMOs, PPO networks are usually larger (in terms of number of providers and enrolled members) and more widely offered by a number of carriers and independent vendors. In addition, PPO networks are generally less expensive to administer than OEHMOs. This means the network sponsor will pass along a lower *access fee* in the retention formula.

Which is the "right" model for your organization? This is a strategic decision. Ideally, this decision should be made before the design process begins.

Decide on an Incentive/Penalty Structure

The combination of network and nonnetwork benefits can work one of three ways when compared with your current program, as shown in Figure 1.

An incentive-based structure can be very appealing in a delicate employee relations environment but, in many cases, it will increase short term plan costs. If the network successfully reduces cost trends, this investment can be recovered. It is wise, however, to estimate the pay-back horizon if such an investment is contemplated.

On the other side, the penalty structure guarantees savings. Both the managed and nonmanaged components have cost reductions built in. The managed side provides equal benefits at "wholesale" cost. The nonmanaged side provides lower benefits at "retail" cost. Each represents a savings from current levels. The employee relations effects from such a structure, however, might prevent its successful implementation.

The compromise design appears to be a reasonable balance for many companies. Where an incentive structure is already in place, it also can be an effective design modification in the third or fourth year of a managed care plan.

Pick your Targets

Managed care networks add a layer of administrative complexity to any benefit plan. Each network represents an incremental cost to the organization in terms of implementation time and maintenance. Even the "national" networks are localized in the services they provide, so employers in multiple locations will need to

---

FIGURE 1

Structure	Network Benefit	Nonnetwork Benefit	Short Term Cost Impact
"Incentive"	Better	Same	Higher
"Compromise"	Better	Worse	Even
"Penalty"	Same	Worse	Lower

consider the number of networks necessary to cover the workforce. This would suggest implementing managed care networks only in those areas where a substantial employee base exists (the definition of *substantial*, however, is open to interpretation). While there is value in a consistent benefit program across all locations, reality suggests that only a portion of any multilocation employee base truly will have access to networks.

Integrate Independent HMOs

Recognize that HMOs are managed care vehicles. The in-network side of a carrier-sponsored OEHMO network is very similar to the local HMO offered beside it. The two products, therefore, must be managed collectively. The design and price of the point-of-service network will influence HMO enrollment, and vice versa. In formulating the message to employees about managed care networks, make sure that it does not conflict with the messages being sent on current stand-alone HMOs.

Now that the concepts of *flexibility* and *managed care* have been addressed separately, let us put the two concepts together.

SOME GROUND RULES

There can be wide variation between two "managed flex" designs, but each can be very effective in meeting different companies' objectives. There are some ground rules, however, that should be followed to ensure that the final design will be attractive to employees, carriers, financial officers and human resource managers.

Manage the High Option Plan

For the most part, the unhealthiest segment of your population will select the richest benefit option available. As more than 70 percent of the average company's claims are incurred by less than 10 percent of the employees, managing the worst risks will have the greatest payoff. No point-of-service network will capture all of the bad risks, but your chances are much better if the high option plan has managed care elements.

Similar selection concerns dictate that all nonnetwork options have some form of utilization control, such as pre-certification and/or case management. Chronic and catastrophic illness will move into the nonnetwork side naturally, as employees reach out-of-pocket limits and cost sharing is no longer a steering

mechanism. The ability to monitor utilization will go a long way toward controlling ultimate expense, albeit not as strongly as a managed care network can.

Maintain Measurable Differences Between Options

Experience has taught that flexible benefit plans work best when employees are
presented clear choices with noticeable differences in value. This allows for better
communication, pricing and administration. The same holds true when manged care
is introduced, but perceived differences are harder to quantify. In an indemnity flex
plan, employees choose among options that may differ by the deductible and
out-of-pocket expense limitations in a given year. In a managed care environment,
employees are making these decisions—in addition to choosing the type of delivery
system. This component will have different value for different people, so the pricing
of a managed flex plan will be less exact. What an employer will want to avoid is
offering a rich managed care option coupled with a low indemnity benefit at a low
option price. This will drive employees intending to use the network into the low
option plan, and excess cash will be provided to high risk employees.

Provide Adequate "Steerage" to Network Providers

The attractiveness of point-of-service networks is that they allow employees to
try the managed care approach without committing to it. It is expected that once
an individual uses the network, that person will stay in the network as long as
there is perceived access and quality.

In order to encourage use of the network, there needs to be some sort of incentive.
As stated earlier, this can be an incentive for in-network use, a penalty for nonnetwork
care or a design that "straddles" the existing plan's benefit levels. The difference
between the nonnetwork benefit and the network benefit is termed *steerage*.

Steerage is important to an employer for two reasons. First, most point-of-service networks charge a fee for each *eligible* employee. High nonnetwork use will
mean these network access fees will be paid for little or no benefit. Second, some carriers
guarantee to their network providers that benefits differences will at least be some
minimum amount. So the availability of some networks may be contingent on steerage.

In general, the marketplace suggests a range of 20-30 percent difference in
value to provide sufficient network steerage. This might be a minimum requirement if a carrier will be assuming any risk.

Use Copayments, Even on the Network Side

Providing 100 percent coverage is very attractive to employees and makes
communicating managed care easier but will likely result in increased utilization
that will severely inhibit the ability to generate cost savings. Even an approach

that drops nonnetwork reimbursements to 70 percent is likely to be only a breakeven proposition. Separate deductibles for hospital confinements on the network side can act to control utilization as well as provide greater degrees of steerage.

Keep it as Simple as Possible

Communicating and administering flexible benefits or managed care is complicated—and doing both is a challenge. Simplicity of design is critical to having a program that will have broad appeal and acceptance. The fewer moving parts between options, the better.

Make a list of the benefit provisions that might differ between options and between in- and out-of-network. If the list has more than six or seven items on it, you may want to revisit the design parameters.

Bear in mind that some of the more detailed plan benefits (e.g., mental health, skilled nursing facility or hospice care) may not be open to design. Carriers typically will have a standard approach, originating from provider contracts, state regulations or system constraints. It is a good idea to preview a suggested design with your carrier early in the process so that minor differences do not result in major problems.

ENROLLED AND OVERLAY MODEL DESIGNS

In a multiple plan environment, managed care can be attached to one or several options. If only certain options are managed, the plan is considered an *enrolled* model, since employees would need to enroll in the option to access the managed care network. If managed care networks are attached to all options, the plan would be an *overlay* model. The indemnity flex options in this model are functioning as the out-of-network half of the point-of-service product.

Enrolled Model Design

In its simplest form, a single indemnity plan with an HMO choice can be considered an enrolled managed flex plan. Employees can choose between two options—only one of which is managed. The choice occurs during the annual open enrollment process.

Let us look at another example, one that offers both a stand-alone HMO as well as a point-of-service network option (in this case, an OEHMO). It might be structured as shown in Figure 2.

Option 1 could be an independent HMO, or it could be an HMO network offered by the same carrier that provides the point-of-service network on option

FIGURE 2

Option	In-Network	Out-of-Network
1	$10 copayment 100% coinsurance	No benefit
2	$10 copayment 90% coinsurance	$250 deductible
3	No benefit	$500 deductible 100% coinsurance

2. The advantage of the latter approach is that experience under all options would be combined in a single risk pool. Thus, the adverse selection so often experienced between HMOs and indemnity plans could be mitigated.

The above approach has certain advantages. It provides HMO-like benefits in the high option and can allow replacement of independent HMOs while still offering similar choices. For those employees not willing to lock into a closed HMO environment, option 2 provides a point-of-service choice. And for those employees with other coverage or a certain amount of risk tolerance, option 3 provides lower benefit levels to minimize upfront premium costs.

Where the enrolled model falls short is in maximizing participation in managed care options. Option 3, while providing what some would consider to be only catastrophic coverage, is still a free choice indemnity plan. Employees enrolled in option 3 might be seeing network doctors or confined in network hospitals, but the employer will not receive the benefit of any discount arrangements because the network option has not been elected.

Overlay Model Design

Making the most of managed care and flexible benefits would lead toward managing all flex options, either in a closed HMO environment or a point-of-service PPO/OEHMO. This type of design opens managed care to the entire population, ensuring that services provided by any network hospital or doctor will be reimbursed at negotiated levels. It also makes a statement about the company's commitment to managed care as a delivery system. If managed care is the wave of the future, such a structure would ease the transition between free choice indemnity arrangements of the past and more restrictive, closed networks of the future.

The design paramenters of an overlay model differ, depending on the type of network utilized. A PPO network, where no gatekeeper exists and normal claim

	FIGURE 3	
Option	**In-Network**	**Out-of-Network**
1	$150 deductible 90% coinsurance $1,000 out-of-pocket maximum	$300 deductible 70% coinsurance $2,000 out-of-pocket maximum
2	$300 deductible 90% coinsurance $1,500 out-of-pocket maximum	$600 deductible 70% coinsurance $3,000 out-of-pocket maximum
3	$500 deductible 90% coinsurance $2,000 out-of-pocket maximum	$1,000 deductible 70% coinsurance $4,000 out-of-pocket maximum

filing procedures apply, can use deductible and coinsurance differentials to create network steerage. A sample program architecture is shown in Figure 3.

Notice in the example in Figure 3 that there are only three moving pieces: deductibles, coinsurance percentages and out-of-pocket maximums. However, communicating this program to employees would be no easy task. If further simplicity is desired, deductibles or out-of-pocket maximums can be equalized between in- and out-of-network segments. What is sacrificed for this simplicity is additional steerage to network providers.

An open-ended HMO design would have slightly different design elements. As primary care provider visits do not require claim filing, the OEHMO network would have copayment schedules instead of deductibles on the network side. In order to control utilization, though, coinsurance can be introduced on other network services as well as *per confinement* deductibles on hospital stays. A sample OEHMO design might look like the example shown in Figure 4.

This design follows the ground rules set down previously: It manages the high option, has real value differences between options, creates steerage to network providers, uses copayments and is reasonably simple. A possible compromise for added simplicity would eliminate the hospital deductible or even equalize the out-of-pocket maximums. As before, the tradeoff for simplicity is reduced steerage.

Both of the examples given use a 90/70 coinsurance level between network and nonnetwork benefit levels. For a company that currently has a comprehensive arrangement with 80 percent coinsurance, implementing this approach would mean that no employee has the opportunity to buy back existing coverage—which often is an important design parameter in first year flexible benefits plans. If a buyback becomes one of your ground rules, you would then need to decide

FIGURE 4

Option	In-Network	Out-of-Network
1	$10 visit copayment 90% coinsurance $1,000 out-of-pocket maximum	$250 deductible 70% coinsurance $2,000 out-of-pocket maximum
2	$15 visit copayment 90% coinsurance $100 hospital deductible $1,500 out-of-pocket maximum	$500 deductible 70% coinsurance $3,000 out-of-pocket maximum
3	$20 visit copayment 90% coinsurance $200 hospital deductible $2,000 out-of-pocket maximum	$1,000 deductible 70% coinsurance $4,000 out-of-pocket maximum

whether the current plan becomes the in-network benefit level (penalty structure) or the out-of-network option (incentive structure).

OUT-OF-AREA CONCERNS

There usually will be two employee groups who will need to receive special handling: those who are located in areas where managed care networks are not available, and those who work within managed care networks but live outside a reasonable service area. These *out-of-area* employees will want the same level of choice as their peers in other locations.

The easiest approach would be to provide these employees with the same benefits as network eligibles. This solution, however, has its pitfalls. If in-network benefit levels are provided, you may be giving away enriched benefits without the advantage of discounted provider fees. If out-of-area employees receive the nonnetwork benefit and this coverage is less comprehensive than existing levels, the effect will be a unilateral cutback, which may have employee relations backlash.

Keeping the out-of-area employees "whole" with their premanaged flex benefits is an option but adds yet another layer of complexity where simplicity is most desirable.

There is no easy answer. The best approach is to keep the out-of-area employee in mind when designing the managed flex plan and attempt to structure options that can be applied to the entire population.

PRICING AND FINANCING

Pricing managed care with flexible benefits is only slightly more involved than pricing flexible benefits alone. However, many more assumptions must be made to create expected costs once managed care networks are a part of your model.

Flexible benefits pricing demands that assumptions be made in the areas of total expected claims, enrollment patterns and adverse selection between options. In addition to these factors, when managed care is introduced assumptions must be made for the following factors as well:

- Utilization differences from higher or lower benefit designs
- Effect of gatekeeper physicians on utilization
- Average discounts from physicians and hospitals
- Additional adminstrative expense
- Potential loss of coordination-of-benefits savings
- Network usage by employees.

As some of the above factors can differ dramatically from network to network, the pricing exercise can be expected to produce less accurate results when applied on a global basis.

On the financing side, most carriers are moving toward offering a range of financing alternatives in response to increased employer demand. The fully insured approach has been and will be available, but usually on the carrier's terms. This might dictate specific benefit levels as well as the ability to offer stand-alone HMOs in addition to the managed care plans.

Self-insured arrangements are becoming more popular, but a word of caution is advisable here. Some networks pay for a portion of services through an all-inclusive monthly fee, or *capitation*. These capitation fees would be charged on a lump sum against your self-insured bank account at the beginning of every month, thus reducing the cash flow advantages typically enjoyed under a self-insured plan.

If a significant portion of eligible employees are seeing nonnetwork providers, another problem exists. The capitation fees are paid (and charged) regardless of network usage, and nonnetwork providers would be paid normal fees for services rendered. The self-insured plan would thus be charged the capitation fees for care that was not delivered plus the fee-for-service charges for care that was delivered—a double hit to the bank account. This can wipe out any cost savings generated by the network, depending on the level of out-of-network "leakage." While this scenario can also play out in an insured arrangement, the carrier would bear this risk.

ADMINSTRATION

Managed flex administration involves a number of functions, including:

- Management of flexible benefit and physician elections
- Transmission of election data to carriers
- Measurement of dollars flowing in and out of the program
- Local network administration
- Claims processing
- Interpretation of periodic management reports
- Ongoing design and pricing activities.

Some of these responsibilities are most efficiently contracted to outside vendors, but even these external relationships require a certain amount of internal management. An important point to remember is that each local network adds an incremental administrative burden, since each network is to some degree managed locally. Ten networks require more time than four networks. This burden can be reduced, but not eliminated, by contracting with a single national carrier.

One decision point is network quality. No national carrier will admit to having the best managed care network in every location. Companies that have compared carriers on a location by location basis have come to this same conclusion. Weighing administrative concerns along with the desire to have the best available network in every city will help decide the direction most appropriate for your organization. What decides quality? Most professionals involved in the managed care arena debate this subject daily. While there is no conclusive answer, networks differ in their provider selection criteria, quality assurance programs and internal utilization management. These areas can provide points of difference that can be used to evaluate one network against another.

Another decision point is geographic concentration. If some of your locations will not have a network available, out-of-area benefits will need to be structured. With this in mind, look at the remaining eligible locations, ranked by number of employees. Draw a line at the point where the small population does not justify the weight of another network.

IMPLEMENTATION

Not allowing enough time to properly install a managed flex paln can destroy months of careful planning. Particularly with OEHMO networks, additional implementation activities are necessary before a network is ready to receive patients. Each participant must elect a primary care physician; these elections must be communicated to the physicians selected; and proper identification cards must be delivered to employees. All of the preceding tasks must be completed before the effective date of the network plan. There also needs to be a clearly defined process for accepting changes in primary care physician elections and enrollment of new employees. For first time managed flex implementation, a six to nine month lead time is not uncommon. For managed care overlay onto an existing flex plan, you should begin implementation activities at least two to three months prior to open enrollment.

ENROLLMENT

Helping employees through the managed flex choice making process is not just a technical challenge—it can in fact decide the success of the overall program. Employees who do not understand the options available to them will naturally resist moving away from current benefits. The fact that managed care networks seek to intervene in existing patient-provider relationships creates additional grounding in present plans.

One of your objectives in communicating managed flex is to encourage network participation, especially by the heavy users of the plan. These employees will accept the network concept only if they believe it is accessible, cost effective and contains quality physicians and hospitals. These are difficult messages to convey, but it is critical that they be delivered simply and positively. Flex will make the communication process easier, as employees see that multiple options are available to suit their particular needs.

Employee surveys and focus groups early in the design process can provide invaluable background for both final design decisions and the communication process. Once the plan is designed, using a combination of media (print, video and employee meetings) may be the most effective way to ensure broad understanding and acceptance.

CONCLUSION

Integrating managed care and flexible benefits allows you to control the cost of your health care plan in a way that is positively perceived by employees. The flex element can create incentives for employees to choose lower cost options and share in health care expenses. The managed care element helps to control utilization once those choices are made. Yet within these controls lies the element of choice, which has been proven to be a powerfully positive influence in employees' perceptions of their benefits.

Creating a successful managed flex arrangement takes a good deal of planning, smart design and pricing, and the willingness to become deeply involved in the administration and communication of the benefit plans. If these convictions are evident in your organization, managed flex may be a refreshing solution in an environment where few solutions exist.

20.   Medical Flexible Spending Accounts: Are They Still Viable?

R. Philip Steinburg   Sharon Klingelsmith

In an age of ever-increasing healthcare costs, employers by necessity are looking at ways to share more of the expense for healthcare benefits with their employees. One such option, the flexible spending account (FSA), first gained attention in the 1980s, and it is now part of a growing arsenal of cost-containment weapons that includes medical review programs, mandatory second opinions, and preferred provider arrangements.

Some employers question the viability of FSAs, citing the risk of increased costs resulting from proposed regulations that would change the method by which these plans are to be administered. There are ways, however, to control the risk so that possible losses under this approach will be minimal compared with rising medical costs. Moreover, FSAs can be an important employee relations vehicle at a time when employees are being asked to assume more of the costs of their healthcare programs through additional premiums or by increasing the deductible and/or copayment amounts under their group health plans. When offered under a cafeteria plan—an arrangement that permits participants to choose either qualifying welfare benefits or cash—FSAs allow employees to use their increased contributions to pay for healthcare services on the same pretax basis as if their employer had paid for it.

HOW THIS ADVANTAGE WORKS

A cafeteria plan is governed by Section 125 of the Internal Revenue Code (IRC), which provides that any dollar amount under the plan will not be included in a participant's gross income solely because the participant could have chosen cash. To receive a tax advantage, elections under a cafeteria plan must be made at the beginning of the plan year and cannot be changed during the year except for certain family status changes, such as birth, marriage, or divorce. In addition, if benefits are not used during the year, they are forfeited.

As one of the welfare benefits under a cafeteria plan, an FSA may be offered reimbursement of qualifying medical expenses. Employees estimate their probable reimbursable medical expenses for the year and agree to have their salary reduced by a specific amount for each pay period. This specified amount is contributed to the FSA on a pretax basis. The employees then receive medical expense reimbursement from their FSAs up to the total amount elected for the year.

The medical expenses eligible for reimbursement are those that are deductible under Section 213 of the IRC. Thus, the employee may use the FSA to receive reimbursement for those higher deductibles and copayments (the costs shifted to the employee) and for other eligible medical expenses that are not covered under the employer's medical plan.

THE RISK-SHIFTING REQUIREMENT

Under FSAs in the past, it has been customary to provide for reimbursement throughout the plan year to the extent that contributions are already credited to a participant's account. Under the new rules, the maximum amount of reimbursement must be available at all times during the coverage period, thereby shifting some insurance risk to the employer. For example, if an employee elects $1,200 of coverage and contributes $100 monthly, he or she must be reimbursed for the total $1,200 even if he or she submits $1,200 of claims as early as the second month, for example.

Thus, the employer bears the risk of an employee incurring large claims early in the plan year followed by the employee's termination of employment or election to decrease contributions because of a change in family status; either situation could result in a cessation of premium payments. Also, because these FSA arrangements are medical plans, they are subject to the healthcare continuation coverage rules set by the Consolidated Omnibus Budget Reconciliation Act of 1985 (COBRA) on the same basis as any other group health plan. As a result, the employer also bears the risk of someone incurring large claims and then ceasing to make further COBRA premium payments. Although losses may be offset by amounts forfeited at the end of the year by employees who fail to use the full amount of their elected benefits, the risk-shifting requirement raises the possibility that losses may exceed forfeitures.

There are several ways employers can minimize the risk under the new regulations governing medical FSAs. First, they can reduce the maximum amount permitted under an FSA. For example, if the maximum has been $5,000, employers might wish to reduce the maximum to $2,000 or $1,000.

Although the law permits changes in elections for family status reasons, it does not require it. Thus, employers could restrict family status elections to events causing an increase in the elected amount. This restriction could be limited to medical FSAs only.

Employers could also change the eligibility rules to try to eliminate those employees with the highest turnover rate as long as the result is not discriminatory under the law. Or, they could restrict items eligible for medical reimbursement. Finally, an employer could charge a small extra premium amount to cover the risk.

OTHER REGULATORY PROVISION

Health plan premium payments are no longer a permissible, reimbursable expense under a medical FSA. This has little impact as far as the employer's health plans are concerned because the direct payment of such premiums through pretax salary reductions may be offered as a separate benefit under a cafeteria plan. The practical effect is that employees may no longer be reimbursed for premiums paid by their spouses to another employer's plan.

The proposed regulations also contain new administrative requirements. To receive reimbursement, there must be a written statement from a third party regarding the expense incurred—including the amount —and a written statement from the participant that the amount was not reimbursed and is not reimbursable under any other health plan coverage.

Although the risk-shifting requirement raises some cause for concern, the possible losses under an FSA will likely be minimal compared with rising medical costs, and the losses can be anticipated. Thus, the FSA remains an important employee relations tool for any employer who wants to share more of the medical cost with employees.

Part 5

ADMINISTRATION AND AUDITING

21. Who Should Administer Your Health Plan?
John C. Garner

An employer has three ways to administer its health care plan: self administration, third party administration, or insurance company administration. Each option has its strengths and weaknesses. This article first examines self administration and then explores in depth third party administration.

A s medium and large employers try to decide who should administer their self-funded health plan, the logical place to start is with the possibility of self administration. Some employers can immediately reject the idea of processing their own claims because it does not fit with their corporate culture. Some companies have focused on keeping headcount low in an effort to be "lean and mean." Others have taken a "back to the basics" approach, ceasing operations that are not primary organizational strengths. These philosophies should be reflected in the administrative areas of an organization, such as human resources and finance—the two most likely candidates for administering medical claims.

SELF ADMINISTRATION

Self administration can have many advantages. When done properly, it can simultaneously reduce administrative expenses, improve employee relations, and provide exactly the right degree of cost containment to suit the organization.

But, all the advantages can become disadvantages very quickly. For example, top management of an organization experiencing financial difficulties might decree an across-the-board 10 percent cut in staff. If the claims office loses staff, it typically encounters problems quickly. This is largely because many participants incur claims just after a layoff, or when one is threatened. Frequently, employees postpone elective surgical procedures (such as for a bad knee), because they are too busy to take time off. After a layoff, they have time for the procedure. Other participants may have been considering an elective procedure, and they decide to go ahead with it after a layoff, figuring they will stop COBRA coverage after they have recovered. When employees think more lay offs may be coming, they may proceed with treatment before they have to pay for COBRA. The result is that the claims office has an increased volume of claims, but fewer employees to process them. This results in delays in processing, which turns an advantage of self-administration into a disadvantage, in terms of employee relations. If the employee relations get bad enough, management may authorize overtime, which turns administrative expenses from an advantage into a disadvantage. In a crisis, claims may be paid without proper scrutiny just to reduce the turnaround time, which destroys the cost containment advantage. Since self administration can turn sour quickly, any organization considering self-administration should be assured of top management's commitment to provide adequate resources.

Adequate resources means a good computer system, good reference materials, good medical and claims consultants, good legal counsel, and adequate office space, as well as enough employees to process the claims. Projecting the administrative expenses associated with self-administration is not an easy task. But experience has shown that an employer's costs can often be less than what a third party administrator (TPA) or insurance company would charge. Obviously, insurance companies and TPAs have economies of scale that help reduce their costs, but employers have some things in their favor, including:

- *Simpler needs.* TPAs and insurance companies have to have computer systems and reports that can fit a large variety of plan designs and employer needs. Even an employer with multiple plans for different business units still has only a limited number of plans that have to be programmed. This can mean that a less complex (and less expensive) computer system may be an option. Similarly, once the standard reports have been created, changes should be infrequent. Insurance companies often need to maintain a large staff of computer programmers to meet the reporting needs of their clients.

- *Lower overhead.* Self-administered employers typically need a very small amount of management devoted to the claims office—perhaps only a supervisor, who reports to the benefits manager. Insurance companies and TPAs usually need a number of layers of management. Similarly, all the administrative support functions are already in place for the employer and may or may not be charged as part of the cost of the self-administered claims office. But the insurance company or TPA has to charge enough to cover the cost. Also, the employer may have unused space and furniture that the claims office can used. Even if the cost accounting process charges the claims office for otherwise unused office equipment, the real cost to the organization is nothing. The selection of a software package for claims processing is sometimes driven by the fact that an organization has an unused or underused computer. If that computer can be used for claims processing, it again holds down the cash outlay for setting up the claims office.

One area of higher costs for many self-administered employers is salary. Insurance companies pay relatively low wages. TPAs typically pay more than insurance companies, which allows them to recruit experienced examiners. Self-administered employers usually fit the claims examiners into their compensation structure, which often results in wages above the market for claims examiners. In the long run, this can hold down costs by reducing turnover.

- *Control*. Probably the best reason for self administration is to control the cost containment process. No third party will ever make exactly the same decisions as the plan sponsor, but self administration puts the plan sponsor in control.

Plan sponsors considering self administration also should be aware that they will lose the third-party buffer. Just as there are employee relations advantages to be gained by processing claims accurately and quickly, there is also no one else to blame when claims are denied or mistakes are made. The biggest danger for a small plan is lack of depth of staff. Even a company with several hundred employees will only need one claims examiner. But what happens when that person goes on vacation, quits unexpectedly, or becomes disabled suddenly?

To promote good employee relations and control costs, an organization has to commit support and resources to a full-time, permanent staff dedicated to claims administration; quality and service, both initially and over the long term; and an advanced computer system. Without initial and ongoing commitment and financial support from top management, self administration will fail.

THIRD PARTY ADMINISTRATION

Most plan sponsors will conclude that using a TPA or an insurance company acting in only an administrative capacity will be more appropriate than self administration.

Although competitive bidding and questionnaires can be used to identify the TPAs with the financial proposals and general characteristics that may best suit a given plan sponsor, the best way to evaluate a claims office is to visit it, see what it looks like, and meet the people there. Some differences between claims offices are too insignificant to have a real influence on quality, but some plan sponsors will prefer one approach to another. Included in this category are such things as:

- *Recruiting*. Some TPAs recruit only experienced examiners, while others hire trainees. Experienced examiners can be productive sooner than trainees, and may bring good ideas from previous employers. On the other hand, trainees can be taught the TPA's approach and will not have bad habits learned elsewhere.

- *Training.* Some TPAs have well-organized, formal classroom training programs, while others have one-on-one on-the-job training.

- *On-line versus batch edits.* Many computer systems are fully on-line with real-time updates, while some systems rely on batch edits done in overnight processing. Batch edits can delay processing, but the most comprehensive edits can only be done in batch processing because they would make response time intolerably long if done on-line.

- *Turnaround-time goal.* A plan sponsor should be certain to find a claims office with turnaround-time goals consistent with its own. Some employers want a relatively long turnaround time to maximize cash flow savings, while others are more concerned with employee relations.

- *Production levels.* Production expectations for examiners can vary widely. All other things being equal, high productivity goals can reduce the cost of processing claims, but accuracy may suffer.

- *Reasonable and customary charges.* There are different ways to determine what is reasonable and customary (R & C) billing for specific procedures and in different geographic areas. The most sophisticated approach is the profiling method whereby data are collected by procedure and zip code. The largest insurance companies collect their own data, but TPAs usually purchase data from the Health Insurance Association of America (HIAA) or MDR. Some carriers merge their own data with HIAA data. A less precise, but simpler and less expensive method is to use a conversion factor, which is applied against a set of unit values for different procedures to determine an allowance for each procedure. Some questions to ask are: How frequently are R & C data updated? What have the savings been? How long is the R & C data retained? If an old claim is received, are current R & C data applied? (If so, that can encourage late filing.) How are claims involving multiple surgery handled? Does the system automatically calculate R & C for multiple surgery, or must the examiner make a manual calculation?

- *Customer service.* Some claims offices have a separate unit that handles telephone calls from employees, while others combine customer service and claims examination into one position. If a participant calls and speaks directly to the examiner who processes his or her claims, communications are direct and can be more effective. Also, if an examiner knows that his or her carelessness will lead to phone calls that interrupt later work and make it hard to meet production standards, he or she may be more careful in the first place. On the other hand, a customer service unit is always available when employees call. A whole unit doesn't get sick or take vacations (as individual examiners do). A customer service unit also allows examiners to concentrate on claims without distractions that can lead to errors.

- *Location.* Today, 800 numbers (if staffed at the proper hours) make it possible to process claims from any part of the country. Nonetheless, some plan sponsors feel more comfortable with a claims office in the same town, state, or time zone.

WALK-THROUGH EVALUATION

Other differences between claims offices are more clear cut as to whether they are advantages or disadvantages. A good way to start an evaluation of a claims office is with a walk-through that follows the workflow. The evaluation should also include a demonstration of the computer system and a discussion of various other aspects of the office. Following is a discussion of each of the most important aspects to be evaluated, with a focus on the questions that prospective TPAs should be asked.

Inventory Module
Many computer systems have modules that allow basic information about a claim to be entered as soon as it is received. A TPA's customer service representative can then respond to inquiries about the status of claims by confirming that it has been received and giving an estimated processing date. Employees would generally rather hear "We received your claim on the 23rd and are now processing claims received on the 19th. We should process your claim in a few days," than to be told there is no record of having received the claim. Confirming that the claim has been received might avoid the expense and delay involved in processing a duplicate submission.

Work Assignments
In some claims offices, claims are not assigned to particular examiners, but are processed on a first-in, first-out basis. This approach may be a deterrent to fraud by examiners because any examiner may be the next one to process a claim for a particular employee. Even so, most claims offices assign examiners to certain clients (or portions of large clients, such as by location or part of the alphabet). It is particularly helpful to have an examiner dedicated to a plan if it has unusual features. Processing certain clients' claims regularly also allows examiners to become familiar with particular claimants, which can speed processing.

Security
There are several important aspects to security in a claims office, but one of the most important is separation of duties. No matter how small a claims office is, claims examiners should not have access to eligibility or provider files. Without such separation, some claims examiners may be unable to resist the temptation to create fictitious employees and/or doctors, pay claims to and/or for them, and have the checks delivered to themselves or an accomplice. The provider,

eligibility, and claims examining functions should be separate, with each subject to audit.

Internal Audits

Internal audits are a vital function of any claims office. They are the first line of defense against fraud, an early warning system to alert management of the need for training or retraining, and a sentinel to keep examiners on their toes. An office that has an auditing plan and sticks to it will be a better office than one that lets the auditing lapse for one reason or another. Ask to see the results of the internal audits; if the office refuses to share them, be suspicious—they may not be doing audits, or the quality of the processing may be poor. Beware of the office that uses a haphazard approach to selecting the claims to be audited. Bias can affect the selection of claims and examiners may learn how to beat the system. A systematic approach, such as auditing every 20th claim (assuming the examiners do not know the starting point) or using a random number generator are the best approaches.

Pre-disbursement audits are preferable to post-disbursement audits, but well-designed post-disbursement audits are better than haphazard audits and much better than no audits. In addition to random audits, targeted audits can improve an office's performance, particularly if a variety of targets are used on a rotating basis. For example, one week physical therapy claims might be audited, the next coordination of benefits claims, and so on.

Individual Limits

In addition to random and targeted audits, certain claims should always be audited. One type of limit should apply to the examiners. Trainees might start with no dollar authority, meaning all their claims are audited, and progress to limits of $500, $1,000, $2,000 or more. The other type of limit would apply to types of claims. For example, all payments over $2,000 not assigned to the provider might be audited. Learning who handles the various types of audits should be part of the evaluation.

Pending System

If a letter has gone out requesting information, does the system keep track of it? Does the system automatically generate a follow-up letter? When the additional information is received, does the whole claim have to be re-entered, or only the new information? Beware of claims offices that do not have a formal follow-up system. Some offices keep a pending folder and send follow-up letters "when they have time." At the other extreme are offices that require examiners to review pended claims due for follow-up before they can process new claims.

Reinsurance

Offices vary as much in their handling of reinsurance as in their handling of pended claims. Some offices file reinsurance claims when they get around to it, which might be every six months. Others have separate reinsurance personnel who do nothing but submit large claims to stop-loss carriers.

Customer Service Hours

When are people available to answer questions? This can be a key issue for national employers, employers whose employees travel frequently, or for a group considering using a claims office in another part of the country.

Coding

What types of diagnostic and procedural codes are used and to what extent? Recording the CPT code is much better than using a two digit type of service code. Data are likely to become even more important in the future and those without it will be at a disadvantage.

Administration Manual

Does the claims office have an administration manual? If so, how extensive is it and how frequently is it used? (If you didn't notice during the tour, look for one on your way out—if it is dog-eared, that is a good sign.) If they rely on a collection of old memos, are they indexed?

Turnover

An annual employee turnover rate of 10 percent is fairly typical of claims offices. A rate significantly higher than that can be an indication of problems.

Stability

In addition to turnover, other indications of stability should be sought. A claims office whose lease is about to expire or that is considering changing computer systems may be about to experience significant problems.

Consultants

Does the claims office have established relationships with consultants? Most claims offices have one medical consultant they use as a resource for most medical questions, but also have access to a variety of specialists they can call upon for help with more complex claims. Other consultants also should be available, including a podiatrist, a chiropractor, a dentist, a claims consultant and, of course, a benefits attorney. The claims office should not only have access to these experts, they should also be willing to spend the money to use them.

Staffing

The total staffing level in the claims office should be discussed. One claims office may need more examiners than another if there is no inventory control, pre-screening, or separate customer service unit, but, as a rule of thumb, an overall staffing level, including clerks and customer service representatives, of about one claims office employee for every 1,000 covered employees is typical.

Production Expectations

Ask what the production expectations are for the examiners and how much mail is received on an average day. Since examiners usually have other duties, the number of examiners multiplied by the production expectation should exceed the average mail.

Backlog

Ask what the current backlog is (also known as on-hand count or inventory). Divide the number by the average mail to get the number of days of work on hand. This will usually be equal to the average turnaround time. In an office with good first-in, first-out controls, 95 percent of the claims will be paid within five additional days (not counting time spent waiting for information from outside the claims office).

Experience and Length of Service

Ask about the number of years of experience in claims and the length of service with the particular TPA for the management, supervisory, and technical staff, as well as the claims examiners.

Cross Training

Does the claims office have personnel who are cross trained in multiple functions? It is helpful to have examiners and customer service representatives cross trained. Cross training is particularly important if the examiners are specialized (i.e., with some handling only coordination of benefits and others only hospital claims, etc.). In addition to asking about the number of people who are currently cross trained, ask about any current or ongoing cross-training programs or plans.

Backlog/Turnaround Time Management

Ask how the claims office management keeps track of the number of claims on hand. A weekly physical count can function as a good early warning system of any problems that may be developing. If claims are never split or combined, and if an inventory module is used, the computer can track the number of claims on hand and identify the oldest claims (although it may not be able to locate them). If claims can be split or combined without computerized tracking, the computer might produce misleading reports.

Turnaround Time

Ask for reports that show the actual turnaround time during the past year. Typically these reports are computer generated, based on the difference between the date received (usually input by the examiner) and the date processed.

Fraud Control

Current estimates are that about 10 percent of health care dollars go for fraud or abuse. Many insurance companies are establishing special units to investigate claims for possible fraud or abuse treatment patterns. Ask about them.

Merit Reviews and Bonus Programs

How does the claims office evaluate its employees? Look for an office that places at least as much weight on accuracy as on production. If the office pays bonuses for high productivity, is high quality also required?

Coordination of Benefits

Ask about COB procedures. How does the office go about identifying claimants with other coverage? What does an examiner do if questions on the claim form about other coverage are not answered? If the employee says his or her spouse is employed but does not have other coverage, does the office accept the answer or call the other employer? What have the COB savings been for the office? How are they calculated? Be aware that some offices inflate their savings by including coordination with Medicare for retirees and others inflate their savings percentage by dividing COB savings by dependent claims (whereas most offices divide by total claims paid).

Medical Necessity

How does the office evaluate whether a claim is medically necessary? Is it up to the examiner to identify certain types of claims or does the system screen for claims that need additional review? Some systems automatically downcode claims that have been upcoded and/or rebundle claims that have been unbundled.

Preferred Provider Organization

Does the system automatically identify PPO providers for your PPO and price the claims appropriately? How are changes to the list of participating providers handled?

Utilization Review

How will your UR organization notify the claims office when an admission has been precertified? How will they notify them of extensions? What does the claims office do with the information? In some offices, paper copies of the precertification are kept in a file that is checked by the examiner. In others, the precertification information is keyed into the system, or data are transferred electronically. Some systems will not permit examiners to pay for hospitalizations that have not been approved, but others rely on the examiner to check the data in a note field.

Hospital Bill Audits

Does the claims office routinely arrange for hospital bill audits? If so, what criteria are used to identify claims to be audited? Does the hospital bill audit company audit all claims or are they screened for cost-effectiveness? How did the claims office select the audit company? Who pays for the audits?

Third Party Liability

If your plan includes a third party liability or subrogation provision, how does the claims office handle such claims? Much follow-up is required for these types of claims; special units or personnel devoted to TPL handling usually do a better job than examiners who have to meet demanding production standards.

Free Form Comments

Examiners need adequate space for entering comments about a family, claimant, and claim. On the other hand, if there are too many comments to wade through they may not be read. Some systems require the examiner to access a separate screen to see all comments; some comments should be highlighted in such a manner that the examiner cannot avoid important messages.

History

How much history is retained on-line? If examiners must leave their work stations to review microfiche or microfilm because history has been purged, they will be tempted to skip doing so. This can lead to problems such as paying duplicate claims or denying claims as duplicates when they are not. The system should have space for multiple iterations of eligibility information. If only the current data are shown, inappropriate payments or denials of older claims may occur for employees who have been rehired, who enrolled then disenrolled from an HMO, or for other reasons.

Disaster Recovery

Special disaster recover plans should be in place to get the system running again as soon as possible after an earthquake, hurricane, tornado, or other disaster. Files should be backed up regularly with the backups stored off site. Arrangements should be in place to use other hardware.

Down Time

Ask about the system's reliability. Down time of 5 percent or more should be a serious concern. Remote locations tied to a central computer via phone lines are most susceptible to down time.

Response Time

When you look at the screen during the demo, pay attention to how long you have to wait for the system to respond. Examiners will tend to lose their concentration if they have to wait 10 seconds every time they make an entry. Try to time your demo for the middle of the day. An office on the West Coast may have great response time in the late afternoon after the East Coast offices have closed, and

East Coast offices can look really good before the West Coast offices have opened.

Software

Ask if the software was purchased or developed internally. If purchased, ask how the vendor was selected. Comparing two or more TPAs that use the same software package might make the comparison easier because you can focus on other issues, but do not assume the software is identical. One office may not have purchased all available features or may have customized the software. Ask about changes to the program—who does the programming and how long should you expect change to take?

CONCLUSION

All the subjects discussed above relate to specific claims offices. You also should think in terms of the entire organization. Typically, insurance companies have many other resources at their disposal, including claims, medical, and legal experts. TPAs usually have fewer such resources, but can compensate for that with their flexibility. If you have unusual needs, such as direct contracting, a desire to be very involved in the claims process, or something else that may be difficult for a large organization to accommodate, then a smaller TPA may be just right for you. You also need to know whether your organization prefers to be a big fish in a small pond or vice versa.

22. Auditing Third Party Administrators

Arthur E. Parry   John D. Fortin

The increasing complexity and changing goals of health benefit plans have imposed sometimes-conflicting requirements on plan administrators. An audit is an effective way to find out whether corporate goals—including cost control—are being met. But before embarking on an audit, the benefits department should have a clear idea of where it is going and how it can get there.

The rampant escalation of health care costs is a significant burden to employers in both the health care and workers compensation benefit programs. During the past 20 years, employers have incorporated numerous cost containment programs into the health care benefits area. These programs have helped curtail the surge of health care costs while improving management of the utilization, quality, and costs of health care.

Statistics clearly substantiate the skyrocketing costs of health care in the United States. Some of the reports indicate the following:

- Health care costs have nearly doubled from 7 percent to 12 percent of the gross national product (GNP) from 1980 to 1990
- Health care costs are expected to surpass 15 percent of the GNP within the next five to six years and, if unchecked, possibly exceed 20 percent of the GNP by the year 2000
- The annual medical cost trend has risen into the 20 percent to 23 percent range and is not expected to improve soon
- Yearly salary increases have plummeted to and stabilized at 4 percent to 5 percent.

In essence, we are paying more and more for our health care. Employee benefit plan providers have aggressively responded to these cost increases by implementing managed care programs that offer cost savings potential to the employer and reduced out-of-pocket expense for the employee.

HEALTH CARE BENEFIT PROGRAM GOALS

The corporate employer, by assuming all or a part of the health care benefit program, is trying to maximize or stabilize benefits to employees while controlling costs and failures of the system brought about through inefficiencies, lack of control, and the offering of unnecessary or unimportant benefits.

The employer may restructure the coverage program by introducing different deductibles, copayment amounts, or limitations on types of accidents and/or illnesses, adding requirements for second opinions on certain types of medical procedures, limiting the definitions of provider, imposing specific reporting requirements on the employee, strengthening offset provisions in the coverage document or in other ways moving the coverage away from what previously had been considered standard. As a result, claims handling is becoming unique in many areas.

The purpose, again, of all such variations, is to control costs while guaranteeing an acceptable form of health care protection to employees and their families. Historically, many programs were offered not only as an employee benefit but, at times, from a somewhat paternalistic approach. The employer "took care" of his employees. The economic pressure of escalating health costs has significantly changed that posture.

GOALS OF THE THIRD PARTY AUDIT

Simply stated, the main objective of a third-party administrative audit is to confirm that the employee health care program is administered wholly in accordance with coverage available, corporate intent, and employee needs while minimizing overhead, inefficiency, and improper settlements. A third-party administration audit examines the understanding of changing factors by the organization's management and those responsible for implementing the payment of claims.

Some audits have shown that the emphasis is on only one aspect of the above—for example, a focus on reduction of claims handling cost while overlooking claim dollar payment control. Others reflect an unevenness in handling either because of poor management or the use of unqualified employees by the administrator. For example, under pressure of incoming claim notices, the third-party administrator may hire subcontractors who have neither the understanding of the program or the supervision given to regular employees. In addition, failure to recognize the legitimate needs and concerns of the employee can prove hurtful to the employer.

There are other areas which affect performance and should be included in a review. The first has to do with the adequacy and availability of data and reports. Sometimes when a company first moves into third-party administration, it has been unaware of what data to collect and what reports are needed. Lack of good statistical data and of an ongoing reporting system prevents interim review of performance costs and problems. Part of the audit can address these subjects and note whether changes are necessary.

Another important area has to do with cost control of claims administration and its effect on claim payments themselves. It is possible that the method of claim settlement (whether by claim or by hour) will not only affect the quality of claim service but also the size of the payments made. This may be aggravated if the company has not audited performance previously. One example is the possible inflating of payments to employees in order to reduce employee complaints (if no company controls or standards are in place).

Audit Problems and Needs

An identification of specific concerns or analysis of real or suspected problems is vital in initiating the audit. The original goals of the corporation may have changed, or the company's financial ability to support the program may be weaker; in fact, the willingness of the organization to continue the program may have been reduced. An interim evaluation of reports, specific claims, and employee attitudes may all require that other factors be reviewed as well. Third party administrators are increasingly putting their fees at risk through performance guarantees, so future audits may be used to verify contractual requirements related to accuracy, turnaround and other criteria. Questions to ask include the following:

- What is intended to be accomplished by the audit?
- Is it part of an overall management audit process?
- Was it necessitated by staff changes, by financial considerations or, possibly, by plan structural revision?
- To whom is the report to be addressed?

The method of audit—whether personal interview, policy and procedure analysis, management control, employee survey, or in-depth file review, or a combination—must also be decided. Specifics will depend on what is to be accomplished by the audit itself. If, for example, files are to be reviewed for specific questions or problems, not only must the goals of the review be agreed upon (adherence to claims philosophy, proper use of authority, qualification and reserving practices, etc.), but the number of files and the type of sample to be used must be decided upon as well. If claims of a certain size or type are to be studied, the assumption is made that a judgmental, not random, sample is to be used. For example, the auditor selects the kind and type of files that will best help in answering specific questions or problems.

A final issue has to do with the currency of claims to be studied. If only "closed" claims are reviewed, long-term trends, including some that are quite far removed from the current period since older claims are more likely to be closed, will be emphasized. As the time period approaches the present, the number of closed claims per period will be reduced. On the other hand, if open claims only are to be reviewed, the emphasis will be on current practice, with a loss of historical trends.

It is important to evaluate all the factors to be reviewed. Dialogue with the individual or group to receive the report should open up possible areas of concern and question that may be covered in the audit itself. If, for example, the company changed its health care benefit program within the last three years, there may be concern as to either employee acceptance of the changes or possibly administrator handling of the changes. If claim costs themselves are a major issue, perhaps administrative auditing of providers as to customary charges, duplicate payments, and erroneous payments, is important.

If the appropriateness of the administrative procedures is a concern then provision is needed to identify such procedures, measure them against employer goals, and audit their implementation. Perhaps excess or reinsurance notification is to be studied. Clear understanding of all requirements will be necessary. Finally, control and handling of copayments, deductibles, or "offsets" may be perceived as requiring analysis. Clear understanding of sample size, type of evaluation, and presentation of audit results will be needed.

Specifics of the Audit

For the purpose of simplicity, we will discuss third party administrator audits under two general headings, management audits and claims audits.

Management Audits

The overall objective of management auditing is to confirm that implementation of the third-party administration is appropriate to the employee healthcare program. Administration should be in accordance with the coverage available, corporate intent, and employee needs while minimizing inefficiency and improper payment. This presumes that the overall goals of the program are in writing, and that the Administrator has such goals and has agreed, in writing, to provide administration in accordance with such goals.

The initial phase of the audit usually involves a meeting with the administrator's senior staff to confirm the above or to clarify areas of concern or possible misunderstanding. These will include a review of the administrator's structure, philosophy, staffing, position requirements, and clinical and statistical support. It will require a review of policy and procedure manuals, specifically with respect to the implementation of the employer program. Each objective that has been translated into a performance goal will be reviewed to determine how measurement is provided. Each step in the claims or servicing process will likewise be measured to permit examination. It may be that specific standards (e.g., claims handling guidelines, reserving requirements, provider requirements, payment controls, or turnaround needs) will have to be "identified" cooperatively with the administrative manager if not previously developed.

Staffing is an important matter and involves adequacy, competence, turnover, peak times, and authorization for substitute or "subcontractor" employees. To the extent that the employer's program is different from standard programs, the need for a "dedicated" staff (utilization of claims personnel solely for that one program) must be addressed.

In initial meetings between employer and administrator management personnel, the purpose of the audit and the standards being used will be established. This will allow rebuttal by the administrator if specific items had not been agreed to or were deemed inappropriate. It is also well to remember that facts are different than opinions. Many people have opinions and some are more supportable and reasoned than others. However, regardless of the professionalism or experience buttressing an opinion, it is not fact. A fact is the result of an audit in which the auditor "counts" the number of variations or errors, and perhaps statistically evaluates these counts in terms of the sample used or the population.

A good audit includes factual information with statistical measures. However, it will take hard work to translate the management audit into a form permitting statistical analysis. Nevertheless, it can and should be attempted.

The following questions are useful for fact gathering:

- How often is the administrator understaffed?
- How long have such understaffings existed?
- How often are unqualified claims personnel used?
- How often are procedures changed without documentation?
- How often is software "down" or computer runs unavailable?
- How frequently are supervisor reports made/required?
- How frequently are coverage verifications made/required?
- How often are provider verifications conducted?

The administrator must also understand that some areas of management control are considered to be of major importance to the employer. These include such items as prompt handling, proper financial controls, authorized payments only, authorized providers only, and involvement of the employer in major questionable matters.

Finally, there are certain subjects that may elude fact gathering but nevertheless are vital to the employer, such as employee reaction to claims handling (usually measurable), administrative staff morale, management competence, and commitment. Many of these matters will require more than management interview, personnel surveys, and document review alone. Many subjects can only be substantiated by actual case review and analysis.

Claim Audits

The auditor will begin by reviewing historical claim reports with both employer and administrator. Such a review will reveal the following:

1. How large the program is (over time, in dollars, in number of claims, etc.);
2. The distribution of major claims or groups of claims;
3. Divisions within the employer group of large subsets (by location, department, employee age, date of hire, etc.);
4. Problem areas (age of claimants, date of hire, functional area, geographical area);
5. Those claims that may require a lower level of analysis (e.g., medical only with no wage loss payment);
6. Patterns in the data that require special analysis; and
7. Gaps in the data, which may require special runs or special handling of individual files in order to provide a certain kind of analysis.

Once the historical review is complete, the actual details of the audit sample and specifics of the review may be initiated. It is important that, when a claim listing (including some narrative, if possible) is utilized for the identification of the claims within the audit, all such files be made available to the auditor (or that reasons acceptable to the auditor be provided if not available). By this means the objectivity of the audit sample is best preserved. To modify the files in any other way could produce a different sample from the one selected to measure the total claim population. If, for example, 25 files from six adjusters representing a certain type of injury or illness in a specific time period were requested, but instead 75 files from two adjusters were supplied, the results would not reflect the same adjuster base and only limited conclusions could be drawn relative to the entire adjuster staff.

What are the specific areas of inquiry in an employee benefit program administrator claim audit? There are many areas, which vary by employer, needs, goals and files available. However, the following are examples of general areas that could be examined by individual case or claim file review:

- **Applicability**: Verification of coverage, limits, date of loss, eligibility of individual, expense and injury.
- **Process**: Method of reporting, timeliness of process, investigation, adherence to claim standards, dealing with physician/providers promptly, contact with injured employee, contact with employer.
- **Reporting**: Reports of individual claims, statistical reporting to the employer, special reports as required or needed by the claim; an area of increasing concern is the proper coding of the claims of active versus retired employees.
- **Reserving**: The nature of the reserving process, when the initial reserve is established, by whom, how it is reviewed, how and when it is charged.

- **Payment**: Timeliness, method, type of accounting and banking used, check register availability, controls in place, number of signatures involved.
- **Authorization**: Authorities and requirements for investigating, reserving, reporting, approving, and making payments, need identification and verification.
- **Offset Verification**: An increasing control within employee benefit payment programs is the use of other parties for payment. These include employees (deductibles), other payors (copayments), reinsurers, and even third parties "liable" for the injury. Verification that all such parties have been involved correctly is needed.
- **Litigation**: What controls or flags exist and how are they used to ensure the prompt involvement of the employer and appropriate handling of all situations that may become lawsuits?
- **Audits of Third-Party Payor Bill**: What controls, reviews, and analyses are in place as to "reasonable and customary," double billing, inaccurate billing, discounts from network providers, etc?
- **Utilization Review (often conducted in a separate audit)**: What is the linkage to the utilization review process, particularly pre-admission certification, concurrent review, and large case management?
- **Employee Handling**: What requirements exist as to handling of employee requests, concerns, rehabilitation, training, overall attitude, etc?
- **Documentation**: The entire claims process should be based on orderly, clear file documentation so that an auditor may trace the file process without gaps in information.

The audit needs to address information from all sources including various health care providers, utilization review companies, psychiatric/chemical dependency vendors, prescription drug administrators, employee assistance programs, HMOs, networks, and insurance carriers.

When claim audits involve a significant number of files, it is necessary to provide for standardized analysis and computer input in order to display the results in an understandable manner and to provide for such statistical testing as is necessary. There should, however, always be written reporting on the process and on specific claims because not all comments and analyses can be tabulated.

Results of the Audit

Whenever an audit is conducted, part of the analysis concerns the appropriateness of the initial requirements. Experience developed under the program is studied and the opinions of participants are evaluated. Many times considerable good to all parties results from the audit.

For example, the following could result:

1. A written claim philosophy is developed because the audit points out the problems in working without such a document;
2. Controls by management and by file are improved;
3. Management, management review, and provisions for staffing changes are strengthened;
4. Control of offset handling is improved;
5. Greater involvement by the employer in one or more phases of the claims handling is achieved;
6. Gatekeeper, payment, and utilization review are improved;
7. A provider network is put in place to assist in both controlling costs and securing services from pre-approved practitioners;
8. Statistical reports are supplemented or the timing of reports changed;
9. Criteria for bill identification, initial screening, and employee ongoing handling are established; and
10. Major changes are recommended because the audit reveals significant opportunities for cost control or claim reduction.

LOOKING AHEAD

As the cost of health care benefit programs increases, greater attention will be given to program administration. It is entirely possible that two major changes will take place in the future. First, much or all of the third-party administration may be brought in-house by the employer for either greater control, better response, or lower expected costs.

Second, there will be pressure to integrate workers compensation and employee health care benefits into a 24-hour care plan supported with managed care programs. Integration offers employers significant possibilities for controlling utilization, costs, and quality. Savings could result from using a single administrative approach; taking advantage of a common, or linked, database with management reports aggregating both health care and workers compensation data; and applying benefits concurrently under employee benefits and workers compensation programs.

In addition, there are specific programs or procedures that will improve employee benefit program costs and services including the following:

- Developing a single provider network (not totally possible now under workers compensation)
- Establishing overall management of claims injuries, the loss process and speedy recovery for injured or ill employees, including the full spectrum of utilization management and case management services
- Obtaining greater consistency in application of medical protocol and adherence to fee arrangements
- Managing the full continuum of claims administration and reporting

- Extending the buying power of the employer across both programs
- Integrating all functions of information systems support and reporting into a common database
- Applying a common philosophy to promote wellness and caring for injured or ill workers and their families

23.   Auditing Your Carrier

Sears, Roebuck & Co. and Marriott Corp. teamed up last year to conduct a joint audit of their managed care programs after discovering they shared a common point-of-service carrier on the West Coast.

The joint effort gave the two companies an opportunity to compare notes about the carrier's performance, a consultant told BNA April 17.

The companies learned they had both chosen The Prudential Health Care System as their carrier for point-of-service networks in Southern California through their participation in the Managed Health Care Association, according to Edward Lipson, a partner with the consulting firm of Ernst & Young.

Lipson assisted the companies in their evaluation efforts while working as head of managed care consulting for William M. Mercer's Medical Audit Services unit.

Both companies began rolling out managed care networks for their enormous and geographically diverse employee populations in 1990. Chicago-based Sears expects its nationwide program will eventually cover the majority of its 519,000 employees who work in retail operations as well as those employed by subsidiaries.

Marriott, based in Bethesda, Md., and best known as an operator of hotels and motels, has more than 200,000 full-time and part-time employees. Marriott's managed care and indemnity plans have about 84,000 participants.

The Sears and Marriott programs are point-of-service plans that allow employees to pick and choose between networks of preferred providers and non-network providers. They can obtain care from non-network providers, but have to pay higher deductibles and copayments.

Reprinted with permission from *Benefits Today*, Vol 8, No 9, pp 135-136 (May 3, 1991). © 1991 by the Bureau of National Affairs, Inc. (800-372-1033)

233

Both companies also sponsor health maintenance organizations and have retained indemnity health plans for those employees in locations where networks are not available.

One notable difference is the two companies' approach to structuring a nationwide program. Sears has contracted with at least three vendors, including Prudential, Metropolitan Life, and CIGNA Employee Benefits Cos.

Sears believes that going with a single carrier would have been a mistake, according to Tim Crow, manager of group insurance benefits/managed care for Sears. Crow described his company's program at an April 8 session of the National Managed Health Care Congress.

Marriott, on the other hand, works primarily with Prudential. Using a single carrier provides administrative ease for a transient employee population like Marriott's and gives the company buying power, explained Brian Marcotte, manager of health plan contracts and services for Marriott, who also participated in the discussion of managed care programs at the conference.

UNUSUAL EMPLOYER PROJECT

The joint audit, an unusual employer project, "actually worked extremely well because both employers were very cooperative with us" and Prudential cooperated as well, Lipson told BNA.

According to Lipson, the two employers separately had reviewed Prudential's qualifications during the feasibility and network selection phases of their programs. As the programs were introduced and the companies began receiving input from employees, Sears and Marriott "felt there were some things that needed to be looked at more carefully," he said.

When Marriott learned Sears had asked Mercer to conduct an audit, Marriott and Sears held discussions and then agreed to go forward with a joint effort.

The plan sponsors sought to exercise due diligence in the selection of managed care arrangements. They also wanted to be able to highlight areas for improvement so they could strive to have the best possible program for employees, Lipson explained. He noted the evaluation focused on several key areas:

- Prudential's provider selection and credentialing process;
- Quality monitoring;
- Provider relations; and
- Medical management of the program.

Lipson explained that medical management—sometimes referred to as "utilization review"—is a term that is broader in scope because it encompasses outpatient as well as inpatient services.

ON-SITE VISITS

"We handled [the evaluation] by going on-site to several of the California locations," Lipson said. "We visited the California headquarters for Prudential in Woodland Hills and also looked at the specific plans in Los Angeles, Orange, and San Mateo." The auditors spent about two-and-a-half days at each location, an intensive visit, he noted.

The auditors first reviewed documents supplied by Prudential, Sears, and Marriott to gain a good understanding of how both managed care programs had been set up. They then interviewed persons instrumental in operating the networks.

"We made a real effort to get beyond the Prudential management to actually talk with some of the staff who are right on the firing line," Lipson told BNA. The auditors sat down with customer service staff members to listen as they handled telephone calls.

Similarly, auditors observed staff nurses taking calls for pre-authorization of hospital services, to determine how the nurses referred matters to the physician advisors backing them up. Hard copies of computer system transactions were examined.

This was done to assess how the actions that were taken on the cases matched up with "what we considered would be the most rigorous medical management standards," Lipson explained. The auditors used standards employed by the best staff-model HMOs as a benchmark, he added. Auditors also made random checks of physician credential files to make sure they were up to date and appropriately filled out. This approach let the auditors get a feel for how the program actually works, as opposed to how it looks on paper, Lipson told BNA.

COMPOSITE AUDIT REPORT

Mercer consultants then prepared a composite report for Sears and Marriott, which was followed by a meeting between the employers and Prudential to discuss actions to take based on the report.

Lipson told BNA that Prudential agreed to make some changes based on the recommendations in the audit report. However, he declined to give specific details. Sears and Marriott could not be reached for comment on the recommended changes made by Prudential.

The joint medical audit appears to be a relatively new practice among employers, but may gain momentum, Lipson speculated. "I suspect we'll see a bit more of that as the employers network together through, for example, the Managed Health Care Association," he said. The Managed Health Care Association is a "users group" of employers that sponsor managed care programs or are planning to offer managed care.

Since a limited number of carriers are sponsoring broad, national networks, "it would be a natural" for employers that need such networks to bank together and examine them, Lipson said. Teaming up for audits might not be possible due to the extent plans vary in benefit design or customized features, he remarked.

"On the other hand, a doctor is a doctor and a hospital is a hospital. If Prudential has Medical Group A and Hospital B and employees use that network, that's where a commonality comes in where employers could do very well," he added.

While Sears and Marriott have no plans to conduct future joint audits, Lipson said it's possible the two companies may team up again should they discover they share carriers in other parts of the country.

Part 6

MANAGED CARE

24. Employers and Managed Care:
What Are the Early Returns?
Helen Darling

The experiences of three large corporations shows that, with careful selection and plan design, managed care offers a promising interim step that can provide some protection against short-term cost problems. But companies of all sizes are likely to find themselves increasingly involved in more direct management of health benefits in order to control rising costs.

As of 1990, 95 percent of U.S employees and dependents were covered by one or more of the many forms of "managed care," according to the most recent Health Insurance Association of America (HIAA) annual employer survey.[1] The prevalence of managed care bears out the view that it is now mainstream medicine and that American physicians are among the most regulated in the world.

However, this statistic may be somewhat misleading. "Managed care" is used to describe everything from the most minimal, superficial utilization review program to the most actively managed staff/group-model health maintenance organizations (HMOs). Not surprisingly, considerable evidence shows substantial variation in the quality and effectiveness of utilization management and other managed care mechanisms.[2]

Enough employers have been involved in managed care for at least five years to ask: What are the early returns? Do employers believe managed care is making a difference? These are difficult questions to answer, because the research that might point to an answer is frequently outdated, often is based on circumstances too specialized to generalize to large groups, or has other methodological or

Reprinted with permission from *Health Affairs*.

statistical limitations. Employers—even large ones with databases and resources—must act upon anecdotal information that would be unsatisfactory to academic researchers. Further, once changes are instituted, many other factors, along
with subsequent program revisions, preclude formal evaluations.

Some employers emphasize the potential of managed care to control health
care costs while not limitnig patients' access to care. The annual cost trend rates
of HMOs and other managed care options during the past few years have been
consistently lower than for the pure indemnity option.[3] Even if the resultant
reductions in outlays for a few years are partly related to "prices" that carriers are
charging, not to a major change in underlying incentives or costs, savings are real
to the affected employer.

For other employers, the importance of managed care lies in improving
quality of care and reducing waste, in the form of unnecessary services and
excessive prices. Some of the nation's largest employers, with the assistance of
knowledgeable benefits executives, are implementing comprehensive health
benefits management strategies that involve them much more than before in the
delivery of care. Analysts and policymakers have long hoped that the private
sector would use its purchasing power in such a way to change the health care
financing system.

In this Commentary, I review trends in managed care from the perspective
of three of the nation's largest employers: General Electric, PepsiCo, and Xerox.
The experiences of these three companies illustrate what corporate America is
doing and what employee benefits managers believe, as reported in face-to-face
interviews in July 1991. These companies reflect a large trend toward active
health benefits management by corporate executives. There seems to be a clear
connection between the amount of pressure on revenues, the ability to pass costs
to the customer (or taxpayer), and an employer's willingness to spend the time,
energy, and staff resource to change its health benefits strategy. Companies under
pressure or determined to manage their costs are working to reduce the amount
of inappropriate or excessive care for which they are paying.

As I compared the experiences of these three corporate giants, with their
very different approaches to managed care, I observed several common threads.
First, no one "right" answer exists for all companies. To be effective, managed
care requires careful selection and proper design. Once in place, it needs continual
oversight. And even in the best-managed environment, measuring its true impact
will remain difficult, in a sphere of activity that is both highly complex and poorly
understood. Nonetheless, managed care does offer a promising interim step that
provides employers some protection from short-term cost problems. The leading-edge employers are trying to go beyond simply purchasing "off-the-shelf"
managed care or leaving the problems to the medical care system. In so doing,
they are struggling with the same challenges and problems that have bedeviled
health policymakers for decades.

WHY FOCUS ON EMPLOYERS?

The employment-based insurance system, which has provided health coverage to most working-age Americans since the 1930s, is the object of scrutiny as the nation wrestles with its health care woes. Some critics view the system as inadequate, to which the number of uninsured or underinsured workers attests. As policymakers look to the employment-based health benefits system as a vehicle to mandate universal health coverage, they must examine how well the current system works for those who are reasonably well insured.

Corporate leaders have never been more concerned about health care costs than they are today. In a recent *Fortune* poll, nearly two out of three business leaders called skyrocketing medical costs one of the worst problems facing American corporations. One-third of them believed that this is the single biggest problem they would face in this decade.[4] Some employers now want federal action to ameliorate the problems and are lobbying Congress to act, but even if Congress were to enact major health system reform by the turn of the century, employers have to deal with problems at hand now. So they are moving ahead with their own health cost containment strategies. With health benefits costs rising 17.1 percent in 1990 to $3,217 per person, on average, employers believe they have to move faster than ever to blunt the increases.[5] If Congress is to rely on the private sector in national health system reform, that sector must prove its ability to provide care of adequate quality while curbing the cost increases eating away at its bottom line. It is at this juncture that managed care enters the discussion.

DOES MANAGED CARE SAVE MONEY?

One need look no further than the trade press and benefits surveys to see what is happening among employers. Managed care premium increases for 1991 were reported to be one-half of the increases for traditional indemnity plans. HMO premiums were in the 10-15 percent range, versus 20-25 percent for indemnity-type insurance. Plans with a preferred provider organization (PPO) option were estimated in the 15-19 percent range.[6] Blue Cross/Blue Shield reported that premium increases would range from 7 to 20 percent, depending on the number and type of managed care features.[7]

Employers tend to compare their own increases to those of other firms or to other published statistics. Beyond mere numbers, however, they look for evidence of quality enhancement or preservation from statistics on questionable admissions and procedures, patient satisfaction data, and monitoring of complaints. Employers who are installing "managed care" programs are doing so partly because they perceive that their costs for those programs are at least slightly lower than their unmanaged fee-for-service plan. However, it appears that the more tightly constrained an employer's outlays are because of reduced revenues or other competitive pressures (including from the global economy), the more willing that employer is to limit employee choices and select the less costly managed care option.

In short, although data point to cost savings connected with managed care plans, it is still not clear that they can save employers as much as one might hope. Administrative costs, so-called network access charges, and other elements of managed care plans can easily end up costing nearly as much as the fee-for-service indemnity plan. Also, costs in the second and third years can rise again if the administrators ("vendors") are not continually monitored and held accountable and if the underlying incentives to use care are not changed. The trade press is full of stories touting the advantages of managed care, especially point-of-service plans, but there is far less talk about failures. There are little hard data of any type, but employers have the flexibility to continually refine ideas and approaches. If one action begins to look like it is not going to produce any savings, within limits, it is possible to not make the change, or make other changes right away. As a result, we will continue to operate with few definitive research results. This is a remarkably dynamic environment.

MANAGED CARE STRATEGIES OF THREE CORPORATIONS

General Electric, PepsiCo, and Xerox are three corporations with different corporate cultures, business strategies, and managed care strategies. All three have been involved with managed care since the early to mid-1980s. They illustrate broader trends among a growing number of large and medium employers. Common to all of these employers is the belief that employers have to take steps to ensure that their employees have the option of selecting high-quality managed care and that they have the information and opportunity to be wiser health care decisionmakers on their own behalf. Other fine examples exist, notably Southern California Edison, whose elaborate delivery system model includes eight primary health clinics that have been surveyed and accredited by the Joint Commission on Accreditation of Healthcare Organizations. I chose these cases, however, because they illustrate the diversity of approaches possible as companies go about trying to implement managed care concepts, what their strategies are, and what they believe are the results.

General Electric

GE spent over $800 million on health care for its employees in 1990, $3,414 per employee for medical care alone. However, costs per employee have risen 38 percent in the past three years and are estimated to increase 13 percent annually. The latter figure, high for any single expense item, is in the low moderate range for health benefits. By national standards, GE's benefits are very generous. The company prides itself on comprehensive benefits programs used as a tool to attract and retain top employees. GE has been involved in managed care since the early 1980s. Charles Buck, staff executive for Health Care Management Programs, was a senior health care executive hired specifically to manage health care costs, a step taken by some other large employers as well. According to Buck, GE's overall cost containment strategy, which has been evolving over the past ten years, can be divided into three categories: utilization review for the fee-for-service, freedom-of-choice plan; incentives to use carefully selected PPOs within the medical plan; and development of enrollment-based managed care options, called Preferred Medical Plans.

GE sees utilization review as a necessary first step, given the significant amount of unnecessary medical care documented in the research literature. GE would rather not be in the position of coming in or paying others to come in late in the medical care process in an "inspect" method of control. This is the least desirable and probably the least effective approach, according to Buck. GE prefers to ensure quality and efficiency as in the industrial model, he explained, by "moving upstream in the quality assurance process: helping the patient navigate the health system, partly by educating and facilitating a questioning process by the patient."

GE is developing specifications for a prototype telephone-based "patient decision support system," known as Nurseline. GE employees and their dependents will be encouraged to call registered nurses for information about health care or health problems. In time, Nurseline will integrate with traditional utilization review, second surgical opinion, and the local provider network (purchasing) strategy. For example, if a patient who has been told he needs prostate surgery would call Nurseline, he would be given information about options and alternative outcomes that he might want to review with the urologist. The nurse might also suggest a local urologist who has an excellent record of conservative practice and good interpersonal skills for talking with patients.

A newsletter for employees aimed at health care decision making is another component of this program. This newsletter is intended as a tool to help both patient and provider be much more informed about medical options. In creating and publishing it, GE has gone considerably further than most other large employers. Its format and information, which includes sophisticated discussions of health care treatment decisions written for a lay audience, differ from some of the better wellness-oriented or health promotion newsletters.

A key to successfully implementing a new health benefits strategy is to make that strategy consistent with the corporate culture that already exists in a company. GE has done this in several ways. First, it regularly runs focus groups to test ideas and approaches. Employees are encouraged to invent solutions to problems they perceive in their health benefits plan. Their concerns can be as specific as needing help finding a physician or deciding about surgery, or as general as knowing what works and what does not. Second, as part of its efforts to understand and influence the health care system, GE is attempting to "map" the health care process, using a management tool already used throughout GE. "Process mapping" involves key participants in the process to produce a flow chart showing every step in the process under examination, no matter how small. This reveals steps that do not add value and allows GE to manage an operation from start to finish.[8]

Another component of GE's health strategy is what GE calls Preferred Medical Plans—network-based alternatives that employees can elect outside the GE plan, with carefully selected physicians, hospitals, and other providers. The company already has Preferred Medical Plans in three cities and plans to develop eighteen more in the next three years. These plans are implemented in a variety of ways, not by a single national carrier, thus enabling the company to be flexible in meeting local needs. A number of criteria, including quality measures, enter into the selection of the best care options in each city. Another part of the scheme is the option of treatment in nationally recognized "centers of excellence." If the patient accepts treatment in one of these centers, GE pays for not only the medical costs but also expenses for transportation, meals, and lodging for the patient and one immediate family member.

In the long run, GE's Buck is betting on enrollment-based options—that is, health plans that must be selected at the beginning of the year and that take responsibility for the care of the enrollee. The preferred model is one in which the patient chooses a primary care physician. Based on this ongoing relationship, the physician and the system have a chance to fulfill their responsibilities for continuing care. This is especially valuable for patients with chronic care needs; it permits an emphasis on wellness, health promotion, and early diagnosis and treatment.

Overall, GE's early returns show added value in what they are purchasing. Annual increases in the low double digits, which are lower than those of other employers, seem to back that up. But because GE is making so many changes at once, it is difficult to quantify which intervention makes the difference. The company has evidence that it is providing more services yet slowing down the rate of cost increase. GE has also learned that it cannot ever let up.

PepsiCo

Although different from GE in both corporate culture and health benefits strategy, PepsiCo shares common elements with GE. One of these is a benefits executive with a great deal of health care-related experience. Dave Scherb, vice-president of benefits for PepsiCo, has both health insurer and HMO management experience.

Although PepsiCo is one of the country's largest employers, a number of its locations employ only a handful of people. With divisions that include Pepsi-

Cola, Frito-Lay, KFC, Pizza Hut, and Taco Bell, PepsiCo's geographic distribution, diverse work force, and demographics make health cost containment a challenge, particularly when it comes to building managed care networks.

The corporate culture of PepsiCo fosters innovation, rapid decision making, and the kind of direct accountability that would make less risk-taking types nervous but can certainly inspire the imaginative. The company thrives on individual choice, accountability, and change. Its chairman believes that one of the worst business advisory statements ever made was, "If it isn't broken, don't fix it." The company's ongoing success reinforces its strategy of devising new ideas each year to improve upon the last year's performance. As far as benefits are concerned, PepsiCo builds in so much individual choice and annual benefit changes that employees view them as normal. PepsiCo has had a flexible benefits plan in place for over a decade—one of the oldest such plans in the industry.

At PepsiCo, a disciplined budgeting process, which has been used successfully since the introduction of flexible benefits in 1980, determines the timing for new managed care programs. Each year, in the first quarter, the benefits staff examines data on prior experience and presents alternatives and estimates of the impact of various options in the second quarter. They decide what to implement in the third quarter and develop communications to "roll out" the changes. In the fourth quarter, employees enroll in their choices, and the cycle begins again.

Some of PepsiCo's most effective managed care programs were developed out of that process, including the high-risk pregnancy program, managed mental health and chemical dependency programs, and HMO and PPO networks. Several years ago, data analysis demonstrated that premature newborns helped make maternity PepsiCo's fastest-growing expense. PepsiCo contracted with a utilization review firm to identify potentially high-risk pregnancies and provide intensive case management through a pilot program for one division. Given the relatively small number of cases and the statistical and measurement problems, Scherb is cautious about offering empirical evidence of the pilot program's effectiveness. Hard data over enough years will soon be available, but in the interim, he can cite the following statistics: Of forty problem newborns identified in the first year of the pilot, twenty were in the new maternity program. Those in the program had medical costs that averaged one-half the costs of the others. (Costs are markers for a number of problems, including pain and suffering of the families.) Based on its apparent success, PepsiCo made the program available throughout the company last year. Employees value the program, as evidenced by positive comments in surveys and their 80 percent voluntary participation rate.

In the analysis and budgeting process, PepsiCo also saw serious problems with psychiatric care. It hired a specialty mental health and substance abuse managed care firm, added case management, and used an employee assistance program (EAP) to encourage early assistance and follow-up help. It also hired another specialty mental health/substance abuse firm with a network for Frito-Lay. In both cases, within two years of implementing these changes, the average length-of-stay went from thirty-six to eighteen days. Psychiatric costs declined by 18 percent within one year of adopting managed care with network providers. Claims costs were almost back to 1987 levels.

Believing that this is still too high, PepsiCo decided to put in a thirty-day inpatient limit, primarily as a tool for case managers. The thirty-day limit can be waived if active case management is present. This shifts the burden of proof from the utilization review firm and case manager to the provider, who must make the case that the care is needed. With limits, Scherb said, "the provider has to show that the care is medically appropriate and necessary. This makes a big difference and also starts the discussion at a more affordable level."

Until PepsiCo began introducing some management, mental health and substance abuse claims were rising at a rate consistent with those of other large employers. After PepsiCo made the changes, their mental health/substance abuse claims costs became third highest, no longer at the top of the list. Maternity occupies that spot, but the data suggest that length-of-stay and cesarean section rates are actually lower than the norm. Nonetheless, in PepsiCo fashion, the benefits staff is tracking data, ready to act if problems arise.

PepsiCo, as do many employers, offers HMOs throughout the country. The geographic dispersion of PepsiCo employees requires the use of national networks (both HMO and PPO) to gain buying power at the local level. However, believing that it had far too many HMOs to exercise adequate management control, PepsiCo began a systematic consolidation of the number of HMOs it offered, using a formal request-for-proposal (RFP) process. At the same time, it developed national PPO networks.

PPO and HMO networks, provided mostly by insurers, are an essential part of a long-term, comprehensive strategy for managing care. PepsiCo believes it is approaching its limits on the costs employees can be expected to share. Through networks, PepsiCo can use its leverage and health care knowledge to help employees get high-quality health care without necessarily increasing their share of the bill. Scherb believes that, over time, the quality of network providers will be the incentive for employees to use network services. That is why PepsiCo has not used negative incentives such as benefit cutbacks to steer employees to its networks.

PepsiCo has had very good success with managed care, Scherb believes. "Second surgical opinion saved a little, but precertification saves a great deal more. . . . Now, with the addition of more sophisticated case management programs and networks, we've continued to hold our annual costs down to single-digit increases." PepsiCo has seen savings of 6-12 percent of hospital and physician charges through the use of networks, but the combination of many actions, not networks, has held down costs. Looking forward, Scherb said:

> In the 1990s, carriers will have to continue to prove that they have high-quality, efficient providers as measured by ever more sophisticated methods. Our networks are using the credentialing and quality

assurance methods known today, but we want providers to continue to prove with solid statistics and outcomes data that their doctors and institutions are better and that they are continuing to reduce unnecessary use. As the state of the art expands, we'll expect our networks to remain at the cutting edge of the quality movement.

Xerox

Xerox purchases health benefits for 55,000 U.S. employees, retirees, and their eligible dependents. Like GE, Xerox has long provided comprehensive, competitive benefits, a policy that is valuable in recruiting and retaining top scientific and technical people in communities such as Rochester, New York, and throughout California. But as have all employers, Xerox has been challenged to blunt the health cost spiral. (Xerox health costs grew 51 percent between 1987 and 1990.) Xerox concluded that shifting more costs to employees was not an acceptable option and that cutting benefits was not desirable.

Xerox employees are clustered in several locations, some of which have a tradition of older, stable HMOs. When Xerox began its most active cost management program, at least 40 percent of its employees—many of them in Rochester—were already enrolled in HMOs. Employees in these communities had considerable choice amoung HMOs. Thus, the Health-Link HMO network, which Xerox offered for enrollment in 1990, is built on an existing tradition of familiarity with HMOs.

For more than six years, Pat Nazemetz, director of benefits at Xerox, has been developing and fine-tuning a bold, imaginative strategy for health care cost management, based on HMOs and nationwide in its scope. The plan was to create a national network of well-managed, high-quality HMOs, applying to the purchase of health benefits the same "Total Quality Management" business strategy that helped Xerox win the prestigious Baldridge award.

Through a lengthy competitive process with twenty-two possible HMO managers, Xerox spelled out in detail its health services requirements. In effect, Xerox asked HMOs if they would not only provide the kind of care Xerox demanded but also help manage other HMOs. Xerox wanted to develop the kind of long-term supplier relationship with their HealthLink HMO managers and HMOs that the Japanese use with such success and that is becoming popular in the United States.

According to Nazemetz, "We were willing to pay a fair and reasonable price. Xerox is a major player in its communities. We always want to be a good corporate citizen. We were not looking for discounts because we did not want to negatively affect the providers that served its employees, and because a long-term, quality-oriented relationship could not be built on simple discounts." At the same time, Nazemetz wanted to ensure that each service area offered competition and a choice for employees. Although Nazemetz continues to refine the original approach, the broad policy direction has remained unchanged.

The components of HealthLink are in place, with Kaiser, Blue Cross/Blue Shield of Rochester, FHP, PruCare, HMO Group, and U.S. Healthcare serving as the six national managers. All billing and reporting will be consolidated under the managers. These managers have already done the thorough on-site surveying and evaluating that permit HMOs to be part of HealthLink.

Beginning in 1991, new Xerox employees will not be offered health coverage outside the HealthLink HMOs. Any Xerox employee hired before that time can remain in the Xerox fee-for-service indemnity plan, but the individual's out-of-pocket costs in this plan can be quite high, thus providing a financial incentive to switch to the managed care option. For example, the annual deductible for the fee-for-service plan is 1 percent of pay (previous year), and the out-of-pocket maximum is 4 percent of pay or $4,000, whichever is lower.

Xerox has gone further than other large employers to exercise its collective purchasing power in identifying high-quality managed health care providers and designing and implementing a nationwide strategy. In so doing, Xerox has accelerated the demands on HMOs to be responsive to employers and directly accountable through detailed, quantitative measures of utilization, quality of care, program effectiveness, and costs.

Because a high percentage of its employees were already enrolled in HMOs and its main locations were in areas with long-standing, strong HMOs, Xerox could implement its HMO-based managed care strategy faster than some other employers could. Early evidence suggests that Xerox is on schedule in its implementation of a tough strategy, and Xerox is confident that it is moving in the right direction. Nazemetz estimates that Xerox's HMO costs are about ten percentage points lower than those of its indemnity plan. As part of its ongoing commitment to HealthLink and to continuous quality improvement, Xerox is working with the National Committee for Quality Assurance (NCQA) and its HealthLink managers to accredit and survey all of its HMOs. In 1991, Xerox planned to complete employee surveys and obtain patient satisfaction data from a national survey. Xerox will also collect baseline utilization and quality data, which it can in turn use to monitor progress in health status.

While the main strategy has been to establish HealthLink as quicky as possible, the indemnity plan also has new elements of managed care to ensure that the indemnity plan's high growth rates are moderated and that Xerox pays only for medically necessary and appropriate care. Xerox now requires utilization review for a hospitalization, including psychiatric and substance abuse treatment. The latter is particularly important, given concerns among all employers that HMO benefits packages discourage patients with high service requirements. Xerox is determined to create a system that takes care of people but also is affordable in the long run.

LESSONS FOR OTHER EMPLOYERS

As these three examples demonstrate, health cost management strategies of leading-edge employers have several elements in common. First, employers are driven by data that document problems and point to causes. Initially, they may have reacted to annual medical claims cost increases that became unacceptable after enough years and growing frustration with no sign of abatement. Second, employers take significant time to develop plans, work with internal groups or task forces, interact with divisional or regional personnel to explore ideas, and meet with external providers and other vendors. Some companies have chosen to, or were forced to, accelerate some of those steps.

Third, as part of that process, employers have learned to stay involved with their suppliers to a degree that would have been unimaginable until a few years ago. In many instances, the employer forced the suppliers or providers to introduce or adapt a program or product. Fourth, the steps they took had to fit with the "corporate culture." What works well or easily in one organization might be counterproductive in another.

Fifth, all have come to appreciate the need for consumers/patients to be knowledgeable and be given the tools to ask questions and make their own health care decisions. Sixth, employers believe, as the benefits managers here described, that high-quality health care will prove to be the most cost-effective and, over the long term, the least costly.

Seventh, employers do not shrink from their roles as buyers of hundreds of millions of dollars of services, which must be continually monitored and actively managed, just like any other major expense. Cost management and quality assurance cannot be "done" and then left to the professionals or the vendors. Financial leverage and technical knowledge are used aggressively to get more return on the investment of their health care dollars. Companies gain because they are slowing the growth of benefit costs that are eating away at their profits. Employees gain because their out-of-pocket costs are reduced and they can get better care if it is managed properly. Finally, and most importantly, employers believe that for the long term, the systems that come closest to truly managing care—well-managed HMOs and gatekeeper-model PPOs—will provide the greatest promise for ensuring high-quality care at a reasonable price.

INCREMENTALISM AS CORPORATE STRATEGY

Health care in the United States is moving toward more oversight and account-ability. Providers, understandably, view it as "micromanagement." Everyone affected laments the added administrative costs due to such management, but employers are not likely to reduce their increasingly direct involvement in health care delivery because the cost management does reduce employers' claims costs relative to their costs if left unmanaged or uncontrolled. They believe they have no choice given their approximately $200 billion annual investment in health care.

It is unknown whether the spread of managed care, with its combination of national systems and regional or local management, will occur with any degree of evenness, competence, and uniformity, or if the wide dispersion, layers of organization, and multiple units of the nation's employers will undermine presumed advantages. Effective execution makes the difference between a shell of a program that simply adds another layer of administrative costs to an already multilayered system and a program that provides useful services to providers and patients alike.

No employer likes to tackle tasks as daunting and thankless as managing health benefits costs. Often, success does not look good enough to gain any accolades from senior management, and every step that moderates the rise in medical claims produces loud complaints. The tougher the reform strategy, such as replacing all other options with an HMO, the more grumbling there is likely to be. Thus, although employer/purchasers are increasingly frustrated by annual increases in the 15-25 percent range, they do not want to move so fast that they either hurt or alienate their employees, thus putting themselves in an uncompetitive situation for recruitment and retention. Employers believe that health coverage is one of the most important benefits they can and should provide to their employees. Because of its importance, managers want to minimize changes with adverse effects.

Yet the ability to pass on cost increases to customers or taxpayers continues to shrink, and employers have less ability to absorb premium hikes at such high levels year after year. The dragging economy has influenced the health benefits market even in the past eighteen months. The recession and the gloomy outlook for the future standard of living have accelerated these realities and made it more essential for some employers to institute more stringent cost sharing and look at capping their outside liability by moving into more comprehensive managed care. Even public employees—who have long had some of the most comprehensive and thus costliest health plans—are beginning to be challenged to give up some of their "first-dollar" coverage or take reductions in other benefits, wages, or jobs.

Degrees of Management

Employers usually follow these steps to reduce medical claim costs: (1) increasing what employees have to pay for coverage, especially for dependents; (2) increasing deductibles and copayments; and (3) introducing new limits in special areas such as mental health and substance abuse ("inside limits").

To date, most employers have been willing to tackle only the most blatant, unnecessary care. Employers with the highest costs and the greatest pressures on their revenues will keep looking for managed care organizations that will give them better and better results. When these methods fail, more aggressive squeezing down on discretionary care and techniques for slowing demand come next. Most employers move unhappily to that stage. Unless government enacts laws that limit price increases affecting all purchasers, employers will take even more drastic steps to limit cost increases, such as limiting their absolute contribution to health plans or providing primary care services in a tightly controlled setting. Direct contracting and purchasing (for more specialized services) will become increasingly attractive to the largest employers in an area. The growing supply of physicians will make it easier to recruit and retain physicians as managers and as clinicians, as well as to provide oversight for the employer.

Integrated Plans

If an employer's younger, healthier workers move first into the managed care programs, and the sicker or older employees stay in the "indemnity" option, an employer will have the worst possible experience. For this reason, employers are looking for integrated plans with carriers and HMOs in which employees' movement in and out of the indemnity option (so-called antiselection) is "priced" in a way that does not cost the employer more money. Until such "integration" is more widely available, employers are pressuring HMOs to hold down their premium increases, partly because employers believe that they are "overpaying." Employers also want evidence that documents their employees' use of services. Since HMOs in the past have resisted employers' demands for more accountability and reduced premiums, employers have come to believe that offering fewer HMOs will give them more leverage and reduce administrative burden. The current trend to consolidate the number of HMOs offered will accelerate. This in turn will make it easier to move to a single option, or very small number of options.

It is not unusual for an employer to announce that it is moving to managed care to avoid having to shift more costs to employees. Companies with the highest per employee costs and the greatest pressure on their own revenues are most likely to feel they have no other choice. Most employers—of all sizes—will go through incremental steps toward less free choice of providers or higher cost sharing if employees want to retain complete freedom of choice.

Unless the economy turns around soon, I foresee much more movement by more employers to the most comprehensive managed care with the most obvious ability to hold down costs. Employers will find it increasingly attractive to deal with one organization, with the adverse risk selection "neutralized" by the integrated plan. At the same time, most costly health care (such as inpatient operations and mental health care) provided outside of an HMO or a PPO will be reviewed by specialized utilization reviewers.

The largest companies will find themselves immersed in "micromanagement" to ensure that they get what they want. Medium and small employers will follow suit to the extent possible. The U. S. health care delivery system is so extensive, complicated, and expensive, no employer of any size can afford not to become deeply involved in finding new ways to limit its outlays. One employer said recently, "I don't like to have to spend so much time on it, but somebody has to control the constantly running meter."

1. Sullivan and Rice, "The Health Insurance Picture in 1990," *Health Affairs* (Summer 1991): 104-115.

2. B.H. Gray and M.J. Field, eds., *Controlling Costs and Changing Patient Care? The Role of Utilization Management* (Washington, D.C.: National Academy Press, 1989).

3. A. Foster Higgins, *Managed Care Survey, 1990* (Princeton, N.J.: A Foster Higgins, August 1991); "Kaiser Debates Point-of-Service, Others Try It On for Size," *Managed Care Report* (26 November 1990): 4; and Group Health Association of America, *HMO Industry Profile, 1991 Edition, Volume 1: Benefits, Premiums, and Market Structure in 1990* (Washington, D.C.: GHAA, 1991), 26-28.

4. "A Cure for What Ails America," *Fortune* (1 July 1991): 43-56.

5. A. Foster Higgins, *Health Care Benefits Survey, 1990* (Princeton, N.J.: A. Foster Higgins, 1991), 4.

6. M. Schachner, "Health Plan Premiums to Increase 10% to 25%," *Business Insurance* (17 December 1990): 3.

7. *Id.*

8. T.A. Stewart, "GE Keeps Those Ideas Coming," *Fortune* (12 August 1991): 41-49.

25. Containing Health Care Costs: Claims Management Review

Carol Johnston

Employee benefits administration costs and their relentless effect on the corporate budget mandate continuous cost containment actions on the part of employers. One of the most effective tactics available for cost control is a periodic review of claims administrator's procedures.

An effective claims management review (CMR) almost always detects areas that the claims administrator can—and should—improve immediately. Once the review is completed, a thorough CMR recommends ongoing strategies for controlling costs in the future. Furthermore, a comprehensive CMR communicates to the claims administrator that the company is committed to health care expense control and to quality claims processing.

Even employers whose administrators use computerized claims processing can benefit from a CMR. Although automated claims processing offers significant advantages—such as improved turnaround time, increased management reporting capabilities, and fewer computation errors—the trade-off, all too often, is quality. A sophisticated computer system does not eliminate the need for well-defined office procedures, careful application of plan provisions, and close coordination between administrator and employer. A CMR can incorporate these issues into a plan that provides direction for future benefit decisions.

FOCUS ON KEY ISSUES

A CMR is a positive way to determine the effectiveness of a claims operation because it provides employers with an unbiased look at the quality and accuracy of the claims administrator's operation. The review offers an in-depth analysis of claims office procedures, staffing, claims payment accuracy, and cost control features. In addition, a CMR includes a review of systems security and capabilities, assessing the availability, timeliness, and value of management information reports.

Evaluation of a claims administrator's performance addresses four key questions:

- How are claims processed?
- Are claims processed according to plan specifications?
- What system and security edits are in place?
- What management data are coded and captured?

To be effective, a CMR must also address the *specific* circumstances of an employer. For example, management may want to use results of the CMR to determine one or more of the following:

- The efficiency of its current claims operation
- What plan design features are overused or underused
- Whether meaningful management reports are available and applied
- How the claims operation compares with industry standards

ON-SITE EVALUATION OF ADMINISTRATIVE PROCESSES

On-site visits facilitate the review and evaluation of the following administrative aspects of a claims handling agency.

Staffing

To determine whether the claims operation is structured so that benefit plans can be administered effectively, a CMR assesses experience levels of claims examiners and evaluates internal monitoring and quality assurance programs. How are the claims examiners evaluated and compensated? What incentives or disincentives are in place for proper claims adjudication? What is the ratio of examiners and customer service representatives to plan participants?

Claims Adjudication

A CMR looks into the interpretation and application of a plan's provisions through automated and manual claims processing procedures. How effective are the procedures used to maintain and apply information about employee and dependent eligibility? Do procedures ensure proper monitoring and adequate control of the workload?

Customer Service Capability

CMRs also evaluate the outcome of customer service inquiries. Are calls handled promptly? Is follow-up timely? Do participants receive correct and current information?

Management Information Systems

During an on-site visit, CMR reviewers examine the use of computer files—including history, plan descriptions, eligibility and other data—for processing claims, preparing management reports, and performing other functions. Is the file data current and accurate? What security procedures are in place? What controls govern the issuance claims payment checks?

FOCUS ON COST CONTROL STRATEGIES

One of the most important facets of a CMR is its evaluation of an administrator's cost controls. A thorough CMR may uncover some of the following "repeat offenders" that often contribute to rising costs.

- Code creep, fee unbundling, and fraud are significant factors in health care costs. How does the claims administrator identify these abuses, and what steps are taken for correction?
- Most claims administrators have hospital bill audit programs for large claims—usually $10,000 or more. How are sizable claims flagged? What type of review is performed? How are recoveries conducted?
- "Pre-existing conditions" among plan participants can be expensive. How are these conditions identified?
- How current is the schedule of "usual and customary charges?" Is there a long lag time between data collection and data use? What percentile limits are used?

- Pending claims can be dormant problems, addressed only when beneficiaries complain. How are pending claims handled? How many are pending, how old are they, and why are they unresolved?

CMR reviewers generally interview claims office management and processing staff to gain insight into characteristic or recurring problems. In addition, reviewers assess current claim cost controls, including coordination of benefits, reasonable and customary cutbacks, and duration guidelines, as well as medical necessity and appropriateness of health care services. Established guidelines for procedures are compared with the claims processors' actual practices.

EVALUATION OF CLAIMS

A CMR includes on-site evaluations of random statistical samples of claims. These analyses test the accuracy of reimbursements. CMRs also study selected claims samples to address specific concerns, such as duplicate payments, missed coordination or subrogation opportunities, or incorrect plan interpretations. Errors detected during a CMR are discussed with the claims administrator's management. Clearly, extensive communication between the review team and the claims administrator is essential to the success of the review.

SYSTEMS AND MANAGEMENT DATA REVIEW

A CMR also includes a review of systems and management data to provide objective evaluation of the system's strengths or weaknesses. Most administrators have installed sophisticated equipment to manage on-line adjudication and such systems promised to generate a variety of management reports. In theory, detailed data collected from submitted claims could provide an employer with valuable information leading to substantial savings in future health benefit administration. For all too many administrators, however, comprehensive data collection has yet to be fully realized.

A thorough CMR includes an analysis of system capabilities as well as current management reports. Reviewers can make recommendations, based on their findings, for capturing and using historical data to control future costs.

A CMR BENEFITS ALL PARTIES

It is important to remember that requesting a CMR does not necessarily imply a question of the integrity of the claims administrator. In fact, most claims administrators will welcome a review as a useful, objective check on their claims-paying operation.

To ensure both fairness and effetiveness, a CMR should be conducted by an independent, objective team with broad experience in benefit administration. The collective expertise should include electronic data processing, benefit plan design, law, and medicine, as well as health care cost containment experience. Reviewers on the team also should have claims processing and administration experience in order to evaluate claims operations knowledgeably.

A properly structured review goes beyond the scope of an accountant's audit or an administrator's internal audit. Claims must be examined at the processing level; much more is involved than numerical accuracy. Along with this greater scope, however, comes greater benefits for the employer, the claims administrator, and the employees.

26.   Controlling Costs With
Point-of-Service Plans

Douglas G. Cave   Larry J. Tucker

The point of service plan is the latest health care cost control method to come down the road. But POS plans are not right for every employer. In fact, in some cases, they can actually cost an employer more. Here are 10 questions every employer should ask before implementing a POS plan.

Many employers feel that multiple-choice health plans have not been effective in controlling spiraling medical costs. Under the multiple-choice strategy, an employer offers a large number of indemnity and HMO plans and sets a fixed contribution level that make employees responsible for the cost differential of a more expensive plan. Employees then should join plans with lower priced premiums, forcing more expensive plans out of the health-plan market.

However, some employers believe their total premium under a multiple-choice program is increasing faster than it would if only a single plan were offered. For this reason, employers have either eliminated or are considering eliminating their current multiple-plan offerings to contract with a single carrier that offers a point-of-service (POS) plan. These plans also are commonly referred to as POS health maintenance organization (HMOs), open-access HMOs and self-referral options. Wells Fargo and Co., First Interstate Bancorp, Bank of America, Hyatt Hotels Corp., Proctor and Gamble, Fort Howard Corp., Ryder System Inc., Allied-Signal Corp. and Citibank are just a few companies that have

Reprinted with the permission of HR MAGAZINE (formerly Personnel Administrator) published by the Society for Human Resource Management, Alexandria, VA.

Exhibit 1   Incentive POS Plan Design

	In-Network	Out-of-Network
Deductible/Copayment	$10/office visit	$300/person
Coinsurance	100%	80%
Out-of pocket maximum	$1,500/person	$1,500/person
Relative value to current indemnity offering*:	1.10	0.98

Relative values were actuarially calculated by Hewitt Assoc. to reflect POS plan design as compared to a sample indemnity plan offering. The values do not consider provider discounts, utilization savings or administrative expense charges.

taken this route. Answers to the 10 most commonly asked questions about these plans follow.

1. HOW DOES A POS PLAN ACTUALLY WORK?

Point-of-service plans usually have five characteristics in common:

- They are generally underwritten by indemnity insurance carriers, although about 15 percent of HMOs offer POS products.
- Each POS plan contracts with a network of providers to control future charge and utilization increases.
- The POS plan network emphasizes the gatekeeper approach, where primary care physicians (PCPs) direct patient care and are placed at some financial risk for medical services delivered.
- Unlike traditional HMOs, employees can go outside the network to receive services from noncontracted providers, but employees who do must pay higher deductibles and coinsurance. In POS plans, therefore, the in-network and out-of-network benefit options are significantly different to give employees the financial incentive to use in-network providers.
- In-network and out-of-network benefits costs comprise a single risk pool.

Examples of several POS plan designs are provided in Exhibits 1 and 2. In these examples, we compare the POS plans to a sample employer's traditional indemnity plan with a $200 deductible, 80 percent coinsurance provision, and a $1,500 out-of-pocket expenditure maximum.

There are two general POS plan designs: an incentive design and a disincentive design. Under the incentive approach, the employer offers more attractive in-network benefits than the traditional plan, and maintains the traditional plan of benefits (or a somewhat lower benefit offering) as the out-of-network option.

Exhibit 2 Disincentive POS Plan Design

	In-Network	Out-of-Network
Deductible/Copayment	$200/person	$400/person
Coinsurance	80%	60%
Out-of pocket maximum	$1,500/person	$3,000/person
Relative value to current indemnity offering*:	1.00	0.83

*Relative values were actuarially calculated by Hewitt Assoc. to reflect POS plan design as compared to a sample indemnity plan offering. The values do not consider provider discounts, utilization savings or administrative expense charges.

Exhibit 1 shows an in-network option with a physician office visit copayment of $10, a 100 percent coinsurance level, and the same out-of-pocket-maximum as the traditional plan. The relative value of this in-network benefit offering compared to the sample traditional plan is about 1.10 or 10 percent higher.

Exhibit 1 also illustrates an out-of-network benefit with a $300 deductible per person, an 80 percent coinsurance level, and the same out-of-pocket maximum of $1,500 per person. The relative value of the out-of-network component is approximately 0.98, or 2 percent lower than the sample traditional indemnity plan.

Alternatively, some employers choose to implement a disincentive POS plan design. Under this approach, the in-network benefits are similar to the employer's traditional plan, and the out-of-network benefits are significantly lower. Exhibit 2 shows sample in-network benefits with the same relative value as the traditional plan (that is, the relative value is 1.0).

However, the value of the out-of-network option is about 0.83, or 17 percent lower than the traditional indemnity plan. The lower relative value is largely attributable to the increased employee cost sharing required on out-of-network benefits.

2. CAN YOU REALLY SAVE MONEY BY IMPLEMENTING A POS PLAN?

Before implementing a POS plan, employers first should determine if the plan can potentially save them money. Omitting this step can be a serious mistake. POS plans are not right for all employers. In fact, evidence shows that implementing a POS plan could actually increase some employers' health-care costs. Employers should consider the following issues in determining potential savings.

- The relative value of the current plan offering compared to the POS plan (in-network and out-of-network benefits).
- Financial incentives used to encourage employees to use in-network providers.
- Current employee participation in HMO plans.
- Discounts obtained from physicians and hospitals.
- Administrative fees charged by the insurance carrier.
- Geographic coverage of the POS plan.

3. WHAT DISTINGUISHES POS PLANS FROM ONE ANOTHER?

The key element to any POS plan's success in lowering medical-cost increases is for network providers to properly manage the health-care needs of plan participants. Yet, no standard methodology exists for establishing and managing provider networks. For this reason, insurance carrier POS plan networks tend to differ in cost efficiency of care, quality of medical services, and accessibility by employees. In choosing a POS plan, each of these areas must be carefully evaluated. The following questions address these issues.

4. HOW DO YOU EVALUATE A POS NETWORK'S COST EFFICIENCY?

In general, a cost-efficient network is one where providers treat medical conditions in the least costly manner possible, while still preserving the quality of care delivered. Two methods exist for evaluating a network's cost efficiency.

Provider Profiling Method

Developing a profile of provider treatment patterns can help determine the efficiency of current network physicians and hospitals. The profiling technique lists key utilization and charge data on each provider and compares this provider-specific data to a set of treatment standards developed by medical experts. Physicians and hospitals significantly deviating from the standards can be identified and brought to the attention of the insurance carrier for corrective action.

Unfortunately, since it is difficult to obtain utilization and charge data on network providers (some insurance carriers consider this information confidential), provider profiling is not always possible. In addition, some POS plans are so new that this data does not yet exist. Thus, the profiling technique generally is limited to monitoring a network's efficiency over time—not for selecting a POS plan.

Contract Analysis Method

The second method for evaluating network efficiency looks at contractual arrangements between the insurance carrier and the network providers. These arrangements form the structural foundation of a network and determine present and future cost efficiency. That is, carriers with contracts that effectively control providers' cost, volume and intensity of services are expected to have the most cost-efficient networks over time.

5. WHAT SHOULD I LOOK FOR IN A HOSPITAL CONTRACT?

The most cost-efficient contracts place hospitals at the greatest financial risk for delivering medical services. There are four types of contract arrangements negotiated between carriers and network hospitals (in order of increasing risk transfer): discounts on billed charges, per diem, per case and capitation.

Discounts on Billed Charges

Employers and carriers have tried to control hospital costs by negotiating discounts on billed charges. However, discounts are not always better than straight-charge arrangements because hospitals have a strong incentive to increase the volume of services to balance the discounts. Some hospitals also try to offset discounts by increasing initial service charges.

Per Diem Contracts

To remove many of the negative effects of discounted-charge arrangements, some carriers are now contracting with hospitals on a per diem bases. The per diem system of reimbursement pays the hospital a predetermined amount for each day a patient is hospitalized. This system transfers more financial risk to network hospitals for services they deliver.

Many hospitals are willing to negotiate per diem contracts because they can negate some of the financial risk transferred to them simply by keeping patients in the hospital longer. Hospitals have an incentive to increase the length of stay because the first days of patient care are the most resource-intensive and costly. The final days of care are relatively inexpensive, so profit from a patient may significantly increase as length of stay increases. Several studies by the RAND Corp. show that the third and fourth days of hospital care are about half as expensive as the first two days.

Per Case Contracts

The hospital's incentive to increase length of stay caused by per diem contract arrangements can be alleviated by moving to per case reimbursement. Under the per case payment approach, hospitals are paid a fixed, predetermined amount for each patient admitted. The amount reimbursed is based on the patient's expected resource needs. This gives hospitals an incentive to reduce both length of stay and the amount of resources used to treat each case.

Case-based payment systems, however, are susceptible to their own negative utilization responses. For example, because decreasing length of stay reduces a hospital's occupancy rate, hospitals have a strong incentive to increase their admission rates to fill empty beds.

Capitation Arrangements

Capitation arrangements transfer the most financial risk to hospitals. Every month, network hospitals receive a sum of money per covered POS member, paid before any services are rendered. The amount of money each hospital receives is based on the expected need (or health risk) of a POS plan's members using that hospital over the month. In exchange for the capitation payment, hospitals are contractually obligated to provide services to covered POS members.

Hospitals providing cost-efficient care profit most under capitation arrangements because they retain all payments not used toward patient care. Therefore, hospitals have an incentive to perform fewer tests and treatments, reduce lengths of stay and decrease admission rates.

However, capitation payment systems also have their own set of problems. For instance, hospitals may withhold necessary medical services to further increase their profit margins, making quality of care a key concern. Carriers should continually monitor network hospitals to ensure that quality of care is not affected.

Moreover, as previously stated, most POS plans are not administered by HMOs, but by indemnity carriers. In certain states such as California, carriers cannot capitate providers unless they are licensed as HMOs by the state. In other states such as Maryland, laws prohibit certain types of capitated arrangements.

Our experience indicates that of the six major carriers offering POS plans in California, one carrier still negotiates discounts on billed charges for all hospital services. Two carriers negotiate per diem arrangements. The remaining three use discounts both on billed charges and per diems, depending on the type of service provided.

Therefore, unlike traditional HMOs—where more than 20 percent reimburse hospitals on a per case or capitated basis—no POS plans currently offered by indemnity carriers have per case or capitated arrangements. Thus, POS plans, still in their early stages of development, probably are not as cost efficient as group/staff model HMOs at controlling hospital expenditures.

6. WHAT MAKES A PHYSICIAN CONTRACT COST EFFICIENT?

As with hospital contracts, the most cost-efficient physician contracts are those that place physicians at significant risk for services delivered. There are three basic types of reimbursement arrangements that can be negotiated with network physicians. These are, in order of increasing risk transfer, discounts on billed charges, relative value scales and capitation.

Discounts on Billed Charges

The most common type of POS network contract for physicians is a discount on usual, customary and reasonable (UCR) charges. For traditional indemnity plans, most carriers define UCR payments for a service based on an area's customary physician charges, using the 90th percentile as a cutoff point. In other words, carriers will allow payments for a service only up to the point where 90 percent of physicians bill for that service.

One problem with the UCR system is its inflationary nature. An area's customary charges are increased as physicians continue to submit bills with charges higher than the current customary level. Therefore, UCR reimbursement rewards physicians who significantly increase their usual fees, because future reimbursement levels are based upon past charges.

Relative Value Scales

To avoid many of the negative effects of discounted UCR reimbursements, carriers have developed alternative payment systems. One such system is a relative value scale (RVS).

Basically, an RVS system differs from the UCR system in that the value among services is expressed in units rather than dollars. A dollar-based conversion factor is then used to translate unit values to actual payments.

The RVS system has at least two advantages over the UCR system. First, an RVS severs the normal link between current physician fees and future reimbursements. Therefore, physicians may significantly increase their usual charges, but payments for services are increased only when the dollar-based conversion factor is updated.

Consequently, physicians have less control over their future payments under an RVS system. Each year network physicians must negotiate with the carrier on how the conversion factor will be adjusted for inflation and other factors.

Capitation Arrangements

The main issues previously discussed regarding hospital capitation also pertain to physician capitation. In particular, capitation transfers the greatest financial risk to physicians; however, certain states prohibit the capitation of physicians.

7. HOW DOES A POS PLAN CONTROL PHYSICIANS' USE OF SERVICES?

Insurance carriers attempt to control volume and intensity of physician service either through physician utilization-review committees or by setting annual-trend performance targets.

Physician Utilization Review Committees

Under this approach, the carrier forms a committee of five to 10 utilization-review experts. These experts are responsible for reviewing and approving the medical necessity of all PCP referrals to specialists as well as all high cost and frequently performed specialist procedures.

Physician utilization-review committees typically deny about 10 percent to 15 percent of all requests for referrals and procedures. After physicians dispute the committee's original denial decision, this percentage can drop to as low as 5 percent. Thus, this process has limited value.

Trend Performance Targets

Due to the committee's low denial rates, many insurance carriers offering POS plans now use annual-trend performance targets for controlling physician volume and intensity increases. Carriers set targets based on what they consider to be reasonable physician price and utilization increases.

If the trend performance target is exceeded, network physicians forfeit a portion of their current or future income. Income reduction can be accomplished either by withholding a percentage of current payments to physicians or by limiting future reimbursements.

8. TO WHAT EXTENT ARE INSURANCE CARRIERS AT RISK FOR SERVICES PROVIDED?

Many employers attempt to shift the risk for providing health care services back to the carrier. This shifting of risk is usually accomplished in one of four ways:

Place a Portion of the Administrative-Services-Only Fee at Risk.

Under this approach, the carrier places a portion of its administrative-services-only fee at risk for several service performance guarantees, including claims turnaround time, telephone response time, patient satisfaction with the POS network, and medical claims cost targets.

The medical claims cost target may be guaranteed from one to three years and works as follows. If health-care costs exceed a certain target, the carrier shares in the financial liability with the employer; if costs are kept below the target level, both the carrier and employer share in the savings.

Obtain a Fully-Insured Product

Under this approach, the employer would pay a fixed premium per month based on the number of employees covered. The carrier is at risk for all claims incurred.

Obtain Aggregate Stop-Loss Coverage with the Carrier

The employer would self-insure all claims up to a specified dollar amount (negotiated with the carrier). The carrier then assumes the risk for claims incurred above this amount.

Negotiate a Trend Performance Guarantee

The employer may be able to negotiate with the carrier for a maximum premium rate increase in future years.

9. HOW DO YOU MEASURE THE QUALITY OF NETWORK PROVIDERS?

Determining the quality of the providers in a POS plan is not an easy process, and measuring it requires technical analysis across a number of measures, including:

Exhibit 3	Measures for Determining Quality	
Utilization Category	**Quality Measure**	**Some Areas to Analyze**
Hospital	Structural	• Accreditation by the Joint Commission on the Accreditation of Health Care Organizations • Certification for participation in Medicare • General characteristics of hospital (e.g., public)
Hospital	Process	• Sanctions by U.S. Department of Health and Human Services • Malpractice compensation • Volume of specific services performed (e.g., cardiac bypass surgery)
Hospital	Outcome	• Case-mix adjusted hospital mortality rates • Case-mix adjusted perinatal mortality rates • Adverse events (e.g., hospital-acquired infections) • Patient satisfaction survey ratings
Physician	Structural	• Medical school training • Board certifications • Hospital admitting privileges
Physician	Process	• Formal disciplinary actions by state medical boards • Sanctions by U.S. Department of Health and Human Services • Malpractice compensation
Physician	Outcome	• Adverse events (e.g., mistakes made during surgery) • Patient satisfaction ratings

- Structural measures—These measures reflect the resources and organizational arrangements in place to deliver care (for example, licensure of facilities and physician board of certification).
- Process measures—These measures reflect activities of providers in the management of patients (for example, number of a certain type of procedure performed).
- Outcome measures—These measures reflect the results or impact of care (for example, health or changes in health status).

More detailed examples of how quality can be measured are provided in Exhibit 3.

10. HOW DO I DETERMINE WHETHER EMPLOYEES CAN ACCESS NETWORK PROVIDERS?

We use the following approach for analyzing employee access to POS network providers.

Distance to Nearest Network Provider

A commonly used method for measuring access to care is to match postal zip codes of employees to network physicians. A good match indicates that network providers are geographically located in the same areas as your employees.

Adequacy of Physician-to-Enrollee Ratios

Adequate patient access to network providers requires the carrier to contract with a certain number of physicians and hospitals for every 10,000 enrollees. If all ratios are above the expected minimum level, employees should have little difficulty obtaining access to network physicians.

Capacity for Providers to Accept New Enrollees

Because hospitals generally do not have a capacity problem, this measure is designed to further evaluate access to network physician services. Physician capacity should be evaluated on an ongoing basis by monitoring employee complaints and administering patient satisfaction surveys.

Maintenance of Existing Physician/Patient Relationships

Studies show that individuals primarily choose their providers based on recommendations from friends and physicians and on the physician's reputation in the community. Geographic location of physicians is an important, although secondary, reason. Therefore, even though the geographic zip code match and ratios of physicians to enrollees may show positive results, employees still may feel there is a problem in accessing high-quality physicians.

Employers should determine how many patient/physician ties are broken in order to gain a better understanding of how many employees may perceive an access problem. In particular, an employer should determine whether those PCPs and specialists currently providing a large volume of care to employees and their families have been included in the network.

NOT FOR EVERYONE

A POS plan is not appropriate for every employer. To determine whether the POS approach is right for you, we suggest working through the following four steps:

Educate Management and Establish Objectives

One of your first steps is to form a managed-care task force. This task force would be responsible for examining all possible managed-care approaches and reaffirming the company's general health-care objectives. These objectives might range from meeting medical expense targets to minimizing adverse employee relations.

Perform a Medical Claims Analysis

Before changing from your current medical cost-containment strategy, you should first evaluate how effectively the strategy is working. An excellent way to measure its effectiveness is to perform a detailed medical claims analysis.

Analyzing medical claims will allow you to determine whether cost increases in specific benefit areas are due to increasing utilization, higher unit prices or both. Higher utilization suggests alternative controls may be necessary, while higher unit prices indicate that alternative hospital, physician or other provider reimbursement mechanisms should be considered.

Problem areas identified from the medical claims analysis may be resolved in a number of ways, only one of which is a POS plan.

Calculate Estimated Savings

As previously mentioned, before deciding on a POS arrangement, you should first determine whether it will save you money. Savings will vary by employer based on such variables as current employee participation in HMO plans, employees' locations compared to geographic coverage of the carrier' networks, and in-network and out-of-network benefit designs.

Identify Carriers Offering POS Plans

If you decide the POS approach is right for your company, the next step is to develop a preliminary list of carriers that could be involved in the bidding process. In formulating this list, you should ask yourself several questions about each carrier:

- How responsive will the carrier be to your specific needs? (For example, a dedicated service representative to answer benefit staff and employee questions, communication materials for employees, claims processing capabilities.)
- Does the carrier's provider network parallel the geographic distribution to your employee population?

- Will the carrier implement your in-network and out-of-network benefit-design options, or will the carrier require you to adopt one of its standard POS plan designs?
- Does the carrier have a mature, stable provider network, or is the carrier's network in the developmental phases?

Following these initial steps should help you determine whether the POS arrangement is worth pursuing. If the answer is yes, make sure you select a provider network that is cost efficient, high quality and accessible to a majority of employees. Take the time to develop a process for selecting and then implementing your POS plan. This action will help maximize the potential for medical cost savings over the long term.

27.   Managing Multiple Providers

A single plan design, not necessarily a single carrier, is a key to successful management of multiple managed care carriers, according to James B. Bronson, corporate director of employee benefits for Sears, Roebuck and Co., and Robert C. Varecha, district manager of benefits administration for AT&T.

Sears Health Care Alliance

Spending $500 million a year to insure 700,000 employees, retirees, and dependents, Sears was concerned about its long-term corporate strategy for health care as well as escalating costs. Like most companies, Sears tried cost shifting, utilization review, and educating employees about health care costs but with little change in overall costs, Bronson said. To begin to address these concerns, senior management formed a group to manage health care for the entire corporation. They found managed care to be a solution to the company's health care cost control and quality needs.

Prior to having a managed care program, Sears employees were covered by a multitude of plans, including four or five HMO choices, depending on their location. Under its Health Care Alliance program, employees make a point-of-service choice of provider. Employees choosing a provider in the network get higher levels of coverage than those choosing non-network providers, Bronson said.

Reprinted with permission from *Managing Employee Benefits*, Warren Gorham Lamont, Alexandria, Virginia, a division of Research Institute of America.

Long-term Strategy

Sears' long-term strategy is to phase in managed care over two to three years to eventually cover 70 to 80 percent of its workforce. It plans to phase out indemnity coverage in all but sparsely populated areas where a managed care network isn't feasible, Bronson said.

Sears has contracted with three providers to make up its managed care network covering 24,000 locations. Although the company wanted to go with a single carrier, it found that "just because a carrier does a great job providing health care in one location is no guarantee it will be able to do the job in another location," according to Bronson.

Implementation

Sears has begun to implement its Health Care Alliance network in western U.S. locations and is moving eastward. "Employee acceptance of managed care seems to be rolling in that direction," said Bronson. Implementation will continue over the next two years.

Before the implementation process began, a pilot managed care program was used to test communication strategy, plan design, and carrier ability to provide services, and to work out carrier relationships. To set up this pilot program, Sears sent out requests for proposals, with questions to determine physician turnover, maturity of network, member services, management of the network, and physician access, and it conducted on-site provider reviews, employee focus groups, and blind employee telephone surveys.

Sears wants to develop long-term relationships with carriers to minimize disruptions to employees' health care, Bronson said. If it experiences problems with a network in one city, the company will work out the problems with the carrier rather than change carriers.

Management

To ease the management of multiple carriers, the network is administered according to Sears' specifications. These include:

- A standard plan design,
- Standard administrative procedures regardless of which network an employee belongs to,
- A common name—Health Care Alliance,
- Standardized communication materials,
- Standard access requirements and service areas,
- Similar enrollment processes,

- Standard transition rules for employees with serious illnesses changing over to the network, and
- Similar risk sharing concepts.

The different carriers had to learn to work together to better balance local and national management. Each network and its management is local and deals with local issues and problems. Sears' corporate management addresses national issues. Bronson described management of the network as more hands-on than management of an indemnity program, with more involvement in the day-to-day dealings of the network.

AT&T: With a Little Help From Its Unions

AT&T developed its National Managed Health Care Network with the help of its two unions, the International Brotherhood of Electrical Workers and the Communication Workers of America. This was one of the first times unions helped develop managed care options for members, according to Robert Varecha. AT&T spends $1.2 to $1.3 billion a year on health care, and the health care issue turned out to be one of the biggest stumbling blocks in past union negotiations, and promised to remain so in the future.

The AT&T plan is similar to the Sears' plan in several respects. Like Sears' employees, AT&T employees annually elect either an HMO or the managed care network, and the employees in the network make a point-of-service choice of provider. Like the Sears' plan, benefits are lower if the employee chooses a provider outside of the network.

Network Implementation

Although AT&T wanted one carrier for employees at all 24 of its sites, like Sears it found this impractical and settled on three carriers. The network implementation process took place on a corporate and local level and involved the coordination of multiple carriers. The corporate level developed:

- The network structure,
- Financial arrangements,
- Administrative processes,
- Systems,
- Enrollment activities,
- Standardized materials,
- Initial member services, and
- Quality assurance.

Local network management sees to the overall alignment of the corporate model, Varecha said. This includes:

- Administration,
- Medical management,
- Provider relations,
- Member services, and
- Quality assurance.

To determine if a network is acceptable, management looks at numbers and locations of providers, types of systems, staffing, and the physical plant, Varecha said. Steering committees have been formed as forums for problem solving.

28.   Case Management:
Issues and Trends
Gary S. Wolfe

Case management continues to be a significant cost containment strategy for high cost illnesses and injuries. Recent polls verify that employers look to case management in an effort to control the few incidents that generate most of the costs. This article will present developments and trends in the case management field: second generation case management products, professional organizations in case management, case manager certification, program standards, selecting a case management program, and legislative activity.

As the profession has matured and proved itself to be a viable cost management tool, second generation case management products are on the horizon and some are already in the market place. The focus of second generation case management products is on controlling high dollar claims for specific diseases. Some second generation products also take the generic case management process and apply those processes to new and different environments.

One highly effective second generation product is management of high risk pregnancies. Case management programs can not only manage premature births after they occur but can manage high risk pregnancy and bring individuals to full term or near full term, preventing some premature births and thus avoiding the associated high medical costs.

Most high risk pregnancy case management programs complete risk assessments on all pregnant women to determine the level of risk. All individuals receive prenatal education via counseling, printed material, and/or videotape. Those women identified as at high risk receive additional attention from a case manager who works with the attending physician to promote a healthy pregnancy and bring the mother to full term without complications, or at least with reduced complications.

These programs are not only very successful in improving quality of care and reducing costs, they also are perceived as a true employee benefit by the employee rather than a cost containment program. It is a program that has an easy buy-in for the employee because of course no one wants a premature infant or sick newborn. Some employers have provided incentives such as waiving the deductible, or giving cash amounts or infant car seats for participating in the program.

Results are measured in different ways, such as reducing overall costs of pregnancies and deliveries, lowering length of stay, increasing compliance in prenatal programs, or assessing level of participation in the program. When evaluating a high risk pregnancy case management program, previous claim history, hospital information or even anecdotal evidence about complications of newborn and pregnancy claims can provide useful information in determining your needs. Return on investment has been reported as 5:1 in some programs.

Other second generation case management programs address chronic diseases such as asthma and diabetes. Individuals with asthma or diabetes have chronic conditions and may need frequent utilization of health services. Using diabetes as an example, a focused case management program seeking to identify individuals newly diagnosed with diabetes can avoid initial hospitalizations and utilize home health care instead for teaching about diets, medication, and blood sugar monitoring. Ongoing case management intervention focuses on education and support to make sure the individual is compliant with the prescribed therapy, thereby avoiding future hospitalizations and complications. This program for an individual newly diagnosed with diabetes can save $15-20,000 the first year. Chronic conditions requiring frequent utilization of health services are excellent opportunities for case management interventions.

Workers compensation is another area in which case management is making a significant contribution. Workers compensation medical costs are skyrocketing faster than group health costs. Although there are many reasons for these escalating costs, very little managed care has been applied to workers compensation. Using generic case management practices, case management has been able to control complicated, high cost workers compensation claims.

FORMATION OF CMSA

Case management is evolving and growing as the whole field of managed care looks at controlling health benefits costs. Many developments are occurring to legitimize case management as a profession: the formation of the Case Management Society of America, accreditation standards being developed by the Utilization Review Accreditation Commission, and the development of certification standards for case managers. These will bring about an acceptance of standards and definitions that will benefit employers by providing a basis for choosing and evaluating case management programs.

In the fall of 1990 a group of case managers met in Chicago to determine if there was sufficient interest to form a national professional association for case managers. Although several local and regional organizations had formed serving case managers' interests, there had been no national effort to form a professional association. The group meeting in Chicago under the leadership of Nell Ann Peck, R.N., founded the Case Management Society of America (CMSA). As stated in the association bylaws, the organization's purpose "is to provide the means by which persons and firms offering services or products within or to the health care case management profession may voluntarily coordinate their efforts to advance the profession in all respects." Goals of the association include:

- To provide the opportunity for the exchange of experience and opinions through discussion, study, and publication
- To promote the professionalism, science, and recognized scope of the practice of case management
- To provide a national forum for professionals actively engaged in case management
- To educate members, health care delivery agency services, medical professionals, insurance health plans and related industries, and the public in the advancement and improvement of quality care, professionals, costs/benefit effectiveness, and the health care benefits of case management
- To develop and encourage high professional standards of performance, competence, service, and conduct for those serving case managers and in case management
- To conduct and cooperate in the conduct of research and courses of study
- To promote the improved public stature and respect accorded the case management profession while meeting the best interests of the profession and the public

CMSA has held two national educational conferences, the last attended by over 500 people; the 1993 national educational conference will be held in San Francisco. Currently the major activities of the association center around government affairs and certification.

One of the early tasks the CMSA took on was a definition of case management. There had never been an accepted definition, leaving the field and profession open to misinterpretation and misrepresentation. After considerable consensus building, the following working definition has been accepted:

"Case management is a collaborative process which assesses, plans, implements, coordinates, monitors and evaluates options and services to meet an individual's health needs through communication and available resources to promote quality, cost effective outcomes."

CMSA also issued a statement concerning the process of case management.

"The case manager should facilitate communication and coordination between all members of the health care team involving the patient and family in the decision making process in order to minimize fragmentation in the health care delivery system. The case manager is the link between the individual, the providers, the payor and the community. The case manager should encourage appropriate use of medical facilities and services, improve quality of care and maintain cost effectiveness on case by case basis. The case manager is an advocate for the patient as well as the payor to facilitate a win-win situation for the patient, the health care team and the payor."

The process of case management should include the following basic elements:

1. Identification of high risk/high cost cases.
2. Assessment of the patient, the patient's needs, and the treatment goals.
3. Development of a treatment plan, in conjunction with the health care team and attending physician that is responsive to the needs and goals of the patient.
4. Implementation of needed services in a cost effective and organized manner.
5. Ongoing evaluation of the treatment plan in relationship to the desired patient outcomes.
6. Evaluation of case management interventions to promote quality service, and evaluation of the effectiveness of case management relative to the desired or optimal outcomes.

The definition and statement developed by the CMSA has been widely distributed and accepted. It has become a benchmark in defining case management services.

Current plans of the CMSA include establishing awareness of the need for national policy changes promoting case management as a strategy to ensure quality and cost-effective health care, and establishing both a regulatory and legislative environment conducive to the growth of case management.

Certification

Currently, anyone can call themselves a case manager. Although the majority of case managers are health professionals (many are registered nurses), there are many others from a variety of backgrounds calling themselves case managers. With a national consensus definition of case management in place, defining case managers is the next important step. Since there is no basic educational program for case managers, and given that many different skills and backgrounds combine to make a good case manager, certification is probably the best method of standardizing the field.

In 1990, a national task force was formed to look at the definition of case management as well as certification of case managers. This task force consisted of representatives from professional organizations involved in case management, including the Association of Rehabilitation Nurses, CMSA, American Nurses Association, Individual Case Management Association (a for-profit association focusing on education), and the National Association of Rehabilitation Professionals in the Private Sector. The task force decided that certification of case managers should be undertaken by the Certification of Insurance Rehabilitation Specialists Commission (CIRSC). This group was selected because of its reputation in standard development and testing, CIRSC was also willing to fund the cost of developing certification criteria. An expert committee was appointed to evaluate the role, function, educational requirements, and experience needed for qualified case managers. It is anticipated that the first testing for certification will occur in April of 1993.

Accreditation

Case management program accreditation is being developed by the Utilization Review Accreditation Commission (URAC). In 1990, the American Managed Care and Review Association (AMCRA)—the trade association for the managed care and utilization review industry that represents HMOs, IPAs, PPOs, utilization review organizations, and other entities—took steps to develop a national voluntary accreditation process for utilization review firms with the establishment of URAC. URAC formed a board of directors representing the major health organizations, including the American Medical Association and American Hospital Association, and organizations representing insurance companies, employers, and unions. AMCRA's position is that voluntary national accreditation is the preferred option to state-by-state regulation. In 1991, URAC published utilization review standards and began accrediting utilization review companies. The next step is to develop accreditation standards for other utilization management programs. Standards are being developed for mental health/substance abuse, and ambulatory care as well as case management. As standards are promulgated and adopted, URAC will then start accrediting such programs. National standards are important because they:

- Bring common understanding as well as consistency in case management
- Establish a basic case management process that causes minimal disruption of the health care delivery system
- Establish standards for the procedures used in case management

- Provide the basis for accrediting case management programs so the accreditation mechanism can be applied efficiently nationwide.

Currently, some eighteen states require utilization review programs to be certified in order to conduct utilization review within their borders. Most of this regulation has taken an anti-managed care position, creating obstacles that don't contribute to the outcome of the utilization review process. One state requires URAC accreditation, and in four states the state certification requirements may be waived if the company has received URAC accreditation. Regulation of case management at the state level will follow utilization review regulation and is under discussion in some states (for example, Maryland). With the development of national standards, state regulation may therefore only increase costs.

With the development of a definition of case management, certification of case managers, and accreditation of case management programs, a new level of acceptance and standard can be expected for case management. These national standards will specify expectations of the profession and define a generic process so people and groups purchasing case management will know what to expect. These standards will be important to employers, patients, and purchasers of case management so there is a common understanding of case management.

EVALUATING A CASE MANAGEMENT PROGRAM

Even with the development of national standards there is a proliferation of different types of case management programs—different in approach as well as outcome. The variety of programs, services and models is important because it allows purchasers to customize services to meet their needs and priorities. Key factors for purchasers to consider in their evaluation of a case management program for potential purchase include the answers to the following questions:

1. *Is the case management program regional or national in scope?* If you have sites in different locations, you want to insure that the case management program can adequately service your needs. If you are primarily confined to one location or region, a regional case management program might be your best choice. Case managers need to be familiar with community resources, physician practice patterns, and costs of services and providers in the area they work.

2. *Is the case management program independent or combined with other utilization management programs?* Case management programs that are part of a utilization management program tend to be more comprehensive then freestanding ones, particularly if the utilization review program provides an excellent system of case identification. If you are looking for a one-stop shop, you would want a combined utilization review/case management program.

3. *Who owns the case management program?* Is the case management program owned individually, a part of an independent utilization management firm, by a carrier, or the group at risk? If the program is owned by the group at risk, the perception is that the goals of providing quality care and controlling claim expense may not be balanced. If these goals are not equal, both you and the patient may lose. If your money is at risk, you may make decisions influencing case management which only focus on the dollar. A case management program not at monetary risk is able to render a decision based upon medical necessity, creating a better balance of the equal goals of quality and cost.

4. *What are the qualifications of the case managers?* There are many individual with a wide variety of qualifications calling themselves case managers. Most case management programs utilize registered nurses with clinical specializations and an understanding of claims and benefits. Other individuals with relevant clinical knowledge and claim experience can also make good case managers. Case managers should be uniquely qualified for each case; specialists in rehabilitation, for example, should not manage premature infant cases. Although there are some generic case management tasks, the same sophistication and specialization required to treat particular diseases and injuries are also required for the case manager.

   You should also look at the turnover of the case managers. High turnover suggests the program is not able to deliver the same quality as a firm whose staff is stable. Another quality indicator is the supervision and management of the staff. You should know how the staff are supervised and the qualifications of the supervisors.

5. *Does the case management program have physician consultants available in appropriate medical specialties?* This is very important. A case management program needs ongoing advice on specific cases from time to time. The case manager may need a review of the medical treatment as well as physician-to-physician dialogue with the treating physician. The availability of specialized physician consultants in a broad range of geographic location is a significant quality indicator of the case management program.

6. *Are the case management services provided by telephone or on-site?* The issues of being telephonic or on-site has become an issue in providing case management services. Some companies only provide on-site case management. That is, they have a case manager physically present at the location of the patient they are managing. This significantly contributes to the cost of case management; in many cases, it can double the costs. Other companies only provide case management by telephone where all work is conducted over the telephone. Without travel time and expenses, case management costs are minimized. Some companies are able to provide a combination of telephonic and on-site services. The important question to

ask is: Does it make a difference? In most cases, telephonic services provide effective case management. In extreme cases, where you may have a dysfunctional treatment team, an incompetent patient with no relatives, or other unusual circumstances, on-site case management is clearly indicated.

7. *How are cases identified?* Identification of cases is very important because if cases aren't identified in a timely and efficient manner you will not realize the benefits of case management. The most effective method of case identification is through utilization review. In utilization review, cases can be identified by diagnosis, length of stay, and/or frequency of admissions. Claims payors should also assist in identifying cases, particularly early claim activity based on diagnosis, as well as flagging claims reaching a certain dollar threshold. Individuals employers can also make referrals to case management. Overall, however, it is the responsibility of the case management program to have a case identification process that works.

8. *Does the case management program have a quality improvement program?* How is quality measured? Are there written standards developed by the case managers and physician consultants to guide the case managers in case work? Is the program monitored with regular feedback to each case manager? What is the appeal procedure if someone wants services that the case manager has denied? The whole issue of quality cannot be understated. If you are purchasing case management services, you should have an excellent understanding of the quality improvement methods used in case management and know the answers to these questions. Case management programs should work with their clients to determine each client's expectations. Setting forth these expectations initially will assist in starting the program.

9. *How are results in case management measured?* Results are somewhat determined by what you wanted when you purchased the case management services. Was it aggressive cost savings? Was it the provision of an advocate for your employees? It is important to delineate those expectations for cost, savings, and quality of care in order to determine the best means of measuring results. Any results reported must be credible and the methodology of measuring results should be explained to and accepted by the client.

10. *How are case management activities and results reported?* Does the case management program make regular written and telephonic reports about specific case activity as well as aggregate activities? Knowing what activity is occurring on cases is important. Many times benefit personnel are asked specific questions about cases, as well as have a general curiosity about what is going on. Aggregate activities should be reported on a regular basis depending on the total number of cases being worked.

LEGISLATIVE ACTIVITY

There is considerable legislative activity, at both the state and federal level, addressing case management. In most instances, case management is perceived by legislators as improving access and controlling costs.

Rep. Ron Wyden of Oregon introduced H.R. 4243, which if enacted would become the Brain Injury Rehabilitation Quality Act of 1992. This bill would amend Title XIX of the Social Security Act to provide coverage, under state Medicaid plans, of case management services for individuals who suffer traumatic brain injuries. It would set standards for marketing brain injury services, create a registry of traumatic brain injuries, develop state specific programs for the prevention of traumatic brain injury, conduct studies, and develop reporting requirements. It would also direct the Health Care Policy and Research Agency to conduct a study to identify common therapeutic interventions used for the rehabilitation of traumatic brain injury patients. This bill should be recognized as a serious proposal because it creates a new federal entitlement and because although it only mandates benefits for Medicaid recipients, Medicaid/Medicare benefits frequently become the basic coverage standard for group health policies.

With the escalating costs and decreased accessibility of health care, as well as changes in the make-up of the Congress, the next few years will see major health care reform. Specific legislation like the Wyden bill dealing with brain injury rehabilitation stand a good chance of moving through Congress and becoming law.

Some states, including California and Florida, have passed legislation affecting case management. In both states, case management is written into proposed legislation concerning workers compensation reform. Florida has already adopted legislation mandating case management on certain workers compensation cases, and California has developed several pilot models and is evaluating the use of case management to improve access and control costs for selected types of cases, such as high risk pregnancies and AIDS. As standards, certification, and accreditation for case management develop and as the general acceptance of case management as an effective method for addressing spiraling costs increases, there will be more legislation.

Case management continues to evolve with the development of second generation case management products, the promulgation of standards, certification and accreditation, and most recently the introduction of federal and state legislation. It is not a panacea (as thought by some) but a cost effective strategy that combined with other strategies, can control health care costs. Benefit staff and other purchasers of case management services will continue to have an important role in helping to shape the case management field.

29. Prospective Screening of Diagnostic Testing: A Valuable Tool

Madelon Lubin Finkel

The elimination of unneeded services is a key to reducing medical costs and enhancing quality of care. Diagnostic tests have been a target of efforts to reduce costs primarily because they are discretionary and often appear to be unnecessary. Believing that the concept of prior review for many diagnostic tests is a good one, this pilot study sought to evaluate prospectively the propriety of diagnostic tests ordered during the first half of 1989 on individuals insured through a major insurance carrier. A physician review found that 21 percent of the tests were deemed inappropriate, leading to the conclusion that prospective review can be an effective means of screening inappropriately ordered tests.

The explosion in the type and volume of diagnostic tests performed throughout the 1970s and 1980s represents a significant yet comparatively neglected factor in rising health care expenditures. The greater utilization of more sophisticated tests in lieu of, or in combination with, previously used simpler ones is as important as the growth in the sheer number of services (volume) and the shift in physician practice patterns for a given condition or diagnosis (intensity).

Ironically, during the past two decades health care costs have increased despite progress in reducing inpatient services: It is the outpatient sector that has seen a huge increase in volume and intensity of services. Recently the rapid escalation of the cost of health care has provided the impetus for the payers of

Reprinted, with permission, from *Benefits Quarterly.*

care to focus attention on high cost, high volume procedures performed on an outpatient basis. Outpatient diagnostic laboratory and X-ray tests, for example, increased 21.2 percent per person from 1987 to 1988, while prescriptions and outpatient surgeries increased 11 percent per person and routine physician visits increased a mere 1.9 percent per person during this same time period.[1] Evidence also shows significant growth in diagnostic clinical laboratory testing done under Medicare Part B. Researchers found that four-fifths of this growth resulted from an increase in the number of services per enrollee. Rapid growth was characteristic of all test types.[2]

Excessive utilization of diagnostic tests, ranging from the comparatively inexpensive complete blood count to the most expensive endoscopies and imaging studies, has become part of the debate over rising health care costs. Diagnostic tests have been a frequent target of efforts to reduce costs primarily because they are discretionary and often appear to be unnecessary.[3,4,5] Hence, utilization review, which has focused on the necessity, appropriateness and efficiency of medical/surgical services by means of prior authorization of hospital admissions and length-of-stay determinations, has been expanded to include a prospective review of services ordered, such as diagnostic tests and procedures. The purpose of such a review is to ensure that appropriate indications exist for the procedure to be performed, to ensure that there is a therapeutic effectiveness and to ensure that the information gained from the procedure is incorporated into a plan for patient care.

Logically, one measure of good care is not having unnecessary tests and procedures performed. Not only do inappropriate services jeopardize quality of care, but they are often very costly. A survey of 720 physicians practicing in central and western Massachusetts, for example, found that the majority felt that major technologies (58 percent), major procedures (57 percent) and inappropriate ordering of diagnostic tests (48 percent) were very important contributions to increasing health care costs.[6] The RAND Corporation estimates that the performance of unnecessary tests adds more than $50 billion a year to the nation's $600 billion health care bill.[7]

The literature abounds with references showing that physicians order more tests than can be justified on the basis of clinical need or improved outcomes for patient care. A recent study[8] found statistically significant differences in the ordering of diagnostic imaging studies among primary physicians who used imaging equipment in their offices and physicians who always refer patients to radiologists, and the patients incurred considerably higher charges for diagnostic imaging than patients who were referred to radiologists. Schroeder and Showstack[9] showed strong financial incentives for physicians to incorporate imaging into an office practice.

In order to guard against unnecessary care, it is necessary to define it and to delineate the circumstances under which a test or procedure is warranted or effective.[10] If the appropriate indications for a test or procedure were clearly

Table 1. Commonly Performed Diagnostic Tests (Inpatient) per 100,000 Population, 1980 - 1987

Procedure	ICD-9	1980	1983	1985	1987	% Change 1980 - 1987
Angiocardiography	88.5	230.0	342.7	548.4	821.0	+256.9
Using Contrast Material						
Cardiac Catheterization	37.21-23	313.0	439.1	578.4	722.1	130.7
CT Scan–Abdominal	88.01	14.3	55.5	97.9	135.7	+849.0
CT Scan–Head	87.03	85.2	214.4	340.5	378.2	+343.9
Endoscopy						
Biliary Tract	51.1-11	4.9	9.0	8.6	17.0	+247.0
Colonscopy (Fiberoptic)	45.23	4.9	18.1	35.4	53.8	998.0
ERCP*	52.91	1.3	8.6	13.9	10.8	+730.8
Small Intestine	45.13	124.6	205.4	221.1	271.0	+117.5
MRI–Brain	88.91	-	-	-	20.7	-
MRI–Chest and Myocardium	88.92	-	-	-	0.7	-
MRI–Spine	88.93	-	-	-	10.8	-
Myelogram	87.21	133.6	173.9	183.9	173.8	+30.1

*Endoscopic retrograde cannulation of pancreatic duct.

Source: National Center for Health Statistics, Hospital Discharge Survey.

defined and widely disseminated, opportunities for misuse would be diminished. To a certain extent, there is a lack of consensus within the professional community regarding appropriate indications for care. Medical education and training, type of practice, the legal system, economic incentives and peer review are some of the factors influencing practice behavior of physicians, giving rise to the situation in which tests could be performed for seemingly questionable reasons.[11]

Researchers from the RAND Corporation examined the propriety of use of carotid endarterectomy, coronary angiography and upper gastrointestinal (GI) tract endoscopy, the latter two being frequently ordered and expensive tests. Under conditions of their study, they found significant levels of inappropriate care use: 32 percent of cases for endarterectomy, 17 percent of cases for coronary angiography and 17 percent for upper GI tract endoscopy.[12] In a followup to this study, the researchers found that inappropriate use accounted for 28 percent of the variance in the county rates for coronary angiography but, for the other two procedures, no significant correlations were found between inappropriateness of use and rate of use.[13] Inappropriate use of the procedures occurred in areas with low usage rates as well as in areas with high usage rates.

Reierstein *et al.* looked at the appropriateness of endoscopy in a large patient population. While fiberoptic endoscopy represents a major technological advance in gastroenterology (GI), the procedures are expensive and can have complications. This study found that 17 percent of all upper GI endoscopies were done for inappropriate reasons and 11 percent for equivocal reasons.[14]

Furthermore, there is ample evidence that excessive utilization of testing occurs especially in the form of unnecessary test repetition. Several factors may account for overutilization or inappropriate utilization of diagnostic tests:

- Misinterpretation of test results or a high degree of false positives, which lead to repeat testing
- Fear of malpractice suit, which provides the impetus for defensive medicine and increases utilization and drives up health care costs
- New technology creates new tests and procedures, but old techniques die hard; it has been observed that when new technologies are instituted, they often are used *in addition to* those they are meant to replace.
- Physician practice habits, too, are a factor. Inexperience or lack of knowledge may cause some physicians to order more tests than are warranted or appropriate.[15]

NATIONAL TRENDS

Table I illustrates the trend in several commonly performed diagnostic procedures. The rates expressed per 100,000 population were obtained from the National Center for Health Statistics (NCHS) and reflect procedures performed in hospitals. Therefore, they should be considered an *underestimate* as many of

Table 2. Most Frequently Performed Radiology and Imaging Procedures, 1988

Rank	Procedure	Total Performed
1	CT Scan–Head	1,399,280
2	Diag. Ultrasound–Heart	967,907
3	Routine Chest X-ray	765,930
4	CT Scan–Abdominal	587,942
5	Diag. Ultrasound–Abdominal	478,698
6	Isotope Vascular Scan	355,826
7	Other CT scan	348,945
8	Isotope Bone Scan	315,480
9	Diag. Ultrasound–Digestive Tract	313,411
10	Isotope Pulmonary Scan	274,494
11	Abdominal X-ray	256,637
12	Lower GI Series	249,069
13	Chest X-ray	246,034
14	Ultrasound–Head and Neck	224,067
15	Ultrasound–Urinary Tract	218,048

Source: National Center for Health Statistics.

these procedures are performed outside of the hospital and are not included in the statistics compiled by the NCHS. The data show a huge increase in the rate of endoscopies, especially in colonoscopies and endoscopic retrograde cannulation of pancreatic duct (ERCP). As gastrointestinal and miscellaneous digestive and bowel disorders are one of the most common causes for admission to a hospital among people ages 40 to 49, 50 to 59 and 60 to 64, those who are admitted under the DRG codes for these conditions would probably undergo a gastrointestinal endoscopy.

The NCHS data also show that rates of computer tomography (CT) scans increased significantly during the 1980s, but widespread use of magnetic resonance imaging (MRI) did not exist prior to 1987. It would be surprising if the 1988 and 1989 data do not show huge increases in the use of this imaging procedure. Table II further demonstrates the most frequently performed radiology and imaging procedures performed in 1988.

PURPOSE OF STUDY

Believing that the concept of prior review for many diagnostic tests is a good one, this pilot study sought to evaluate prospectively the propriety of diagnostic tests and procedures by ascertaining the degree to which these services were delivered in accordance with established professional standards (quality of care). The overriding consideration of this review process was that the proposed test be warranted and appropriate before it was performed and to ensure that repeat studies would be done at medically appropriate intervals. This study did not attempt to address strategies to reduce physician ordering of tests; others have presented such a discussion.[16]

NEED FOR PROCEDURE-SPECIFIC GUIDELINES

Numerous professional associations have developed or are in the process of developing guidelines to establish criteria for standards of care. These guidelines delineating the indications and contraindications for care have been developed by consensus to establish standards of care.[17,18,19] The American Medical Association (AMA), the RAND Corporation and a consortium of academic medical centers are in the process of jointly developing practice guidelines and standards for dozens of frequently performed procedures. Additionally, medical necessity guidelines for numerous procedures have been issued as part of the Blue Cross and Blue Shield Association's Medical Necessity Program[20,21] in cooperation with the following medical specialty organization: American College of Radiology, American College of Physicians, American College of Nuclear Physicians, American College of Neurology, Society of Nuclear Medicine, American Association of Neurological Surgeons, American Academy of Pediatrics and American College of Obstetricians and Gynecologists. An annotated *Directory of Medical Practice Guidelines* has been prepared by the editors of *Report on Medical Guidelines and Outcomes research*. The standards of care used in this study were based on the above guidelines.

METHODOLOGY

The pilot study sample consists of individuals across the United States, insured through a major insurance carrier in 1989, who were recommended to have an elective diagnostic test or procedure performed. Clearly it is not cost effective to require a review for every diagnostic test. Rather, it is important to focus on the frequently ordered, expensive diagnostic tests since the cost savings potential for a reduction in excessive or inappropriate utilization of such tests is much greater. Any emergency test or procedure was automatically excluded from the review process.

This prospective review program, implemented as a new benefit in January 1989, became part of the insurance company's established utilization review/managed care program in which the insurance company required prior notification from the attending physician.

Once notification was made, the insurance company sent a facsimile to Sentinel Review Services, Inc., of Millwood, New York, a nationwide review organization whose purpose is to conduct such reviews. All reviews were carried out by board-certified physicians affiliated with major medical centers in the New York City area. The physician reviewers are certified in the following specialties: pathology, colon/rectal surgery (one a certified endoscopist), cardiology and radiology. It is important to note that the physician reviewers are not associated with the insurance company nor with the attending physician. They are impartial reviewers who receive a flat fee per case for Sentinel Review Services.

Upon notification of review, the physician reviewer contacts the attending physician for verification of the proposed test or procedure and for explicit information (i.e., demographic factors; pertinent medical history, including results of any tests previously done; pertinent prescription drug treatments; and result of any therapies tried). Once the physician reviewer has all of the pertinent information, a review of the case is made. All reviews are conducted within 24 hours of notification, thus avoiding any inconvenience or delays in testing due to the program requirement. The reviewing physician has the opportunity to discuss the recommendations with the primary physician and to explain why the test or procedure should not be done, if such a determination has been made.

The medical propriety and necessity of the requested test or procedure is determined on the basis of specifically designed medical criteria and guidelines as discussed earlier. Procedures that are reviewed include CT and MRI scans, myelograms, angiograms and endoscopic procedures.

FINDINGS

Forty-eight cases were reviewed during the first six months of 1989 (see listing in Table III). In almost 21 percent of the cases, the physician reviewers felt that the test or procedures should not be performed, as it was not medically indicated based on the procedure-specific guidelines. While the total number of cases reviewed is small, the high rate of nonconfirmation is indicative of the proportion of diagnostic tests performed for possibly questionable medical reasons. The following case studies illustrate a few of the cases for which the proposed procedure was deemed inappropriate.

Case Study 1

A markedly obese 62 year old male had been diagnosed as having a submucosal lesion in the distal sigmoid and a smaller one in the distal descending colon, both

Table 3. Diagnostic Procedures Review

Procedure	Agreed	Not Agreed	% Not Agreed
Cardiac Cath.	4	–	–
CT–Abdominal	1	–	–
CT–Ankle	1	–	–
CT–Back	1	–	–
CT–Chest	1	–	–
CT–Head	4	–	–
CT–Spine	2	–	–
Colectomy	–	1	100.0
Colonoscopy	6	3	33.3
Cytoscopy	5	1	16.7
Endoscopy–GI	1	1	50.0
Gastrectomy	1	–	–
Gastroscopy	2	1	33.3
Bone Scan	1	–	–
MRI–Back	–	2	100.0
MRI–Spine	2	–	–
MRI–Foot	1	–	–
Myelogram	4	1	20.0
Sigmoidoscopy	1	–	–
Total	38	10	20.8

of which were diagnosed in the course of removal of two adenomatous polyps of the proximal rectum. His physician at this time wanted to perform a colectomy. The patient described no obstructive bowel symptomatology or abdominal discomfort. After review of records and previous operative findings, the physician reviewer felt that the lesion was most likely to be a benign one and not likely to produce any obstruction in the near future, if ever. It was deemed that the procedure was not warranted or appropriate and that the operation posed a significant risk in this less-than-good risk patient, who also had a past medical history of coronary occlusion with subsequent angioplasty done four years earlier.

Case Study 2

A 36 year old male with lumbar strain had been recommended to have an MRI. After examination of pertinent history and findings, the physician reviewer deemed that the MRI was not called for at this time as conservative treatment had not been tried. It was recommended that physical therapy, pain medication and muscle relaxing medication should be tried first. The patient subsequently recovered without having the MRI.

Case Study 3

A 59 year old female was recommended to have a cystoscopy. She had a left ureterectomy three years previously for Grade III transitional cell carcinoma. She was taking mitomycin and having cystoscopies every three to six months. The previous three cystoscopies performed over the past year and a half were negative. The reviewer felt that annual cystoscopies were indicated.

DISCUSSION

Until recently, there have been few pressures within the system to limit price or to discourage utilization of diagnostic services. Unfortunately, few mechanisms have been developed to ensure the appropriateness of outpatient diagnostic procedures. Fiscal realities dictate, however, that the economic consequences of excessive and inappropriate utilization of diagnostic tests should not be ignored any longer. The volume and cost of the proliferation of diagnostic tests have provided the impetus to focus attention on this component of health care.

This study, and others like it, clearly show the need to formulate and disseminate uniform guidelines and standards for commonly performed tests and procedures. Both a review of the literature on the topic of diagnostic testing and an analysis of data compiled by NCHS make it clear that the reliance on medical technology has exploded in the absence of agreed-upon practice guidelines. It is hoped that the development of meaningful guidelines and standards will mean that physicians will be less inclined to prescribe or perform unnecessary tests or surgery. The guidelines will serve as a consensus on the correct way to practice medicine. While it is essential to develop standards and guidelines for specific tests, prior authorization is another method for screening inappropriate procedures.

On the basis of the pilot study, it is concluded that a prospective review of diagnostic testing can be an effective means of screening inappropriately ordered tests. The majority of persons for whom a test was deemed inappropriate did not subsequently have the procedure performed. No complaints were received from either the patient or the physician about the program. As retrospective review studies of this sort have shown, diagnostic tests are being performed for questionable reasons. In this study, the recommendations for the tests were reviewed prospectively, thus potentially obviating the need for the procedure to be performed. The cost savings potential is obvious. Yet, cost containment's objective should not merely be a reduction in the number of procedures performed, but the elimination of those that are performed inappropriately. The enhancement of quality of care is an intended byproduct of prospective review.

1.   Corporate Health Strategies. *Information Management Bulletin,* Spring 1989.

2. G Dodds and L Etheredge, "Trends in Laboratory Testing Under Medicare Part B," *Health Affairs,* Summer 1989, 111-115.

3. FF Griner, "Use of Laboratory Test in a Teaching Hospital: Long-Term Trends: Reductions in Use and Relative Cost," *Annals of Internal Medicine,* February 1979, 243-248.

4. AM Epstein and BJ McNeil, "Relationship of Beliefs and Behavior in Test Ordering," *American Journal of Medicine,* May 1986: 865-870.

5. SA Schroeder, "Strategies for Reducing Medical Costs by Changing Physicians' Behavior: Efficacy and Impact on Quality of Care," *International Journal of Technology Assessment,* 1987, 39-50.

6. HL Greene, RJ Goldberg, H Beattie *et al.,* "Physician Attitudes Toward Cost Containment," *Archives of Internal Medicine,* September 1989, 1966-1968.

7. *Business Insurance,* 26 March 1990.

8. BJ Hillman, CA Joseph and MR Mabry, "Frequency and Costs of Diagnostic Imaging in Office Practice—A Comparison of Self-Referring and Radiologist-Referring Physicians," *New England Journal of Medicine,* December 1990, 323 No. 23: 1604-1608.

9. SA Schroeder and JA Showstack, "Financial Incentives to Perform Medical Procedures and Laboratory Tests: Illustrative Models of Office Practice," *Medical Care,* 1978, Vol 16, No. 4: 289-298.

10. LL Leape, "Practice Guidelines and Standards: An Overview," *Quality Review Bulletin,* February 1990, 42-49.

11. VR Fuchs and AM Garber, "The New Technology Assessment," *New England Journal of Medicine,* 6 September 1990, 323, No. 10: 673-677.

12. MR Chassin, J Kosecoff, RE Park *et al.,* "Does Inappropriate Use Explain Geographic Variations in the Use of Health Care Services?" *Journal of the American Medical Association,* 1987, 2533-2537.

13. LL Leape, RE Park, DH Solomon *et al.,* "Does Inappropriate Use Explain Small-Area Variations in the Use of Health Care Services?" *Journal of the American Medical Association,* 2 February 1990, 263, No. 5: 669-672.

14. O Reierstein, J Skjoto, CD Jacobsen *et al.,* "Complications of Fiberoptic Gastrointestinal Endoscopy: Five Years' Experience in a Central Hospital," *Endoscopy,* January 1987, 1-6.

15. FL Ham, "The High Cost of Medical Technology: Who's to Blame?" *Business & Health,* July 1989, 22-31.

16. JS Spiegel, MF Shapiro, B Berman *et al.,* "Changing Physician Test Ordering in A University Hospital," *Archives of Internal Medicine,* March 1989, 549-553.

17. JT Kelly and JE Swartwout, "Development of Practice Parameters by Physician Organizations," *Quality Review Bulletin,* February 1990, 54-57.

18. Committee on Endoscopic Utilization, "Appropriate Use of Gastrointestinal Endoscopy," American Society for Gastrointestinal Endoscopy, 1986.

19. KL Kahn, ed., *Indications for Selected Medical and Surgical Procedures* (Santa Monica: RAND Corporation, 1986).

20. Blue Cross and Blue Shield Association, *Medical Necessity Guidelines on Cardiac Care* (Chicago: Blue Cross and Blue Shield Association, 1984).

21. Blue Cross and Blue Shield Association, *Issues Guidelines to Reduce Diagnostic Imaging Procedures* (Chicago: Blue Cross and Blue Shield Association, 1984).

30. Direct Contracting:
Utah's Managed Approach Saves State Millions
Louis Kertesz

The State of Utah's managed care approach for state employees may serve as a model for other states' plans.

By directly contracting with providers and establishing standard fees for services, the Utah Public Employees Group Health program has held health care cost increases to 6.6 percent in each of the past three years.

In fact, over just the past two fiscal years, which end June 30, the state's aggressive management of health care for 75,000 employees, dependents and early retirees who are not yet eligible for Medicare has saved the state at least $10 million, according to Joan Ogden Actuaries of Salt Lake City.

Had the state not taken such measures, its medical cost hikes would have approached the 15 percent to 20 percent faced by other Utah employers in the last two years, she said.

Employers' health care costs nationwide increased an average of 18.6 percent in 1988, 16.7 percent in 1989 and 17.1 percent in 1990, according to consultant A. Foster Higgins & Co.

Consultants say employers would do well to study and apply the techniques Utah used to assertively manage health care costs.

Utah's techniques include:

- Directly contracting with providers to participate in its managed indemnity plan, based on provider profiles developed in-house and—since mid-1990—with the help of statistical criteria used by its consultant.
- Establishing standard fees for most surgical and outpatient procedures, which inhibits costly "unbundling" of services.
- Encouraging competition among the state's health maintenance organizations.

And to reduce health care costs, Utah has developed programs like paying plan members in the managed indemnity plan for good loss experience and rewarding all employees for adopting healthier lifestyles.

Although not every employer can contract directly with providers, "where certain factors are present, it's worth serious exploration by every major employer," said Glenn Meister, a principal with A. Foster Higgins in Los Angeles.

"There's evidence here," as there is with other major employers that have directly contracted with providers, "that when an employer has enough market share in a given area to go directly to the providers and structure these arrangements," the resulting benefits are significant, Mr. Meister said.

Directly contracting with providers can "truly pay dividends not only from the fixed-cost standpoint" but also in the "philosophical change" in the way care is provided and obtained, he said.

"My one caution would be from a liability standpoint," Mr. Meister observed. When employers direct employees to certain providers based on specific information, "they need to be careful about the underlying information they're using," because if it is wrong, "it could come back to haunt them."

But that caution should not deter an employer with a strong market presence from exploring the possibility of directly contracting with providers, Mr. Meister asserted.

Many employers could make use of Utah's "information-based approach" to "assertive management" of provider behavior, agreed David Rinaldo, a consultant with TPF & C, the benefits consulting division of Towers, Perrin, Forster & Crosby Inc. in Valhalla, N.Y. Mr. Rinaldo helped Utah determine the most efficient providers for its preferred provider organization.

Linn Baker, director-public employee group insurance at the Utah State Retirement Board in Salt Lake City, said he has taken a "market-based approach" that focuses on price and competition in steering Utah's successful attack on health care costs.

"It comes as no surprise to me as an economist to know that the marketplace isn't working" in keeping health care costs down for most employers, Mr. Baker said.

"How can the marketplace work when the people who are ordering or purchasing the care—the doctors—aren't paying for the care?" Mr. Baker said.

"Physicians purchase the majority of health care services; employers and the government pay for it," he explained.

However, physicians "don't know what the price of the care is and they don't care. We as consumers have no way of knowing before we have some major medical situation occur what the cost is going to be," he said.

Mr. Baker said he believes the elements of managed care, like preferred provider networks and utilization review, are "necessary" but added that "they don't seem to be controlling the costs."

"It seems to me people ought to be talking about why the marketplace isn't working and what we can do to make it work," he asserted.

Under the Utah Public Employees Group Health program, employees and retirees can enroll in a self-funded traditional indemnity plan, a self-funded managed indemnity plan with a PPO feature—at a lower cost—or two health maintenance organizations.

Half the plan members are enrolled in the managed indemnity plan with the PPO feature, 41 percent in the traditional indemnity plan and 9 percent in the HMOs.

The first step in designing Utah's system was setting up a PPO eight years ago, Mr. Baker explained. That was done after studying provider profiles to screen out those who were inefficient, he explained.

A year and a half ago, the screening process for 1,700 primary care physicians was greatly enhanced by the use of statistical criteria known as Harrington Patterns, which are used to measure proper patterns of treatment.

The criteria were developed by a physician, Donald Harrington, who founded a company called Concurrent Review Technology Inc. in Shingle Springs, Calif., to license the criteria, TPF & C's, Mr. Rinaldo explained.

The Harrington Patterns were developed by using a series of "consensus panels of board-certified, knowledgeable physicians" who agreed on certain treatment norms for various procedures, according to Mr. Rinaldo.

Mr. Rinaldo and TPF&C helped process the data on providers furnished by the state of Utah and, using the Harrington criteria, developed a set of reports and physician profiles for the state.

The Harrington Patterns not only helped Utah choose panels of physicians but also help the state continually review and adjudicate treatment, Mr. Baker added.

For example, one Harrington criterion is the maximum number of office visits normally required for treatment of a specific illness as well as the tests normally prescribed for that condition. "A physician who routinely exceeds this maximum is identified as potentially aberrant." Mr. Rinaldo said.

The Harrington Patterns are "a very powerful screening tool that really allows you to identify the most questionable physicians in an area and does so using clinically validated criteria, so you can approach a physician on a professional basis and discuss the reasons why his profile is so far from the norm," Mr. Rinaldo said.

"We found that some physicians as much as 80 percent of the time were ordering lab tests that had nothing to do with the diagnosis," Mr. Baker explained.

In addition, TPF&C periodically provides Utah with updated information on the providers' Harrington Patterns. "We do the analysis and present the results on a continuous basis to ensure that the (physician's) behavior has in fact been modified," Mr. Rinaldo said.

In addition to more accurate provider selection criteria, the Utah plan also has negotiated standardized fees for bundled services—or so-called global fees—for 95 percent of surgical procedures.

A year and a half ago it expanded those fees to include a "facilities charge" and anesthesia charges for outpatient services.

"Eight years ago we found there were consultants out there who were increasing physicians' incomes by telling them how to unbundle their services," Mr. Baker explained.

"Then they come to the insurance companies and the claims payers and teach them how to bundle them back up. It's like a game we're playing," he continued.

"A la carting" has always been a problem, he said, but it recently has become much worse, with doctors "feeling the pinch" of managed care and greater competition for the health care dollar.

By negotiating global fees with providers, the Utah plan is assured of stable prices for procedures.

For example, "a normal delivery is $1,000," Mr. Baker said. "Doctors are told, 'We don't care whether you do an ultrasound or other tests, the fee remains $1,000,' " he said.

Global fees were developed inhouse with input from the medical community. The state adopted as the fee it would pay the 50th percentile of physician charges for a group of services essential to a certain procedure, like child delivery.

Using the same method, Utah also has negotiated fees for office procedures, Mr. Baker said.

Once a physician completes a procedure, like a delivery, the physician receives immediate payment by depositing a medical claim draft into his or her bank account.

"Physicians have to call us when the baby is delivered, and we give them an authorization number for their draft" so the drafts can be deposited, Mr. Baker explained.

"Physicians like it because it's immediate cash—it eliminates the claim. We like it. It controls utilization, plus it gives us a very good price," he said.

Doctors attach a copy of the medical claim draft to the itemized bill when it's sent to the plan, and the bill is retrospectively reviewed for appropriateness.

The Utah plan also has negotiated global fee arrangements with University Hospital in Salt Lake City, which is affiliated with the University of Utah, and LDS Hospital in Salt Lake City for heart transplants and with University Hospital for bone marrow transplants.

The fee is the same regardless of whether the patient is covered under the state's traditional indemnity plan or the plan with the PPO option.

And, the fee structure places University Hospital at risk for part of the cost of bone marrow transplant. Under this arrangement, the plan pays a base fee of $90,000, and the hospital is at risk for the next $70,000, if those costs are incurred. Costs beyond that $160,000 level are shared equally by the hospital and the plan.

Utah's preventive care program is also cost-effective in that it does not pay indiscriminately for a "generic" routine physical exam. "A routine physical exam can cost $300 and include a lot of unnecessary tests," Mr Baker explained.

"So we went to the health department and found out what people were at risk for at different stages of their lives, and what we should be paying for that is cost effective," he explained.

For routine physicals, the plan pays for only those tests specified as appropriate for the member's age.

Other cost-containing elements in the Utah plan include:

- Partial premium rebates for members enrolled in the PPO with few claims.

  Utah encourages employees to join its PPO—and to stay healthy—with its "Prevention Plus" program, which offers premium rebates of up to $240 per family, $160 for a family of two and $120 for individuals with few claims.

  The rebates decrease as a member's claims costs rise.

- Encouraging rural members of the traditional indemnity plan to ask non-PPO providers to accept preferred provider fees.

  Those employees had been willing to drive long distances and use preferred providers for some outpatient services in return for lower copayments.

  But, rural hospitals were complaining that they were losing a great number of patients, Mr. Baker explained.

  So plan members were encouraged to persuade rural providers to charge the preferred provider price.

- Paying employees to exercise, stop smoking and make other lifestyle changes to reduce their health risks.

  Utah pays the cost of employees' attendance at a workshop on lifestyle changes and then pays them for making healthy changes to their lifestyle. For example, an employee can earn $100 by giving up smoking and up to $60 a year for exercising regularly.

  What makes the program effective is "not the money—it's the incentive" to make changes that ultimately control the cost of health care for those employees, Mr. Baker said.

  Last year, 4,067 employees attended the workshops. Of those, 1,476 received a bonus for exercising, 843 received at least $30 for losing weight, 139 received a bonus for lowering their cholesterol level, 77 received the smoking cessation bonus and 57 received a bonus for lowering their blood pressure.

- Devising prescription drug reimbursement schedules that encourage employees to shop for the best price for drugs and immunizations.

Utah has set up its own drug card program, after unsuccessfully trying out a program from a large drug company.

That company "approached us several years ago and offered us a drug card for wholesale purchases, and the first year our costs went up 80 percent," because "it was too easy to use our drug card. After a $3 to $5 copayment, the consumer doesn't know what the drug costs. Even if he's using the more expensive drug, it still costs only $5," Mr. Baker explained.

Since the large drug company could not make the changes the Utah plan wanted, "we decided to do our own drug card program. Currently, our preferred druggists will accept 90 percent of wholesale as payment in full. If our employees go to the preferred druggist, they have to pay 10 percent and the dispensing fee, so our cost is 80 percent," Mr. Baker said.

As for the dispensing fee, the druggists were told, "Set whatever fee you want, but our cardholders have to pay it, and we're going to tell them to shop around for the best dispensing fee," he continued. The result was "our average dispensing fee went down about 40 percent. The marketplace worked," he asserted.

The Utah plan also encourages its employees to be smart consumers when it comes to children's immunizations. "Some pediatricians are charging $38, but the health department charges only $16" for immunizations, Mr. Baker explained.

"So we said we'll give the employee $15 and the employee will choose whether to make the large copayment," Mr. Baker said. "And, it's working."

Even with all of these efforts, Utah believes its health care costs will increase by 10 percent in the fiscal year ending June 30, 1992.

Aggressive techniques can do so much, Mr. Baker said, "and after that, we're in the stream like everyone else."

So, beginning in July, the Utah plan will become even more aggressive in attempting to control rising costs by establishing a "Designated Service Plan."

Through this program, the state will designate the most efficient providers for 20 high-volume inpatient procedures.

Initially, members of the PPO and the indemnity plan will be able to use the designated service providers and receive more generous benefits than if they used preferred providers, Mr Baker explained.

The state envisions later expanding the designated service plan and making it a stand-alone plan, like its PPO. A lower premium for the designated service plan would be an incentive for employees to join.

The program will be phased in over the course of a year.

The plan is an attempt "intervene before the selection" of providers, Mr. Baker explained. Employee health care booklets will feature categories of services with the designated providers listed in each category, he said. The booklet will be designed "as an educational tool for employees," with details and explanations of the costs of procedures, Mr. Baker said.

Utah also is attacking cost increases in its HMO arrangements.

In its negotiations with its two HMOs—FHP Health Care of Fountain Valley, Calif., and Intermountain Health Care of Salt Lake City—Utah specifies that it wants a three-year contract and that annual premiums cannot increase more than the increase in the Consumer Price Index for medical care in Utah.

Utah also insists that there not be any provisions in the HMO benefit package—like a cap on the prescription drug benefit—that result in excluding high-risk individuals.

"We're also concerned that the HMOs selected have panels of physicians that don't overlap. We refer to that as a vertical system. We want these vertical systems to compete with one another, and if you're offering the same benefits and the same providers, I'm not sure you've really accomplished one of the reasons you're offering alternative plans," he explained.

Part 7

MANAGED MENTAL HEALTH CARE

31. Seeking Sane Solutions: Managing Mental Health and Chemical Dependency Costs

Brenda Ballard Pflaum

When benefit managers scrutinize health care plan costs these days, they often uncover disturbing trends related to treatment of mental and chemical dependency disorders. These costs seem to be rising faster than overall plan costs. In fact, many companies are seeing mental health and chemical dependency costs grow at a rate as much as twice that of their plan's overall rate.

While corporate benefit managers may view increases in the costs of treating mental and chemical dependency disorders as excessive, no one is sure what constitutes a reasonable level of cost. On one hand, available data suggest that mental and chemical dependency disorders have historically been inadequately diagnosed and undertreated. A study conducted by the National Institute of Mental Health (NIMH) found that almost one-third of the adults in our country are likely to suffer from a mental illness or chemical dependency disorder some time during their lives. The study also revealed, however, that a surprisingly small portion of those needing help actually receive it. Only about one-third of those reporting a mental health problem within the six months before the study had actually sought help from a doctor or mental health specialist.

"Seeking Sane Solutions: Managing Mental Health and Chemical Dependency Costs," by Brenda Ballard Pflaum, which appeared in the Sept. 1991 issue, was reprinted with permission from the *Employee Benefits Journal*, published by the International Foundation of Employee Benefit Plans, Brookfield, WI. Statements or opinions expressed in this article are those of the author and do not necessarily represent the views or positions of the International Foundation, its officers, directors, or staff.

On the other hand, there is ample evidence that treatment for mental and chemical dependency disorders is not delivered efficiently. Benefit managers and insurers alike cite anecdotal tales of treatment patterns that seem to be driven more by health plan reimbursement than objective medical decision making.

Historically, there has been a tendency to view utilization of mental health and chemical dependency treatment as discretionary. When tough choices have to be made about the allocation of health care dollars, those services deemed discretionary are often the first ones targeted. Consequently, as health care costs have escalated, many companies have cut back on coverage for mental and chemical dependency disorders.

One survey conducted last year found that nearly 60 percent of companies now impose a lifetime maximum on mental health benefits. Others set various types of plan limitations, including maximum annual payouts both for overall expenses and for outpatient expenses, and various dollar or duration limits on outpatient benefits.

But a backlash may be emerging. Some providers are arguing that "knee-jerk" responses on the part of corporations anxious to reduce costs are jeopardizing access to much needed care. The *Wall Street Journal* recently reported that, according to the medical community, the cutbacks are beginning to hurt patients and their families. The article cites stories of families left in crisis because benefits have run out, leaving them without access to needed care.

THE CASE AGAINST BENEFIT CUTBACKS

While cutting benefits may be the easiest choice available to benefit managers, in the long run it may not be the best choice. There is growing evidence that untreated *behavioral problems* (a term that can be used to encompass the total range of mental and chemical dependency disorders as well as less severe adjustment and situational problems) can result in significant indirect costs from increased absenteeism, low productivity and diminished performance. Furthermore, research suggests that untreated behavioral problems drive considerable utilization of other health plan benefits. Consequently, cutbacks in behavioral benefits may merely fuel greater utilization of medical benefits, resulting in no overall cost savings.

Underlying coverage decisions is a view that sufferers of mental and chemical dependency disorders are not seriously ill. But this view may not be accurate. A recent study strongly suggests that at least one mental health disorder is as debilitating as serious physical disorders. Researchers with RAND Corporation have looked at the functioning and well-being of patients with depression and have concluded that the day-to-day functioning of depressed patients is as impaired as that of patients with major chronic medical conditions. Some of the medical conditions to which depression was compared included diabetes, hypertension, advanced coronary artery disease (ACAD), angina, arthritis, gastrointestinal, back and lung problems. The researchers found that the only chronic conditions that were more debilitating than depression were current active heart conditions.

Data such as these may begin to explain why people who suffer from behavioral problems tend to be high utilizers of health care. There is, in fact, astounding research that attributes more than 50 percent of the average primary care physician's time to the treatment of physical manifestations of mental and chemical dependency disorders, including such ailments as headaches, backaches and gastrointestinal problems.

Acknowledgment of this relationship may further our understanding of how treatment of behavioral problems impacts overall health care utilization.

For a number of years researchers have debated the existence of what has become known as the *offset effect*. The *offset effect* describes a process in which the cost of psychotherapy may be offset by savings in medical expenditures.

Several studies have shown that an individual's total health care expenditures will drop significantly after mental health treatment is begun. For example, one set of researchers performed an analysis of multiple controlled studies and found widespread and persistent evidence of a lower rate of increase in medical expenses following mental health treatment. The authors of the study concluded that his finding argues for the inseparability of mind and body in health care.

Another study utilized data from the Federal Employee Benefit Program and compared 26,915 families having at least one member who had received mental health treatment with a randomly selected group of 16,468 families where no member had received mental health treatment. The data indicated that, before treatment, the total health care costs of those families receiving treatment were considerably higher than those of similar families not needing treatment. The researchers found that costs increased continuously for the treated families during the 36 month period before treatment began. Once care was begun, however, a decrease in total health care costs was seen—even when the cost of mental health treatment was included. This study strongly suggests that when one family member becomes sick, not only will he or she be a high utilizer of care but so will the rest of the family.

USING PLAN DESIGN EFFECTIVELY

A case can be made that current benefit plan design drives inefficient use of care. While employers have become increasingly vocal about the rising cost of mental health and chemical dependency treatment, many providers of care have been quick to point out that treatment patterns have responded to the financial incentives set up by insurance coverage. And those incentives strongly favor hospitalization—the most expensive setting for treatment.

Traditionally, health insurance plans have not covered inpatient and out-patient mental health treatment equally. The dominant plan structure today is full benefits (usually 80-100 percent) for inpatient treatment and severely reduced benefits (typically 50 percent) for outpatient treatment. Underlying this plan design has been the concept of *moral hazard,* which can be defined as a risk resulting from uncertainty about the insured's ability to control health care purchases. Since purchase of outpatient mental health treatment is deemed discretionary, moral hazard suggests that utilization will rise as the cost of treatment goes down. In the early evolution of coverage for behavioral benefits, the insurance industry feared that offering full plan coverage for outpatient treatment would result in excessive claims resulting from lengthy psychotherapy, some of which might be for treatment of legitimate mental illness but much of which would represent the pursuit of happiness of self-actualization.

Research appears to verify the belief that lowering out-of-pocket payments for outpatient treatment tends to increase the demand for services. Using data from the health insurance experiment, RAND Corporation researchers found that insurance plans with lower coinsurance rates (smaller out-of-pocket payments) cause significantly higher use of outpatient psychotherapy services. However, the researchers also found that even where outpatient benefits are generous, expenditures on outpatient psychotherapy amounted to only about 4 percent of total plan expenditures.

Ironically, attempts to minimize the cost of discretionary use of outpatient benefits has led to benefit structures that encourage high cost treatment. Currently, inpatient mental health treatment accounts for as much as 70 percent of total mental health costs. Compared to inpatient treatment, outpatient treatment can be a bargain. At average room rates, the cost to keep a person suffering from depression in the hospital for six months can run in excess of $100,000. In contrast, six months of out-patient therapy at two sessions a week would run around $5,000 to $6,000.

Not only does skimpy coverage appear to restrict utilization of outpatient services, but generous coverage appears to drive long inpatient stays. Evidence suggests that once an individual is hospitalized, the duration of the stay may be determined more by reimbursement than clinical factors. Frank and Lave examined the factors affecting the length of stay of Medicaid psychiatric patients. The results indicated that length of stay is negatively affected by limits on the number of days paid for by Medicaid. Data from the State of Illinois also suggest that length of stay is correlated with payment. (See Exhibit 1)

Research studies have attempted to compare the effectiveness of inpatient and outpatient treatment in order to better understand why inpatient treatment predominates. Kiesler, in a review of the literature, found that outpatient treatment generally produced results equivalent to or better than those of hospitalization. This finding seems to provide further evidence of the influence of reimbursement levels on treatment patterns.

Exhibit 1 Length of Stay by Payment Source

Self-pay	13.5 days
Medicare/Medicaid	14.0 days
HMOs	14.6 days
Commercial Insurance	30.6 days

In addition to driving inefficient care, current plan design restricts providers' ability to prescribe flexible treatment settings. Most plans cover a narrow range of treatment settings. Coverage of inpatient and outpatient treatment may be well defined. Other settings, however, may be either ignored or clearly included. Many clinicians today believe that for efficient treatment to take place there must be plan design flexibility that will allow for reimbursement of less traditional modes of treatment such as partial hospitalization, day treatment, halfway houses and after care.

MANAGING COST BY MANAGING UTILIZATION

In dealing with the cost of behavioral disorders, plan sponsors are faced with the daunting task of providing ample access to care under a health care system that has yet to adequately define *appropriate care*. There are forceful arguments for putting mental health and chemical dependency benefits on par with medical benefits. But once benefits are improved and care is more readily accessible, the challenge is to manage utilization in such a way that care is provided efficiently and in the appropriate setting.

In order to better manage the cost of mental health and chemical dependency benefits, many companies are adopting programs to influence and control utilization. A recent survey by American PsychManagement (APM), a managed care company, showed that more than 70 percent of companies were either considering installing a mental health managed care program or actually had one in place.

Management of utilization can take may forms. At one end of the spectrum is utilization review of hospital admissions, which may include recertification, concurrent review and case management. The goal of utilization review is to prevent unnecessary hospitalizations and to minimize the length of those stays that are necessary. Under this approach, the patient has freedom to select any provider of care, but care that is not certified by utilization review may not be fully reimbursed.

At the other end of the managed care spectrum is utilization that is delivered exclusively through a network of providers that may be at risk for management of the costs. The patient must seek care through this network in order for care to be covered. This type of program utilizes a gatekeeper to evaluate the severity of the problem and direct the patient to the appropriate mode of care.

Between these points on a continuum, there are many options for managing mental health and chemical dependency costs and many ways to access programs. As the cost of mental health and chemical dependency coverage has grown, so has the number of vendors offering management services. In fact, the field has become so packed that it is difficult to sort through the options.

Experience with managed mental health programs is beginning to show that certain key issues should be considered in determining the structure of a managed program.

Control of Access to the System

Employees and their dependents are not well-informed consumers of care. The decision to seek care, especially care for adolescents, may be precipitated by a crisis. Entry into the system may come through an emergency room or may be influenced by the provocative advertising of hospital-centered intervention programs. Even where individuals seek entry to the system from a primary care physician, they may find themselves being inappropriately treated. Several different research studies have found that less than one-half of patients with major depression are identified and diagnosed by primary physicians.

It is important that entry to the system be controlled by a gatekeeper who is qualified by virtue of training and experience and refer psychiatric and chemical dependency disorders.

No Established Criteria for Care

There are no standard, national guidelines for treatment of psychiatric and chemical dependency disorders. While treatment patterns for medical problems may vary somewhat based on severity of illness, there is general agreement on many aspects of how care should be rendered. For example, if a parent calls a utilization review number requesting hospitalization for a child needing a tonsillectomy, the review organization will probably deny the request based on knowledge of the appropriateness of performing tonsillectomies on a outpatient basis. If, on the hand, a parent calls a utilization review number requesting hospitalization of a child diagnosed with depression, there are few hard and fast rules to guide the review organization in determining the appropriateness of admission. The diagnosis of depression may describe conditions ranging from mild to suicidal.

Because there are few objective standards for care, selection of the vendor to do the screening is important. The selection process should scrutinize the vendor's criteria for review. Plan sponsors should be wary of vendors that claim their review criteria are proprietary. If the managed care program involved a network of providers, these providers should be screened not only on the basis of their credentials but also on the basis of their typical practice patterns. Any ownership interest in treatment facilities or other types of self-serving financial agreements should also be investigated.

Early Intervention

Various studies have confirmed that the earlier treatment is started, the less costly overall treatment will be. If not treated, most mental health and chemical dependency problems will grow over time from mild to serious. As the problem progresses, the sick individual and, in many cases members of his or her immediate family, will become heavy utilizers of health care. At some point the problem will peak—often at a point of crisis—and treatment will start. The later in this progression treatment is started, the longer it will take for the individual and the family to return to health and full productivity.

Large Cases Costly

As with most health care utilization, a small number of people may drive a major portion of mental health and chemical dependency costs. A recent study by the University of Pennsylvania showed that 7 percent of the total Medicaid population in Philadelphia incurred 44 percent of all psychiatric charges.

Case management targets those individuals at high risk for hospitalization—especially those who have been hospitalized before. Mental health and chemical dependency problems tend to be chronic. Unlike physical illnesses that generally are either self-limiting, treatable or fatal, mental health and chemical dependency problems can continue indefinitely. Health plan utilization data will often show a pattern in which a few claimants with chronic problems cycle through repeated periods of inpatient treatment.

Case management can be effective in minimizing the cost of these chronic cases. Effective case management, however, requires considerable flexibility in plan design because preventing hospitalizations will often require a creative intermediate treatment alternative.

The jury is still out on how effective managed programs will be over the long run. However, empirical evidence available at this point suggests certain characteristics that should improve a program's effectiveness. These include the following:

- The program should provide a full range of coverage for mental health and chemical dependency treatment. Benefits should not be severely limited, and intermediate treatment settings should be covered.
- The program should incorporate a gatekeeper mechanism that helps individuals and their families identify providers and appropriate levels of care.
- The program should encourage early identification of problems.
- Providers associated with the program should be selected on the basis of prior treatment patterns that are philosophically consistent with the management goals of the program.
- The program should provide for followup as well as identification of high risk cases.

USING EMPLOYEE ASSISTANCE PROGRAMS FOR MANAGEMENT

Since many plan sponsors already maintain an employee assistance program (EAP), these programs are becoming popular gatekeeper mechanisms for managed programs. One advantage of using an EAP is that it offers highly visible and easy access to initial help, which may prevent the employee form wasting benefit dollars by "shopping" for a provider.

It is important to understand, however, that the mere existence of an EAP will not necessarily result in cost effective utilization of services. Historically, EAPs have not had cost management as one of their mandates. If, for example, an EAP automatically funnels alcoholics into a 28 day hospital program or sends troubled adolescents to a psychiatric hospital, then the EAP may not be effective in managing costs.

In order to be effective, EAPs need to control entry into the health care system. The EAP should channel employees into treatment settings on the basis of an assessment of the severity of the problem. Ideally, the EAP will refer employees and dependents to a network of providers that are selected on the basis of prior cost effective practice patterns. The EAP will also need to follow employees and dependents through treatment and closely monitor those suffering from chronic conditions.

USING UTILIZATION REVIEW

Many utilization review firms offer review of mental health and chemical dependency utilization. Some firms specialize in this area, providing targeted services.

A utilization review program is an administrative function overlaid onto fee-for-service medicine. The review process takes place after the employee or dependent has entered the health care system and has been evaluated by a physician or other provider. Therefore, this approach does not encourage early identification of problems nor does it control access to care. Consequently, a utilization review program by itself may not provide optimal management of mental health and chemical dependency costs.

To overcome these deficiencies, a utilization review program can be linked to an EAP. In this arrangement, The EAP provides an intake function and then refers the employee to an appropriate level of service. If hospitalization is recommended, the admissions must be approved by the utilization review organization. Ongoing monitoring of care, followup and case management services would also be provided by the review organization.

USING PPOS/EPOS

Some companies are using preferred provider organizations (PPOs) or exclusive provider organizations (EPOs) as the primary means for employees to access care. As with other managed care programs, utilization for a PPO or an EPO for mental health and chemical dependency treatment will generally involve certain contractual agreements between the plan sponsor and the network, and the benefits structure will be used to channel employees into the network.

A PPO arrangement generally allows a point-of-service selection of provider. Plan design can either encourage use of network providers through a better benefit structure (positive channeling) or can discourage use of nonnetwork providers through reduced benefits (negative channeling). In the agreement with the network, the plan sponsor agrees to encourage employees to use the provider. In return, the provider network may agree to discounted fees and to certain utilization review requirements.

An exclusive provider organization eliminates employee choice of provider. The network becomes the only source of reimbursable care. Employees must use the network providers if they want benefits to be paid by the plan. As with PPOs, discounted rates are negotiated with providers, and the providers are subject to certain utilization review requirements.

A PPO or an EPO can work in conjunction with either an EAP or with a utilization review (UR) program. A recent study conducted by William M. Mercer found that specialized UR coupled with a specialized PPO can offer an extremely effective means of preventing unnecessary inpatient utilization for psychiatric and chemical dependency disorders. Approximately half as many inpatient days were approved for cases subject to specialized utilization review plus PPO. In this study, board-certified psychiatrists examined full medical records and found no significant differences in quality of care between UR-only and UR/PPO cases. These data seem to substantiate the importance of having providers involved in the process of managing the cost of care.

THE IMPACT OF HMOs ON MENTAL HEALTH AND CHEMICAL DEPENDENCY COSTS

One of the most significant reasons for a plan sponsor to consider a carve-out plan may be that it provides a way for dealing with costs associated with employee use of HMOs. Discussions of rising mental health and chemical dependency costs often ignore the impact of HMOs on indemnity plan costs. HMO utilization can add to indemnity plan costs in two ways: adverse selection costs and disenrollment costs.

Adverse selection occurs when the worse risks in a total employee population select a plan. Many employers believe that the offering of HMO coverage results in adverse selection against the indemnity plan because HMOs tend to attract a younger and healthier covered group. This adverse selection generally increases the per capita cost of the indemnity plan.

One factor that appears to strongly influence adverse selection against an indemnity plan is the limited level of mental health and chemical dependency benefits provided under typical HMOs. The most common HMO benefit structure is a maximum of 30 days for inpatient care and a maximum of 20 out-patient visits.

Data suggest that employees who have any expectation of needing mental health or chemical dependency services will select indemnity rather than HMO coverage. Consequently, the indemnity plan will have a disproportionate conception of costs related to treatment of mental and chemical dependency disorders. This factor may account for at least part of recent rapid increases in mental health and chemical dependency costs as a percentage of overall indemnity plan costs.

A second factor influencing mental health and chemical dependency costs under indemnity plans is what may be called the cost of HMO *disenrollment*. Recent research strongly suggests that HMOs underdiagnose mental and chemical dependency disorder. RAND Corporation researchers investigated the detection of depression in patients enrolled in fee-for-service and prepaid plans. The researchers found that among the depressed patients of medical clinicians, those receiving care financed by prepayment were significantly less likely to have their depression detected or treated than were similar patients receiving fee-for-services care. In a second study of mental health services in HMOs and fee-for-service plans, RAND researchers found differences in the costs incurred by patients. In comparing the overall cost related to treatment of mental health services, the study showed that participants in a fee-for-service plan with no cost sharing incurred 2.8 times the cost of pre-paid participants.

In a financial offset study analyzing the long-term costs incurred by employees seeking help through its EAP, McDonnell Douglas found disturbing patterns among those who sought treatment through an HMO. The study found that employees who sought mental health care through their HMO were four to five times more likely to quit or be fired within four years than those who used the EAP. Daniel C. Smith, director of the McDonnell Douglas EAP, has suggested that this finding points to serious flaws in the ability of HMOs to identify and treat mental health and substance abuse problems. Smith has said that this startling difference in outcome indicates that "something is . . . dramatically wrong" with the quality of mental health and substance abuse care that prepaid health plans provide.

These studies strongly suggest that employees who disenroll from HMOs come back into the indemnity plan with undiagnosed or untreated mental and chemical dependency problems. These studies also suggest that a primary cause for disenrollment from an HMO may be the inability to access adequate care for mental and chemical dependency disorders.

To deal with the impact of HMOs on indemnity costs, a carve-out plan must enroll both indemnity plan and HMO participants. All eligible employees then receive care for mental and chemical dependency disorders through the carve-out plan and its provider network. The carve-out serves to neutralize those HMO design disincentives that drive indemnity plan costs unreasonably high. It also assures that all employees and dependents needing care have equal access to appropriate providers and are diagnosed and referred before minor problems become costly ones.

—EBJ

PROS AND CONS OF CARVE-OUT PLANS

A newly emerging trend in management of mental health and chemical dependency costs is the carve-out plan. A carve-out involves placing coverage of mental health and chemical dependency benefits with a single vendor that has responsibility for management of the cost. The contract will generally specify some type of risk assumption on the part of the vendor. The carve-out plan may be open only to those employees who have opted for indemnity plan coverage, or it may also include employees enrolled in HMOs.

Because the single vendor has responsibility for all utilization, the design of a carve-out plan will need to channel employees into a provider network. A carve-out can be structured in two ways. It can function as a point-of-service plan where benefit coverage is reduced if care is received outside the network. It can also function under an exclusive provider organization/health maintenance organization (EPO/HMO) model where benefits will be paid only if care is received from network providers.

One of the most highly visible examples of a carve-out plan was established last year by IBM. IBM signed a five year contract with American Psych-Management (APM) to manage the plan, which will eventually cover over 650,000 domestic beneficiaries. As a part of the contract, APM agreed to place at risk a part of its administrative-services-only fee. The plan includes all the features of an EAP, a utilization review program and a PPO. Benefit incentives will be used to encourage employees to use the network.

As mental health and chemical dependency costs continue to rise, carve-out plans may become more attractive as a way to integrate improved benefit design with medical management. One argument for a carve-out plan is the possibility of producing more accurate utilization data, since the incentives to "game" plan design by coding mental health and chemical dependency costs as medical problems are diminished. Another important reason for considering a carve-out plan is that it provides a way to deal with costs associated with the offering of HMOs (see side bar).

The major argument against a carve-out plan is that it increases complexity of plan administration and communication. Advocates of carve-outs argue, however, that the administrative burden is more than offset by the greater ability to manage costs. It also appears likely that any additional communication required may ultimately pay off by helping employees become better consumers of mental health and chemical dependency services.

PREVENTION

Mental health specialists cite increasing stress on the job as a primary factor in increasing rates of anxiety and depression. A survey conducted by the New York Business Group on Health found that 25 percent of the workforce at companies surveyed suffer from anxiety and stress-related illness, with about 13 percent suffering from depression.

In considering methods to better manage the cost of mental and chemical dependency disorders, companies should not overlook the area of prevention. Preventive programs can take many forms and may range from approaches as simple as a stress management workshop to as complicated as altering corporate culture. It seems clear, however, that efforts to better manage mental health and chemical dependency costs can be greatly enhanced by programs designed to reduce workplace stress.

1. DF Anderson, "How Effective Is Managed Mental Health Care?" *Business and Health,* September 1988, pp 34-35.

2. RG Blumenthal "Survey Finds 25% of Work Force Has Anxiety Disorder, Stress-Linked Illness," *Wall Street Journal,* October 20, 1989, p B3.

3. RG Frank and JR Lave "The Effect of Benefit Design on the Length of Stay of Medicaid Psychiatric Patients," *Journal of Human Resources* 21, No 3, pp 321-337.

4. HD Holder and JO Blose "Changes in Health Care Costs and Utilization Associated With Mental Health Treatment" *Hospital and Community Psychiatry,* October 1987, pp 1070-1075.

5. CA Kiesler "Public and Professional Myths About Mental Hospitalization: An Empirical Reassessment of Policy-Related Beliefs." *American Psychologist* 37 pp 1232-1339.

6. WG Manning et al, "How Cost Sharing Affects the Use of Ambulatory Mental Health Services," *Journal of the American Medical Association,* October 10, 1986, pp 1930-1934.

7. E Mumford et al. "A New Look at Evidence About Reduced Cost of Medical Utilization Following Mental Health Treatment," *American Journal of Psychiatry,* October 1984, pp 1145-1158.

8. G Ruffenach "Slashes in Mental Health Benefits Start to Hurt Patients, Medical Officials Say," *Wall Street Journal,* March 19, 1991, p B1.

9. KB Wells et al "Use of Outpatient Mental Health Services in HMO and Fee-for-Service Plans: Results From a Randomized Controlled Trial." *HSR: Health Services Research,* August 1986, pp 453-474.

10. _____; "The Functioning and Well-Being of Depressed Patients, Results From the Medical Outcomes Study," *Journal of the American Medical Association,* August 18, 1989, pp 914-919.

11. _____; "Detection of Depressive Disorder for Patients Receiving Prepaid or Fee-for-Service Care, Results From the Medical Outcomes Study," *Journal of the American Medical Association,* December 15, 1989, pp 3298-3302.

12. R Winslow "Spending to Cut Mental Health Costs," *Wall Street Journal,* December 13, 1989, p B1.

13. _____. "IBM Moves to Cap Mental Health Costs." *Wall Street Journal,* July 27, 1990, p. B1

32.   New Systems to
Manage Mental Health Care

Mary Jane England   Veronica A. Vaccaro

Faced with unabated health care cost increases over the past fifteen years, businesses look more and more to managed care for solutions. Early managed care arrangements focused narrowly on cost, triggering a fierce debate over access and quality concerns. The debate over managed care in mental health practice has been particularly bitter and controversial. The contention is stimulating new managed, or organized, mental health systems that are fundamentally different from earlier arrangements. Major U.S. companies are beginning to show that these new systems enhance early detection of mental health problems, offer a broad scope of services, provide continuity of care, reduce cost shifting to individuals, grant generous and protective benefits, and improve the overall quality of care. Of no small consequence, these systems also contain costs.

THE IMPETUS BEHIND MANAGED MENTAL HEALTH CARE

In 1990, employer/purchasers saw another 21 percent increase in their health care expenditures, despite cost containment efforts spanning more than a decade.[1] Mental health and chemical dependency services, with reported cost increases of up to 60 percent per year, are a prime target for managed care.

Employers report that mental and substance abuse disorders are among the most frequent short-term disability cases. Both the number and duration of these cases are on the rise, driving up the expense of both disability and health insurance.

Quality Concerns

In addition to rapidly increasing costs, purchasers have identified several quality-related problems as they choose from available mental health and chemical dependency services. First is overuse of hospitalization, the most costly and restrictive treatment setting. Adolescent care provides a striking illustration. Between 1986 and 1988, inpatient charges for adolescent care grew by 65 percent.[2] Much of this increase was market driven. During the mid-to-late 1980s, diagnosis-related group (DRG) regulations and the comparative return on investment between psychiatric and general hospitals generated and explosive growth in psychiatric beds. Beds were filled through sophisticated marketing campaigns targeting adolescents, which resulted in alarming increases in expenditures and consequent distrust of the psychiatric community by purchasers.

Second, services are purchased without indication of clinical effectiveness, making it difficult to identify good care and good providers. The scientific literature shows that a variety of biopsychosocial interventions are effective, but few accepted guidelines exist to direct individuals to appropriate treatment. Moreover, indemnity plans are designed with an assumption that individuals are knowledgeable about their choices for care. The lack of guidance often results in inefficient and inappropriate use of services.

Third, traditional benefit plans contain a financial incentive to use hospitalization rather than ambulatory services by providing more generous inpatient coverage. Designed as a way to protect those most in need of mental health services, this practice often discourages early intervention. Furthermore, the scope of services covered is limited to inpatient and outpatient care, excluding such intermediary services as partial hospitalization, residential care, day or evening treatment programs, and in-home family counseling.

Fourth, service delivery is fragmented. Examination of the utilization data of a member company revealed that two-thirds of individuals who were hospitalized did not receive follow-up ambulatory care. Because of the chronic nature of mental and addictive disorders, coordination of medical and support services increases the effectiveness of treatment. But case management is unavailable in traditional indemnity plans.

Finally, few mechanisms exist to detect mental health problems early. Costs can be lowered if care is provided before hospitalization is necessary, but benefit plans often lack incentives for early and easy access to care.

Changes in Practice

Application of the core managed care technology—utilization review and selective contracting—has led to drastic change in mental health practice.[3] Participants in the 1991 Utilization Management Survey conducted by the National Association of Private Psychiatric Hospitals (NAPPH) reported that most care is managed, with 78 percent of admissions requiring precertification and 74 percent undergoing concurrent review.[4] Approximately 28 percent of employers use special mental health provider networks, and approximately 22 percent of employee assistance programs (EAPs) are integrated with mental health benefits to facilitate early access and continuity of care.[5] Generally, it is less and less common for patients to receive treatment in the fragmented, unmanaged fee-for-service system.[6]

The core technology has proved effective at containing costs. Utilization review with use of a specialized provider network reduces unnecessary inpatient use and the associated expense.[7] But the growth of managed care in mental health practice has not been without its problems. Purchasers whose costs keep rising implement utilization review and discount contracting. Out of sheer frustration, they also limit mental health benefits. Providers, subjected to frequent and time-consuming review of their work, harshly criticize these techniques as discriminatory, intrusive, insensitive to patients' needs, and extraordinarily burdensome.[8] Both sides agree on the importance of improving quality of care and health status. But until recently, quality improvement was a token effort, and no reliable models existed to assess the status of care.

Discussions of managed care in mental health practice are plagued by disputes over objectives. Concern exists about whether care is being managed, resulting in coverage for appropriate and necessary treatment, or whether cost is being managed and access to necessary care is actually being restricted. Providers report problems with one managed care technique: utilization review. NAPPH reports that review criteria are often sketchy. Forty-five percent of hospitals state that utilization review takes considerable staff time and that utilization review firms "rarely or never have specific review criteria."[9] The absence of privacy safeguards in the utilization review process leads some clinicians to censor medical records and report diagnoses that carry less stigma, to protect patients.[10] The integrity and efficacy of the review process are still in question, as is the effect on cost shifting to the public sector.[11] Finally, there has been no significant examination of the effect of utilization management on the long-term outcomes of mental health care.[12]

Managed Care and Quality

Providers and purchasers share concern about the effect of managed care arrangements on treatment outcomes. In the current managed care environment, providers compete most often on the basis of price rather than quality. But as managed systems mature, providers that cannot demonstrate that their services are both of high quality and cost-effective will have difficulty competing for contracts. Quality assessment and improvement are, in fact, the next challenges for managed care.

To be measured, quality must be defined. What are the desired outcomes? What variables are meaningful to measure? Are data systems in place to measure the desired variables? Contracts between purchasers and network providers are beginning to spell out quality expectations. A case in point is the quality assurance approach in IBM's new mental health plan. In 1990, IBM contracted with American PsychManagement (APM) to establish nationwide network of providers to serve its 700,000 employees, dependents, and retirees. APM also manages the network and provides utilization review and case management services. Overseeing APM's activity is an independent advisory board, comprising nationally recognized mental health experts. The board is responsible for enhancing access to the highest possible quality of care.

IBM's quality expectations pertain to clinical staff and provider network credentials and characteristics, the integrity of operations (resource referral line, utilization review, case management, and employee assistance program), beneficiary satisfaction, and clinical outcomes. Practice patterns and the case management process will be audited. In addition to doing oversight of clinical matters the board is working with APM and Value Health Sciences to develop national consensus practice standards for adolescent inpatient care and adult substance abuse care.

Many purchasers, like IBM, view practice profiling as a first step in the development of practice guidelines. Profiling is a "statistical technique which involves identifying a provider's pattern of practice and comparing it with similar providers' patterns, by way of one centralized data base."[13] Looking at patterns of care over time helps to identify uniform approaches and reward high-quality, cost-efficient providers. It also reduces the need for utilization review and is, therefore, less intrusive in the provider/patient relationship.

Profiling is a new technology for mental health practice and is consistent with successful strategies focusing on quality rather than price. A recent study by New Directions for Policy reports that companies have reduced health care costs by 20 to 50 percent by "aggressively pursuing quality, eliminating waste and inefficiency, and rewarding good performance by providers."[14] Honeywell, Southern California Edison, and Southwestern Bell are among the featured companies using value-based purchasing with financial incentives to direct beneficiaries to high-quality providers.

MANAGED CARE CASE STUDIES IN MENTAL HEALTH

Over the past three years, several large employers introduced managed systems of care that differ significantly from previous arrangements. Although each company takes a slightly different approach, all are applying scientific advances in mental health practice to organized finance and delivery systems. Key components of all the systems are selective contracting, utilization review, comprehensive individualized services, easy access, and quality assessment and improvement. Because these systems are so new, conclusive longitudinal data pointing to their level of effectiveness are not yet available. But early examination reveals that employers using these systems are expanding benefits and containing costs.

McDonnell Douglas

In 1989, the McDonnell Douglas Helicopter Company introduced a managed mental health care program based on experience gained from analyzing its parent company's employee assistance program conducted between 1985 and 1989.[15] The study confirmed the cost-effectiveness of EAP case management of mental health benefits and projected cost saving of $2.1 million over four years, after considering individual and family medical costs, absenteeism, and turnover.

The McDonnell Douglas program uses EAP case management with a carefully selected provider network. "Basically, the benefit has no rules," said Daniel C. Smith, director of Employee Assistance and Risk Management Services for McDonnell Douglas.[16] The case manager authorizes treatment in a variety of inpatient, outpatient, and intermediary settings based on individual needs. The company covers 80 percent of charges for approved services, regardless of treatment setting, with 50 percent coinsurance for treatment obtained outside the network. "The EAP-delivered system enhances early case finding and easy access to benefits," Smith said, "as well as providing long-term management of care." Case mangers track individuals for two years after hospitalization.

During the first year, 17 percent of the covered population used benefits, up from 10 percent the previous year. At the same time, per capita costs declined by 34 percent. Reduced costs were attributed to a 50 percent decrease in psychiatric and a 29 percent decrease in chemical dependency admissions, a 47 percent reduction in average length-of-stay, and lower provider payments through negotiated rates. The company is also monitoring patient satisfaction. From the 1,172 individuals who received treatment, there were no complaints regarding quality, accessibility, or quantity of care.

First Chicago

The First National Bank of Chicago implemented a comprehensive mental health program in 1984.[17] Major components of the program are utilization review, an EAP/wellness program, and expansion of the mental health benefit. More intermediary services are covered, and ambulatory services are reimbursed at a more generous rate. Inpatient benefits include 85 percent coinsurance after a $250 deductible for the first $6,666.66 of covered charges and 100 percent thereafter, up to a million-dollar lifetime benefit. Outpatient care that is determined to represent an alternative to inpatient hospitalization, such as day hospitalization, medication management, and intensive outpatient programs, is covered at 85 percent. Other outpatient care is covered at 50 percent.

The program has resulted in a significant decrease in the inappropriate use of hospitalization, while enhancing the accessibility of ambulatory services. During years of consistent nationwide increases in the cost of mental health services, total spending on mental health benefits for First Chicago's estimated 13,000 covered lives has increased only slightly. Over the past five years, total inpatient spending decreased by 59 percent, while total mental health expenditures increased by 3 percent. This was accomplished without coverage limits or benefits cuts. Furthermore, while the number of employees using short-term disability leave for mental health diagnosis has increased, the average length of disability has decreased from a high of 47.7 days in 1988 to 30.3 days in 1990.

Pacific Bell

In 1991, Pacific Bell expanded services, through U.S. Behavioral Health, from chemical dependency services only (in use since 1988) to all mental health care for its one-quarter million covered lives. The program combines utilization review with a specialized provider network and is integrated with employee assistance and health promotion programs. Network provider services are covered at 80 to 90 percent, with a $100 inpatient deductible and minimal copayments.[18] Services outside the network have separate $400 deductibles for mental health and chemical dependency services, with 50 percent of charges covered.

Quality assurance activities include a sophisticated practice profiling system that generates information on appropriateness of treatment recommendations, compliance with treatment criteria, and recidivism rates for individual providers and the entire network. Data are compared with regional and national cost and utilization statistics. Credentialing and recredentialing, continuing education for network providers, and patient satisfaction surveys are other components of the quality assurance program.[19]

IBM

In 1990, IBM introduced its new mental health program, which expanded benefits. "IBM wants to offer benefit plans that meet the needs of employees and are cost effective," according to William Matson, manager of Health and Welfare Programs for IBM.[20] When employees use the network, the company covers 100 percent of first-year charges for inpatient care, after a deductible. After the first year, 80 percent is covered. Outpatient care is covered at 80 percent for the first $15,000, after a deductible. From $15,000 to $25,000, the company covers 50 percent of charges. A resource referral service directs individuals to the most appropriate level of care, and case managers coordinate services. Among other responsibilities, the case manager can authorize care not normally covered under the benefit.

Chevron

The Chevron Corporation, concerned that some of its health maintenance organization (HMO) enrollees were in plans that did not have adequate mental health and chemical dependency care, implemented a specialized provider network and utilization review program for its 128,000 covered lives in 1989. The new program expanded coverage to include a variety of intermediary services such as partial hospitalization and evening alcohol treatment programs and created an incentive to use ambulatory care.

The mental health benefit covers 90 percent of charges in the outpatient setting, 80 percent for inpatient care. The chemical dependency benefit has a lifetime limit of $20,000 and covers the first $5,000 at 100 percent, with the balance covered at 80 percent. Inpatient days are limited to forty-five days annually and ninety days lifetime. There is no limit on outpatient days. During the first year of the program, EAP use increased by 60 percent. Although the benefit covered twice as many lives as the previous year, total plan costs rose to $9.8 million from $9.2 million.[21] Much of the saving is attributed to a 21 percent decrease in hospital admissions.

Digital

Digital Equipment Corporation, also concerned with the quality of mental health and chemical dependency care delivered through its HMOs, has undertaken an intensive evaluation of HMOs' treatment of depression. The effort developed from Digital's participation in the Outcomes Management Project, sponsored by InterStudy.[22] Digital will be using a version of the outcomes module for major depression and dysthymia, an assessment tool developed by a team of clinicians led by G. Richard Smith of the University of Arkansas. "At present, the outcomes module includes seven domains," Smith said, "diagnosis, prognosis, general and disease specific functioning, symptom severity, remission, relapse, and medical care utilization."[23] The information can be used for a variety of purposes, some of which are to select providers, monitor care, and improve provider network performance.

These and other employer-initiated efforts are attempting to address the cost and quality problems discussed earlier. Although the early evidence is anecdotal, continued evaluation will build a substantial database and refine the practice of value-based health care purchasing. Undoubtedly, the most important innovation of these new managed systems is the development of models to evaluate quality. Assessment and improvement of network performance should eventually lead to less micromanagement by purchasers and their agents, and more quality variables on which to judge providers.

THE FUTURE OF MANAGED MENTAL HEALTH SYSTEMS

As our attention centers on reform of the U.S. health care delivery system, experimentation with organized systems of care must continue. The regulation of managed care is a prominent issue at the state level, with some states enacting laws that restrict or increase the expense of utilization review and selective contracting. Unfortunately, the outcome of this movement may be less cooperation between purchasers and providers in an era when more is needed.

Exciting innovations in mental health service delivery are on the horizon. A mental health care system that combines the strengths of the public and private sectors can bring about lasting reform. A prototype for this new service delivery approach is the Mental Health Services Program for Youth, a national demonstration project funded by The Robert Wood Johnson Foundation. The five-year, $20.4 million effort "is the largest national initiative to date, public or private, to improve services for children with serious mental illnesses," according to a foundation report.[24] Through this program, eight states are developing organized systems of community-based care. Services are integrated at the community level and include participation by health, child welfare, juvenile justice, mental health, and education agencies. Private purchasers have begun to use the integrated services in their communities. Mental health experts agree that the program likely will affect norms for clinical practice and financing mechanisms, as well as the direction of public policy and programs.

As scientific advances make mental health treatment more effective and specific, purchasers, providers, and policymakers will need to work together to refine the components of an improved health care delivery system—a system that combines the strengths of the public and private sectors and is designed to promote easily accessible, high-quality health care at an affordable cost.

1. A. Foster Higgins and Company Research and Survey Services, *Mental Health and Substance Abuse Benefits Survey* (Princeton, N.J.: A. Foster Higgins, December 1990).

2. R.G. Frank, D.S. Salkever, and S.S. Sharfstein, "A New Look at Rising Mental Health Insurance Costs," *Health Affairs* (Summer 1991): 116-123.

3. A. Broskowski, "Current Mental Health Care Environments: Why Managed Care Is Necessary," *APA-Professional* (30 November 1990): 39.

4. *National Association of Private Psychiatric Hospitals' 1991 Utilization Management Survey* (Washington, D.C.: NAPPH, June 1991).

5. A. Foster Higgins, *Mental Health and Substance Abuse Benefits Survey;* and Buck Consultants, *Employer-Sponsored Alcohol/Substance Abuse and Mental Disorders Treatment Benefits* (Secaucus, N.J.: Buck Consultants, 1991).

6. J. Gabel et al., "The Changing World of Group Health Insurance," *Health Affairs* (Summer 1988): 48-65.

7. D.F. Anderson, "How Effective Is Managed Mental Health Care?" *Business and Health* (September 1989): 34-35; and P.J. Feldstein, T.M. Wickizer, and J.R.C. Wheeler, "The Effects of Utilization Review Programs on Health Care Use Expenditures," *The New England Journal of Medicine* 318 (1988): 1310-1314.

8. G.L. Tischler, "Utilization Management of Mental Health Services by Private Third Parties," *American Journal of Psychiatry* 147 (1990): 967-973; and NAPPH, *1991 Utilization Management Survey.*

9. NAPPH, *1991 Utilization Management Survey.*

10. S.S. Sharfstein, O.B. Towery, and I.D. Milowe, "Accuracy of Diagnostic Information Submitted to an Insurance Company," *American Journal of Psychiatry* 137 (1980): 70-73.

11. Tischler, "Utilization Management of Mental Health Services."

12. *Id.*

13. Washington Business Group on Health, "Physician Profiling: A Strong Tool to Influence Medical Practice," *Quality Resource Center Update* (Washington, D.C.: WBGH, Summer 1991), 6-7.

14. J. Meyer, S. Sullivan, and S. Silow-Carroll, "Private Sector Initiatives: Controlling Health Care Costs" (Washington, D.C.: New Directions for Policy, March 1991), distributed by The Healthcare Leadership Council, Washington, D.C.

15. "McDonnell Douglas Corporation Employee Assistance Program Financial Offset Study: 1985-1989" (St. Louis: McDonnell Douglas Corporation and Alexander Consulting Group, 1990).

16. Daniel C. Smith, director, Employee Assistance and Risk Management Services, McDonnell Douglas Corporation, personal communication, 15 August 1991.

17. W.N. Burton et al., "Quality and Cost-Effective Management of Mental Health Care," *Journal of Occupational Medicine* (April 1989): 363-366.

18. "Pacific Bell Contracts with CIGNA to Administer Managed Care Network," *Spencer's Research Reports* (Chicago: Charles D. Spencer and Associates, 13 April 1990), 4-5.

19. From background information on U.S. Behavioral Health, 2000 Powell Street, Suite 1180, Emeryville, California 94608.

20. "Economics and Efficacy of Mental Health Care," comments by William Matson, manager of Health and Welfare Programs, IBM, at Health Agenda 1991, Annual Conference of the Washington Business Group on Health and the National Association of Manufacturers, Washington, D.C., 30 January 1991.

21. "Mental Health Benefits Costly, Managing Care Controversial," *Managed Care Report* (6 August 1990): 5-8.

22. P.M. Ellwood, "Outcomes Management: A Technology of Patient Experience," 99th Shattuck Lecture, Annual Meeting of the Massachusetts Medical Society, 21 May 1988, *The New England Journal of Medicine* 318 (June 1988): 1549-1556.

23. G. Richard Smith, Department of Psychiatry and Behavioral Sciences, University of Arkansas, personal communication, 16 September 1991.

24. "Developing Community-based Systems of Care," *Family Matters* (Fall 1991).

33. Integrating EAPs with Managed Care

Ronald J. North

Two years ago, Campbell Soup Company incorporated managed behavioral health care services into an established employee assistance program (EAP) at three sites. The pilot program, which covered nearly 10,000 lives, would provide Campbell Soup with a barometer of the effectiveness of managed care. If successful, Campbell's internal Employee Assistance Department would use the results and data obtained to support an EAP-based managed care program for its approximately 40 sites nationwide.

Campbell's set out to meet three strategic objectives through the pilot program:

- to reduce psychiatric and substance abuse costs by 20 percent;
- to provide the most effective and efficient treatment; and
- to improve or maintain employee satisfaction with health care service delivery.

After its first year, the program exceed the company's expectations. At sites where the program was implemented, behavioral health costs were reduced by 36 percent, and behavioral health costs as a percentage of all medical costs were reduced from 11.5 to 6.7 percent. The objectives of providing high-quality treatment and improving or maintaining employee morale were also met.

Since completion of the pilot program in April 1991, Campbell's has established the managed care program—dubbed the "Quality Care Program"

Reprinted from EAP Digest, Jan/Feb 1992 with permission of Performance Resource Press, Inc., 1863 Technology Drive, Troy, MI 48083.

(QCP)—at 10 additional sites across the country with the goal of bringing all appropriate sites on board by mid-year.

For EAP managers evaluating managed care services, and grappling with the seemingly incompatible goals of providing quality health care while reducing health care expenditures, the following insights were gained while working with Campbell Soup on the program's design and implementation. The experience overturned some conventional assumptions regarding managed care and indicated the need to address several key considerations at the beginning of the process. Among these considerations:

- *Saving money is not the only goal of managed care services.* In fact, where cost savings is the only goal, the effort is likely to fail because employees feel that a fundamental employee right is being taken away. On the other hand, when the focus and message are on providing the right treatment the first time and improving the quality of health care services, managed care services can be positioned as an enhancement to the employee's health care benefit, not a restriction. As inefficiencies in the delivery of health care are eliminated, cost reduction follows.

- *Managed care represents a long-term commitment to changing the way that companies deliver health benefits.* This commitment requires employee education about making smart health care choices and what making the right choice means for both the individual and the company. In some cases, companies will have to say "no" to a provider's recommendation for hospitalization when less restrictive, but equally effective, treatment modes are available. This can be a difficult concept for companies, but is necessary to achieve long-term goals.

- *Benefit plans may need to be restructured in order for managed care services to be effective.* Campbell's EAP is voluntary; employees have a choice as to whether or not to use it. To encourage use of the program, benefits are structured around incentives. For example, if the indemnity plan provides 50 percent outpatient reimbursement and the EAP/managed care program provides 80 percent reimbursement, employees will likely be motivated to at least try the EAP.

- *Managed care services should be client- versus criteria-based.* While client-based programs such as Campbell's use a case-by-case analysis to determine treatment plans and referrals, most managed care programs base treatment decisions on pre-defined categories or diagnoses. Utilization Review (UR)—the most common form of criteria-based program—is not a substitute for case management. For medical/surgical cases, UR decisions are relatively clear-cut. Yet when applied to substance abuse and mental health cases, a UR approach can alienate employees, create serious liability problems for the company, and lead to union grievances.

Campbell Soup has contracted with a network of EAP counselors as case managers who provide face-to-face assessments for employees requiring managed care services or EAP counseling. Counselors may treat the employee who needs short-term care or refer the employee to the most appropriate provider. Either way, the case manager actively monitors the employee's progress beyond treatment. Utilization review is used by Campbell's only as a general guideline for rigorous case management.

- *On an individual, case-by-case basis, managed care may require spending more money in the short term in order to achieve long-term goals.* Campbell's program is flexible to meet the treatment needs of employees. For example, where inpatient substance abuse treatment is determined to best serve the individual, that treatment is covered by the plan. This may require spending more on an individual's treatment than other alternatives, but by treating the problem correctly the first time, the likelihood of further treatment is reduced.
- *External managed care programs that are "slapped onto" as opposed to integrated into existing benefit programs can alienate the workforce.* Workers and unions may feel that "choice" is being taken away and that they are being "forced" to use an alternative program. Traditionally, however, EAPs are respected by employees and are already playing a key internal role at the company. For these reasons, EAPs are in a stronger position than external vendors to effectively provide managed care services.
- *An integrated EAP and managed care program provides important information that can be leveraged across the company.* At one Campbell's plant, the program identified increased EAP usage during periods when employees were required to work double shifts. These extended work hours caused a high level of stress, and relationship and marital problems ensued. Recognizing this pattern, the EAP/managed care program now regularly schedules educational workshops on stress and relationship issues prior to periods requiring double shifts.

MANAGED CARE MISCONCEPTIONS

In addition to carefully considering company readiness for a managed care program and the specifics of program design, it is important to understand the common misconceptions about EAP-based managed care models and other forms of managed care. Again, Campbell's is proving that managed care activities can meet corporate objectives without sacrificing employee needs. Achieving this balance is facilitated when quality, employee satisfaction, and cost reduction are given equal priority.

The following is a series of commonly held myths regarding managed care and some suggestions for how to counter these myths with senior management.

Myth: Every company needs a managed care program.

Fact: Every company does not need managed care. To determine a company's needs, a cost/benefits analysis and claims history should be conducted.

Doing so determines the potential return on investment to be realized by applying managed care concepts. Such an analysis also provides baseline information about areas such as: current provider usage patterns; EAP utilization rates; factory and office areas contributing most heavily to health care costs; and the costs of behavioral health care as a percentage of total annual health care expenditures.

Should a company's behavioral health care spending fall at or below the national average, managed care can still be effective in improving the quality of health care services, getting employees back on the job more quickly, and ensuring a high level of employee satisfaction with health benefits.

Myth: Managed care is focused on limiting the length-of-stay in inpatient drug, alcohol, and psychiatric treatment centers.

Fact: Managed care is less concerned with reducing a day or two of hospitalization than it is with eliminating overtreatment or mistreatment of serious mental and behavioral illnesses. For example, treating an adolescent with serious psychiatric problems in a residential, free-standing facility for 90 days (approximately $150/day) may be preferable to what might be "prescribed" in an unmanaged program (45 days inpatient at a psychiatric center at $900 to $1,000 a day). In this hypothetical case, it is not a medical necessity for the adolescent to be in a medical facility, accumulating charges associated with a variety of staff members and hospital services. In addition, the milieu of a free-standing residence might prove more positive than a hospital psychiatric ward.

Myth: Every good EAP counselor can be a good case manager.

Fact: Case mangers may be called upon to assess the full range of mental health and substance abuse problems. Biological mood disorders combined with substance abuse problems, or simultaneous mental health and medical problems, are commonly encountered. As a result, PhD-level experience is especially helpful. Companies may need to reassess the abilities of their EAP clinicians. As the goal is to put the most effective case management network in place, case management training may be the best answer. It may also mean that some EAP clinicians may need to be replaced.

At one Campbell's Soup plant, a qualified case manager works closely with an EAP counselor who is well liked by employees and familiar with Campbell's program. Employees access the EAP counselor when it is determined that short-term counseling (up to eight sessions) is needed and the case manager when the presenting problem is more severe.

Myth: Companies can continue to offer full indemnity health care plans without having to sacrifice anything.

Fact: Economic forces will eventually force companies to address the enormous financial toll traditional health care plans are taking on the bottom line. The result? These costs will have to be off-set somewhere, whether in freezes on salary increases, new hirings, or capital expenditures. Employees should be made aware of the realities of these trade-offs.

Myth: Instituting managed care programs interferes with an EAP counselor's ability to perform the job for which he/she is trained.

Fact: While many managed care providers design elaborate procedures and "rules" for how clinicians should address serious behavioral health problems, Campbell's program took a different approach. Campbell's focused on developing a network of highly-trained and highly-effective EAP case managers, relying on their expertise and skill to make the right treatment decisions within the program's broad goals—effective, efficient treatment, reduced costs, and improved employee satisfaction. The program offers counselors both the freedom and responsibility to make the right treatment decisions.

Campbell Soup's community-based EAP case managers also understand the social, cultural, economic, and religious influences in their particular communities, enabling them to use the techniques and methods they think will work best.

Myth: Employees who have serious problems will leave the company anyway.

Fact: They may not leave—they may stay with the company for many years, draining the company's health care benefits and impacting the available workforce. When Campbell's employment records were reviewed, many individuals had been with the company for 20 or 30 years. It is in the company's best interests to offer programming that addresses employee's health care needs.

Myth: Managed care providers leave hospitals and other treatment providers in the dark about what kinds of care will be authorized and funded.

Fact: While managed care providers have often refused to share their criteria for authorizing care, a number of providers now recognize that the sooner this information is made available to treatment providers, the sooner the two can begin working together for the benefit of employees.

Part 8

MEETING NEW REQUIREMENTS

34. Responding to the New Rules: Choosing Assumptions and Implementing SFAS 106

Anna M. Rappaport   George Wagoner

In 1990, the Financial Accounting Standards Boards issued Statement of Financial Accounting Standards No. 106 (SFAS 106), specifying methodology for employers' accounting for postretirement benefits other than pensions.

SFAS 106 changes accounting from a pay-as-you-go-or cash basis to an accrual basis. While most employers will probably adopt SFAS 106 in 1993, the majority will have measured these liabilities at least once in 1992 or earlier years and will have already studied the impact of the new rules. Because of Securities and Exchange Commission (SEC) rules, many employers are disclosing liabilities before adoption, but often as a range of values. Because many employers have studied the costs of the current plans and because they wish to reduce those costs by the time of adoption, employers are considering alternative assumption setting and adoption strategies and revising their postretirement programs as they adopt SFAS 106. The decisions they are making today will affect the pattern and level of future earnings. This article reviews some issues relative to the adoption of SFAS 106. While SFAS 106 requires accrual accounting for all benefits other than pensions provided to retirees, the authors limit analysis and comments to retiree medical benefits. Much analysis will be drawn from three surveys conducted by William M. Mercer, Incorporated (Mercer). These surveys are:

1. Analysis of valuation results and actuarial assumptions used in over 130 valuations completed in 1989 and 1990 (the March 1991 Valuation Survey)

2. Analysis of valuation results and actuarial assumptions used in over 200 valuations completed in 1991 (the March 1992 Valuation Survey)
3. Analysis of over 2,000 employers' responses to a survey about plan design changes (the February 1991 Plan Design Survey).

Note that an actuarial valuation is the process used to determine costs under SFAS 106. In the two valuation surveys, Mercer has analyzed the assumptions and the SFAS 106 results of actuarial valuations of retiree health benefits covering over three million employees and retirees. Most of these benefits were unfunded (i.e., there was no trust fund in which cash was being accumulated before benefits were due, so that cash was paid from company operations in the year benefits were due) as of the valuation date. In addition to the two valuation surveys, the authors provide some results from the Mercer February 1991 Plan Design Survey to which over 2,000 employers responded. This survey shows that employers are adopting strategies to reduce liabilities. The analysis from all three surveys provides data information that is helpful to employers in interpreting their own results and setting strategy.

This article presents an analysis of the results of the valuations and a summary of assumptions that have significant impact on the valuation results. A summary of the results includes:

- The "new" SFAS 106 expenses and liabilities as a multiple of current pay-as-you-go costs
- The impact of plan design changes
- The relationship of total liabilities (the present value of all future benefits, or EPBO in SFAS 106 terminology) to past service liabilities and to current year expenses
- The specific "building blocks" of the current year's expense.

Following the summary of results, this article:

1. Reviews assumptions that are unique to medical plans.
2. Reviews assumptions that also pertain to pension plans.
3. Discusses differences between pension valuations and postretirement medical valuations.
4. Discusses the value of forecasts for these benefits.
5. Reviews special issues that companies should consider when adopting SFAS 106.

BASIC SFAS 106 CONCEPTS

Before SFAS 106, companies accounted for postretirement benefits other than pensions on a pay-as-you-go basis, where the cost recognized is the cost for claims (or current insurance premiums) for benefit payments in the current year. SFAS 106 specifies that accounting for these benefits will change to an accrual basis similar to that used for pension plans. With accrual accounting, the expected lifetime value of the benefit is calculated and recognized as a cost over the working lifetime of the employees. Due to the nature of medical increases, current costs calculated on an accrual basis will almost always be greater than pay-as-you-go costs. In addition, the employer must also recognize the transition obligation—the expense that would have been accrued on an employer's books had the employer been accounting according to SFAS 106 since the inception of the plans being valued. Because the transition obligation can be enormous relative to current pay-as-you-go costs, SFAS 106 allows employers the option of recognizing the past service cost immediately or amortizing that cost over 20 years.

The starting point in an actuarial valuation for determining an employer's postretirement expenses under SFAS 106 is the estimation of the present value of all employer-provided postretirement benefits, which is called the expected postretirement obligation, or EPBO. These calculations look at the expected benefits to be paid over the lifetime of all active employees, retirees, and dependents covered in the plan. They take into account the probability that benefits will be paid, the expected amount of benefits to be paid, and the time value of money. The parameters chosen for each of these items are called actuarial assumptions. The EPBO can also be viewed as the amount of money that, if invested today in a lump sum, would allow the plan sponsor to pay for all benefits to current plan participants. The amount of benefits to be paid is based on the plan design, the anticipated claim experience under the plan, and expectations as to future changes in medical cost. EPBO calculations must be based on the "substantive plan," which is the plan as understood by the employer and the employees. The substantive plan reflects the design as written in the plan document(s), past practices with regard to change of the plan such as consistent changes in the level of retiree contributions or deductibles, and formal corporate policy with regard to ongoing changes.

Once the EPBO is calculated, the lifetime value of the benefit must be spread or "attributed" over a period beginning on the date the employee is hired (or begins to have credited service under the plan's benefit formula) and ending on the date the employee becomes available for full benefits. This attribution of the EPBO divides the EPBO into segments:

1. A segment that represents the prior accruals based on past service known as the accumulated postretirement benefit obligation (APBO)

2. A small segment to be accrued in the current year for employees not eligible for retirement (representing the value of the benefits charged to the current year) called the service cost.

3. A remaining segment, reflecting the value of amounts which will be accrued in future years. The SFAS 106 rules and actuarial theory specify how this division takes place. The EPBO is the equivalent of the present value of

benefits in pension terminology, and the APBO is the equivalent of the accrued liability.

At adoption of SFAS 106, the excess of the APBO (amount attributed to past periods), less existing plan assets, is an unrecognized obligation that exists when the rule is first applied. this is called the transition obligation. Employers can either recognize this obligation immediately or amortize it over the employees' average remaining service period, or 20 years, whichever is longer. Immediate recognition means that the entire amount is charged to the profit and loss statement in the year SFAS 106 is adopted.

The retiree medical expense during a fiscal year—the hit to the bottom line—is called the net periodic postretirement benefit cost (NPPBC). It is calculated as follows:

+   service cost (current year's accrued expenses for employees not eligible for full retirement benefits)
+   interest cost on APBO
−   return on the plan assets (zero for unfunded plans)
+   amortization of transition obligation
±   amortization of benefit increases (decreases)
±   gains and losses

———————

=   NPPBC (net periodic postretirement benefit cost)

The service cost can be considered to be the value of benefits assigned to a given year. The difference between the service cost and NPPBC equals the amount needed to recognize the cost of past benefits not yet expended, plus the amount needed to make up interest because benefits are not funded. In most cases, a retiree health plan will have a much higher expense than a pension plan with a similar service cost because the retiree health plans are generally unfunded. Because the plan was unfunded and had utilized pay-as-you-go accounting, current expense must include amortization of the recognized liability and interest on the ABPO without any offsetting income on assets. As shown in the division of NPPBC later in this article, these factors make the expense far higher than the service cost.

The consequence of recognizing cost in accordance with SFAS 106 and not funding the benefits as they are expended is that an unfunded liability will build and will be shown on the books of the plan sponsor. This liability will equal the accumulated net excess of the amount expended over the cash outlays.

WHAT VALUATIONS HAVE SHOWN

The following paragraphs present an analysis of the SFAS 106 valuations from our March 1991 and March 1992 Valuation Surveys. The analysis compares the

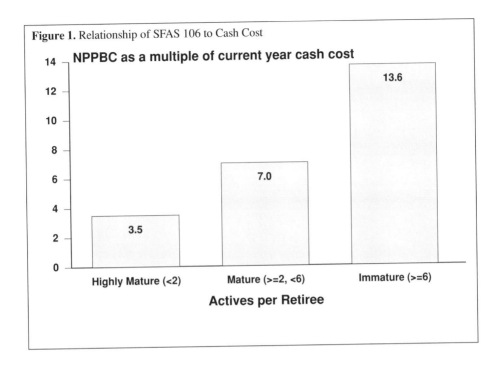

Figure 1. Relationship of SFAS 106 to Cash Cost

NPPBC as a multiple of current year cash cost

Highly Mature (<2): 3.5
Mature (>=2, <6): 7.0
Immature (>=6): 13.6

Actives per Retiree

SFAS 106 NPPBC to the pay-as-you-go cost. The 1992 comparisons show different results from the 1991 comparisons, reflecting the steps that employers have already taken to reduce the value of their benefit promises and, therefore, their liabilities and SFAS 106 expense. In most cases, these changes had little impact, if any, on existing retirees and cash costs.

As discussed above, the current year expense—the NPPBC—will generally be greater than the cash cost. Based on Mercer's March 1991 Valuation Survey, the NPPBC is approximately seven times greater than the pay-as-you-go cost, on average. The seven times multiple in the 1991 Valuation Survey has been reduced to approximately five times in the 1992 Valuation Survey. To provide a better measure of how costs may change based on the specific makeup of an employer's population, the relationship of NPPBC to pay-as-you-go cost based on the number of active employees per retiree is summarized in Figure 1.

As Figure 1 demonstrates, the NPPBC as a multiple of cash cost (pay-as-you-go cost) decreases as a group matures because of the decreasing relative impact of active employees on the expense. Table 1 shows three companies with the same number of retirees, but a very different number of active employees. Amortization of the transition obligation over 20 years is assumed.

The level of NPPBC and its relationship to cash cost are materially affected by an employer's decision to amortize or immediately recognize the transition obligation. When there is immediate recognition of the transition obligation, there is a very large charge in the year of transition, and lower expenses for the next

Table 1.

Company	Retirees	Actives	Cash Cost* (Retirees Only)	NPPBC* Retirees	NPPBC* Actives	NPPBC* Total	NPPBC as a Multiple of Current Year Cost
A	1,000	1,000	1,000	2,000	1,000	3,000	3.0
B	1,000	4,000	1,000	2,000	4,000	6,000	6.0
C	1,000	10,000	1,000	2,000	10,000	12,000	12.0

*Dollars in thousands

Table 2.

Company	Retirees	Actives	Cash Cost*	NPPBC* Retirees	NPPBC* Actives	Total	NPPBC as a Multiple of Current Year Cost
Before change	1,000	10,000	1,000	2,000	10,000	12,000	12:1
After change	1,000	10,000	1,000	2,000	5,000	7,000	7:1

*Dollars in thousands

20 years. Almost all of the valuations in the March 1991 Valuation Survey assumed that the plan sponsor would choose amortization of the transition obligation.

For the March 1992 Valuation Survey, the NPPBC as a multiple of cash cost decreased when compared to the March 1991 Valuation Survey for all levels of population maturity. This was primarily because of changes in plan design for future retirees leading to reductions in benefits, but also because some valuations were done with somewhat more aggressive assumptions and some plan sponsors assumed an immediate recognition of the transition obligation. The March 1992 Valuation Survey reflected plan design changes consistent with what companies reported they were doing in the February 1991 Plan Design Survey. These two studies covered different samples of plan sponsors, but confirmed consistent action to reduce benefits.

Two thousand employers responded to the 1991 Plan Design Survey and showed that 61 percent of companies with 5,000 or more employees had made a postretirement benefit plan change, and 41 percent of companies with less than 5,000 employees had made such a plan change.

Using Company C from Table 1, Table 2 shows the impact on NPPBC of a plan design change reducing benefits for future retirees by 50 percent. The benefits for current retirees are identical on Tables 1 and 2. For any company, the relationship of NPPBC to cash will depend in large measure on the plan design and the number of actives per retiree.

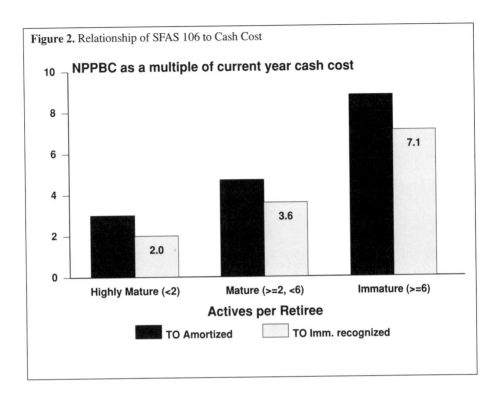

Figure 2. Relationship of SFAS 106 to Cash Cost

Combining the March 1991 and the March 1992 valuation surveys produces the results seen in Figure 2. The major components of the NPPBC, particularly in the first few years of the calculations, would be service cost, interest cost, and amortization of the transition obligation where applicable. The division of the expense into these components is shown in Table 3, with and without amortization of transition obligation.

The information in Table 3 is significant for understanding the level of cost for providing retiree health benefits. The service cost represents the value of the benefits assigned to the current year; the interest cost (without an offset for interest on assets) represents the consequence of having an unfunded plan; and the amortization represents "catch-up" since costs were recognized on a pay-as-you-go basis in the past. From 67 percent to 90 percent of the average cost in this situation is due to having had an unfunded plan with prior pay-as-you-go costs. For pension plans, the cost will more typically be an amount close to, or less than, the service cost. This is due not to the value of the benefits being currently earned, but rather to the fact that the pension plan is funded and has had accrual cost recognition for many years. As mentioned earlier, SFAS 106 NPPBC can be reduced by funding, but this is essentially a trade between the SFAS 106 NPPBC and investment income to the plan sponsor.

When the transition obligation is recognized immediately, the future NPPBC for the next 20 years is reduced by the amount of the amortization (which is no longer needed), and cost is now split between the two components as long as the

Table 3. Components of NPPBC If Transition Obligation Is Amortized

Description	Number of Actives per Retiree	Service Cost Percent	Interest Cost Percent	Amortization, Percent
Highly mature	Less than 2	10.2%	55.4%	34.2%
Mature	2 or more, but less than 6	21.5	48.9	32.0
Immature	6 or more	32.3	40.8	26.6

Table 4. Components of NPPBC If Transition Obligation Is Recognized Immediately

Description	Number of Actives per Retiree	Service Cost Percent	Interest Cost Percent
Highly mature	Less than 2	15.5%	84.5%
Mature	2 or more, but less than 6	30.5	69.5
Immature	6 or more	44.2	55.8

plan is unfunded). Table 4 shows the split of the cost and also can be viewed as the split after the end of the amortization period.

SURVEY ASSUMPTIONS

In the calculation of liabilities and expenses according to SFAS 106, many of the actuarial assumptions that must be made are similar to those used for pension valuations. However, for medical valuations, SFAS 106 requires the use of important assumptions that are unique to this calculation. These assumptions include medical claim costs by age for the current year and medical claim costs by age trended forward for as long as any current or future retirees would be projected to be receiving benefits (typically, projections would be required to 2080 or 2090).

The survey results presented also focus on the discount rate and are followed by a discussion of issues related to the discount rate.

Claim Cost and Aging Factors

In order to value retiree health benefits, it is necessary to construct a grid of medical claim costs by age. If possible, claim costs should be based on actual plan sponsor claim data, split between pre-65 and post-65 claims. Ideally, there should be enough participants for experience to be considered credible and statistically valid. The number of retirees and dependents covered by the group is also needed. Based on the March 1992 Valuation Survey, the median claim cost for a typical pre-Medicare retiree (age 61) would be approximately $3,000, and the median claim cost for a typical post-Medicare retiree (age 72) would be approximately $925.

Currently for most employers, there are not enough retirees and not enough detail in the claim data to analyze actual claim experience age by age. Hence, aggregate experience for pre-Medicare plans is first developed and then "aging factors" based on a national data bases are used to help develop costs by age.

Data on aging are available from some government sources, as is analysis of large group claims. This data indicates fairly rapid increases in cost at the middle ages and a slowing of the increasing pattern of claim costs between ages 75 and 80. Some situations show a flattening of plan costs by age at the higher ages. This is partly influenced by a shift to more long-term care benefits (not covered by the typical employer plan) at the very high ages and by the structure of Medicare benefits.

For some employers, there are barriers to direct development of claim costs, which include:

- Too small a number of retired participants
- Lack of consistent data on claims and individuals covered
- Too short a period of claim experience data to develop a credible claim pattern
- Major plan benefit or eligibility changes so that past claim data (even with adjustments) is not reflective of the current or future plan experience.

Where directly developed claim costs are unavailable (or not credible), there are a number of strategies that can be used. These include:

- Developing claim costs for the total retiree pool and using actuarial modeling techniques to split these into pre-Medicare and post-Medicare claim costs, by age
- Using expected costs for the active plan and adjusting for differences between expected active and retiree plan experience; the minimum adjustment is for age, and usually an adjustment is also made to recognize more adverse experience for retirees at the same age as actives
- Using premium rates if an insured arrangement is in place and adjusting them to be appropriate for the retiree group
- Using a similar technique that is possible with COBRA rates
- Estimating based on experience with other plans with similar benefits, demographics, and geographic characteristics.

Where one of these techniques is used initially, it is important to develop actual retiree experience as soon as feasible. If there is not a credible base of retirees, this will not be feasible for some time. Likewise, if a new plan is adopted where there was none previously, estimates based on actuarial relative value adjustments must be used initially.

In developing claim costs, it is also important to be sure that the technique used will give reasonable results form year to year. It is undesirable for results to fluctuate too much from year to year. Using several years of experience is one method to help smooth fluctuations. More years of experience provides for more life years of data. If available, it is suggested that three to five years experience be used to develop a claim cost. The experience of the earlier years should be adjusted for changes in medical cost levels (trend) and plan design changes already implemented in order to bring all years to a comparable basis.

Another special situation arises when there are differences in benefits (often modest) between location and separate experience by location. Claim costs often vary a great deal without being justifiable by differences in benefits or average costs by geographic area. In such cases, the actuary must consider which locations are large enough to be credible and whether or not it would be better to pool experience and then to make adjustments for plan design on an actuarially expected basis.

Medical Benefit Trend Rate

The trend rate measures the year-to-year change in health care costs under the plan. For SFAS 106 purposes, the impact of aging should not be included in the trend assumption. The trend rates must reflect the long-term rate of experience of the plan. It is common to use a higher trend rate initially, reflective of recent years' experience, and grade it down over time. Essentially, this is a compromise between what has happened recently and what is sustainable over the long term. If medical cost increases continue at rates higher than the increases in GNP over time, medical costs will reach an intolerable level. Currently, medical costs are about 12 percent of GNP. It is common to test the ultimate percentage of GNP for medical care that is implied by the trend rate. Opinions differed as to the limit on this figure, but amounts over 20 percent imply a very different society, and the authors think that Americans will demand a major change in the health care delivery system by the time medical costs reach 15 percent of GNP. The trend rate should consider the plan's benefit structure so that it reflects underlying changes in the costs of medical care, as well as the plan provisions and covered population. Employer costs can increase more rapidly than general medical costs because of the specific plan design, because of cost shifting from public sector programs to employer sponsored plans, and from one plan to another. The 1992, 1995, 2000, and the ultimate trend from the March 1992 Valuation Survey are shown in Table 5. The results of a SFAS 106 valuation are quite sensitive to changes in medical trend. A 1 percent decrease in medical trend produces approximately a 12 percent to 18 percent decrease in the APBO.

Table 5.

Percentile	1992 Trend	1995 Trend	2000 Trend	Ultimate Trend
20th	12%	9%	7.5%	6.4%
40th	14	10.5	8.0	7.0
Median (50th)	15	11.0	8.7	7.0
60th	15	11.0	9.0	7.5
80th	15	12.0	10.0	8.0

Table 6.

Percentile	Discount Rates by Valuation Year		
	1989	1990	1991
20th	7.50%	8.00%	8.25%
40th	8.00	8.50	8.50
Median (50th)	9.00	9.00	9.00
60th	9.00	9.00	9.00
80th	9.00	9.00	9.00

Table 7.

Percentile	Discount Rate Minus Ultimate Trend Rate
20th	.5%
40th	1.5%
Median (50th)	1.5%
60th	2.0%
80th	2.5%

DISCOUNT RATE

In paragraph 31, SFAS 106 states: "Assumed discount rate shall reflect the time value of money as of the measurement date in determining the present value of future cash outflows currently expected to be required to satisfy the postretirement benefit obligation. In making that assumption, employers shall look to rates of return on high quality fixed income investments currently available whose cash flows match the timing and amount of expected benefit payments."

There are important differences and similarities in the situation for pension and retiree health: SFAS 87 calls for using an interest rate at which the liabilities can be settled and which reflects the current market. Settlement of pension liabilities is very common through the purchase of annuities, and a bond portfolio can be used to match pension liabilities.

However, settling retiree health is generally not feasible, and matching is much more difficult as the medical plan cash flows generally get relatively much larger further out in the future because of the medical trend. The retiree health discount rate should reflect the interest rate on a long-term bond portfolio. As the

Table 8.

Discount Rate	Number	Percent
Under 8.00%	20	5.7
8.00–8.24%	42	12.0
8.25–8.49%	15	4.3
8.50–8.74%	76	21.7
8.75–8.99%	29	8.3
9.00–9.24%	107	30.5
9.25–9.49%	18	5.1
9.50–9.99%	31	8.8
10.00% and over	13	3.7
Total	351	100.0

Table 9.

Interest Rate	January		
	1990	1991	1992
PBGC immediate	7.25%	7.25%	6.50%
Government long term	8.66	8.32	7.80
Term			
Corporate long term	9.85	9.68	8.61
Corporate intermediate	9.49	9.23	7.27

retiree health liabilities are "longer in duration" than the pension liabilities, an interest rate .5 percent to 1.0 percent higher than the settlement rate for pension liabilities may be justified as long as there is a positive yield curve. A positive yield curve occurs when long-term rates are greater than short-term rates. The longer duration of retiree health liabilities is a consequence of the fact that these benefits increase with medical trend, whereas pension benefits are generally dollar amounts determined at retirement without any built-in indexing for inflation.

Based on the Mercer valuation surveys, the median discount rate used for 1989-1991 valuations was 9.0 percent. The range of discount rates from the Mercer valuation surveys are summarized in Table 6 according to a valuation year. As with medical trend, the SFAS 106 valuation is very sensitive to changes in the discount rate. For typical valuations, an increase in the discount rate of 1 percent causes the APBO to be reduced by 10 percent to 16 percent. It is common to look at the spread between the discount rate and the salary scale for pension plans, as both are influenced by inflation.

Because the postretirement health plan calculations are so sensitive to both medical trend and discount rates, and because both rates are partially driven by underlying general inflation, it is important to consider the "corridor" between discount rates and the ultimate trend rate. However, it is important to note that medical trend is also driven by a number of other factors including cost shifting and utilization. Relationships from the March 1992 Valuation Survey as shown in Table 7.

Actuaries working with retiree health have discussed whether the ultimate trend rate should be less than the discount rate. There is general agreement that the ultimate rate can be below the discount rate and that this reflects considerable change from the current environment. There is also agreement that this needs to happen, at least at the level of medical care in general.

Pension Versus Retiree Medical Discount Rates

The SFAS 106 discount rate assumption can be compared to assumptions used for pension accounting in accordance with SFAS 87. The practice is indicative of how corporate America has interpreted SFAS 87. Mercer has analyzed the 1990 fiscal year annual reports for 351 major companies and has found that the rates shown in Table 8 were used for pension calculations. The range of SFAS 87 rates shown in Table 8 indicates a wide range of latitude in interpreting SFAS 87.

External indices, which could be considered in developing discount rates for both purposes, include the interest rates as of January 1990, January 1991, and January 1992, as indicated in Table 9. The difference in the corporate intermediate and long-term indices shown in Table 9 confirms the higher rate for long-term bonds, refereed to earlier as a positive yield curve. The significant drop in rates during 1991 brings considerable uncertainty about the discount rate which will be used for 1992 valuations. It is very possible, in fact, that discount rates will be decreased in 1992 valuations.

Other Assumptions

In addition to discount rates, other assumptions with pension counterparts are retirement rates, termination rates, mortality rates, and disability rates. As discussed below, the magnitude of impact of these assumptions can be significantly different for pension plans than for other postretirement plans. However, the authors feel that these decremental assumptions should be consistent with the pension assumptions unless there is a specific reason to indicate otherwise. The increased sensitivity of financial statements relative to these assumptions may indicate a need to reexamine the pension assumptions at this time.

Termination Rates

It is much more important that termination rates be reflective of experience in a retiree health valuation compared to a pension valuation. For pension valuations, termination rates, after benefits are vested, are generally used. The benefits paid on vesting are calculated as part of the valuation. Since vested benefits are paid, the termination rates do not have a great effect on results. In contrast, retiree health benefits generally are lost if employees leave before retirement eligibility at the present time so termination dates have a major effect on the cost. This presents a major challenge. There are two actuarial approaches to the analysis of turnover. The first approach is to complete detailed gain and loss exhibits as part of the annual valuation. Such an analysis will show how close the impact of turnover rates in the actuarial valuation is to actual experience. The appropriate theoretical model for the second approach, a more extensive analysis of this issue, is to do a "turnover study" and analyze the rates of termination by age and length of service. Experience to date may be a key factor in expected experience, but in some cases it is not. Many organizations have been through downsizing in the last five years, and have changed so that recent experience is unusual and would not be valid as an assumption for the future. Experience prior to the recent period might also not be valid. This requires the actuary to work with the plan sponsor and jointly formulate their best judgment about future turnover.

Retirement Rates

Retirement rates are also different in impact. Most pension plans reduce benefits to reflect the longer payout period when people retire early. In some cases, the adjustment is actuarially equivalent; in others, those who retire earlier get a benefit worth more. Retirement rates are important to the pension valuation, but again their effect is dampened by the adjustments in benefits for early retirement.

In contrast, retiree health benefits are higher before medicare eligibility because there is no reduction for benefits already paid by Medicare. The plan cost per capita pre-Medicare is often three to six times the plan cost after Medicare eligibility because there is no reduction for benefits already paid by Medicare. The plan cost per capita pre-Medicare is often three to six times the plan cost after Medicare eligibility. A retiree at age 55 gets ten pre-Medicare years and then benefits supplementing Medicare, whereas an age 64 retiree gets only one pre-Medicare year. In addition, if an employee retires early, there are more years of benefit payments but no decrease in annual benefit to reflect the longer payout. This makes retirement rates much more important to the SFAS 106 valuation.

The same theoretical solution applies to developing retirement as well as termination rates, and the same practical difficulties relating to the unusual circumstances of the last few years exist.

SFAS 106 VERSUS SFAS 87

Mechanically, SFAS 106 looks a lot like the corresponding pension accounting rules as set forth in SFAS 87. Therefore, on first examination, it seems reasonable for plan sponsors to expect results on adoption of SFRAS 106 not unlike what they experienced when adopting SFAS 87. However, that will not happen in most cases.

Although pension expense sometimes went down when SFAS 87 was adopted, in most cases retiree health expense will go up by a considerable multiple. Pension expense was already based on accrual accounting, and costs were recognized over employees' working lives under prior pension accounting rules. Pension plans were also funded. For many organizations, the change to SFAS 87 slowed down the speed of cost recognition and made such cost recognition more uniform among plan sponsors. Where a plan had assets greater than the value attributed to past benefits in accordance with the rules, this amount—the "transition asset"—was amortized and served to reduce pension expense. In contrast, retiree health benefits have generally been funded on a pay-as-you-go basis, with no plan assets. As a result, there is generally a large transition obligation, but no interest income to offset the interest on the liability already accrued.

A consequence of having an unfunded plan is that expense will increase each year simply because the plan is unfunded. This is another difference between retiree health and pensions. Note that if a plan sponsor chooses to fund the plan, its SFAS 106 expense will be reduced over time, but there is an offsetting reduction in investment earnings in the underlying business. The net effect would be zero if after-tax earnings in the business and the benefit plan fund were exactly the same. The funding decision is very different for pensions and retiree health. Because pension funds are subject to minimum funding by federal law, there is no choice about funding. Funding retiree health, however, is a business decision.

Another key difference between retiree health and most pension plans is that the pension plan benefits generally are not indexed for inflation after retirement, whereas the health benefits are usually effectively indexed (by virtue of increases as medical costs increase) at a rate significantly greater than the cost of living index (CPI). This factor will also serve to substantially increase the retiree health care costs that must currently be recognized under SFAS 106. Some plan sponsors are changing their plan design to limit the future increase in their share of retiree health care costs.

For all of these reasons, it is important to be careful in interpreting retiree health valuations and building expectations. Although knowledge of pension accounting is a base, it is important to focus on differences as well as similarities.

Value of Forecasts

The expected pattern year by year of SFAS 106 costs is very different from the expected pattern of SFAS 87 costs. SFAS 87 costs can be volatile depending on asset returns, particularly in a well-funded plan, but there is no expectation that they will generally increase in the long run as a percentage of payroll. In contrast, SFAS 106 costs generally will increase year by year because of the following factors:

1. Health care benefit increases in recent years have been more than assumed.
2. Changes in demographics—in particular, increases in the number of employees eligible for future benefits—will increase the costs of an ongoing plan.
3. For unfunded plans (more than 95 percent of postretirement medical plans), costs will increase as interest cost increases without any corresponding offset for investment income.

The level of increase in SFAS 106 costs is surprising to most plan sponsors accustomed to much less significant year-by-year changes in pension costs. Cost increases may also be exacerbated by claim costs going up faster than expected in accordance with the actuarial assumptions in the valuation.

Experience with plan sponsors who have done multiple year valuations has frequently indicated that costs are increasing faster than expected and that they are surprised by the "expected increases," as well as by the increases due to actuarial gains and losses.

Forecasts can be helpful in evaluating the long-term implications of funding, different assumption strategies, and different plan design strategies. In some situations, the first year's effect of a change is misleading as the long-term effect can be different. For example, companies considering the possibility of using a defined contribution approach may find that the short- and long-term costs implications are radically different. Assumption changes that reduce the short-term NPPBC may very well increase the long-term NPPBC. Forecasts are important in helping a company to evaluate any major changes over time and to understand the dynamics of SFAS 106 over time. A company considering a comprehensive strategy to manage the benefits is probably also considering other human resources changes, and may be expecting a variety of changes in benefits and workforce.

SPECIAL ISSUES—COMPANIES IN TRANSITION

As companies change from accounting on a pay-as-you-go basis to an accrual basis, there are a number of issues they should consider. Key among these issues are the following:

- Whether to adopt early, or wait until the latest possible date
- Whether to recognize the full transition obligation immediately, or to amortize it
- Whether to change benefits before adoption of SFRAS 106

SFAS 106 requires large U.S. employers to adopt the new accounting rules for fiscal years beginning after December 15, 1992. However, employers can adopt SFAS 106 sooner if they desire. Employers with financial results that are either significantly better or worse than anticipated often decide to adopt SFAS

106 in the same year as the unusual experience. Typically, they feel it is better to explain several unusual occurrences in one year than to explain occurrences for several years. Early adopting and onetime transition will put a large liability on the balance sheet. Most employers, however, probably won't adopt SFAS 106 until the requirement date.

For those who do not adopt early, disclosure of the anticipated financial impact of SFAS 106 is required under Staff Accounting Bulletin 74 of the Securities and Exchange Commission. Specifically, "Where the registrant has made reasonable estimates based on the existing plan, but has not yet identified a specific plan change(s) that will occur before the adoption of Statement 106, . . . SAB 74 requires the disclosure of the amount of the present liability under the current plan and its effect on earnings . . . if it is probable that [any of] the intend change[s] will occur before the adoption of Statement 106, . . . registrants should disclose the impact of the plan that is probable of being in place upon the adoption of Statement 106 rather than the existing plan."

In addition to deciding when to adopt SFAS 106, employers also must decide whether to immediately recognize the transition obligation or to amortize it over the remaining working lifetime to retirement of active workers, or 20 years, if greater. Average remaining lifetime as an amortization period should be used for a plan that covers retirees only. Concern about loan covenants or the desire to keep unbroken history of earnings per share growth are two typical reasons to amortize the transition obligation. The primary reasons for immediate recognition—assuming the balance sheet would allow such—is the feeling that investment analysis will not penalize a company for recognizing its full postretirement liability initially. In fact, because earnings will not be reduced by amortization of the transition obligation in future years, investors might actually favor the employers that immediately recognize their transition obligation.

Many employers are currently considering postretirement medical design changes, and the timing of such changes. Some employers are hurrying to make the changes before they adopt SFAS 106, while other employers are holding off on changes temporarily. The primary reason for making changes quickly is to lower the SFAS 106 liability upon adoption or upon disclosure under SAB 74. For employers that are delaying changes temporarily, the primary reason is to allow more time to study their postretirement coverage options. Employers should develop objectives for the entire retirement program, develop design options, and prepare communication and implementation plans consistent with the objectives.

Because the difference between accrual and cash accounting can be substantial, the many decisions on how to accrue need to be carefully considered. Each plan is unique and has components that weigh differently in importance.

The authors believe that the vast majority of employers now offering relatively high benefit postretirement plans other than pensions will, if they have not already done so, review their plans and make some changes—even if minor—to reduce SFAS 106 cost.

CONCLUSION

SFAS 106 has focused attention on postretirement benefits other than pensions. Employers implementing SFAS 106 are making decisions that will affect their level and pattern of earnings. The increased focus on retiree health has caused many employers to examine these benefits and, as in any other benefit plan review, the company's reason for having the benefit and its ability to pay for the benefit. At the same time, employers have been reexamining the entire retirement package. The results of the various Mercer surveys show that many companies have already taken steps to reduce their liabilities for retiree health. The medical benefits promised to future retirees will likely be different from those received by retirees today. The future benefits will reflect a compromise between the needs of the retiree, the needs of the company and their ability to pay, and the interests of society. It will be a great challenge to employers to set policy and find the appropriate balance for their companies.

35. Financing or Funding Options for Retiree Health Benefits

Paul M. Millholland

Some major corporations have decided to reduce costs and cost volatility by prefunding retiree health obligations. But before embarking on that course, an employer should carefully review all of the options—and the tax implications of each.

On December 20, 1990, the Financial Accounting Standards Board adopted new accounting rules for retiree health benefits by issuing Statement of Financial Accounting Standards Number 106. The new rule, which becomes effective December 15, 1992, requires companies to recognize their "net periodic postretirement benefit cost" as an expense on their income statements. They must also recognize on their balance sheets the actuarial present value of the benefits, attributable to the accrual period, in excess of plan assets.

To calculate Financial Accounting Standards Number 106 (FAS 106) liability, the employer must first determine the "expected postretirement benefit obligation" (EPBO). This consists of two parts: the present value of employees' future service benefits, and the past service benefits that have already been earned. The value of these past service benefits is known as the "accumulated postretirement benefit obligation" (APBO). The unfunded, unrecognized APBO in existence when the FASB rules are first applied is known as the "transition obligation." It may be recognized immediately, or over a period equal to the longer of either the employees'

351

average remaining length of service or 20 years. It is from these figures that the employer calculates the net periodic postretirement cost that must be shown as an expense on the employer's income statement. In general, company expenses for these benefits will be higher under FAS 106 because of the need to amortize the accumulated obligation plus expense benefits as earned rather than as paid. One of the things FAS 106 does not require is prefunding.

Once the liability has been calculated, there are essentially two issues that a company needs to address relating to the financing or funding of that liability. First, a company may want to consider ways to reduce its liability, if any. The extent of the liability is determined by the nature of the employer promise. Thus, if an employer offers no retiree health benefits but creates a vehicle for employees to save for such coverage, the employer may have no FAS 106 liability. The second issue concerns the extent to which a company wants to provide for financing the liability (i.e., setting aside funds in advance to pay for retiree health benefits but not formally dedicating the funds for that purpose) or prefunding the liability (i.e., setting aside funds during an employee's working years that are restricted to specifically providing retirement health benefits).

REDUCING LIABILITY

FAS 106 liability may be reduced by decreasing the level of benefits, changing the method of Medicare integration, altering the age and/or service requirements for benefit eligibility, increasing the retirees' contributions, changing to a defined contribution approach, capping employer-paid premiums, providing no company retiree health benefit plan but giving employees the option of buying group annuities, or increasing pension payments to allow the retiree to purchase private coverage.

Many companies have already implemented some of these methods. For example, IBM announced in July 1990 that it would cap spending on retiree health benefits for employees retiring after December 31, 1991. Those who retire and are under age 65 will have a cap of $7,000 per person per year. Those eligible for Medicare receive up to $3,000 per year.

Another example is Warner-Lambert, which is reducing its FAS 106 liability by combining a cap with prospective elimination of company retiree health benefits, softened by an increase in pension payments. The company has capped its cost for retiree health benefits at $150 per month for an individual and $300 per month for a family, for employees that retired before January 1, 1992. Employees retiring January 1, 1992 or later will receive a separate pension benefit of $8 per month per year of service to purchase private medical insurance. The company has made arrangements with an insurance company to make insurance coverage available to its retiring employees, but the retired employee is free to purchase insurance from any source or not purchase coverage at all.

FINANCING OR FUNDING CONSIDERATIONS

Some employers believe they can earn a higher rate of return by investing the money in their business than they can earn on fund investments to pay for retiree health benefits. Other companies may simply lack the cash necessary to fund the liability. There are also stringent limitations on the tax deductibility by the employer and the payment of tax-free benefits to employees. In addition, there are many grey areas on the tax side because there has been very little guidance from IRS. For these reasons, not many employers have decided to set aside funds to specifically prefund their retiree health care liability. On the other hand, companies that decide to maintain retiree health benefits may be able to reduce costs and cost volatility by prefunding their retiree health obligations even if only on a limited tax-favored basis.

Options

Following are some of the options available to employers who choose to fund their retiree health liabilities, with the corresponding advantages and disadvantages for companies and employees.

Transfer of Surplus Pension Assets to a Section 401(h) Retiree Health Account
The Omnibus Budget Reconciliation Act of 1990 (OBRA '90) created Internal Revenue Code (Code) Section 420, which allows for a limited transfer of surplus assets to a 401(h) account to pay for current retiree medical liabilities. Transferred assets cannot be used to prefund future liabilities; therefore, this transfer does not reduce the future FAS 106 liability. It is a way to put funds into a separate account within a defined benefit pension plan to finance current year retiree health expenses. The transfers can be made once a year through 1995. Once a transfer is made, the employer cannot reduce per retiree health costs for the next five years. In addition, the employer must fully vest all potential beneficiaries as if the plan had been terminated immediately before the qualified transfer. The transferred assets may not be used to discriminate in favor of highly compensated employees. Money transferred and not used to pay health benefits must be transferred back to the pension plan account or it is subject to the excise tax on asset reversions. The transfer cannot reduce the level of pension assets below the full funding limitation (the lower of 125 percent of current pension liabilities for accrued benefits or 150 percent of termination liabilities).

Transfers are less attractive than they might have been at one time because of the requirements of immediate vesting and maintenance of level spending for five years, the current year cost rule, and the excise tax on asset reversions. However, employers that have been paying for retiree health benefits on a pay-as-you-go basis can now use excess pension assets to reduce current retiree health benefits costs. The transfer of excess pension assets is advantageous primarily to employers with overfunded pension plans and large current year liabilities. Cash flow is increased since retiree health costs do not have to be paid out of the current year's operating income. The disadvantage of the transfer is that it reduces the current tax deduction for medical benefits. It also hastens the time when the employer must begin making tax-deductible contributions to the pension plan. Retiree health benefits provided through this type of 401(h) plan are tax-free.

401(h) Medical Account in a Pension Plan

Companies may put up to 25 percent of their total aggregate pension contributions (excluding those for past service credits) into a 401(h) medical account that is part of a pension plan. This 401(h) contribution is tax deductible and earnings accumulate tax-free, two major advantages. This vehicle is available to employers with defined benefit plans that have not reached the full funding limits. These accounts can also be part of a money purchase pension plan to which the employer makes annual contributions, in which case the full finding limit is never reached. The 25 percent limit still applies as do the 415 limits. Because accumulated funds are restricted to the payment of retiree medical benefits, the employer may use these assets to offset the FAS 106 liabilities. This is another advantage for the employer. The disadvantage is that this option is not available to companies with fully funded pension plans. Retirees have the advantage of receiving tax-free health benefits through a 401(h) medical account.

Consolidated Edison of New York and Central Illinois Light Company are making employer contributions to a 401(h) medical account to prefund their retiree health benefit liability.

Profit-Sharing Plans

The amounts allocated to participant accounts may be used to provide incidental life, accident, or health insurance. "Incidental" means the total premium for all three coverages combined may not exceed 25 percent of the employer contributions and forfeitures allocated to the participant's account.

This approach provides employees the ability to build up more money in their profit-sharing plan, which can be used to pay for increased retiree contributions for medical benefits in retirement. Thus, employees use a certain part of their account balance to pay for their retiree medical expenses. The company can either designate the contribution percentage allocated for this purpose on behalf of all participants, or let each employee designate his or her own percentage.

The money when distributed to pay retiree medical benefits is considered by some to be a taxable distribution; others assert it may be tax-free if the plan itself buys retiree medical coverage and then pays medical benefits. In other words, this is grey area, subject to challenge. If this arrangement restricts amounts in the plan to the provision of retiree medical benefits, the funds can offset employers' accumulated FAS 106 liability. In addition, the employer has the advantages of tax deductible contributions and tax-free buildup of the funds.

Employee Stock Ownership Plan (ESOP)

Employee stock ownership plans (ESOPs) can also be used as a method of providing assets for employees to draw upon in paying for retiree health benefits. The ESOP may be a separate plan, or used as a means of financing the employer's contributions to a 401(k) plan. Contributions by the employer are tax deductible. Employees benefit from the tax-deferred aspects of the plan, but distributions from the ESOP are taxable to the employee when received.

Gillette Company has begun to shift the cost of retiree health benefits from the company to employees and used an ESOP to provide money for employees to pay for retiree health benefits. Employees who were hired before July 1990, and retire after December 31, 1991 will be responsible each year after retirement for an increasingly larger share of their retiree health benefits premium, which can be paid from their ESOP. Employees hired after July 1990 and who retire after December 31, 1991 will have to pay the full cost of their retiree health benefits premium, again using assets from the ESOP. All employees who retired before December 31, 1991 are grandfathered into a company-paid retiree health plan.

Boise Cascade uses a combination of a 401(k) plan and an ESOP, which was instituted in 1989. They use an ESOP to match employee contributions to their 401(k) plan. One half of the company stock goes into a separate account to provide money for employees to pay for retiree medical benefits. ESOP stock is allocated on the basis of years of service. Employees retired before 1989 are not involved in the ESOP arrangement but do pay a portion of the cost of their retiree medical benefits.

Defined Contribution Accounts

The defined contribution concept, commonly used to provide retirement benefits, is gaining employer appeal for welfare plans as well. In such cases, the employer is promising a specified dollar amount toward health benefits, versus the open-ended and potentially unlimited promise of health benefits. Employees are usually given a fixed dollar amount for each year of service. The dollars or credits accumulated at retirement may then be used toward the payment of premiums for retiree health benefits. If the employee has the option of taking the accumulated amount in cash, it would become taxable income when received.

The Pillsbury Company, The Vons Companies, Inc., and Weyerhaeuser Company are a few of the companies using the defined contribution approach.

Corporate Owned Life Insurance

Corporate owned life insurance (COLI) is another method an employer can use to finance retiree health benefits, in that the employer makes a specific investment to give the corporation itself the money to pay its retiree health costs. The company usually purchases life insurance on part or all of the active work force. As deaths occur, the company collects life insurance proceeds tax free. The company also has the option of borrowing against or withdrawing the cash value of the policy if necessary to create a positive cash flow to meet all or part of the benefit costs. The primary advantages to the employer are the tax-free death benefits and the buildup of earnings on a tax-deferred basis. In addition, interest on policy loans up to $50,000 is deductible. The retiree health benefits are still provided from a retiree health plan separate from COLI and are tax-free.

There are some considerations to keep in mind in using COLI as a way to finance retiree health benefits. There must be a transfer of risk from the employer to the insurance company (including asset performance), although some carriers will allow outside investment managers to give direction. Assets may be maintained in a separate account but the credit worthiness of the carrier needs to be considered because the death benefit claim is still at risk. A switch of carriers may be made at any time, tax-free. At the state level, there are insurable interest laws that have to be dealt with, and in this regard some states require employee consent to insure the life of the employee. This may or may not present an employee relations and/or an administration problem.

Group Annuities

An employer may provide employees with the option to purchase group annuities while they are working to provide a stream of income in retirement to pay for retiree health benefits. Some have interpreted an IRS regulation as permitting both the health care-related distributions and the earned interest to be tax-free, although if employer contributions are used the inside buildup is taxed. Others have challenged this interpretation, so the tax treatment of group annuity payments under these circumstances is currently unclear. The major attraction to the employer is that it is a way to shift responsibility for the cost of retiree health benefits to the employees while allowing employees to save for their retiree health benefits, possibly in a tax-favored manner.

Ball Corporation of Muncie, Indiana is using a variation of this approach for salaried employees hired after 1989. All salaried employees are eligible to participate, regardless of hire date, but must contribute at least 2 percent of pay via payroll deduction or lump sum payments. These after-tax contributions are invested in group annuities set at a fixed rate of interest. Retirees obtain private health insurance and pay out-of-pocket health expenses. These bills are then submitted to the company, which reimburses the retiree tax-free out of their annuity account. It is important to note that the IRS has not by any means blessed this approach.

501(c)(9) Trust or Voluntary Employee Benefit Association

A 501(c)(9) trust, also called a voluntary employee benefit association (VEBA), can be used for investing employer contributions to pay for retiree health benefits, but deductible contributions are limited by law. In particular, the funding maximum is calculated by disregarding future medical inflation. Employer contributions to the trust are tax deductible, which is one advantage, but the disadvantage is that the trust earnings are subject to a maximum 31-percent unrelated business income tax (UBIT). Employers do not face the above deduction limit or UBIT, however, if the trust is established under a collective bargaining agreement. Funds in a VEBA, which are assets that offset the retiree health benefit liabilities of active employees, may be dedicated to reduce FAS 106 liability. This is another major employer advantage. The primary advantage to the retiree is that health benefits provided through a VEBA are tax-free.

Ameritech, Bell South, and Westinghouse are some of the companies using 501(c)(9) trusts for prefunding retiree health liabilities through employer contributions.

Trust Owned Life Insurance

Trust owned life insurance (TOLI) is a recently established approach that allows COLI to be combined with a VEBA to provide employers some tax advantages not found in a VEBA or COLI alone. Employer contributions to the VEBA are used by the trust to buy life insurance on some or all of the individuals who will be entitled to retiree health benefits. The TOLI premiums are thought to be tax deductible, subject to VEBA deduction limits, although some IRS spokesmen have informally suggested otherwise.

The major advantage is that the cash value can be used as an offset against the FAS 106 liability. Another key advantage over the stand-alone VEBA is that there is interpreted to be no unrelated business income tax on the inside buildup in the TOLI because cash value accumulation is tax sheltered. As with COLI, the death benefits are tax-free and interest on policy loans up to $50,000 is deductible. Retirees receive health benefits tax-free since funds in the VEBA are for the specific purpose of providing retiree health benefits.

The same considerations apply in using TOLI as a way to prefund retiree health benefit liabilities as with using COLI as a financing vehicle (described previously).

HSOP

A HSOP is an Employee Stock Ownership Plan (ESOP) that has qualified as a money purchase pension plan and is combined with a 401(h) medical account. HSOPs were developed to add two advantages not present in ESOPs: providing tax-free medical benefits to retirees and having earmarked assets to count toward the FAS 106 liability. Although the IRS approved the first such plan, which was created by Procter & Gamble, it has since directed all of its field offices not to issue determination letters on HSOPs, pending a comprehensive review. There is speculation that IRS will disallow such plans, in part because of revenue implications, if they were adopted on a wide scale.

Employee Contributions Toward Prefunding Vehicles

Employers may also want to consider whether or not these prefunding vehicles can receive employee contributions. In addition to reducing the cost to the employer, the advantages and disadvantages to employees under the different options should be considered. These are determined by the taxability of their contributions and of their benefits.

Some vehicles, such as TOLI, do not lend themselves to employee contributions. Where employee contributions could be made, they would be voluntary and made with after-tax income. Also, there would be no additional tax advantage at the time the benefit was received. As a result, there is no particular incentive for the employee to participate unless the employer discontinues health benefits at retirement for active employees who do not contribute. Another disadvantage of asking employees to contribute is that it may leave the employer with the dilemma of what to do about employees who choose not to participate.

If employees contribute to an employee-pay-all VEBA, the inside buildup of the fund is tax-free but individual employees may not receive a refund of their contributions. Over time, the employee contributions (and earnings thereon) reduce or eliminate the employer's FAS 106 liability. One of the primary concerns is whether sufficient funds can be accumulated to pay for medical benefits over the retiree's lifetime.

36. Key Issues in Plan Design for the 1990s and Beyond

Anna Rappaport   Beth Vorwaller

Retiree health benefits have become a topic of increasing focus and visibility as the implementation date for SFAS 106 approaches. In 1992, it is clear that retiree health is a significant part of an increasingly difficult national health care environment, and that public policy is in need of reform. There is widespread recognition that these benefits are costly; employers are seeking ways to manage the cost while employees are realizing how important these benefits are. This article provides an update on retiree health benefit issues and a review of the current situation. It will summarize the challenges facing the government in its effort to bring about health care reform and the challenges employers and employees face in managing their benefits without a longer-term definition of public policy.

THE NATIONAL HEALTH CARE ENVIRONMENT

Today's major health policy concern does not focus on the retiree, but rather on the uninsured. There are an estimated 37 million Americans without any health insurance coverage. Generally, these do not include the poor who are covered by Medicaid nor Medicare eligible retirees. The uninsured include many of the near poor as well as working individuals without coverage, many of the unemployed, and some retirees not yet eligible for Medicare.

The government's primary concern involving health policy for the uninsured is how to develop a national approach so that there is coverage for all Americans.

At present, the system of providing health care benefits in the United States is essentially employer based and voluntary. Government sponsored coverage is available only to the poor, those over age 65 with coverage under the Social Security system, and certain individuals with disabilities.

Economic pressures have created strains on both the government and private systems which exist today. Government programs have gradually been reduced. Reductions in these programs for the poor have meant lower reimbursement to providers and fewer people covered in some cases. In Oregon, there are limitations on the types of treatment covered. Reductions in government programs produce cost shifting that affects individuals, providers and employers.

Health care costs constitute about 13 percent of the Gross National Product (GNP) and are continuing to increase as a percentage of GNP. This is partially a result of increasing prices, but also a result of better and more extensive technology and changing utilization.

In addition to government's general concern about health care and the role of public policy in health care reform, are the following specific concerns about retiree health care benefits:

- Medicare policy
- Regulation of Medigap policies
- Possible extension of ERISA and employee benefit law to include retiree health benefits
- Taxation of benefits
- Funding requirements
- COBRA application

Medicare Policy

Reimbursements

The biggest changes in Medicare in the last decade have been changes in the method of reimbursing hospitals and, more recently, physicians. The Medicare reimbursement systems are designed to provide a certain level of reimbursement and have, in the case of hospital reimbursements, resulted in increases in charges for private pay patients.

The impact of the changes in physician reimbursement are still developing. It is very possible that Medicare reimbursement levels will continue to be controlled and will increase less rapidly than health care costs generally. This will result in employer plans being asked to pay a greater share of the total cost.

Eligibility

Social Security has modified its retirement ages so that the age for receipt of full benefits will gradually increase from 65 to 67 for persons born after 1959. Medicare eligibility, however, remains at age 65 regardless of year of birth. There has been no move within public circles to increase these ages, and there has even been some suggestion that reducing them would help eliminate the coverage gap for early retirees. Many observers feel, nevertheless, that increases in retirement ages are quite likely since the demographics point to a vast increase in the elderly population.

Primary Status

Medicare is currently secondary to employer plans for employees who are working and over age 65, but primary for retirees covered by employer programs. It is possible that this could change and Medicare could become secondary for retirees covered by an employer program. This would probably cause many employers to discontinue post-Medicare retiree coverage.

Benefits Covered

Another area of uncertainty relates to the specific benefits covered by Medicare. Medicare does not include any coverage for prescription drugs, and only includes very limited long-term care coverage. It also has limits on covered hospital care, so that some elderly are left with uncovered catastrophic costs.

In 1988, Congress enacted the Medicare Catastrophic Coverage Act (MCCA), which filled some of the gaps, but did not deal with long-term care. The drug coverage in this legislation was also quite limited. The changes were to be financed by the elderly by a combination of tax increases and Medicare premium increases. However, MCCA was repealed the following year after a great deal of protest about its financing. The coverage gaps still remain and there seems to be little short-term interest in addressing them.

Financing

Medicare is currently financed by taxes on workers, Medicare premiums, and general federal revenues. The portion of the Medicare financing that is from premiums (i.e., paid by the elderly) is small, but it would have increased significantly under MCCA. Although MCCA was repealed, parallel changes were made to Social Security. Social Security benefits were entirely tax free for many years. However, today up to 50 percent of Social Security benefits are taxed for recipients with incomes of over $25,000.

Regulation of Medigap Policies

Medigap policies are individual insurance policies that supplement Medicare coverage. As part of the 1990 federal budget legislation, new requirements were enacted for Medigap policies. Insurers are required to offer no more than ten standard plans that have been developed by the National Association of Insurance Commissioners. These policies generally cover Medicare deductibles and co-payments, though some cover Medicare ineligible items such as drugs and additional long-term care within predefined limits. Insurance companies must now provide a six-month open enrollment period for new Medicare Part B enrollees. During this period, the insurance company cannot deny insurance or discriminate in the pricing based on the retiree's health status or medical condition.

Possible Extension of ERISA and Employee Benefit Law

The government has set out very specific laws governing pension benefits. These include mandatory prefunding, vesting, benefit accrual, and joint and survivor requirements. Although there are uncertainties with regard to specific issues, there are numerous rules which have become so complex that compliance is a major issue for many employers.

In contrast, retiree health law is much less well-defined, but has been the subject of a great deal of litigation. It remains an area of uncertainty as to whether retiree health benefits will become subject to the same types of requirements as pension plans.

Important issues relating to "ERISAfication" include the effect it would have on employers' benefit security and other compensation and its effect on the federal deficit.

On the surface, it appears that imposing such rules would have a positive effect from the perspective of employees by enhancing benefit security. However, this may not be the case. It is unclear whether imposing such rules would enhance security, or whether it would simply cause employers to abandon their plans. For employers, there is a delicate balance.

Taxation of Benefits

Pension contributions are generally deductible at the time they are made with investment income tax deferred. Benefits are generally taxable when paid. For retiree health, most benefits are provided on a pay-as-you-go basis, although there is limited tax-favored prefunding available. Benefits are generally not taxable when paid so that rather than being tax deferred, prefunded amounts are tax free.

Benefits can also be paid from profit-sharing or pension plans, but there is some uncertainty involving the tax status of amounts provided as incidental benefits from profit-sharing plans. Some experts argue that this can be done on a tax-free basis. Clarification is possible within the next couple of years, although at present there is no activity by the government to clarify.

Funding Requirements

There is currently no requirement to prefund for retiree health benefits. Voluntary prefunding is possible to some extent through the use of voluntary employees' beneficiary association (VEBAs) or 401(h) accounts. One of the issues discussed over the last few years is a potential change in funding rules to encourage and make prefunding easier. It has been argued that this will increase participant security and make employers more willing to sponsor plans.

COBRA Application

COBRA currently requires employers to offer continued coverage for 18 months, but not beyond Medicare eligibility. There have been proposals to extend COBRA so that employers are mandated to continue coverage for retirees until they reach Medicare eligibility.

The biggest concern for a pre-Medicare eligible retiree is access to affordable coverage. It is not uncommon for a pre-Medicare retiree to incur costs two and one-half times that of an active employee. For example, a plan with a COBRA rate of $100 per month per person could have a cost for early retirees of as much as $250 per month per person.

The availability of COBRA coverage for the early retiree would help the access problem, but it might well hurt those retirees who currently have coverage with a greater subsidy, as employers might be inclined to discontinue more liberal coverage.

CHALLENGE TO EMPLOYERS

The financing of health care in the United States is centered around employers, and employers today are under increasing cost pressure. Businesses are facing tougher competition both at home and abroad, government entities are under budget pressure, and not-for-profits are finding it harder to get funding from traditional sources. All of this means more pressure on labor costs which translates into pressure on benefit and compensation costs. Rising health care benefits costs are absorbing a greater part of each compensation dollar, leaving less for other benefits and pay increases. Employers have been seeking ways to manage and control their health care costs (both for active employees and retirees).

Furthermore, in response to these economic pressures, many organizations have downsized and have encouraged early retirement through special early retirement window programs. This has increased both the number of employees eligible for retiree health and the period of time that they will get benefits prior to Medicare eligibility.

The employer's challenge is balancing the needs of the organization with the needs of the employee. For a privately-owned company, this can be viewed as balancing shareowner and employee interests. This is particularly difficult today because dollars available for total compensation are often growing slowly, and sometimes not at all, while demands for benefits are increasing. The individual without employer-sponsored health benefits may find coverage unavailable, and will certainly find it expensive.

Employers are finding a variety of different ways to balance these competing demands. Some are increasing productivity, generating more resources for both shareowners and employees. Others are managing labor costs by limiting direct compensation and working to keep benefit costs down.

In this environment, a change in the recognition of retiree health costs would be particularly difficult. The situation is tougher because many employers have traditionally run their businesses on the basis that there was no cost until the benefits were paid.

The strategy management takes involves a variety of different issues. The employer must review its policies, as well as the needs of the retiree, weighing the risks of the employer and the employee and determining who is responsible and to what extent. Complicating the issues is our changing demographic makeup. Management's strategy for retiree health is often a focus on total retirement income, and a change in design and/or financing of one or more components of the retirement package.

Retiree Need

The entire population needs a method for financing medical care. In any year, most Americans will have some medical expenses, and a few will have very large expenses. In a typical employer plan, 1 percent of the employees account for 30 percent of the claims, 3 percent account for 50 percent of the claims, and 10 percent account for 75 percent of the claims. The expenses of the average family without severe illness may be viewed as budgetable, with the benefit plan viewed as a means to cover unusually high expenses.

Medicare eligible retirees get Medicare, so their residual needs are quite different from the needs of the general population. Medicare covers a very substantial part of the acute needs of the retiree, but with substantial gaps. The biggest gaps for the Medicare beneficiary are:

- Very long-term acute care hospital stays
- Very high doctor bills, diagnostic test bills, etc.
- Long-term care, including nursing home and community-based care
- Some outpatient prescription drugs
- Physician charges in excess of the Medicare limits on allowable cost
- The costs of services not covered at all by Medicare

Congress has changed the method of payment to physicians. In 1989, when it repealed the Medicare Catastrophic Coverage Act, it also enacted the Resource Based Relative Value System (RBRVS) for paying physicians. At this point, it is unclear precisely what this will mean for employer plans, but it appears likely that it will result in more cost shifting to employers and ultimately the retiree. Employer plans may also decide to adopt RBRVS as their method of payment. It is quite possible that PPOs will adopt this method of payment.

Many employer plans that include post-Medicare coverage find that prescription drugs account for 30 percent to 40 percent of plan costs after age 65. This is a major area for consideration in a Medicare supplement.

Risks to Retirees and Employers

Identification and analysis of risks provide a context for employer policy development. From the employer's point of view, retiree health continues to be a risky and difficult benefit to manage. Some of the risks include:

- **New technologies.** These are more expensive, and may prolong life, adding periods of extremely costly treatment.
- **Medicare risk.** Essentially this refers to the possibility that the employer's share of the cost will go up as Medicare changes or becomes secondary.
- **Inflation.** Medical prices have increased much more rapidly than general prices in the United States.
- **Litigation.** Employers may find that they have assumed obligations that they did not intend to because of court interpretations.
- **Employee relations risk.** Supervisors and others with apparent authority may make legally binding promises that the employer did not intend to make.
- **Public policy.**

The risks have not changed and they are expected to continue.

As mentioned earlier, medical costs as a percentage of GNP have risen steadily to about 13 percent. Employer health care plan costs have often risen much more rapidly than total health care spending due to the design of the programs and the interaction between government and private spending.

From the employees' point of view, the risks seem to be growing. The greatest risk is not having coverage at all, and not being able to get it because of evidence of insurability issues. The next greater risk relates to having access to affordable coverage.

Employer Policy

Retiree health benefits policy needs to be developed within the context of the employer's general benefits policy. Benefits policy can be defined along a spectrum ranging from compensation to entitlement. A purely entitlement-oriented employer would offer fully paid retiree health. A compensation-oriented employer would not offer the benefit at all. Most employers have adopted a middle position in their total compensation and benefits arrangements, and many are redefining their policies today, with a move more toward a compensation orientation. This is being implemented in retiree health programs with a variety of strategies including:

- Discontinuance of benefits in some situations
- Stricter eligibility rules
- Greater cost sharing
- Limiting employer obligation for future cost increases

Employer policy also needs to be developed within the general context of retirement policy. There is no consensus today about the importance, desirability, and relevance of "career employment" as a goal of human resources policy. The traditional retirement program in larger organizations was designed to reward and foster career employment, and many individuals spent large portions of their working years with a single employer. Some organizations view career employment to be just as important today as in the past, whereas others feel that it is an outdated view of working patterns.

Actual employment patterns during the 1990s still indicate that many organizations have a lot of long-term employees who will be reaching retirement age in the next ten to 20 years. Quality is a growing concern of American organizations. It is very possible that an outgrowth of the quality movement will be a new focus on career employment.

A second key issue in establishing a retirement policy is the early retirement objectives. Some employers think that it is important to support and encourage early retirement, whereas others do not. Some feel that it will become important to encourage people to work longer as demographics change.

An employer's orientation regarding entitlement and retirement policy will generally determine the overall position on retiree health benefits. An employer who is entitlement oriented and wishes to support career employment is very likely to offer these benefits. An employer who wishes to encourage early retirement is also likely to offer these benefits even if the employer is not concerned about career employment or entitlement. A compensation-oriented employer not focused on career employment is relatively unlikely to offer these benefits.

Who Pays?

In addition to the employer's need to determine whether or not to offer the benefit through an employer plan, there is the additional question of who should pay for the benefit. This should be considered in the context of the level and adequacy of the retirement benefits, and the overall policy toward retirement. Currently, there is a shift in employer philosophy to more individual responsibility for retirement.

Demographic Issues

There has been a major trend to earlier retirement over the last 30 years, and in recent years, retirement trends have been driven by downsizing and corporate restructuring. Labor force participation rates in the last two years, however, indicate a leveling off, meaning retirement ages may again be beginning to rise.

The level of retirement benefits available is a key determinant of retirement age. People tend to retire when they can afford to do so without substantial loss of living standards. Retiree health is an important factor in early retirement decisions; employees without retiree health are often reluctant to retire prior to Medicare eligibility. The absence of coverage is often a barrier to early retirement.

The age mix of the population will change drastically over the next 20 years. There was a much larger number of people born annually between 1945 and 1965 than in the years before or after. This group has often been called the "baby boom." Today, the workforce is aging; there will be fewer young entrants to the workforce in the 1990s than in the 1970s and 1980s.

There was also a major influx of women into the workforce during the 1970s and 1980s. That, too, is likely to be much more gradual, as today over 75 percent of the women in the prime working ages are already in the labor force—the potential for expansion of female labor force participation is much less.

These labor force trends must be considered together with the downsizing of the last few years. In 1992, there are a surplus of qualified people for most jobs. (There are a few exceptions, particularly in the health professions.) It is not yet clear how this situation may change over the next decade, particularly as the economy improves. There is divided opinion as to whether there may be shortages of skilled labor and where.

Plan Design

Retirement Package Integration In light of the recognition of retiree health benefits as an important part of the retirement package, it is important to step back and look at the entire package on an integrated basis. More and more employers are dealing with retirement plan issues where one set of objectives and retirement policy control the entire package.

Pension Benefit Consistency Many employers are changing their retiree health plan design to make it look more like part of the pension benefit. This includes introduction of benefits linked to length of service at retirement. Traditionally, company support for retiree health benefits was the same regardless of length of service once employees were eligible. Today, it is much more common to see a program where the required retiree contribution varies by length of service.

A related change is to revisit eligibility for the benefit in light of the company's retirement policy, so that the benefit will be offered only to those employees who have longer service. Some employers are raising the retirement age for retiree health eligibility. Pension benefits are typically actuarially reduced for early retirement, thereby providing little financial impact. If a retiree retires early under a typical retiree health plan, the retiree and their spouse receive that many more years of benefits.

Employers are also reviewing the rules for dependent eligibility and the corresponding subsidization for family members. Pension benefits are actuarially reduced to provide for joint and survivor coverage. Traditionally, single and family retiree health benefits are provided with the same subsidization for each person. This usually results in a greater benefit to the retiree receiving family coverage.

Medical Benefits Coverage Change   Some of the employers' plan design efforts are focused on the medical coverage itself. Examples of changes to coverage include:

- Services covered
- Method of Medicare coordination
- Deductibles and copayments

In many cases, the medical plan is similar in benefit structure to the active employee health plan (at least before Medicare eligibility).

Plan design changes range on a spectrum from making one or more of the above changes to more radical approaches involving major changes in direction.

New Design Approaches   In some cases, employers are looking at tradeoffs between cash retirement benefits and retiree health. In other cases, they are looking at using defined contribution plan benefits to fund retiree health.

Several employers have discontinued retiree health coverage and instead are providing preretirement savings vehicles for retiree health expenses. The preretirement savings can be in the form of any savings program, but the most widely publicized programs have involved the use of employee stock ownership programs (ESOPs). Purchase of company-sponsored coverage is then made with the ESOP balance. This arrangement could work well in the long term, but retirees in the near future would have little time to save.

When employers discontinue their programs, it is often through a phase out rather than a sudden and immediate elimination of the benefit. For example, one employer provides for an election at the time of retirement, so that the employee can apply the entire ESOP balance at retirement to purchase retiree health and then the coverage will be provided. Additional retiree contributions may be required depending on the balance and the plan cost. The company is gradually phasing out company support beyond the ESOP over time.

Another approach that has gotten a lot of publicity, but has been actually implemented by only a few employers, is to require preretirement contributions to purchase postretirement coverage. There are many design issues involved in offering such a program, including:

- What happens on early termination?
- What is effectively "guaranteed" at retirement?
- How are funds held and invested?

Retiree Flex Plans   Flexible benefit plans (flex plans) for active employees are very popular. However, the benefit options do not automatically extend to retirees, nor are they necessarily appropriate. Therefore, the employer needs to consider how to handle retirees in this situation.

Where flexibility is offered to active employees, the possibilities to consider for retirees include the following:

1. Continue coverage at the last election in the flex plan, or allow a one-time election at retirement;
2. Continue the flex plan with periodic elections;
3. Do not use the flex plan for retirees—automatically offer all retirees one of the options in the flex plan (at least pre-Medicare) and possibly use a different post-Medicare flex plan design; or
4. Use an entirely different program for retirees.

When independently structured, flex plans for retirees can be handled in a variety of ways. One approach is to offer a choice of the prior coverage with relatively high contributions and a more catastrophic coverage option requiring a lower contribution. This approach makes sense when the prior coverage was generous or not well designed to coordinate with Medicare, but the employer does not want to eliminate the prior coverage as an option.

Another approach is to establish a pool of credits (possibly linked to length of service) and give the retiree choices as to their use. Choices can focus on lifetime versus pre-Medicare spreading of funds, and single versus family coverage, as well as different medical options. One large company's program, implemented several years ago, includes these choices, but it appears that this idea is complex and so has not caught on widely.

Another option is the possibility of offering a choice between traditional coverage and long-term care coverage. Both are needed, but if one spouse has traditional coverage, the other may prefer long-term care. The authors are not aware of any situations where this has been implemented.

Benefit Capping   One very popular idea is putting a "cap" on the employer's cost or subsidization level. Under this approach, the employer limits support to the amount provided in a given year or some percentage of that amount. For example, an employer may say that their support will be limited to the amount provided in 1996. Alternatively, the employer may say that the amount provided will be limited to 150 percent of the current level. Another option is to have the amount limited to the current cost level increased not more than 5 percent per year. Implementing a cap has the following features:

1. Current coverage is continued at present levels;
2. Accounting costs under SFAS 106 are drastically reduced;
3. The employer generally postpones the problems of dealing with the issue of large future liabilities;
4. In a negotiated situation, the cap can become an attractive negotiating item; and
5. The company can "buy time" for major changes, allowing it to learn more about what other employers are doing and to see how the national health policy debate unfolds before committing to a new design.

   This can be a good strategy where radical long-term change may be needed, but it is not yet the right time to introduce radical change.

Tiered Approaches and Transition   It is very common for employers implementing changes to grandfather existing retirees and perhaps a subset of active employees (usually at least those currently eligible to retire). Different grandfathering approaches are then used depending on how far away from retirement a group is.

   It is also very common to offer a time period when people can retire under the "old plan." The plan change may be announced several months or even a year before the effective date, and serves as an "early retirement window." This approach will encourage many people to retire, and needs to be evaluated from that perspective. It may support company human resource objectives, but in some cases, it will not.

   Over the last few years, there have been many early retirement windows or other restructuring programs including workforce reductions and severance programs. For companies offering such programs that do not subsidize retiree health, it has been common to offer a benefit through to Medicare eligibility as part of the window.

Managed Care   The same managed care approaches applicable for active employees would extend to retirees prior to Medicare eligibility, if the active benefit is extended to retirees. For Medicare-eligible retirees, the plan design needs to "wrap around" Medicare and, therefore, managed care approaches must be different.

However, the issues may be different for retirees than for active employees. The costs for early retirees are a lot higher on average than for active employees, and the incidence of chronic and serious illness is greater, making managed care an even a more critical issue. In addition, retirees have more time and may become more frequent users of medical services so that consumer behavior is more important.

Large case management is a good idea for retirees and offers the potential to be quite effective. The greatest difficulties occur where there are seriously ill persons with multiple problems.

Prescription drugs are a key area for retiree managed care, both before and after Medicare eligibility. Drug costs and utilization for the elderly are much higher than at younger ages. In addition, many of the elderly use multiple prescriptions concurrently (often from different physicians), and drug interactions are often a problem. Costs are increasing rapidly in this area, but improving technology is offering new opportunities for drug management.

Health maintenance organizations (HMOs) are another area with a potential for managing care that has largely not been realized. In limited situations, HMOs have offered very attractive retiree coverage at a reasonable cost. This possibility should be considered whenever there is relatively heavy use of HMOs among the active population.

Long-Term Care

Long-term care refers to coverage to protect retirees for expenses associated with assistance with daily living. A significant part of the medical cost of the elderly, and particularly the costs not covered by Medicare, are long-term care expenses. There is a growing recognition of the seriousness of this issue and many employers are studying it. A number have implemented voluntary self-paid long-term care insurance programs. Some have referral services for elder care.

This is an area without easy or neat solutions. The problem has been recognized on the national level, but nothing is being done to solve it at this point. It is anticipated that there will be a great deal more employer emphasis on this issue in the years to come.

Funding

As indicated in the public policy section of this article, there are questions about policy regarding funding. In the meantime, more employers are considering prefunding retiree health benefits. There are several issues involved in decision making about prefunding, including:

- Cash management and effective management of company resources

- Benefit security
- Implications for customers and pricing of product or service (applies primarily to utilities and defense contractors)
- Perceptions of the company by financial community

During the last year, an increasing number of companies have evaluated prefunding as an option. Those organizations that can recover the benefit cost (to the extent funded) by increasing the price charged to customers are most likely to prefund. Others may prefund in the years ahead, but it is too early to tell whether there will be a large number of companies adopting this strategy.

Communicating Effectively with Retirees

Implementing change and preparing employees for change is significantly dependent on effective communications. Communications is key to building expectations and defining legal rights. As employers are implementing complex plan changes that involve tiered and transition approaches, it is particularly important to communicate effectively with all groups of employees.

37.   ADA: Impact on Medical Benefit Plans

Joseph A. Brislin

The purpose of this article is to review the provisions of ADA, the legislative history and the EEOC's final regulations that pertain to insurance. The analysis will review what an employer and plan sponsor can and cannot do under the existing regulations. There is a discussion of the many unanswered questions regarding benefits limitations in an employee benefits plan that adversely affect an individual with a disability.

The Americans with Disabilities Act (ADA) became effective on July 26, 1992. ADA and the Equal Employment Opportunity Commission's (EEOC) regulations specifically state that it is not the intent of the law to disrupt the current nature of insurance underwriting or current insurance industry practices related to sales, pricing, underwriting, administration or other services, claims, and other insurance-related activity.[1] This appears to cover entities that establish, sponsor, observe or administer employee benefit plans that are either subject to state law or self-insured plans.[2] Under ADA, however, the covered entity may not use the insurance exemption of ADA as a subterfuge to avoid the purpose of the act.[3] Neither the act nor the regulations are clear as to what constitutes a *subterfuge*.

A *covered entity* under ADA includes an employer, union and joint union-management committee.[4] A covered entity must provide equal employment

"Impact on Mecical Benefit Plans," by Joseph A. Brislin which appeared in the March 1992 issue, was reprinted with permission from the *Employee Benefits Journal*, published by the International Foundation of Employee Benefit Plans, Brookfield, WI. Statements or opinions expressed in this article are those of the author and do not necessarily represent the views or positions of the International Foundation, its officers, directors, or staff.

opportunity that includes accommodations that permit an employee with a disability to enjoy equal benefits and privileges of employment as are enjoyed by employees without disabilities.[5] The covered entity may not enter into a contractual relationship with an organization that provides fringe benefits to the employees of a covered entity that has the effect of subjecting an individual with a disability to discrimination prohibited by ADA.[6]

WHAT ARE ADA's PROVISIONS ON INSURANCE PROGRAMS?

ADA[7] and EEOC regulations[8] provide that the act shall not prohibit or restrict:

(1) an insurer, hospital or medical service company, health maintenance organization, or an agent, or entity that administers benefit plans, or similar organizations from underwriting risks, classifying risks, or administering such risks that are based on or not inconsistent with State law; or

(2) a person or organization covered by this Act from establishing, sponsoring, observing or administering the terms of a bona fide benefit plan that are based on underwriting risks, classifying risks, or administering such risks that are based on or not inconsistent with State law; or

(3) a person or organization covered by this Act from establishing, sponsoring, observing or administering the term of a bona fide benefit plan that is not subject to State laws that regulate insurance.

(4) Paragraphs 1,2, and 3 shall not be used as a subterfuge to avoid the purpose of the ADA.

The appendix of the EEOC's regulations provides some further guidance on the insurance exemptions in ADA.[9]

The exemption is limited to those who establish, sponsor, observe or administer benefit plans such as health and life insurance plans. It applies to self-insured employers that are not subject to state laws as well as employers that provide plans subject to state laws. It does not apply to plans not involving benefits, such as liability insurance plans.[10]

The purpose of the provision is to permit the development and administration of benefit plans in accordance with accepted principles of risk assessment. The provision is also not intended to disrupt the current nature of insurance underwriting or current insurance industry practices in sales, underwriting, pricing administrative and other services, claims and similar insurance-related activities based upon classification of risk as regulated by the state.[11]

The provision is not meant to disrupt the current regulatory structure of self-insured employers. These employers may establish, sponsor, observe or administer the terms of a bona fide benefits plan not subject to state insurance laws.[12]

Under this provision, ADA is not violated even if the insurance activity results in a limitation on individuals with disability. However, the limitation cannot be a subterfuge to evade the purpose of ADA.[13]

WHAT ELSE WILL THE EEOC REGULATE?

When the EEOC published its proposed regulations, the agency requested comments on the following insurance issues:[14]

- What are the current risk assessment of classification practices with respect to health and life insurance coverage in the area of employment?
- Must risk assessment or classification be based on actuarial statistics:
- What is the relationship between *risk* and *cost*?
- Must an employer or insurance company consider the effect on individuals with disabilities before making cost saving changes in its insurance coverage?

In its comments to the final regulations issued July 16, 1991, the EEOC stated:

> In the NPRM, the Commission raised questions about a number of insurance-related matters. Specifically, the Commission asked commenters to discuss risk assessment and classification, the relationship between "risk" and "cost," and whether employers should consider the effects that changes in insurance coverage will have on individuals with disabilities before making those changes. Many commenters provided information about insurance practices and explained some of the considerations that affect insurance decisions. In addition, some commenters presented a wide range of opinions on insurance matters, and the Commission will consider the comments as it continues to analyze these complex matters.[15]

> The divergent views expressed in the public comments demonstrate the complexity of employment-related issues concerning insurance, workers' compensation, and collective bargaining agreement matters. These highly complex issues require extensive research and analysis and warrant further consideration. Accordingly, the Commission has decided to address the issues in depth in future Compliance Manual sections and policy guidances. The Commission will consider the public comments that it received in response to the NPRM as it develops further guidance on the application of title I of the ADA to these matters.[16]

There will be more rulings and interpretations on ADA's effect upon employee benefits plans. The questions of when does risk underwriting become a subterfuge and what is equal access to insurance are still unanswered. There will undoubtedly be numerous lawsuits regarding medical plan limitations that have an adverse effect upon an individual with a disability. An entity covered by ADA that sponsors an employee benefit plan should review the current plan with its legal advisers and insurance consultants. The covered entity should also keep abreast of developments in the law and make a thorough analysis of ADA requirements before benefit changes in an employee benefit plan are made.

WHAT ARE THE RESTRICTIONS ON MANAGING A MEDICAL INSURANCE PLAN?

There are specific insurance-related prohibitions placed upon employers and plan sponsors under the EEOC's final regulations. They may not:

- Make an employment decision based upon a speculation that an individual may cause increased health insurance premiums or workers' compensation costs.[17]
- Have an attitudinal concern regarding insurance or workers' compensation costs that creates a barrier or excludes a qualified individual with a disability.[18]
- Refuse to make reasonable accommodation that enables employees with disabilities to enjoy equal benefits and privileges of employment as are enjoyed by employees without disabilities.[19]
- Reduce the level of health insurance benefits offered to employees and their dependents simply because an employee has a dependent with a disability.[20] This is true even if providing the benefit would result in an increased health insurance cost for the employer.[21]
- Use voluntary medical examinations that are part of an employee health program for the purpose of limiting health insurance eligibility.[22]
- Use the fact that the individual's disability is not covered by the employer's current insurance plan or would cause the employer's insurance premiums or workers' compensation costs to increase as a legitimate nondiscriminatory reason to justify disparate treatment of an individual with a disability.[23]
- Deny a qualified individual with a disability equal access to insurance or subject a qualified individual with a disability to different terms or conditions of insurance based on disability alone, if the disability does not pose increased risks.[24] Decisions not based on risk classification must be made in conformance with nondiscrimination requirements.[25]
- Use any of the permissible insurance underwriting as a subterfuge to avoid the purpose of ADA.[26]

WHAT IS PERMITTED IN MANAGING A MEDICAL INSURANCE PLAN?

Specific insurance-related actions that are permitted under the EEOC's final regulations are:

- Information obtained from an employment entrance exam permitted under ADA may be used for insurance purposes permitted under ADA.[27]
- A plan may continue to offer policies that contain preexisting clauses even if they adversely affect individuals with disabilities, so long as the clauses are not used as a subterfuge to evade the purpose of ADA.[28] There is, however, no guidance on the time period that a preexisting condition clause may exclude or limit coverage.
- A plan may offer an insurance policy that limits coverage for certain procedures or treatments to a specified number per year. For example, a health plan may limit benefits to five blood transfusions per year to all covered employees. This is not discriminatory because a hemophiliac employee may require more than five transfusions annually.[29]
- A plan may place limitations on reimbursements for certain procedures or on the types of drugs or procedures covered. Examples are limits on the number of permitted X-rays or noncoverage of experimental drugs or procedures. If the employer has limitations, they must be applied equally to individuals with or without disabilities.[30]
- An employer may have a benefit plan that does not address the special needs of every individual with a disability as long as the plan is uniformly applied to all employees.[31]
- A plan may reduce the amount of medical insurance coverage for all employees, even if the reduction has an impact on employees with disabilities who are in need of greater medical coverage.[32]
- A plan may continue to conduct voluntary medical exams or inquiries as part of an employee wellness or health program. Examples are blood pressure monitoring, weight control counseling, cancer detection and administering of prescription drugs such as insulin.[33] The medical records that are developed from the voluntary exam must be maintained in a confidential manner.[34]
- An employer may continue the use of its workplace alcohol and drug abuse program that is consistent with other federal and state laws and regulations.[35]
- An employer may prohibit or impose restriction on smoking in places of employment that are consistent with other federal and state laws and regulations.[36]

WHAT IS A SUBTERFUGE UNDER ADA?

The caveat to the insurance exemption under ADA is that the coverage limitations may not be a *subterfuge*. A *subterfuge* is defined as evading the purpose of ADA, and the legislative history expressly indicates that the term *subterfuge* will be narrowly interpreted. Congress specifically rejected the definition of *subterfuge* in the U.S. Supreme Court's decision in *Public Employee Retirement System v. Betts.*[37] In *Betts,* the court held that a pension plan was not a subterfuge to evade the purpose of the Age Discrimination in Employment Act, unless it were intended to discriminate based upon age. In rejecting the *Betts* interpretation, Congress intended that *subterfuge* under ADA does not require purposeful intent.[38] Also, both the EEOC's appendix and Congressional history establish that benefit plans established before the passage of ADA are not automatically considered bona fide.[39]

There is some legislative history as to ADA's subterfuge caveat on the ability to classify risk in accordance with state laws. An insurer may not "refuse to insure, or refuse to continue to insure, or limit the amount, extent or kind of coverage available to an individual, or charge a different rate for the same coverage solely because of a physical or mental impairment, except where the refusal, limitation, or rate differential is based on sound actuarial principles or is related to actual or reasonable anticipated experience."[40]

In relationship to being able to charge different rates or to limit coverage based upon recognized risk classification, the legislative history provides:

> Moreover, while a plan which limits certain kinds of coverage based on classification of risk would be allowed under this Section, the plan may not refuse to insure, or refuse to continue to insure, or limit the amount, extent or kind of coverage available to an individual, or charge a different rate for the same coverage solely because of a physical or mental impairment, except for the refusal, limitation, or rate differential based on sound actuarial principles, or is related to actual or reasonably anticipated experience.

> For example, a blind person may not be denied coverage based on blindness independent of actuarial risk classification. Likewise, with respect to group health insurance coverage, an individual with a pre-existing condition may be denied coverage for that condition for the period specified in the policy but cannot be denied coverage for illnesses or injuries unrelated to the preexisting condition.

> Specifically, point (1) makes it clear that insurers may continue to sell and to underwrite individuals applying for life, health, or other insurance on an individually underwritten basis, or to service such insurance products.

> Point (2) recognizes the need for employers, and/or agents thereof, to establish and observe the terms of employee benefit plans, so long as these plans are based on underwriting or classification of risks.[41]

The legislative history is clear that an employer may not refuse employment to an individual because of the individual's effect upon the cost of a medical plan. ". . .[E]mployers may not refuse to hire an individual with a disability because that individual, or that individual's family, might insure higher health care costs for the employer in the future. Allowing the fact of such increased costs to justify employment discrimination would effectively gut the protections of the ADA for individuals with disabilities."[42]

UNANSWERED QUESTIONS

The issues of what is considered to be a *subterfuge* and what is *denial of equal access* are not entirely clear. The EEOC's regulations do not provide much assistance. There are several questions that remain unanswered. Many cost containment actions taken in employee benefit plans by plan sponsors are designed to discourage the use of the plan by the group of individuals who utilize a benefit the most heavily. Is this permissible?

How much risk underwriting justification must the employer be prepared to demonstrate to justify a cost containment policy or benefit change?

What is the meaning of the requirement that the employer must make reasonable accommodation that enables employees with disabilities to enjoy equal benefits and privileges of employment as are enjoyed by employees without disabilities in relationship to insurance? For example, the employer's medical plan has a preferred provider hospital and doctors. If the employee goes to the specified hospital or doctors, the medical charges are paid in full. If the employee goes to an alternative hospital or doctor, the plan pays 80 percent of the medical charges and the employee pays the remaining 20 percent. The employer employs a qualified individual who is paraplegic. The disabled employee is treated by a nonpreferred doctor and hospital under the plan. Going to the PPO hospital is a hardship on the disabled employee compared to going to a nearby hospital where the disabled employee's doctor practices. Does the employer have to make a reasonable accommodation? Or, if the PPO arrangement is based upon sound actuarial principles and risk classifications, is it a complete defense?

An employer or covered entity may not enter into a contractual relationship that has the effect of discriminating against the employer's employees. A *contractual relationship* includes an organization that provides employee benefits to the employer's employees.[43] How much risk and underwriting information and justification must an employer, plan sponsor or trustees receive from a PPO, HMO or insurance carrier that offers the plan? What justification must a multi-employer plan provide to employers that participate in the plan under the terms of a collective bargaining agreement?

Can the plan sponsor establish a plan or amend a plan to explicitly exclude or limit the benefit levels for a specific illness or affliction such as AIDS? Court cases have previously held that such limitation on AIDS does not violate ERISA.[44] Can the plan continue to have caps and limits for specific treatment or conditions such as the limit for mental, nervous and chemical dependency?

An employer that learns of an employee's or dependent's disability and then takes action to reduce or limit benefits based upon that knowledge will be subject to a challenge of subterfuge. However, the insurance market frequently will deny renewal of insurance coverage for an employer that has an employee or dependent that will have prolonged medical treatment. Also, many insurance carriers will only write group coverage for small employers on the condition of the insurability of each employee and dependent. Will an employer or plan sponsor faced with this dilemma have a defense of acceptable underwriting or is this a denial of access that is prohibited under ADA?

Many plan sponsors are faced with the dilemma of allocating coverage to retirees, surviving spouses of deceased employees, disabled employees, employees on layoff as well as the actives and their dependents. Will plan sponsor and trustee action to allocate the available funds, change benefits and increase the amount of self-payments fall within ADA's exemptions of "acceptable principles of risk assessment"? Will the plan sponsor have to give more consideration to the effect of a benefit change upon a person with a disability than to the other categories of participants in making allocation decisions?

What will be the relationship between risk and cost when a plan considers making a benefit modification or changing an eligibility requirement?

What will be the effect upon pension plans and life, as well as long- and short-term disability benefits?

PRACTICE TIPS

In reviewing its insurance plan, an employer or plan sponsor should:

- Be prepared to justify any differences in premium costs, self-pay rates and benefit limitations. The justification must be based upon state insurance law risk classifications or sound actuarial principles.
- Identify all of the benefit limitations, caps, exclusions and rates in the plan that could have an effect on a person with a disability. Assure that each of these limitations is based upon accepted principles of risk assessment under state law or accepted principles of risk assessment.
- For any differences in premium and coverage limitations in the plan, have the insurance carrier certify, in writing, that the differences and limitations in the medical plan are based upon and rated in accordance with accepted principles of risk assessment. If the plan is self-insured, the plan's professional adviser who advises on underwriting should provide the certification. Obtaining a *hold harmless agreement* from the carrier or adviser is advisable.

- Assure that the plan sponsor's decision to modify the benefits or add an exclusion or limitation is based upon acceptable underwriting principles and risk classification, and not for the purpose of excluding or denying access to persons with disabilities.
- Assure that all employees have equal access to the benefits in the medical plan. Employees with disabilities cannot be offered different terms and conditions of insurance based upon their disabilities alone. For example, a plan sponsor cannot offer insurance to a disabled employee with an unlimited preexisting condition exclusion and all other employees with a six months' preexisting condition exclusion.
- Assure that employment decisions or plan decisions are not based on an individual's effect upon the medical plan. For example, the employer has two qualified applicants. One applicant has a heart condition. The employer cannot refuse to hire the applicant with the disability because the heart condition may have adverse consequences on the cost of the medical plan.
- Consider ADA's applications and the accepted principles of risk management to plan provisions, such as:
    —Limitations in substance abuse
    —Limitations on mental health benefits
    —Proof of insurability
    —Case management
    —Exclusion of certain providers
    —Separate benefit schedules for specified diseases or medical conditions
    —Exclusion of specified diseases or medical conditions
    —Rates and premiums based upon smoking or other lifestyle choices such as exercise, diet, etc.
    —Limits of payments on specific illnesses or diseases such as transplants, heart surgery, etc.
    —Limitations based upon going to a specific doctor or hospital for treatment
    —Cost shifting or premiums and copayments to employees
    —Utilization management
    —Coordination of benefits
    —Eligibility rules
    —Penalties or incentives to encourage plan participants to use less costly alternatives, such as second opinions, ambulatory surgery, deductible or copayment based upon the provider, inpatient and outpatient limitations
    —Flexible benefits.
- Review the plan's eligibility rules to assure that they do not have an effect of denying equal access to coverage. Once the bona fide rules are established, do not make exceptions.
- Consider requiring a signed acknowledgement of understanding from a participant who makes a voluntary election to reject coverage. For example, the plan requires a partial self-payment when an employee elects coverage

for a spouse. If a spouse is enrolled upon initial eligibility, there is no preexisting condition exclusion. However, if coverage is rejected, the spouse may only apply during an open enrollment period, and there is a six month preexisting condition exclusion. If spousal coverage is rejected, the employee and spouse should sign a written acknowledgment indicating a complete understanding of the eligibility rules and the consequences of their rejection.

CONCLUSION

The Americans With Disabilities Act will have a significant impact upon plan sponsors and the administration of an employee benefit plan. Prior to the July 26, 1992 effective date, a plan sponsor or trustee should meet with the plan's attorney, provider and other insurance advisers and review the effect ADA will have upon the plan. The EEOC will be issuing additional interpretive rules before the effective date of ADA, and there will be numerous court challenges after the effective date. Plan sponsors and trustees should keep abreast of the developments as they occur. Before a benefit change or premium adjustment is made, it should be reviewed with legal counsel to assure that it conforms to ADA's insurance exemption. Plan sponsors and trustees should have legal counsel, the provider and the plan's insurance advisers develop the documentation that will enable the plan to establish ADA's insurance exemption to defend any legal challenge.

1. 42 USC 12201(c); 29 CFR 1630.16(f).

2. *Id.*

3. *Id.*

4. 42 USC 12111(7) and 29 CFR 1630.2(c).

5. 29 CFR Appendix 1630.2(o).

6. 42 USC 12112(b)(2) and 29 CFR 1630.6.

7. 42 USC 12201(c).

8. 29 CFR 1630.16(f)

9. 29 CFR Appendix 1630.16(f); 1630.14(c);1630.5.

10. 29 CFR Appendix 1630.16(f).

11. *Id.*

12. *Id.*

13. 42 USC 12201(c); 29 CFR 1630.16(f).

14. 56 Fed Reg 6579, February 28, 1991.

15. 56 Fed Reg 35726, July 26, 1991.

16. 56 Fed Reg 35527, July 26, 1991.

17. 29 CFR Appendix 1630.2(m).

18. 29 CFR Appendix 1630.2(n).

19. 29 CFR Appendix 1630.2(o).

20. 29 CFR Appendix 1630.8.

21. *Id.*

22. 29 CFR Appendix 1630.14(d).

23. 29 CFR Appendix 1630.15(a).

24. 29 CFR Appendix 1630.16(f).

25. *Id.*

26. 42 USC 12201(c); 29 CFR 1630.16(f); 29 CFR Appendix 1630.16(f).

27. 29 CFR Appendix 1630.14(b).

28. 29 CFR Appendix 1630.5

29. *Id.*

30. *Id.*

31. *Id.*

32. *Id.*

33. 29 CFR 1630.14(c); 29 CFR Appendix 1630.14(c).

34. *Id.*

35. 29 CFR 1630.16(b) and (c).

36. 29 CFR 1630.16(d).

37. 492 US 158 (1989) Congress overruled *Betts* when it passed the Older Workers Benefit Protection Act in 1990.

38. 136 Congressional Record H4624 (Daily edition July 12, 1990); 136 Congressional Record H4626 (Daily edition July 12, 1990); 136 Congressional Record S9697 (Daily edition July 13, 1990); Joint Explanatory Statement of the Committee of Conference HR Rep No 596, 101st Cong, Second Sess (1990); HR Report 596.

39. 29 CFR Appendix 1630.16(f); 1981 Rep No 85, 1990 House Education and Labor Report 37 and 1990 House Judiciary Report 71.

40. Committee on Labor and Human Resources Report, S Rep No 101-116, 101st Cong, 1st Sess 85 (1989); Committee on Education and Labor Report, HR Rep No 101-485 Part 2, 101st Cong, 2d Sess 136-137 (1990).

41. Committee on Labor and Human Resources Report, S. Rep. No. 101-116, 101st Cong., 1st Sess. 85 (1990).

42. Congressional Record H4623 (July 12, 1990).

43. 42 U.S.C. 12112(b)(2).

44. McGann v H&H Music Co 12 EBC 1838 (SD Tex 1990); Alexander v Choate, 469 US 287 (1985) (where there was a § 504 challenge on limitations on inpatient coverage under Medicare).

38. ADA: Impact on Workers' Compensation
Richard Pimentel   Michael J. Lotito

Answers to the seven most commonly asked questions about workers' compensation under ADA.

In July 26, 1990, the Americans with Disabilities Act was signed into law. Thus began one of the most ambitious social experiments in our history. The ultimate goal is the integration of persons with disabilities into every segment of society.

The Equal Employment Opportunity Commission (EEOC) enforces Title I of the ADA—the employment provisions. It issued final interpretive regulations on July 26, 1991. While many questions were answered in this body of law, others are still open. One of the least clear but most important issues is how the ADA will interact with workers' compensation. The following are responses to the most commonly asked questions regarding workers' compensation and the ADA.

1. Are injured workers going to be a significant factor in the ADA?

We estimate that the majority of the ADA complaints will come from existing employees. Of those, many will be related to an industrial injury. This is true for a number of reasons.

First, there is a greater responsibility for reasonable accommodation for an existing employee than an applicant. This additional responsibility is to identify and reassign an employee with a disability who cannot do his or her regular job with or without a reasonable accommodation to a vacant position that the person

Reprinted with permission from Milt Wright Associates, Northridge, Calif.

could do. This involves a lateral transfer or possible demotion; a promotion is not required.

Second, the potential for a discrimination claim is very clear in a workers' compensation situation. The nature of the impairment is known to the employer through the workers' compensation procedure. The worker was obviously qualified to do the job before the injury (disability), so the question now becomes whether the worker has been discriminated against because of his or her status as an individual with a disability. A closely related issue is whether the person also was discriminated against for filing the workers' compensation claim if the individual is denied a job opportunity.

Third, workers' compensation litigation is exploding. With an attorney involved during the workers' compensation portion of the claim, it is more likely that many of these cases will eventually evolve into ADA complaints since the ones allegedly discriminated against already have access to legal advice.

2. Are injured workers individuals with disabilities?

While the ADA does not specifically identify injured workers as individuals with disabilities, it does not exclude them either. Therefore, if an injured worker otherwise meets the ADA's definitional tests, that person will have the same rights as other qualified individuals under the Act.

Consequently, if an injured worker has a mental or physical impairment that substantially limits a major life activity, has a record of such an impairment, or is regarded as having such an impairment, he or she will be an individual with a disability. The employer will then have a duty not to discriminate and to provide reassignment.

3. Why should ADA complaints under workers' compensation cause employers any more difficulty than any other complaints?

The problems that will potentially be created under workers' compensation are significantly more difficult and complex because the workers' compensation system itself is in disarray: costs are skyrocketing and out of control; litigation is increasing at appalling rates; and the preponderance of American companies have little or no regulation, policy or procedure for reasonably accommodating industrially injured workers for return to work after an injury.

Indeed, some companies see the workers' compensation system as an extension of their termination process, often declining to return an injured worker unless they are "100 percent recovered." Vague management policies regarding the injured worker lead to confusion, animosity and eventual litigation. The ADA makes these issues even more crucial because of the potential punitive damages, up to $300,000 for discriminating against a qualified individual with a disability.

To illustrate, assume a person is injured on the job. The resulting condition is significant enough to constitute a disability under the ADA. The employer refuses to consider the person eligible to return to work unless he or she is fully recovered. Thus, the employer does not engage in a requested discussion with the employee about job restructuring or other accommodations that may be possible. This scenario is discrimination under the ADA, which can lead to punitive damage liability in addition to any workers' compensation liability.

Finally, traditional workers' compensation medical-report formats and content will not be in accord with the informational requirements that employers will need under the ADA. Physicians who work in the workers' compensation field will be, by and large, unprepared to generate the kind of medical reports needed for employers to make valid decisions under the ADA.

At the same time, employers are rarely including a workers' compensation component in their overall ADA strategy, an omission that is flagrant because of the high number of industrially injured workers.

4. What will be the most common litigation issues for injured workers under the ADA?

General complaints will encompass all possible forms of discrimination. However, we predict some potentially dominant issues:

- Failure to offer reasonable accommodation to allow the worker to perform the job in which he or she was injured.
- Failure to reassign the worker to a vacant position that the worker is qualified to do with or without a reasonable accommodation.
- Issues involving whether the worker is a "direct threat" (see question five).

Workers' compensation procedure within an overall ADA compliance strategy should address each of these three issues in detail. It should include a step-by-step decision-making procedure with delineated authority and responsibility. The company's "ADA Czar," risk management, workers' compensation carrier and attorney, and labor counsel all should be involved.

5. What is "direct threat" and is it an important issue with injured workers?

Perhaps no ADA issue will be more explosive than the question of "direct threat." Defined in the statute as a significant risk of substantial harm to "others," the EEOC added the concept of risk to oneself in the proposed and final administrative rules.

Disability groups are expected to vigorously contest the EEOC's rules on this point. They argue that there is no justification in any of the legislative history to add harm to oneself to the rules. They contend, instead, that stereotypical fears about persons with disabilities hurting themselves on the job have been used as an excuse not to hire persons with disabilities. The EEOC will probably argue that the burden of proof for "direct threat" for an employer is so exacting that employers could not discriminate in this arbitrary way. The ultimate outcome of this issue is unclear.

For an employer under current rules to deny employment or reinstatement under the "direct threat" provisions, the employer must demonstrate that the worker represents a "significant risk of substantial harm to the health or safety of the individual or others that cannot be eliminated or reduced by reasonable accommodation."

This determination must be made on a case-be-case basis. The most current medical evidence available and specific knowledge of the individual's precise situation is required. Assumptions, fears and stereotypes are forbidden. Specific factual findings will be necessary for the following points:

- Duration of the risk.
- Nature and severity of the potential harm.
- Likelihood that the potential harm will occur.
- Imminence of the potential harm.

But even if this is made, the next step in the analysis is to determine whether or not the risk can be eliminated or reduced through reasonable accommodation. Thus, the injured worker who wants to return to work, but is denied the opportunity to do so based on the employer's fear of a re-injury to the person that would exacerbate the company's worker compensation experience rating, will argue:

- That fear is never relevant, since re-injury to the person cannot be considered based on the precise wording of the statute;
- Even if risk to self is a legitimate factor, the specific situation does not constitute a "direct threat";
- Even if the situation is a "direct threat," the risk of harm can be eliminated or reduced through an accommodation so that the person will only be an "insignificant risk of substantial harm" or a "significant risk of insubstantial harm."

6. Will my doctor be able to help determine whether the person is or is not a direct threat?

By July 26, 1991 (the effective date for Title I for employers with 25 or more employees), only an incidental number of doctors are likely to be aware of the intricacies of a direct threat analysis. Therefore, employers will have to develop step-by-step procedures for dealing with incomplete declarations of "direct threat" or face possible expensive litigation. In essence then, all medical questions under the ADA are really legal in nature.

Furthermore, because of the degenerative and unstable nature of many work injuries, it will be difficult to be as definitive as the regulations demand. For example, back conditions may be more difficult to evaluate for "direct threat" than paraplegia. Moreover, regulations maintain that only current ability to perform the essential functions of the job may be considered for purposes of "direct threat." Employers will, we predict, litigate this interpretation.

Employers may fear that an injured worker, even though technically able to perform a job today, may become incapacitated in the future. This would lead to another compensation claim, increasing the employer's experience rating. The EEOC takes the position that increased workers' compensation costs, like medical insurance, are not a defense to an ADA claim.

Therefore, the employer's alternative is to deny the person the opportunity to return to work based on future capacity or risk the possibility of increased costs for insurance if the person returns and has a re-injury. This choice is not appealing. Thus, we believe an employer confronted by this dilemma will have little choice but to litigate to gain some flexibility. Currently, the regulations prohibit the employer either defense.

7. What should we do to prepare to deal with the workers' compensation aspects of the ADA?

Each organization is different and needs to develop procedures of its own. However, the following are general steps that should be considered:

1. Bring human resources and health together to begin a unified approach to the ADA and workers' compensation.
2. Review return-to-work, decision-making procedures regarding reasonable accommodation and "direct threat" issues.
3. Check with your workers' compensation insurer to determine what they are doing to limit needless ADA exposure for your organization from claims management and workers' compensation litigation decisions.
4. Develop comprehensive, essential function analysis tools to help determine reasonable accommodation responsibilities and "direct threat" evaluations.
5. Review collective bargaining agreements on the issues of job reassignment and job restructuring for the ADA and workers' compensation purposes.
6. Meet with local physicians, physical therapists, rehabilitation counselors and medical staff to review reporting and consulting needs under the ADA.
7. Implement training to change the attitudes of your management team to become open to reasonably accommodating injured and ill workers.

8.   Remember human resources is an important department, but the ADA is just too large and all-encompassing for any one department to handle all the compliance issues alone. Workers' compensation is just one of many multi-departmental issues that must be acted on. It may be advisable to consult with knowledgeable counsel to develop a preventive compliance strategy now.

39. Managing the Legal
Risks of Managed Care Programs

Barbara B. Creed   Maureen E. Corcoran   Marcia Leitner

No reported cases to date have held employers liable for the negligent selection of network providers. But employers must be aware of their potential liability as they become more and more involved in the management of the health care employees receive.

Many companies have instituted various managed care programs, such as preferred provider organizations (PPOs) or utilization review organizations (UROs), in an effort to control escalating health care costs. To avoid losing cost savings from these programs to lawsuits, employers need to be aware of the potential for legal risks in their implementation. This article reviews recent court decisions and theories of liability in this area, and it includes practical suggestions to assist employers in evaluating and managing the risks of managed care.

CORPORATE NEGLIGENCE

Employers setting up PPO networks or contracting with established PPO networks must be aware of the potential for liability for the negligent selection and retention of network providers under the doctrine of corporate negligence. This doctrine has been widely accepted by the courts as a viable theory for holding hospitals liable for the negligent selection of staff physicians. Recently, courts have begun to extend this doctine to find HMOs liable for the negligent selection of their physician networks.

In *Harrell v. Total Health Care, Inc.,*[1] the Missouri Supreme Court found that an HMO may be liable for harm suffered by patients due to the HMO's negligent selection of contracting physicians. In applying the doctrine of corporate negligence, the court reasoned that by limiting its members' choice of physicians to those selected by the HMO, there was an unreasonable risk of harm to members if the HMO selected physicians who are unqualified or incompetent. Therefore, the HMO owed a duty to conduct a reasonable investigation of physicians' credentials and reputation in the community. Despite its finding, the court granted the HMO immunity from liability based on a state law protecting HMOs from liability for the malpractice of contracting physicians.

There are no reported cased to date that have held employers or PPO sponsors liable for the negligent selection of network providers. However, as more employers contract with provider networks and channel their employees to these networks, the likelihood of employer liability in this area will increase.

If an employer is contracting with a PPO sponsor to set up PPO networks rather than contracting directly with providers, it is less likely that a court would find the employer liable for the negligent selection of a provider. However, a court may determine that the employer has a duty to ensure that its PPO sponsor chooses quality providers.

OSTENSIBLE AGENCY

Under the theory of ostensible agency, an employer may be held vicariously liable for the acts of physicians contracting with an employer or PPO sponsor. Although the physicians are independent contractors the courts can find liability if the employee reasonably believes that these physicians are agents of the employer (i.e., "ostensible agents").

Courts have generally found that a hospital can be liable for the negligence of independent physicians under the theory that the physicians were its ostensible agents. In reaching their conclusions, the courts have noted that the patient looked to the hospital for care and that the hospital, not the patient, chose the physician.

In *Boyd v. Albert Einstein Medical Center,*[2] a Pennsylvania court extended the theory of ostensible agency from the hospital setting to the HMO setting and held that an HMO can be liable for the acts of its participating physicians.

Two factors relevant to the court's finding of ostensible agency are whether the patient looks to the HMO rather than the physician for care and whether the HMO "holds out" the physician as its employee. Based on these factors, it is possible that a court could find that a network provider was an ostensible agent of the contracting employers.

If an employer is contracting with a PPO sponsor rather than directly with providers, it is less likely that employees will view network providers as ostensible agents of the employer. In addition, an employer can minimize its liability exposure by emphasizing in its employee communications that the provider networks were established by a PPO sponsor and that the providers are all independent contractors. Language in the PPO directory for plan members should directly disclaim any warranties of the physicians' quality of care and should advise members that *they* are responsible for choosing a physician.

Employers can minimize their liability exposure by carefully selecting the PPO sponsor and by investing the procedures used to implement their own thorough credential verification procedures.

A primary concern is whether the PPO sponsor independently verifies each provider's credentials or whether the sponsor relies upon a provider's having medical staff privileges at a hospital. This depends upon the hospital's representation that the credentials of providers on its staff have been adequately investigated.

A shortcoming of relying on the hospital's verification of credentials is that if a hospital takes a few "shortcuts" in its investigation and admits an unqualified physician to its medical staff, a PPO sponsor may in turn rely upon the faulty review process of the hospital and include the physician in its network. The result may be that the PPO sponsor and the employer are liable to the patient for the negligent selection of the physician. Because of the shortcoming inherent in relying on the hospital's method of verifying credentials, it is important that the PPO sponsor independently verify the credentials of each network provider.

In 1990, the federal government established a National Practitioner Data Bank to track malpractice judgments and limitations on privileges for physicians, as well as other health care providers. Access to the Data Bank is limited to health care entities. Thus, employers—and many PPOs—cannot directly access the Data Bank at this time. However, employers and PPO sponsors can require each contracting physician to obtain a copy of his or her current Data Bank file and submit the file as part of the PPO application and renewal process.

In order to minimize liability risks, employers should thoroughly investigate the procedures for verifying credentials used by PPO sponsors to ensure that they include, as a minimum:

- Verification of current licensure and/or certification;
- Verification of board certification, if applicable, and adequate education, training, and competence;
- Verification of current hospital staff privileges, if applicable, and investigation of any denial or restriction of privileges;
- Investigation of any successful or pending challenges to the provider's license, registration and/or certification;
- Investigation of the provider's defense of professional liability actions;

- Evidence of adequate professional liability insurance; and,
- A review of the physician's file with the National Practitioner Data Bank.

For providers who do not obtain hospital privileges, the PPO sponsor may want to do a more thorough investigation of the provider's experience, competence and involvement in professional liability actions. The PPO sponsor should also institute a quality assurance program, whereby it can continuously evaluate the quality of care rendered by each provider and review credentials before renewing the provider's membership in the network. Providers who are not delivering quality care must be removed before the contract renewal date.

Utilization review in a managed care system means that requests by a treating physician to perform certain procedures, to admit a patient to a hospital or other facility for an elective procedure, or to prolong a length of stay are reviewed by the nurses and physicians hired by the payor (the HMO, insurer, employer or claims administrator) to determine if the admission or treatment is medically necessary under the plan's criteria for payment. The review includes an evaluation of the appropriateness of the setting as well as the level of treatment for the condition.

This prospective determination of medical justification for services theoretically affects only payment, since patients can choose to accept uncovered treatment. In reality, many patients will refuse treatment not covered due to financial restraints. In recommending treatment that will not be paid for, physicians are also likely to be influenced by financial considerations. In a managed care plan, the treating physician may decide not to provide care that the URO has determined will not be covered. If a patient suffers a bad result, the payor may be sued on the theory that a defect in the utilization review process resulted in the patient's failing to receive necessary or appropriate medical care.

For example, in *Wilson v. Blue Cross of Southern California*,[3] a California court ruled that a third-party payor that denies payment based on an improper utilization review decision may be liable for injuries to the patient if the denial of payment was substantial factor in causing the patient's injuries.

The potential for liability arising from defective utilization review stems from the same legal theories described in the preceding discussion on setting up a PPO network. The doctrine of ostensible agency can be used to hold employers liable for the acts of a URO if the organization is seen by the plan member as an agent of the employer.

An employer may also face liability for negligence in the hiring or selection of the URO under the doctrine of corporate negligence if it does not exercise care to investigate the quality of the services provided by the contracting URO or if it fails to terminate the contract if it learns of problems with performance.

SUGGESTIONS FOR LIMITING RISK

The following are some methods of limiting potential risks arising from selecting and contracting with UROs:

- The employer should thoroughly evaluate the credentials of the URO's staff. In particular, the employer should ensure that URO staff nurses are appropriately licensed and that the URO has board certified physician specialists available to review specialty cases.
- The employer should thoroughly investigate the URO's track record, its financial stability, and the reputation of its physician reviewers in the medical community.
- To limit its exposure on an agency theory for the acts of the URO, the employer should identify the URO as a separate entity to plan members. Independent contractor status should be clearly delineated in the certificate of coverage, summary plan document, brochures, and other member communications.
- Care must be taken to monitor the URO without exerting control over the URO's work. Otherwise, the URO's status as an independent contractor could be jeopardized.
- The employer should seek a hold harmless and indemnification clause in its contract with the URO.
- The contract should require the URO to maintain general and professional liability insurance with adequate limits of liability. The employer should be named as an additional insured on the policy.
- The employer should examine the URO's method of review. The employer must evaluate carefully the URO system design to ensure that it applies criteria consistent with plan standards.
- The URO appeal mechanism must be timely and reasonable, leaving adequate time for preparation of the appeal. The treating physician, hospital or facility and patient should all be allowed to appeal.
- The employer should monitor the URO's performance for adherence to the contract and plan terms and it should retain the right to review any changes by the URO in the utilization review program during the term of the contract.

Generally, the Employee Retirement Income Security Act of 1974 (ERISA) preemption of state law claims offers employers some protection from large awards for tort damages under state law. However, employers with ERISA plans may have a false sense of security regarding the tort liability protections available under ERISA. Several courts have found that third-party payors may be liable for the personal injuries of ERISA plan members and that such claims are not preempted by ERISA because they do not "relate" to the benefit plan.[4]

An employer's best protection against legal liability is to select carefully its PPO sponsors and utilization reviewers, to structure and monitor its contractual relations with these entities to minimize liability risks and to communicate clearly to its plan members its relationship with these entities.

1. 781 SW2d 58 (Mo 1989).

2. 547 A2d 1229 (Pa Super 1988).

3. 222 Cal App 3d 660 (1990).

4. 555 A 2d 147 (Pa 1988), *Independence HMO, Inc. v. Smith*, 733 F Supp 983 (ED Pa 1990).

Part 9

THE NEW EMPHASIS ON QUALITY

40. Assessing the Quality of Managed Care Systems: A Purchaser's Dilemma

Margaret O'Kane

While the state of the art of quality assessment has advanced considerably in the last ten years, we are still far from having the complete set of measures which will be necessary to evaluate the quality of health care systems in a valid and reliable way. But there are some good single point measures which, while they are not sufficient to make a judgment about total system performance, at least allow a glimpse into the quality of the system. As these measures are developed and enhanced, the technology of health care performance assessment promises to improve and become more useful to purchasers and consumers.

In 1990, the Institute of Medicine developed a definition of quality health care:

> The degree to which health services for individuals and populations increase the likelihood of desired health outcomes and are consistent with current professional knowledge.

This is a good definition because, while it recognizes the paramount importance of evaluation of outcomes, it also acknowledges that the relationship between the process of medical care and the patient's outcome is not a perfect one. Good medical care can at best *increase the likelihood* of good outcomes. This is not to minimize the importance of ensuring that the latest medical knowledge informs how the patient is actually treated, and the definition acknowledges this. The definition also includes the notion of caring for the health of a population, which goes beyond conventional sickness-related health care and involves more proactive ways to preserve health like prevention, screening, and health promotion activity.

Quality of care refers to the proper application of medical knowledge to a particular clinical issue, or as it is sometimes stated, "the right thing done right." In a quality interaction with a health care provider or system, the patient will receive the right treatment when indicated, and no treatment when no treatment is indicated. But in addition to determining what is the right treatment, the quality provider or system must be able to provide the treatment in a competent manner.

To illustrate the point, we can simplify a complicated example. If a patient presents with coronary artery disease, there are a series of decisions that must be made that have an impact on the ultimate well-being, or outcome, of the patient. The cardiologist must decide among a variety of diagnostic procedures, some of them risky, weighing the additional information to be obtained from the tests against the risk to the patient of performing the tests. If the disease is sufficiently severe, the physician will have to decide between treating the disease medically, with drug therapy, or surgically, with coronary artery bypass surgery. Again the risk must be weighed against the benefit. But aside from the immediate surgical risk to the patient, there is a longer term issue, because in general the disease will continue to progress even after the surgery. If the patient has surgery too early in the course of the disease, his or her lifespan may actually be shorter than if he or she had been treated with drugs and then operated on at a later date.

But, continuing our example, let us assume that the patient is a good candidate for surgery, that surgery is "the right thing." Now it will have to be "done right." Where the patient has the surgery and who performs it will have a dramatic impact on the patient's outcome. A complex set of factors, including the skill of the surgeon, the competence of the heart-lung bypass machine team, the quality of the intensive care and general nursing care, and many other factors, medical and non-medical, will have an impact on the outcome of the patient. Studies of the outcomes of cardiac bypass surgery have shown that mortality rates can vary dramatically across hospitals, even adjusting for differences in patients.

Additionally, there are patient-related factors such as the patient's age, the severity of his or her illness, additional illnesses that the patient may be suffering from, the patient's family support system and even his/her will to live, which may play an important role in the outcome. This makes the assessment of which providers "do it right" a complex task.

And is it not important to back up a step and see whether the system could have been more effective in preventing the patient's coronary artery disease in the first place? Early interventions such as cholesterol screening or smoking cessation programs could perhaps have prevented or delayed the episode of angina or myocardial infarction which precipitated the patient into the cardiac care system in the first place.

This example serves to illustrate the complexity of making an assessment of the quality of care of a health care system. While the state of the art of quality assessment has advanced considerably in the last ten years, we are still far from having the complete set of measures which will be necessary to evaluate the quality of health care systems in a valid and reliable way. But there are some good single point measures which, while they are not sufficient to make a judgment about total system performance, at least allow a glimpse into the quality of the system. As these measures are developed and enhanced, the technology of health care performance assessment promises to improve and become more useful to purchasers and consumers.

QUALITY OF SERVICE

Besides the issues of technical quality, there are issues of quality of service in any health care delivery system. Quality of service generally refers to how the system performs in meeting the members' non-clinical needs. Important areas of quality of service include appointment waiting times, telephone response times, competence of handling claims, courtesy, and responsiveness in solving problems and providing information. While quality of service issues are often closely related to quality of care issues, they are generally easier to assess through customer satisfaction surveys.

For the corporate purchaser, the problem is in trying to make comparisons of enrollee satisfaction among systems which are using different and non-comparable survey methodologies.

Relationship Between Quality and Cost

As with many goods and services, the relationship between quality and cost is not a direct one. That is, paying more for health care does not assure higher quality. If unnecessary care is provided, it may even diminish quality. But even if the care provided is necessary, an efficient delivery system will deliver the same level of quality at a lower cost than will a less efficient one. The problem for the purchaser today is that there is little available information on the quality of the systems with whom they are contracting. Without this information, it is impossible to know whether lower-cost providers are more efficient or whether they keep their costs down by withholding care or providing lower quality care.

Increased Purchaser Interest in Quality

As health care costs have risen to record levels over the past decade, purchasers have increasingly turned to managed care systems in an attempt to mediate the rate of increase. Concerned about a possible adverse effect on quality, many purchasers began to ask for information on the quality of care and service which various managed care systems offer. Increasingly, large corporate purchasers issued requests for proposals which asked for detailed information on quality and even began sending in their own review teams. Many managed care organizations complained that time spent responding to these reviews took time away from their own internal quality control activities. Others expressed concern that the information requested had little to do with quality or reflected outdated notions of reactive quality assurance rather than more proactive total quality management.

At the same time, the federal government launched a new system to review HMOs with Medicare risk contracts and instituted a requirement for external quality review of capitated Medicaid programs. Many states began a more in-depth review process for licensure. Again, these review systems often were heavily targeted to locating and punishing "bad apples" rather than systematically and continuously improving the performance of a system.

The proliferation of reviews as well as increasing purchaser frustration with their own review processes led to the launching of the National Committee for Quality Assurance (NCQA) as an independent external review organization in 1990. Originally established under the wing of the major trade associations for managed care, the Group Health Association of America and the American Managed Care and Review Association, NCQA was spun off as an independent entity with funding from the Robert Wood Johnson Foundation and matching money from managed care organizations.

THE NATIONAL COMMITTEE FOR QUALITY ASSURANCE

Increased demand for information on the quality of managed care systems led to development of a unique accreditation program for managed care organizations. Governed by a Board of Directors of managed care executives, purchasers, independent quality experts, and union and consumer representatives, the National Committee for Quality Assurance is now the leading external review organization for managed-care organizations.

NCQA accreditation is based on an in-depth review of the plan's systems for medical and quality management, as well as evaluation of the quality of care rendered by the organization, as reflected in its medical records.

The Review Process

The review begins with an off-site phase in which extensive documentation submitted by the plan is reviewed against the NCQA standards. This is followed by an on-site visit, typically two to three days, during which the review team validates the preassessment information, and reviews the functioning of the plan's systems through extensive review of documentation and interviews. After the visit, the team prepares a report which assesses the plan's compliance with each of the NCQA standards.

The report is reviewed for consistency of interpretation, edited by the NCQA staff, and submitted to the NCQA Review Oversight Committee, which makes the actual accreditation decision. Plans may be fully accredited; accredited with recommendations (where there are minor areas of non-compliance with the standards which must be corrected within ninety days); provisionally accredited (where areas of non-compliance are more substantial, but could be corrected within twelve months); or denied accreditation. The term of full accreditation is three years.

NCQA Reviewers

NCQA review teams typically consist of an administrative reviewer and two or more physician reviewers. Administrative reviewers are non-physician clinicians or quality assurance experts with extensive experience in quality assurance in managed care. Physician reviewers are medical directors or directors of quality management from managed care organizations. The strong operational experience of NCQA review teams is one of NCQA's unique strengths and provides a value in the review process that goes beyond the evaluation of conformance to the NCQA standards.

Areas of Review
The review process consists of an in-depth review of the plan's systems for quality improvement and medical management, as well as a review a sample of the plan's medical records. The highlights of each portion of the review process are described below.

Quality assurance. The first and most intensive area of NCQA review is an organization's own internal quality control systems. To meet NCQA standards, an organization must have a well-organized, comprehensive quality assurance program accountable to its highest organizational levels. The program's scope and content must be broad, covering the full spectrum of services included in its delivery system; the program should focus on important aspects of care and service and address clinical issues with major impact on the health status of the enrolled population.

Quality assurance must be coordinated with other management activity. Contracts with physicians and other health care providers must be explicit about the need to cooperate with the plan's own quality activities or about the contractor's delegation of quality assurance responsibilities. An organization must actively monitor any delegated quality assurance activity.

Finally, and most importantly, an organization must be able to demonstrate program effectiveness in improving its quality of care and service.

NCQA establishes compliance with its standards by thorough review of an organization's quality assurance program description and related policies and procedures, quality assurance studies, projects and monitoring activities, quality assurance and Governing Body minutes, interviews with key staff, tracking of issues uncovered by the quality assurance system to ensure resolution, and documented evidence of quality improvement.

Credentialing. The review process also includes a thorough review of an organization's credentialing system. NCQA requires that the managed care organization conduct primary verification of such credentialing information as license, malpractice history, good standing of hospital privileges, DEA certificate, etc. Additionally, for IPA-model organizations, NCQA requires the managed-care organization to conduct a structured review of primary care physician offices prior to contracting.

An important part of ensuring delivery system integrity is periodic recertification or reappointment of providers. Aside from reverifying the "paper" credentials, NCQA requires an organization to conduct periodic performance appraisal to include information from quality assurance activity, risk and utilization management, member complaints, and member satisfaction surveys. Organizations delegating credentialing responsibility retain responsibility for ensuring that it meets NCQA standards.

Compliance with credentialing standards is ascertained by reviewing an organization's credentialing policies and procedures, sampling individual provider files, conducting interviews with relevant staff, and tracking issues identified through the complaint system or quality assurance findings.

Utilization management. Utilization management, a keystone of effective managed care, is an important determinant of both the cost and the quality of a managed care organization. NCQA standards for utilization management seek to establish that an organization has an organized system for utilization management, that review decisions are made by qualified medical professionals, that the organization has written utilization management protocols based on reasonable scientific evidence, that there are adequate appeals mechanisms for physicians and for patients, that decisions and appeals are processed in a timely manner, and that the utilization management system monitors for underutilization as well as overutilization. An organization must actively monitor any delegation of utilization management.

The process includes review of utilization reports and committee minutes as well as interviews with relevant staff.

Member Rights and Responsibilities. To meet NCQA standards, an organization must have written policies that recognize such member rights as voicing grievances and receiving information regarding the organization, its services, and practitioners. These written policies must also address such member responsibilities as providing information needed by the professional staff and following practitioners' instructions and guidelines.

NCQA requires an organization to have a system for resolving members' complaints and grievances, to aggregate and analyze complaint and grievance data, and to use the information for quality improvement.

NCQA standards require communication to members of certain types of information about how the health plan works, including: the organization's policies on referrals for specialty care; provisions for after-hours and emergency coverage; covered benefits; charges to patients; procedures for notifying patients about terminations or changes in benefits, services, or delivery sites; procedures for appealing decisions regarding coverage, benefits, or relationship to the organization; disenrollment procedures; and complaint and grievance procedures. The standards require that member information be written in readable prose and be available in the languages of the major population groups served.

Organizations must have mechanisms ensuring confidentiality of specified patient information and records.

Finally, an organization must have mechanisms to protect and enhance member satisfaction with its services, including member satisfaction surveys, studies of reasons for disenrollments, and evidence that the organization uses this information to improve its quality of service.

Preventive Health Services. Managed care organizations have traditionally prided themselves on their commitment to preventive health services. Moreover, because they serve defined populations, they are in a better position than the fee-for-service system to ensure that preventive services are used appropriately. NCQA preventive services standards require development of "specifications" —clinical policies or practice guidelines—for the use of preventive services, communication of this information to providers and patients, yearly measurement of performance in the delivery of two such services chosen from a list developed by NCQA. These results are audited by NCQA.

In its next development stage, NCQA will develop a common measurement system for this important dimension of clinical performance.

Medical Records. NCQA supplements management systems review with a sample of ambulatory records to assess both the quality of documentation and the quality of care. NCQA physician reviewers, guided by a twenty-one item medical record review form, assess the adequacy of diagnosis, the appropriateness and continuity of care and the use of preventive services.

Who Does NCQA Accredit?

NCQA reviews organizations that deliver managed health care services, including traditional staff and group model HMOs, network and independent practice association model HMOs, mixed models, and open-ended HMOs or point-of-service products. Certain other network-based systems may also qualify.

Eligible organizations must provide comprehensive health care services to enrolled members through a defined benefit package in both ambulatory and inpatient settings, have been in operation and actively caring for members for at least eighteen months, have an active quality management system, and have access to essential clinical information on its patients.

One current important developmental project is NCQA's Michigan Project.

NCQA Michigan Project

Generated out of the auto companies' interest in purchasing the best quality health care at the best price for their employees, the Michigan Project is a unique approach to comparing performance data and service variables across different HMOs. The project is a collaborative effort involving Ford, GM, Chrysler, the United Auto Workers' Union, eight southeast Michigan HMOs and NCQA.

The project's goal is to produce comparable data on each participating HMO which is for use by external customers such as the auto companies. The project has four components: an NCQA accreditation review; a criteria-based technical quality assessment; a consumer satisfaction survey; and, a mental health and substance abuse program review. The final products will be "report card" for each HMO that address each component of the review and an NCQA accreditation decision.

The auto companies will use the information to begin to ascertain the quality of care and service delivered by their participating managed care organizations. The information will be used to establish baselines and benchmarks for HMO quality improvement, enhancing opportunities for HMOs to prove to both employer groups and consumers their successes in improving the quality of their care and service.

FUTURE DIRECTIONS

NCQA's clear directions for future development are to integrate specific measures of system performance into the review process. The new NCQA review process is currently the most thorough and comprehensive review process for managed care organizations. However, NCQA intends that the process will continue to evolve. Eventually, its systems review will be supplemented and enhanced by data on performance—clinical, quality of service, and member satisfaction. To this end, NCQA will work with recognized experts to develop and pilot test state-of-the-art quality measures.

NCQA is committed to the twin goals of improving quality and providing quality information to purchasers of managed care systems. For purchasers who are seeking reassurance that the systems to whom they are entrusting their patients put together health care delivery systems based on quality, that they continuously monitor and seek to improve the performance of their systems, and that member rights are guaranteed and member satisfaction is an organizational goal, NCQA offers a review process which is unparalleled in terms of its depth, comprehensiveness and integrity.

41. A Quality-Based Strategy to Control Costs

M. Daniel Sloan

Quality improvement strategies have enabled manufacturers to reduce costs while making dramatic improvements in quality. Now, health care purchasers and providers are turning to quality improvement. They're finding that communication, uniform statistical methods, and long-term partnerships can pay dividends.

By the year 2000, Seattle might be one of the first U.S. cities to boast, "Our health care costs are going down every year." During the '80s, scores of Puget Sound manufacturers committed to the international quality model. Because the continuous quality improvement model frequently measures success by counting money saved through decreased costs, these companies have been rewarded with higher profits. Quality pays well.

During the past year, five Seattle hospitals, a regional health maintenance organization, and a prominent benefits administrator have formally committed to this same quality improvement model. These health care leaders believe high-quality service costs less. As one executive told me, "We've raised the quality of our service without increasing expense. We know this works."

For the first time in history, manufacturers (the largest health care purchasers) and health care suppliers (hospitals and doctors) share a common management philosophy. There is a mutual commitment to the three simple principles of quality improvement: communication, uniform statistical methods, and long-term partnerships.

408

Health care buyers, even small ones, cam benefit from this significant and visible trend. If you live in a quality-focused community like the Puget sound region, act now and apply the principles.

COMMUNICATION

Communication requires cooperation, and cooperation means reciprocity. Speak with your health insurance carrier on a regular, scheduled basis. First, find out what you must give to get better rates. Negotiate, but expect them to tell you a nonsmoking, drug-free population is less expensive to insure. The reasons are no secret:

- Tobacco is the single leading cause of premature death in the United States.[1] Bladder cancer, pancreatic cancer, laryngeal cancer, and lung cancer share a common risk factor: smoking. Smoking is responsible for 17 percent of all cardiovascular deaths.[2]
- Around the country, emergency room personnel treat illnesses caused by epidemic cocaine abuse every day. Cocaine intoxication causes seizures, cardiac arrhythmias, respiratory arrests, and virtually every psychiatric symptom.[3]
- The second leading cause of premature death is alcohol misuse and abuse.[4] Illnesses related and attributable to alcohol abuse include alcohol psychosis, alcohol polyneuropathy, alcohol cardiomyopathy, alcohol gastritis, alcohol dependence syndrome, acute alcohol toxicity, pneumonia, tuberculosis, and a host of other disorders categorized as alcohol debilitation.

Quality improvement begins with prevention. If you want a quality health process, you must remove these causes of morbidity and mortality.

Next, ask what the medical cost offset effect is. This effect was defined when dozens of clinical studies suggested that quality mental health services reduced the demand for expensive medical and surgical services by up to 80 percent.

For instance, Aetna's Federal Employees Health Benefits Program compared 26,915 families having at least one member receiving mental health services to 16,468 families with no members receiving mental health services. Families that received mental health care experienced 36 consecutive months of decreasing health care costs.[5] These savings were achieved well in advance of the U.S. government's Diagnosis Related Group cost containment efforts.

Speak with your employees regularly and explain the information you get from your insurance carrier. Ask them for strategy suggestions. Some might volunteer to quit smoking, and others might volunteer themselves and their families for drug testing in exchange for reduced health insurance rates. Some will tell you stories about how biofeedback or therapy got them off expensive medication.

QUALITY CONTROL STATISTICAL METHODS

It is next to impossible to reduce variation without the prudent use of quality control statistical methods. Control charts are essential to the economic control of quality.

Many still cringe when they hear the "S" word. Fortunately, learning quality control statistics is more like learning a simple language than leaning complex mathematics or accounting. Keeping a control chart is as easy as connecting dots, and drawing a flow diagram is like drawing a map. Control charts, flow diagrams, histograms, and Pareto charts are just pictures: their simplicity is a source of strength. Statistical pictures let manufacturers streamline processes and help production workers reduce defects to fewer than 10 parts per million. Hospitals and insurance companies are using these pictures and information to reduce variation in service quality, reduce errors, and improve service times.

Health care givers (doctors, nurses, and psychologists) must now learn to use statistical reasoning to diagnose patients' disease processes. Physiology is only one process that must be sampled. Care givers must also monitor the emotional and behavioral processes that contribute to disease.

The statistical implications for medical data management are significant. For example, blood pressure readings are reported as a ratio of two variable measurements, a systolic over a diastolic pressure. An example of a normal reading is 120/80. Unfortunately, the ratio is neither an accurate nor a precise diagnostic measure; it fails to display variation. Control action must be guided by a knowledge of process variation. (See Figure 1.)

The health care industry standard, a blood pressure ratio, does not give physicians or nurses the power to differentiate common cause and special cause variations. Consequently, special causes are often treated as common causes and common causes are often treated as special causes. W. Edwards Deming calls this type of hit-and-miss control action "tampering."[6] Tampering can keep any process, including a physiological process, in a state of statistical chaos.

Statistical methods require a rational sampling plan. Systolic and diastolic measurements must be graphed using individual and moving range charts.

The absence of statistical reasoning from the health care profession's academic curriculum is one of the core issues facing health care purchasers.

BUILD A LONG-TERM PARTNERSHIP

Partnerships thrive on teams that work toward a common goal. Quality improvement supplier contracts focus on the measurable and specific goal of decreasing costs.

Figure 1. Individual and Moving Range Charts

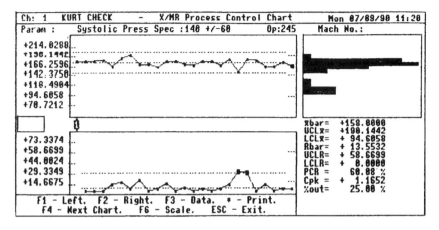

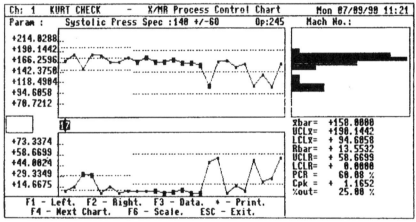

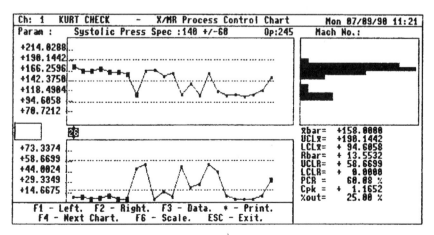

Figure 2. Causes of High Health Care Costs

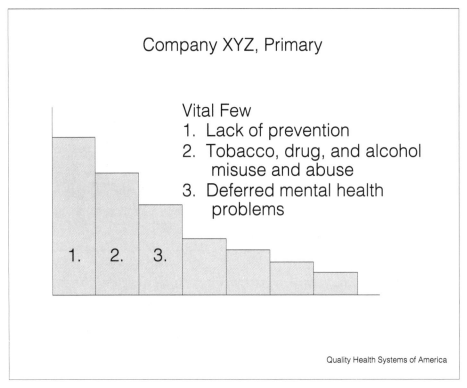

The supplier agrees to share with the purchaser the benefits of decreased costs through annual price reductions. The purchasing partner returns the favor by giving the supplier more business.

A force-field analysis displays the opposing pressures that surround proposed health care purchaser-supplier contacts:

Supplier	Purchaser
Fill hospital beds	Minimize use of hospital
Use high technology	Minimize use of technology
Set own quality standards	Set supplier quality standards
Increase revenue per patient	Decrease expense per employee
Use enumerative statistics	Use analytic statistics/QC methods
Provide discount pricing	Attain lowest total cost
Sign annual contracts	Set long-term agreements

The compelling need to produce high-quality health services at a decreasing total cost can overcome force-field obstacles. Supplier certification partnerships work every day for manufacturers like Motorola, AT&T, Boeing, Weyerhaeuser, Ford, General Motors, Hewlett-Packard, Xerox, IBM, and hundreds of others. Supplier certification partnerships can work for health care purchasers, too.

A SEVEN-STEP EMPLOYER INITIATIVE

The book *The Quality Revolution and Health Care: A Primer for Purchasers and Providers* (Milwaukee, WI: Quality Press, 1991) outlines a strategic purchasing plan for reducing the cost of health care.[1] The seven-step approach (which follows) integrates the work of Walter Shewhart, W. Edwards Deming, and J.M. Juran with current health care industry quality improvement tactics. Richard Schonberger's tagline, "world-class," is used to emphasize the similarities between industrial and health care quality models.

1. *Adopt a world-class health care philosophy.* Insist on the integration of medical science, behavioral science, education, and the use of statistical process control for all diagnosis and treatment interventions. This means corporations should give themselves permission to conduct their business transactions using the same quality business principles.

    As a former vice president of marketing for a licensed 305-bed hospital, I am convinced health care suppliers can meet the same quality standards as other suppliers. Once a company specifies its health care standards, the market will respond.

2. *Build a consensus for quality health care.* Employees are now empowered to control their production processes. They must be empowered to control their own health care processes. Empowerment builds consensus.

    This means patients will be sampling their own processes and, when required, keeping control charts. Patients must have free access to medical records.

3. *Establish policies to screen job applicants for tobacco and drug use.* Refuse to hire anyone who fails this quality control screen.

4. *Establish an off-site, confidential employee assistance program (EAP) or buy an EAP service from a provider that delivers quality-controlled therapy services.* EAP therapy services facilitate the medical cost offset effect. (Quality

Figure A. Supplier Certification

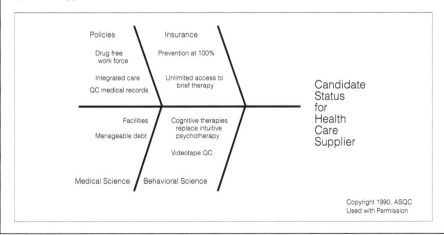

Policies
Drug free work force
Integrated care
QC medical records

Insurance
Prevention at 100%
Unlimited access to brief therapy

Cognitive therapies replace intuitive psychotherapy
Videotape QC

Facilities
Manageable debt

Medical Science / Behavioral Science

Candidate Status for Health Care Supplier

Copyright 1990, ASQC
Used with Permission

control therapy means counseling and therapy sessions are videotaped and flow diagrams are used to reduce variation in counseling methods.)

5. *Negotiate for quality, world-class service.* Expect ever-increasing quality of service and ever-decreasing costs. Health care suppliers committed to quality will be willing to make this commitment. Quality savings can be shared with the customer in the form of annual price reductions.

6. *Establish a world-class health care supplier certification program.* Existing supplier certification standards can be applied to health care suppliers. All suppliers can be expected to meet the same quality standards for leadership, statistical process control, strategic quality planning, and employee education.

7. *Establish a cost-of-quality health care accounting system.* Prevention investments must be measured in total dollars saved.

Communication, uniform statistical methods, and long-term partnerships have improved companies' products over the past 10 years. They can improve the quality of companies' health care benefits in the same ways for the same reasons.

Quality can reduce the total cost of care. One day, the quality of preventive health care will be so high that the proliferation of today's medical centers will be remembered as needless complexity. Prevention, education, and clinical teamwork can make high-quality, low-cost health care a reality.

Figure B. Costs of Quality

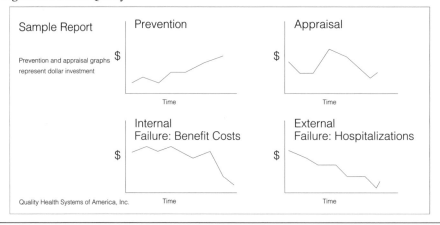

Imagine how the three principles of quality improvement and supplier certification can be used to reduce health care costs.

Management and employees at the XYZ company use quality control statistics to identify the primary causes of its high health care costs (see Figure 2). All employees, insured dependents, the insurance carrier, and the preferred health care providers review the information together, increasing communication. They develop an action plan for improvement based on shared statistical data, design a health care delivery process that reduces costs for every party, and set specific cost reduction goals.

The health care purchaser and the health care supplier sign a long-term contract. Annual price reductions and failure-to-perform penalties are specified by this supplier certification document.

Frequent communication, shared statistical data, and teamwork lead to a signed contract; the partnership begins. Shared cost reductions begin a process of never-ending improvement.

Over time, employees become healthier by improving individual and family lifestyles. The need for technologically intensive (meaning expensive) health care service diminishes, reducing costs.

Physicians work on cooperative clinical teams with nurses and mental health professionals. They standardize diagnostic and treatment processes using flow-charts. Control charts improve the accuracy and precision of drug therapies. This results in uniformly high service quality and delighted customers.

Hospitals use statistical process control to streamline operations. High-quality hospital care reduces relapses, and discharged patients stay healthier longer.

Actuarial data are presented using the uniform statistical methods of quality control. The pictures (charts) show the quality improvement team that the insured population is a reduced risk; as a result, premiums decrease for health care purchasers, large and small. The lowered premiums attract business, which increases volume for certified quality health care providers.

This make-believe vision is a reality for manufacturing plants all around the United States. Suppliers deliver higher quality, less costly goods just in time for the production process. This was impossible and improbable 10 years ago. Continuous quality improvement is now a way of life with visible benefits: bigger profits for both partners.

High-quality service, measured by decreasing costs, can become a health care service industry reality too when management shares a common philosophy. Communication, a common language, a common goal of reduced health care costs, and long-term partnerships can make it happen in our lifetime.

1. *Healthy People: The Surgeon General's Report on Health Promotion and Disease Prevention* (Public Health Service, 1979).

2. RW Amler and H B Dull, *Closing the Gap: The Burden of Unnecessary Illness* (Oxford and New York: Oxford University Press, 1987), p 47.

3. NS Miller, MS Gold, and RL Millman, "Cocaine," *American Family Physician,* February 1989, pp. 115-120.

4. *Healthy People: The Surgeon General's Report on Health Promotion and Disease Prevention.*

5. HD Holder and JO Blose, "Changes in Healthcare Cost and Utilization Associated with Mental Health Treatment," *Hospital and Community Psychiatry,* October 1987, pp 1,070-1,075.

6. WE Deming, *Out of the Crisis* (Cambridge, MA:MIT Center for Advanced Engineering Study, 1986), pp 327-330.

42.   Quality vs. Cost: How Should Employers Evaluate Providers?

Paul J. Kenkel

Employers have generally tried to control health care cost increases by focussing on the cost of services provided. The result—at best—has been to slow the rate of increase. Now, some employers have concluded that a focus on quality may be the best approach.

Hospitals in Cleveland will spend hundreds of thousands of dollars co-operating with the city's business community in a data-gathering project that eventually may tell consumers where to find the area's best health-care bargains.

Some 30 providers are supporting the project, known as Cleveland Health Quality Choice. The effort will try to pick out which hospitals provide the best services at the best prices. It will take at least another year of experimentation and consumer education before Cleveland healthcare managers know whether the idea has a chance of working.

But in a business coalition-led project in St. Louis, providers balked at supporting a scheme that sought to publish a price list of hospital services for area consumers. Coalition executives are mulling over their next moves—steps that may alter their relationships with providers.

Business-led initiatives to compare medical quality and prices in cities such as Cleveland and St. Louis are becoming commonplace. Employers in at least a

Exhibit 1. Where business groups are scrutinizing hospitals in quality and price issues

	Date begun	People covered	No. of hospitals	Price/cost studies	Quality surveys	Direct contracts
The Alliance Denver	1984					
Midwest Business Group on Health Chicago	1987	Represents 140 employers in nine Midwest states		√[1]	√[1]	√
Central Iowa Quality Health Services Purchasing Demonstration Des Moines	1991	100,000		√[2]	√[2]	
Business Coalition on Health New Orleans	1991		6[3]	√	√	
Prospective Pricing Initiative St. Louis	1988	500,000	2	√		
Greater Cleveland Health Quality Choice Cleveland	1989	300,000	30	√	√	
Lehigh Valley Business Conference on Healthcare Bethlehem, PA	1990	80,000		√		√[4]
Memphis Business Group on Health Memphis, TN	1986	200,000	15	√		√
Buyers Healthcare Cooperative Nashville, TN	1988	140,000	20	√	√	√
Foundation for Health Care Quality Seattle	1988	Covers population, providers statewide		√[5]	√[5]	
Alliance Purchasing Initiative Madison, WI	1990	50,000	3	√	√[6]	√
Healthcare Network of Greater Milwaukee Milwaukee	1986	150,000	13	√	√[7]	√

1. Total quality management demonstration projects underway in Chicago, Milwaukee and Kingsport, TN. 2. Studying cardiac care, maternity and child health, mental health and substance abuse. 3. Six hospitals submitting proprietary data; Medicare reports on 254 hospitals also used. 4. Contracts for prescription drugs, laboratory services. 5. Studies on lower-back pain and obstetrics care in conjunction with the University of Washington. 6. Studies on administrative services and clinical care. 7. Participant in total quality management demonstration project sponsored by Midwest Business Group on Health.

dozen cities have initiated projects that try to compare outcomes, costs and other measurements of quality care (See Exhibit 1).

Such efforts, most of which got started within the past year or two, reflect a growing interest among corporate healthcare purchasers frustrated in finding ways to cap medical expenses, which have been running ahead of most consumer prices for years.

Because no one knows for sure why medical bills keep rising, such groups have begun collecting healthcare data for use in building new purchasing systems they hope will provide the answer and bring results.

In two of the most advanced projects, planners in Cleveland have zeroed in on quality; St. Louis purchasers have tried to tackle price. The tale of those two cities' efforts to pry open the secrets of controlling costs provides a vivid contrast in the way purchasers have tried to solve the cost-containment puzzle.

RANKING QUALITY IN CLEVELAND

In Cleveland, healthcare payers wanted to know whether it was possible to create a quality-ranking system for the area's 30 hospitals.

"There were various assumptions about hospitals and quality, but it would come down to pretty subjective factors," said Patrick J. Casey, executive director of the Health Action Council of Northeast Ohio, a Cleveland-based coalition of benefits managers.

Hoping to get solid answers to their questions, planners in Cleveland this summer began testing a system that will measure hospitals according to three standards: severity of illness, risk and patient satisfaction.

Providers collected hospital data on severity of illness last December and conducted a survey measuring patient satisfaction in February. Planners then began sorting data according to preset quality indicators of non-critical care in March. Planners chose Washington-based APACHE Medical Systems to collect the data.

By this time next year, the business-provider coalition hopes to begin ranking hospitals in several categories of services according to preliminary quality indicators. The project involves such nationally known Cleveland-area companies as Nestle Enterprises, Parker-Hannifin Corp., BP America and Reliance Electric Co.

The Cleveland participants are hopeful that the project in the long run will save purchasers money on healthcare bills and reward quality hospitals with more business based on selective contracts.

"The key, I think, is whether all parties will continue to work together in good faith," said Terry Hammons, M.D., director of the Center for Quality Assessment and Utilization Management at University Hospitals of Cleveland. He also is a member of the coalition's steering committee that's working on the development of critical-care quality indicators.

EDUCATING EMPLOYERS ON QUALITY

Providers are gambling that Cleveland employers will learn how to use the quality data they have collected in ways that are profitable to hospitals.

Hospitals have operated for years under pacts with managed-care companies based primarily on price. Now they hope purchasers will use quality rankings based on severity of illness, risk and patient satisfaction measurements to channel patients to them in new selective contracting arrangements.

"Business has to hold up this part of the bargain (to use the data)," said Powell Woods, vice president of human resources of Solon-based Nestle Enterprises and past president of the Health Action Council of Northeast Ohio, a coalition of benefits managers.

That's why the provider-business coalition this fall will begin offering workshops to help benefits managers become better healthcare purchasers.

They will have to learn how to understand and use various measures of hospital quality and efficiency so they can redesign their companies' benefits packages. Some 50 large companies and dozens of smaller firms representing 300,000 people are participating in the project.

Some healthcare executives believe it may take several years before companies' benefits managers become adept at picking and choosing among the services that area hospitals offer.

"This (project) will take a long time to shake out," said Burt Bundgus, president and chief executive officer at Emerald Health Network, a Cleveland-based preferred provider organization.

"It's not business as usual. You've got to change a lot of old patterns," said Thomas S. Roos, director of employee benefits at Parker-Hannifin Corp., a Cleveland-based heavy equipment manufacturer, and chairman of the coalition's incentive benefits committee.

His group will offer its first workshop in October. The workshops will use simulated data because actual data won't be available for use until next July.

"There's no question that the thrust of the project is to do some patient channeling. The idea would be to offer incentives in various benefits plans to make these things happen." he said.

Parker-Hannifin is among a handful of companies in Cleveland that already make extensive use of elements measuring price and quality that are needed to fashion a managed-care program based on direct contracts with selected providers. The level of sophistication among purchasers declines rapidly after that first tier of companies, he said.

Even so, the education program should give hospitals that score well on the quality indicators some new opportunities to contract directly with purchasers or work out other special service agreements, he said.

"I see a real movement here in this city with more direct contracting and more choices," Mr. Roos said.

"This (project) is a real good opportunity for healthcare providers to meet customers' requests for service," said Pete M. Dawson, director of physician and managed-care development at Meridia Health System, the Mayfield Village-based parent company of four hospitals in suburban Cleveland.

"Sometimes we don't focus enough on what we need to do to supply our customers. After the quality assessments are published next year, hospitals will have plenty of information to work with," he said.

Many area physicians naturally are skeptical that "we'll stay the course and use good data that will eliminate random variations and reflect adequate risk adjustment factors, but all the parties involved still have a strong commitment to do it right, he said.

The real test will come next year when it comes time to decide whether the quality indicators give a reliable picture of how well providers are doing and whether they should be made public, he said.

PROJECT'S COSTS

The project won't come cheap. Budget estimates by providers in Cleveland have run as high as $6 million, but the city's business representatives think such figures are inflated.

"It's important from a business standpoint that others take a look at market reform. I don't want to scare them off with a figure I'm not happy with," Mr. Casey said.

To make the project's cost worthwhile for hospitals and purchasers, planners this fall will begin teaching corporate benefits managers how to interpret the data for use in overhauling their companies' health plans in 1992 and beyond.

Many observers believe the process of involving purchasers and providers in every step of the project that's being pioneered in Cleveland stands the best chance of making healthcare more efficient.

"We're trying to set community standards for evaluation of healthcare. This has never been tried anywhere else in the country," said Pete M. Dawson, director of physician and managed-care development at Meridia Health System, the Mayfield Village, Ohio-based parent company of four hospitals in suburban Cleveland.

The Cleveland project has moved along relatively smoothly because representatives from business, hospital and medical communities were willing to get down "in the trenches" together to hammer out agreements on how to measure quality, said Ralph S. Pollock, associate director of health policy of the Center for Health Ethics and Policy at the University of Colorado, Denver, and a consultant on the Cleveland project.

"It became theirs in the end. They invested in the thing. Quality is a long-term vision," Mr. Pollock said.

The project isn't operating in a vacuum. It's part of Cleveland Tomorrow, a decade-old coalition of political, business, labor and health interests formed to restore the city to national prominence. The health quality project began in 1989.

MORE THAN PRICE

From the beginning, the rising cost of healthcare was a major issue with purchasers in Cleveland. Unlike the project in St. Louis, however, which got started about the same time as Cleveland's quality initiative, price wasn't the central criterion.

"It's not just price; it's value. And now we've added another dimension called quality," Mr. Pollock said.

In the beginning of the project, "there wasn't a consensus that looking at quality had a relationship to the cost side of it," Mr. Casey said.

As they studied the issues, the planners in Cleveland began to see a probable relationship between value and cost. "What you pay is important, but what you get for what you pay is also important," Mr. Casey said.

"People can get together on issues of quality and value," said Michael Pine, M.D., a Chicago consultant hired by the Cleveland coalition to boil down non-critical data into a useful quality-measurement system for use by purchasers.

"When you start talking about outcomes, that matters to people. Everyone has a common ground," he said.

Because the data-gathering project had broad community support, "providers knew this was a real ball game and that this was something they should pay attention to," Meridia's Dawson said.

But hospitals worried that with current technology it wasn't possible to compare hospitals fairly. If they were to cooperate, they wanted a level playing field. "You're always nervous when you're going to be compared," Mr. Dawson said.

DRAWBACKS

One of the biggest drawbacks in comparing quality has been the lack of established quality indicators, Dr. Pine said.

Although quality assessment is a relatively young science, purchasers and providers have been steeped in mountains of technical data produced by vendors hustling to share market share.

"There's enough data to do a credible job badly," Dr. Pine said. "None of these pieces (of technology) is the solution. As far as any of the individual pieces are sold as solutions, everyone suffers."

Other concerns arose as a result of efforts to keep the project manageable and on schedule. To do so, planners compromised on the scale of what they could measure efficiently.

For example, planners decided to designate the use of certain antibiotics in the treatment of urinary tract infections as a quality indicator. "When you're sitting at the table making compromises, you'll accept them more readily," Dr. Pine said.

In another compromise, planners decided not to look at outpatient care. "You've got to accept those kinds of roughness around the edges," said Bruce Wilkenfeld, vice president for professional services at the Greater Cleveland Hospital Assn.

Even so, the project will be able to measure quality of care for inpatient surgical, obstetrical and medical diagnoses according to such risk-adjusted outcome indicators as lengths of stay, adjusted mortality rate, unplanned returns to the operating room and readmissions within 30 days, planners said.

The project will cost hospitals $7 to $8 per discharge, which is relatively inexpensive compared with more elaborate proposals that might have cost as much as $25 per discharge had the coalition adopted them, Mr. Wilkenfeld said.

Hospital staff members collected the intensive-care data and helped conduct the patient satisfaction surveys as part of their daily office routines. The gathering of non-intensive-care data may require hospitals to pay overtime, he said.

"The glue that hold this project together and that has driven it from the beginning has been the commitment from businesses as represented by the CEOs to use the data," Mr. Casey said. Their message to hospitals was, "'We're going to reward you for collecting this data.' That makes it all the more meaningful."

ST. LOUIS' PROBLEMS

Providers' uncertainty about how purchasers would use the data helped to stall the St. Louis initiative, said David Aquilina, a Minneapolis consultant who helped collect and analyze data for use in that project.

Mr. Aquilina said the initiative got bogged down over the central question of whether it was reasonable for the purchasers of healthcare in St. Louis to ask only one question: "What's the price?"

Few hospitals cooperated with the business group because the pricing plan ignored three other factors involved in most healthcare purchasing decisions: quality, service and location. The project also failed to take into account possible variations in consumer demand for services, said Richard Grisham, president and chief executive Officer at St. Anthony's Medical Center in St. Louis.

Members of the St. Louis Business Health Coalition wanted 37 St. Louis-area hospitals to submit guaranteed prices on 205 inpatient services. The coalition specified 205 services for the price list because they demonstrated easily measured variances in severity and outcome, Mr. Aquilina said.

The coalition wanted to publish the prices as a guide for consumers who would then consult the list to find out what price they could expect to pay at area hospitals. Coalition members represented such major employers as McDonnell Douglas Corp., Anheuser Busch Co., Ralston Purina Co. and Monsanto Co.

The coalition didn't collect data directly from the hospitals but built its list based on a comparison of 500,000 records of patients younger than 65 that were stored in a data base managed by Westborough, Mass.-based MediQual Systems, which uses a severity index called MedisGroups to make comparisons.

Only two hospitals submitted full retail pricing information as requested by the coalition by the Feb. 28 deadline. The coalition had hoped to publish its first price list in April.

Since March, coalition members have met with the "key hospitals" in St. Louis to get a better understanding of what issues need to be resolved to get the project back on track.

"I suppose we were a little unrealistic in assuming this would not take an incremental process," said James C. Stutz, the coalition's executive director.

The initiative "was seen (by providers) as a fundamental change in their way of doing business. It seemed straightforward to us," he said.

St. Louis providers were more uncooperative from the start than their Cleveland colleagues because the price initiative represented an immediate threat to profits, Mr. Aquilina said. "I'd find it much easier to cooperate (in Cleveland) because I wouldn't see either an immediate threat or reward on my bottom line," he said.

SPECULATING ON WINNERS

As the quality project in Cleveland moves into the testing phase, speculation is mounting as to who will emerge as the project's eventual winners and losers.

Coalition members hope the data system will work according to plan and reveal discernible levels of quality among providers.

"I don't know how clear the demarcation will be between the best and the rest. Our hope is there will be real clarity (in the data)," said Powell V. Woods, vice president for human resources at Nestle Enterprises and former president of the Health Action Council.

Healthcare purchasers want to reward the best providers, Mr. Casey said. "I think that's pretty well accepted by everybody. It's a part of life, a market approach, and (winning and losing) is implied," he said.

"If we did nothing, there would be winners and losers. This (quality project) sets up a different way of establishing who they are," he said.

The project won't rate hospitals, only the services offered, Mr. Wilkenfeld said. That way, the data should reveal where hospitals are strong as well as where they are weak.

It may help some hospitals see where they need to upgrade or drop services. Others may gain new opportunities to exploit the areas where they excel, he said.

43. Clear Goals Necessary to Pick Among Broad Field of Providers

Louise Kertesz

This article suggests a method for choosing quality providers.

Employers faced with a dizzying, ever-expanding array of managed care products can use a two-step process to select a provider.

First, employers should clarify their goals, experts advise. Then, only after their expectations are clear, should they evaluate key features of managed care organizations with which they may contract.

In setting managed care goals, employers must first decide "how restrictive they want to be with their employees. Many times the employer doesn't have a sense that there are trade-offs here," warns Dr. Thomas Mayer, a principal with William M. Mercer Inc. in Los Angeles.

For example, an employer may not realize that "a very large network interferes with the ability to actually get good cost savings," Dr. Mayer explained.

Employers should focus on function, not form, when choosing a managed care program, agreed Kathryn Abernethy, national practice leader for employee benefit consultant TPF&C, a division of Towers, Perrin, Forster & Crosby Inc. in Arlington, Va.

She advised employers to ask themselves two basic questions about any managed care program:

- Does it work?
- Does it make sense?

Exhibit 1. Top 10 General Service HMOs

Ranked by number of employees and dependents in employer groups as of June 30, 1991.

Plan (Sponsor)	Employees and dependents in employer groups	Participating employer/ payer groups	Tax status	Corporate headquarters
Kaiser Permanente Medical Care Program (The Permanente Medical Groups, Kaiser Foundation Hospitals, Kaiser Foundation Health Plans)	**5.9 mill.**	**43,447**	NFP	**Oakland, CA**
Blue Cross & Blue Shield Plan HMOs (Blue Cross Blue Shield Assn.)	**5.2 mill.**	N/A	Varies	**Chicago**
CIGNA Healthplan Inc. (CIGNA Corp.)	**2.2 mill.**	N/A	FP	**Hartford, CT**
United HealthCare Corp.	**1.4 mill.**	N/A	Varies	**Minneapolis**
Aetna Health Plans (Aetna Life & Casualty Co.)	**1.3 mill.**	**10,000**	Varies	**Middletown, CT**
U.S. Healthcare Inc.	**1.2 mill.**	**11,423**	FP	**Blue Bell, PA**
Health Insurance Plan of New York	**997,519**	**7,292**	NFP	**New York**
Prudential Health Plans (The Prudential Insurance Co. of America)	**971,509**	N/A	FP	**Roseland**
Health Net	**819,145**	**2,371**	NFP	**Woodland Hills, CA**
Sanus Corp. Health Systems	**661,000**	**3,615**	FP	**Fort Lee, NJ**

Note: Humana Health Care Plans (HMO & PPO) reports 1.6 mill. members as of June 30, 1991.
Source: BI survey.

"Employers throughout the '80s have been reacting to 25 percent increases in (health insurance) premiums and throwing a dizzying array of products at that problem, so now it is not unusual to have 12 different products at one site," pointed out Dr. Roger Taylor, national leader of the Wyatt Co.'s health care practice in Washington, D.C.

"The advantage is that there are thousands of options. The disadvantage is the confusion it creates, which is all the more important reason" for employers to first decide which managed care strategy is best for them, Dr. Taylor said.

Exhibit 2. Top 10 General Service PPOs

Ranked by number of employees and dependents in employer groups as of June 30, 1991.

Plan (Sponsor)	Employees and dependents in employer groups	Participating employer/ payer groups	Tax status	Corporate headquarters
Blue Cross & Blue Shield Plan PPOs (Blue Cross Blue Shield Assn.)	13.9 mill.	N/A	Varies	Chicago
USA Healthnet Inc. (Columbia American Corp.)	8.5 mill.	112	FP	Phoenix
The Affordable Network	5.0 mill.	1,885	FP	Downers Grove, IL
Preferred Health Care Ltd.	3.3 mill.	43	FP	Wilton, CT
MetLife Network (Metropolitan Life Insurance Co.)	2.9 mill.	247	FP	Norwalk, CT
Preferred Health Network (Blue Cross Blue Shield Assn.)	2.7 mill.	12,000	FP	Long Beach, CA
Anthem Health Systems, Inc. (Associated Group Insurance Co.)	2.6 mill.	N/A	FP	Indianapolis
Beech Street	2.5 mill.	86	FP	Irvine, CA
Prudential Health Plans (The Prudential Insurance Co. of America)	2.2 mill.	N/A	FP	Roseland, NJ
Aetna Health Plans (Aetna Life & Casualty Co.)	2.0 mill.	9,000	FP	Middletown, CT

Source: BI survey.

"The industry has advanced to the point where companies can now choose the best vendor for managed care and the best networks and the best claims payer. That could be one company or three or more companies," he explained. But, in making those choices, an employer must determine "what's the most value to be added."

While employers' expectations about managed care differ, by and large employers are seeking "increased accountability . . . both from a cost and quality standpoint," said Michael Thompson, vp of managed medical operations at The Prudential Insurance Co. of America in Roseland, N.J.

In deciding which managed care organizations to contract with, employers should "narrow down the choices to those that have demonstrated a strong history of quality and cost (containment) and employee satisfaction and that are willing to work with (employers) to comply with the specific standards which they ask of them," Mr. Thompson asserted.

But determining a health maintenance organization's or a preferred provider organization's commitment to quality is no easy task.

"What an employer wants to know is whether they are getting good value for their money . . . Everyone still is struggling with how an employer assures themselves of that," noted Marsha Gold, director of research and analysis at the Group Health Assn. of America, an HMO trade group in Washington, D.C.

In attempting to evaluate an HMO's quality of care, employers "are struggling to see how much they should do themselves and how much to rely on other bodies, like the National Committee on Quality Assurance," whose accreditation process "is still evolving," Ms. Gold said.

"It's increasingly becoming an issue that not only the HMOs themselves have their own quality program but that (the program) meets the guidelines of an external validation organization" like the NCQA, Mr. Thompson said.

Prudential, which Mr. Thompson says was the first organization to seek external accreditation of its HMO operations on a national level, has been working toward nationwide accreditation of its network for two years.

When assessing a managed care program, employers must evaluate its specific features. In doing so, employers will find that no organization will be perfect.

"You do have to make some compromises," said Timothy Borchert, a consultant with Hewitt Associates in Lincolnshire, Ill.

But, evaluating the characteristics of a managed care organization "will give the employer the necessary information for understanding its strengths and weaknesses. And where compromises need to be made, the employer will know what those issues are up front," he continued.

That information will facilitate communication, both with the managed care provider and with employees, Mr. Borchert said.

In evaluating managed care firms, employers should consider: provider selection; provider contracts; quality management; accountability to employers and members; financial strength; how premiums are determined; and history of past premium increases.

Evaluating how providers are chosen is one of the most important steps. Employers should ask whether the organization "just sent out an open invitation or first screened the doctors to only those that met certain criteria, and if so, what were the criteria," said Mercer's Dr. Mayer.

"It's our feeling that you do want to limit the network somewhat. If all providers were efficient and effective, we wouldn't be in the straits we're in," he explained.

"The employer has to be able to figure out if the PPO just went out and contracted with any hospital willy-nilly or if the contracting was supported by an analytic process that let them evaluate on cost, efficiency and quality," agreed Gene Guselli, who is general manager of Private Healthcare Systems Ltd., a consortium of insurers based in Lexington, Mass., that offer PPO products nationwide.

Proper provider selection is one of eight components of a PPO accreditation program operated by American Accreditation Program Inc. of Reston, Va., and endorsed by the American Association of Preferred Provider Organizations, Mr. Guselli observed.

Employers should ask if the organization has a physician application policy that asks "to see all the right things," including a current medical license, proof of medical malpractice insurance, board certification and a license to dispense narcotics, Dr. Mayer added.

But the important thing is to verify that the organization has followed up on the information provided on the application, he said.

"Often during a vendor evaluation (for a client), we make an on-site visit. Years ago, we just did a request for a proposal, but we feel that's probably not adequate any longer. At the site visit, we randomly select some of the credentialing files and audit them. We ask, 'Did you indeed get the 12 pieces of information you asked for . . . and did you sue the information appropriately?'" Dr. Mayer explained.

"Where I get disappointed is I see people spending a million dollars on credentialing and then not acting on the information they create from that process," he said.

The credentialing process is "in some sense very loose," agreed Hewitt's Mr. Borchert. "Where things fall down is that very few HMOs will go back and find out if a physician has lost licensing in other states . . . (and) few HMOs actually go in and look at practice patterns before signing physicians up," he continued.

The criterion of physician board certification "is a good example of where the system breaks down," Dr. Mayer asserted. While certification by the American Board of Medical Specialties, a unit of the American Medical Association, is "the gold standard," board eligibility—which managed care organizations often claim for some of their providers—is "meaningless," he added.

A physician who is board eligible has the training necessary for certification but hasn't passed the credentialing exam. "I may have taken the exam and failed it 30 times, but I can still say I'm board eligible, Dr. Mayer explained.

But lack of board certification also can be misleading.

"Often the most highly regarded providers are not certified" because they were trained before a board was recognized by the AMA, Dr. Mayer noted. "It's the role of the medical director" of the managed care organization "to sort those out," give a waiver to the good physicians and eliminate the others, he said.

"The best advice to an employer is to ask (the managed care organization) to describe what its credentialing process is" in order to compare different organizations, said Judith Wilson, director of HMO-USA, a national network of Blue Cross & Blue Shield Association HMOs based in Chicago.

An employer should also evaluate whether the contract that a managed care organization has with its providers encourages both efficient and quality care.

"It's important that physicians have a stake in how well a plan does," asserted Robert Crane, senior vp at Kaiser Permanente Medical Care Program in Oakland, Calif.

"Employers need to find out whether or not the payment systems that PPOs have in place with hospitals and physicians create incentives for efficient care," agreed PHCS's Mr. Guselli.

"The doctor will make the most reasonable decision where there's no profit in making an unreasonable decision and where he shares in the risk of the cost," said Mercer's Dr. Mayer.

Plans maintain various contracts with primary care physicians, specialists, hospitals and ancillary care providers, Dr. Mayer explained. It's important to examine each contract because "its possible for one sentence in a contract to invalidate all the incentives you work for," he asserted.

Employees also should expect a managed care organization to have quality management programs in place that mirror those in other areas of American business, it's generally agreed.

"Much of American business has identified 'total quality management' as a means by which they can improve their own business. Similarly, I believe that in health care there is significant room for improvement using those techniques. So a reasonable question to ask plans is whether or not and how those tools are being used within the network," said Kaiser's Mr. Crane.

Kaiser is "at an early stage" in implementing total quality management. "We're making a major commitment in improving our activity in this area. We're trying to learn from some of the most successful companies in the U.S.," he said.

"It isn't something that the health industry as a whole is deep into. We're the leaders here, but we have a long way to go," Mr. Crane asserted.

"Quality management is getting the right people in and monitoring what they do," explained Mercer's Dr. Mayer.

Several managed care experts emphasize that an employer should ask a managed care organization to explain how it monitors its providers and processes.

One way to do that is to retrospectively review the care that was delivered before an employee is admitted to a hospital, said BC/BS's Ms. Wilson.

For instance, if someone is admitted in a diabetic coma, it could be a sign that the person may not have received appropriate care in the doctor's office and that previous treatment should be reviewed, Ms. Wilson explained.

One of the components of the AAPI credentialing process is "whether there is an integrated continuous quality control process in the PPO," observed PHCS's Mr. Guselli.

"We give our medical management people very sophisticated information technology products," which are a prelude to total quality management, said Skip Creasey, vp of sales and marketing for managed care and employee benefit operations at Travelers Insurance Co. in Hartford, Conn.

For example, computerized systems can track patterns of treatment and monitor various patterns of treatment and monitor various procedures for medical appropriateness. That gives medical directors a "tool" with which to "approach a physician" and help that physician improve quality and cost effectiveness, he explained.

Larger insurers are going to be in "a little better position" to pursue total quality management because that kind of information technology is quite costly, Mr. Creasey asserted.

Ms. Wilson of BC/BS emphasized that monitoring involves "an educational component." For example, "a doctor just doesn't become a good gatekeeper." An HMO must monitor the doctor's referrals "to make sure they make sense," she said.

An employer should ask what sort of training or continuing education is available to network doctors and whether regular meetings are held to discuss the organization's goals, Ms. Wilson said.

Employers also should try to assess whether "the health plan holds itself accountable to employers and to the employees who choose it," Kaiser's Mr. Crane said. "Does it measure satisfaction and act on those indicators? Is the plan willing to provide information to the employer" regarding cost and value? he explained.

"The employer needs to (have) a good sense of whether this is a customer-sensitive organization," agreed PHCS's Mr. Guselli.

"Take a look at their satisfaction surveys to find out what their members think of them," advises Art Berarducci, a consultant with TPF&C in Boston. Although those surveys most often are not publicly available, HMOs will make them available to employers that are close to signing a contract, he said.

Employers should also look closely at the financial strength of the managed care organization.

"Any good HMO these days is running in the black," asserted Mr. Berarducci.

"Few employers actually look at the financial strength of an HMO today . . . though it is a very important part of selecting an HMO," said Hewitt's Mr. Borchert. He advised employers to scrutinize the HMO's balance sheet and determine what kind of safety net "is available to pay claims if the HMO goes under."

Another area to evaluate is the managed care organization's premium, which can be seen as its "accountability as it relates to the employer's own experience," Prudential's Mr. Thompson said.

"HMOs have historically community rated, but more and more employers are looking to rating tied to their own experience," Mr Thompson explained. "Where there are enough employees nationwide and where permitted by law, we do offer flexible rating arrangements," he said.

Many HMOs have adopted the strategy of "shadow pricing, or coming in with rates just under the indemnity plan price," said Hewitt's Mr. Borchert. "That has not been the most effective" strategy for employers and "now more and more HMOs are willing to experience rate."

"I'm not a big fan of community rating," said Travelers' Mr. Creasey.

"It tends to hurt the guy with the healthy group. We'll see more and more modified community rating," which blends community and experience rating, "but we'll be moving toward an experience rating because of the problems you have in trying to do a little of both," he commented.

Employers should examine a health maintenance organization's history of premium increases to determine if it has exceeded the industry average. That trend "tends to be 13–15 percent these days," TPF&C's Mr. Berarducci observed.

Employers "should consider an HMO's track record" when it comes to premium increases, agreed Kaiser's Mr. Crane.

"Over the last 10 years, our average increase has been in the 10 percent range," Mr. Crane added.

An organization "having the right elements structurally can give an employer some assurance that the financial results are going to be better than average," he explained.

"Rates that fluctuate widely from year to year are not desirable," Mr. Crane warned employers.

One large purchaser of managed care builds rate stability into its contracts with HMOs.

In Utah, the state employee group insurance plan insists on three-year contracts. "We tell them they can't increase their premium more than the Consumer Price Index for medical care in Utah," said Linn Baker, director of public employees group insurance for the state.

Utah also makes sure that any health maintenance organization it chooses does not avoid high-risk employees by such methods as limiting prescription drug benefits or making reimbursements for durable medical at a lower rate than other expenses, Mr. Baker said.

Besides these features, other indicators of a managed care organization's efficiency include: hospital utilization; membership and provider turnover; and "systems integrity," in which doctors help design a managed care plan.

Part 10

COMMUNICATION STRATEGIES FOR COST CONTROL

44. Communicating the Managed Care Plan

David Lally

In the scramble for solutions to contain exploding health care costs, employers, the insurance industry, and the government alike have seized managed care as today's "savior."

Yet what does managed care really mean? And is it really effective in controlling health care costs? Is it the savior we've all been looking for? Perhaps so; but like all remedies, it relies on the skills and commitment of those who implement it.

For managed care to work, it must be clearly defined by employers and their insurance partners so that employees—the ultimate health care consumers—understand why managed care is necessary, what managed care can do, and how they as participants in the process can help to maximize savings potential. Employees must also realize that managed care itself is in a state of evolution, and as a result, they must be open to—and even expect—changes in their health care coverage.

All this adds up to the fact that employers need to create an environment of active employee involvement in managed care initiatives to make them effective. And the foundation for this involvement must be an ongoing process of education.

Insurance brokers are in a unique position to help employers convey the realities of health care in America today. Those who advise benefit managers on employee communications strategy have an opportunity to add value to their products and services as well as to enhance client relationships.

Reprinted by permission of David Lally and *Broker World.*

UNDERSTANDING THE BIG PICTURE

Employers and their employees need access to facts. When it comes to understanding health care, it helps to start with an explanation of the problem on a national level and then relate it back to the individual employee and his/her employer. All ideas should be communicated clearly and concisely. The following outlines key points that should be included in any employee education program.

Nationally, health care costs currently outpace overall inflation three to one. As a result, medical coverage is consuming a larger share of every company's financial resources each year. To make these figures more personal, employees should understand that ever-increasing medical costs may be a contributing factor to smaller pay increases, fewer jobs, and possibly even decreased competitiveness in the marketplace. Increased health care costs are also taking a bigger bite out of employees' own disposable income in the form of higher copayments, premium contributions, deductibles, and out-of-pocket maximums.

If properly explained through communication tools such as newsletters, videos, and employee meetings, these financial facts directly relate the impact of the health care crisis to employees' own pockets. The use of graphs and charts can be very effective in communicating financial information in printed materials.

Employees should also be advised of the key factors responsible for driving up costs:

- **Medical inflation** has been surging ahead of general inflation for more than a decade, and there are no signs of it subsiding. Prices in the medical care component of the Consumer Price Index (CPI) have risen an average of 8.1 percent per year since 1981, while the overall CPI has risen only 4.7 percent per year. Price increases have been compounded by advances in technology that have led to common use of expensive diagnostic tools. The cost of the new technology is staggering (for example, a magnetic resonance imaging (MRI) machine is over $1 million)—and someone must pay the bill.

- **Cost-shifting**. Due to budget problems of their own, federal and state governments are reducing payments for Medicare and Medicaid patients. Because these programs don't fully reimburse providers' normal charges, they result in the shifting of some of these costs to patients who are covered by private insurance plans. With Medicare patients accounting for almost half of all hospital expenses, a growing part of the bill will be picked up by private insurance plans.

- **Unnecessary surgical procedures**. The Rand Corporation found that as much as 25 percent of all surgical procedures are unnecessary, particularly hysterectomies and coronary artery bypass operations. This underscores the need to train employees to question tests and treatments ordered by physicians and to involve them more closely in their medical care.

THE NEED FOR MANAGED CARE

Although little can be done regarding medical inflation, employees need to understand that a variety of medical delivery systems, utilization management techniques, and plan designs—known collectively as managed care—can be used to help stem cost shifting and to significantly reduce the incidence of unnecessary medical care. This is where employee involvement plays the biggest role.

For instance, employees should be told that to combat cost-shifting, managed care plans negotiate reduced fees with specific groups of health care providers, including physicians, hospitals, and labs. For example, most of ITT Hartford's managed care networks have negotiated arrangements with selected providers that average at least 15 percent below the usual charge.

To help prevent unnecessary care, they should also know that managed care programs share three common features:

- **Provider involvement**. Doctors in provider networks have agreed to certain treatment guidelines aimed at providing appropriate health care in the most cost-effective way.
- **Monitoring care**. Through the timely management of the care process, ineffective or unnecessary treatment is reduced or eliminated. This point must be handled carefully to insure that employees learn about the role of utilization management in a positive manner—not as a system that "denies" them access to medical care.
- **Incentives for network usage**. Unnecessary and costly care can best be eliminated through the use of a provider network. To encourage the use of participating providers, employees will often get increased benefits for using network physicians versus employees who go outside the network for their care. This financial incentive deserves to be featured prominently in all communication materials.

After employees understand basic tenets of managed care, the next step is an explanation of specific types of managed care programs, including health maintenance organization (HMOs), preferred provider organizations (PPOs), or exclusive provider organizations (EPOs)—and why employers have chosen a particular managed care option.

In addition to explanations of the different types of managed care plans, employers should also define different managed care terms, such as utilization review, primary care physician, and gatekeeper. It's important that employees learn what is meant by managed care for them to clearly understand and embrace it.

Brokers should advise their clients that once employees have been given a grounding in managed care principles, employers should influence employees' attitudes and behaviors to maximize cost containment. Their objective should be to help employees become better health care consumers. This includes teaching employees to question physicians on the need for treatments and tests rather than just accepting what doctors say as gospel, and modifying the belief that expensive treatments are better because they cost more. Employees must also understand that if they don't want to participate in the managed care system, they must share the financial consequences.

AVOIDING THE "HMO DILEMMA"

Insurance brokers should explain to employers how various managed care programs can affect their overall benefits plan. If employers educate their employees properly, they should see more people using managed care plans. However, an employer offering a community-rated HMO option may have a financial headache when too many younger (and usually healthier) employees gravitate towards the HMO, while generally less healthy workers stay with a company's traditional indemnity plan. The result is increasing costs for both the indemnity plan (through higher risk) and the HMO (through community rates higher than the associated risk). While managed care concepts used by HMOs can provide health care at a lower cost, in most cases employers are not sharing sufficiently in the HMO's cost savings due to community rating. Simply bringing everyone back into the current indemnity plan and giving up the advantages of managed care is certainly not a long-term solution.

So what's the answer to the "HMO Dilemma?" One alternative brokers can recommend is a point-of-service (POS) plan which gives employees the freedom to choose their own providers and employers the ability to manage costs under a single plan. Many companies are caught in the trap of giving too many health care options to their employees. For example, it is not uncommon for companies to offer multiple HMOs, a PPO, and an indemnity plan. This can confuse employees as well as make it extremely difficult for employers to effectively monitor their managed care options. By limiting the number of selections or moving to a single POS plan, employers have a much greater chance of gathering, tracking and understanding their managed care claims experience data—which translates into savings for the company and its employees.

ACCENTUATE THE POSITIVE

The process of making employees more informed—and therefore better—health care consumers is an ongoing effort. Employees must learn to expect changes in health care until employers find a solution that works. Employers must communicate the reasons behind any changes as well as anticipate the needs and concerns of employees.

To do that, brokers should recommend that clients keep the communication flowing 12 months a year—not just during enrollment periods. Health care is undergoing tremendous upheaval, and employees need to be kept informed of what's happening so that any changes in health care benefits, employee contributions, and other issues will be met with acceptance—not surprise or discontent. A series of newsletters detailing the issues listed above, videotapes on plan conversion, informational packets, payroll stuffers and/or employee meetings are all effective communication tools that can be utilized throughout the year. In addition, employers should notify employees that they have year-round access to someone who can answer questions on the company's insurance plan(s) and other health care issues.

As a further service for their clients, brokers can become a resource for information employers need to educate employees on the state of health care in the US as well as their specific plan. Insurance carriers can provide booklets, newsletter copy and statistics on topics including general health care issues, the HMO dilemma, and definitions of managed care that can be useful when developing employee communications. Don't overlook other sources of information including trade journals and government agencies that you can give to benefits managers to help make their jobs easier.

Employers have a variety of ways to determine the success of their educational efforts: the number of people who enroll in managed care plans, network usage, cost savings, and the number of inquiries received about the plan.

However, to get an even better handle on employees' thoughts and opinions, brokers should recommend that benefits managers conduct focus groups or employee surveys before and after the educational program. This is one of the most effective ways in which employers can learn what employees know, what they need to know, and how satisfied they are with the company's efforts.

For managed care to succeed, employees must shed their passive behavior of the past and become active participants in the health care system. Employers along with insurance professionals must do all they can to make employees true partners in the fight against health care inflation. Education is the key!

45. Controlling Costs Through Medical Consumerism

Donald W. Kemper

In the search for ways to control health care costs, wise employers are inviting employees to become part of the managed care team. Through employee communications and training in medical self-care and consumerism, companies are gaining a triple benefit: lower health care costs, higher quality, and better satisfied employees.

Most efforts to contain health care costs have centered on controlling the provider, the supply side of the health care equation. HMOs and other managed care strategies, for example, achieve their savings by placing financial incentives on providers to avoid unnecessary procedures. While this strategy has worked well to reduce hospitalizations and some elective surgeries, it has failed to alter the upward spiral of health care cost increases facing employers at every insurance renewal.

SUPPLY VERSUS DEMAND

Some employers are now adding a new element to their health care strategies called "demand-side" cost containment, where the efforts are centered on the employee, not the provider. Demand-side advocates point out that the employer's greatest cost control resource is the employee's own control over medical decisions since no medical test, medication, or procedure can be administered without the permission of the person who receives it. Any change in employee demand for services yields a direct and measurable impact on the use and cost of medical care. The challenge is to help employees make better decisions about the care they need and how best to get it.

How much savings can come from employee-controlled decisions? The potential might surprise you. A 1991 Milliman & Robertson report[1] suggests that up to "53 percent of our current health care costs are medically unnecessary." The services provided result in no significant benefit to the patient.

MEDICAL SELF CARE

Medical self-care is what the individual does for himself to recognize, prevent, and treat specific health problems. Today, about 80 percent of all health problems are cared for at home without any help from a health professional.[2] Because of its breadth of impact, self-care is arguably the most important part of our health care system. And yet, it is generally overlooked as a strategy for health care improvement.

The primary goal of self-care programs is to improve the quality of health care. Through better information, better doctor-patient communication, and self-confidence in health care decisions employees improve the quality of care they give and receive. Informed employees provide higher quality care at home and get higher quality care from their health professionals. The additional benefit of cost reduction is important, but it comes only if the quality and appropriateness of care improve as well. No matter how low the cost, health care is no bargain if it provides no benefit.

Self-care programs are inexpensive, easily implemented, and enthusiastically received. Unlike participation in fitness, stress, or nutrition programs, self-care programs often involve 90 to 100 percent of eligible employees. In addition, self-care programs produce measurable benefits that are visible from day one. First year return on investment ratios average around 2.5 to 1. As a bonus, self-care programs invariably create increased support for health promotion efforts. For these reasons, health promotion professionals are exploring ways to include self-care and medical consumerism in their program development plans.

Self-care is not wellness, but it's close. Self-care and wellness are both pieces of the health promotion pie. Although closely related, they are also distinctly different. Both self-care and wellness are based on self responsibility for health, both motivate people to make changes, and both reinforce each other. However, self-care programs usually focus on the immediate treatment of disease or symptoms, while wellness programs deal with longer term prevention of chronic disease in asymptomatic individuals. As a result, self-care programs usually have a more immediate impact on health care costs.

MEDICAL CONSUMERISM

Medical consumerism is the individual's role in medical decision making. It is what the individual does to determine the costs, risks, and benefits of treatment and provider options, before agreeing to a particular treatment plan. It helps people improve the quality of care they receive without incurring unnecessary costs.

Traditionally, medical consumerism has been stymied by a lack of access to information. Lack of access to medical records, journals, and handbooks has limited the consumer's ability to participate as full partners in medical decisions. Now that an increasing amount of medical information is reaching the public through journals, newsletters, and self-care handbooks, a more active role for consumers is evolving.

Giving people access to medical records and information increases their involvement in medical decision making. People who fully understand their medical problems are better able to contribute to their solutions.

However, good information is not enough. Medicine is not an exact science; outcomes are never certain. There are several alternative approaches for treating most medical conditions. The question is who decides on which alternative is best.

Without strong consumerism, treatment decisions are often determined for patients by their physicians. Surprisingly to many, physician decisions are not based solely on science. Large variations in practice patterns, even in geographically related communities, demonstrate the problem. For example, for a similar number and mix of people, Boston doctors prescribe about twice the number of carotid endarterectomies than doctors from New Haven.[3] On the other hand, the people of New Haven are much more likely to get a coronary bypass than are Bostonians. Similar variations can be seen for hysterectomies, back surgeries, hip replacements, and scores of other procedures and hospitalizations. These differences cannot be explained by measures of the population's health. Rather, they seem to be due primarily to differing values of the physicians in each community.

With strong consumerism, these decisions are made using the same outcomes information but with the values of the individual rather than those of the physician. The results can be significant.

Three Medical Consumer Models

The chart below describes three models of typical medical consumers.

- Model #1: Doctor's Choice
- Model #2: Shared Choice
- Model #3: Consumer's Choice

Medical Consumer Models

You may follow different models for different doctors or situations.

Model #1: Doctor's Choice

Description

You rely on the doctor's advice with little questioning.

Your trust in the doctor replaces the need to seek other alternatives.

You do not ask many questions or offer much information unless asked.

Message

"I'm looking for a doctor that will take charge of all my health problems. I plan to rely on your judgment in all medical decisions."

Situations

You have one main doctor you trust to provide or coordinate care.

In emergencies where split second decisions are critical.

Model #2: Shared Choice

Description

You expect your doctor to discuss alternatives and develop a shared treatment plan with you.

You are comfortable asking questions and expressing concerns or ideas.

Message

"I'm looking for a doctor who will involve me fully in treatment decisions and give me access to my medical records. I will share responsibility for choosing among treatment alternatives."

Situations

You are confident your ideas will improve the quality of care you get and believe your ideas will help keep costs down.

You do not have a regular doctor who provides or coordinates all your care.

Model #3: Consumer's Choice

Description

You listen to the doctor's assessment of alternatives but reserve the right to decide what to do yourself.

Message

"I like to make up my own mind about which tests and treatments are best for me, but I need your help to diagnose my problems and identify alternative treatments."

Situations

Fragmented Care: You are bounced from specialist to specialist with no one physician coordinating overall care.

Alternative Medicine: You wish to try a nonmedical approach.

Until recent years, most Americans followed the Doctor's Choice model. They did what the doctor said with little question or concern. That model is still appropriate for many situations.

Today, however, many people are changing to Shared Choice relationships in which they and their doctors jointly decide on treatment plans. Some even have moved to the Consumer's Choice model where they take full control over treatment decisions. The smart consumer knows when to use each model to his or her best advantage.

How Medical Consumerism Contains Costs

Encouraging medical consumer skills results in cost savings in three ways.

1. *Better home care.* Self-care education is the most basic part of medical consumerism. Effective education can improve both the competence and confidence with which people manage health problems. When the consumer is informed and activated, unnecessary care is avoided and needed care is obtained more quickly. As shown below, self-care education efforts consistently result in significant medical care savings. The savings come in three areas: the avoidance of unnecessary care, the substitution of home care for professional care, and the prevention of illness complications due to early home management of health problems.

2. *Better communication.* Another area of savings comes from helping doctors avoid mistakes. The typical doctor sees 20 to 40 patients in a day. He or she may have only 10 minutes to think about each case and make a treatment plan. As in any field, high volume and time pressures often lead to mistakes. Because the patient has only one person to worry about, he or she can help the physician avoid errors in judgment or execution. By actively communicating with the doctor and asking a few basic questions, the individual greatly reduces the chance of mistakes.

   Good communication also impacts the cost of malpractice. Some malpractice attorneys cite poor communication between the patient and the doctor as a contributing factor in 90 percent of their cases. Improved communication not only reduces the chance of error, it increases the patient's understanding and acceptance of the risks involved.

3. *Risk-averse choices.* Perhaps the most significant area of savings from medical consumerism comes in the patient's natural aversion to risks. People are more reluctant than their doctors to accept high risks for side effects from medical procedures. This is particularly true when the benefits of the procedure are not certain. Studies of men concerned with enlarged prostate glands show that after learning the probable costs, risks, and benefits of surgery, they became much more conservative than their doctors in opting for surgery.[5]

HARD DATA EVALUATIONS

At least seven controlled evaluations of comprehensive self-care programs have been reported in the medical literature.[6-14] All seven studies involved the distribution of at least one self-care guide along with various combinations of workshops, incentives, and additional communications aimed at improving the quality of medical decisions made at home.

Ten Action Steps To Reduce Costs Through Medical Consumerism

Employers can reduce costs by systematically implementing a step-by-step plan to encourage medical consumer skills among employees. Each of the following steps is practical, well-demonstrated, and cost effective.

1. *Become an Active Medical Consumer Yourself.* You will be better able to promote medical self-care professionally if you practice it personally.
   - Find a good doctor and express your desire to be actively involved in medical decisions that affect you.
   - Prepare for every office visit by writing down your symptoms and the three questions you would most like answered. Ask the most important question first.
   - Always ask for the benefits, risks, and costs of any proposed treatment, and always ask for at least one alternative.
   - Learn where to look for help. Libraries, books, subject matter experts, and other resources are increasingly available.
   - Keep your own set of medical records. Written records will greatly improve your ability to manage health problems.
2. *Build Self-Care Concepts into All Health Promotion Efforts.* Every medical screening, health promotion program and risk reduction intervention provides an opportunity to reinforce the message that the employee is in charge of his or her own health. Review every program with an eye toward strengthening that message.
3. *Increase Access to Medical Information.* The biggest barrier to effective self-care is inaccessible information. Work to make medical records available to employees and help them gain access to a basic medical library.
4. *Provide Self-Care Training and Resources to Employees.* Build a case with your employer for offering self-care training and a self-care handbook to all employees. One short workshop and an inexpensive handbook is enough to introduce employees to the self-care concept and give them the basic tools for improving medical care decisions.
5. *Eliminate Consumer-Squashing Language.* Review the language in your health plan and your health promotion communications. Work to eliminate language and requirements that limit the employee's ability to manage his or her own health. Take out requirements for physician approvals when possible. Rely on the self-responsibility of the individual.
6. *Support Care Counseling Systems.* Encourage your workplace to contract with care counselor services such as those provided by Employee Managed Care Corporation of Seattle or The Traveler's Informed Care Program. These services allow each employee to consult with a nurse counselor by telephone. The nurse's job is to make the employee an expert in his or her own health problem.
7. *Identify Consumer-Friendly Providers.* Support local efforts by employees and others to identify providers who fully educate patients about all the options. Help to highlight provider efforts to encourage medical consumerism among their patients.

8. *Reward People Who Use Consumer Skills.* Work to introduce incentive systems within your company's health care plan. Employees who are committed to actively managing their health care will create savings for their employer. Find a way to recognize that contribution. Non-monetary incentives and recognition can be as effective as cash payments.

9. *Track Changes in the Consumer Models.* A sample survey of employees can determine how many follow a shared choice medical consumer model. Repeat the survey annually to track how those numbers change as you introduce self-care education and support programs throughout the workplace. Set a goal to encourage shared choice doctor-patient relationships among 40, 50, or 60 percent of employees by a given date.

10. *Promote Self-Responsibility in Health Care Reform.* In the debate for health care reform, little attention has been given to how people can be helped to help themselves. Add your voice to those who are beginning to call for a greater level of personal responsibility to be included in health care reform. Then, insist that educational approaches such as those discussed above are widely promoted and provided within any new health care program.

All seven of the studies demonstrated a reduction in visits to physicians. Although some studies lacked statistical significance, the magnitude of the reductions is relatively consistent, ranging from 7 to 24 percent.

Other findings of the studies included:

- Eighty one percent of participants read at least half of the book[6]
- Thirty-five to thirty-eighty percent of participants used the book for a specific health problem during a six month study period[7,12]
- None of the studies reported any harm to the subjects because of inappropriate decision making. Questions on harm were specifically asked in one study[9]

EMPLOYER SPONSORED SELF CARE PROGRAMS

Medical self-care programs are becoming an important part of employer sponsored health promotion efforts. The goals for self-care programs generally include quality enhancement, cost reduction, and employee satisfaction.

Union Pacific Railroad

Union Pacific Railroad has a long history of offering innovative health promotion programs to employees. They have even converted railroad cars into mobile fitness centers for the benefit of employees in remote locations. In 1989, Union Pacific (UP) began planning ways to introduce medical self-care into its broad-based employee health promotion program. The challenge was to find a way to get the self-care message to both employees and spouses throughout the broad network of UP facilities across the nation.

Strong union involvement in the planning was present from the beginning. Union representatives quickly realized that the medical self-care program was a win-win situation for employees and the company. They were invited and encouraged to help design the program. Their involvement and ideas helped to foster program acceptance by employees.

In order to reach both employees and spouses, Union Pacific mailed a copy of the *Healthwise Handbook* and a videotape introducing the book to each employee's home. The packet also included a letter, a self-care quiz, and a brief evaluation form. Over 33,000 union and non-union employees received the packets in late 1991. Employees who returned the quiz and evaluation were eligible for a drawing that included a trip for two to Hawaii and three $1,000 cash prizes. Because the quiz included information presented in the video, it encouraged greater employee participation.

Union Pacific's medical director, Dennis Richling, MD, is a strong supporter of medical consumerism and self-care. His visible leadership and personal letter encouraging employees to view the video and use the book added to the credibility and success of the program.

The implementation of the program was coordinated by UP Wellness Center director, Joe Leutzinger, who worked to increase employee awareness in advance of the mailout. Leutzinger believes that "both UP and its employees benefit from the program. It's part of a managed-care effort, where UP gives employees the knowledge and skills to avoid unnecessary medical expenses. This helps UP to not pass on health care costs to employees."

Future plans for UP include adding an electronic self-care guide to their company-wide computer network so that employees can have ready access to the book and receive updates as medical science changes.

Montana Power Company

In 1985, following several years of rapidly increasing health care costs, Montana Power Company decided to help their employees reduce their own health care costs. Instead of raising deductibles or reducing benefits, they implemented a program of educational seminars, self-care communications, and the CareWise care counseling service offered by Employee Managed Care Corporation of Bellevue, Washington.

The CareWise service offers employees toll-free access to CareWise nurses who help employees become experts in their own health problems. The nurse helps the individual understand the medical problem and the treatment options available. They also assist in developing questions to be asked at the next physician visit, in order to better prepare the person to make a good decision about the treatment plan.

The CareWise nurses do not practice medicine; they do not diagnose, nor do they provide any treatment. Their sole purpose is to coach, counsel, and inform the individual so that he or she can become a better medical consumer. One inquiry may last 5 minutes and be over; the next may take several hours and involve a review of recent medical articles and the opinions of medical experts in a particular specialty. The nurse does whatever is required to get the information needed for the next step in the treatment process.

A follow-up employee survey was conducted after fifteen months of the CareWise service. As compared to a pre-CareWise survey, the number of employees responding that the company cared about their health increased from 54 percent to 74 percent.

The CareWise program has been offered continuously at Montana Power since the spring of 1986. The company's average cost increase over that period has been between 12 percent and 13 percent, far lower than the average 21 percent annual increase before the program. The program costs about 1.5 percent of the company's medical expenditures. Keith Kovash, manager of risk management and benefits, says, "The system provides our workers with the answers they need to understand and make appropriate health care decisions."[15] By providing the tools employees need to take control of their health care, Montana Power has saved millions of dollars in health care costs.

CAMSCO

CAMSCO is a small Campbell Soup Company subsidiary located in Dudley, Georgia. In 1987, Rose Mary Beasley, a nurse at CAMSCO, became interested in medical self-care as a way to improve employee health and add to the cost containment effort among CAMSCO's 200 employees. She approached management with a budget of several thousand dollars and a plan for introducing self-care at CAMSCO. After a year of planning and becoming certified as a self-care instructor, Beasley presented self-care workshops to all CAMSCO employees.

According to Beasley, "CAMSCO implemented a medical self-care workshop program to reduce employee health care benefit costs, and it worked." Following the program implementation in late 1988, medical costs for CAMSCO employees dropped 16 percent in the first year and 30 percent in the second. Although no formal study was done to attribute the cost savings to the self-care program, Beasley felt that there was no question about employee enthusiasm for the program. "They loved it. I could tell they were using the book. They would bring the book to me and ask me questions."

TRENDS AND FUTURE

There is a fast-moving trend by employers to introduce consumerism and self-care programs to employees. HMOs and health plans are also maneuvering to increase communications and educational programs that reinforce the consumer's role in health care decision making. These demand-side solutions to quality and cost control are not the complete answer to the health care crises. However, many companies are now realizing for the first time that without employee involvement, long-term health care cost control is not possible.

1. DV Axene, RL Doyle, and AP Feren, "Analysis of Medically Unnecessary Health Care Consumption," Milliman & Robertson, Inc., October 4, 1991.

2. JD Williamson, and K Danaher, *Self Care in Health* (London: Croom Helm, 1978).

3. JE Wennberg, JL Freeman, and JW Culp, "Are Hospital Services Rationed in New Haven or Over-Utilized in Boston?" *The Lancet*, May 23, 1987.

4. DK Kemper, KE McIntosh and TM Roberts, *The Healthwise Handbook* 10th edition (Boise, Idaho: Healthwise, Inc., 1991).

5. W Geber, "A Tool for Better Care," *HMO Magazine*, September/October 1991, p. 24.

6. DK Kemper, "Self-care education: impact on HMO costs," *Medical Care* 20(7): 710-718 (1982).

7. SH Moore, J LoGerfo and TS Inui, "Effect of a self-care book on physician visits," JAMA 243(22): 2317-2320 (1980).

8. DM Vickery and JF Fries, "Letter to the editor," JAMA 245(4): 341-342 (1981).

9. K Lorig, RG Kraines, BW Brown, and N Richardson, "A workplace health education program that reduces outpatient visits," *Medical Care*, 23(9): 1044-1054 (1985).

10. DM Vickery, J Kalmer, D Lowry, M Constantine, E Wright, and W Loren, "Effect of a self-care education program on medical visits," JAMA 250(21): 2952-2956 (1983).

11. EC Nelson, G McHugo, P Schnurr, C Devito, E Roberts, J Simmons, and W Zubkoff, "Medical self-care education for elders: a controlled trial to evaluate impact," *American Journal Public Health*, 74(12): 1357-1362 (1984).

12. DM Vickery, TJ Golaszewski, EC Wright and H Kalmer, "The effect of self-care interventions on the use of medical service within a medicare population," *Medical Care*, 26(6): 580-588 (1988).

13. JP Leigh, N Richardson, R Beck, C Kerr, H Harrington, CL Parcell, and JF Fries, "Randomized controlled study of a retiree health promotion program," *The Bank of America Study*, February, 1990.

14. JP Leigh and JF Fries, "Health habits, health care utilization and costs in a sample of retirees," California, Blue Shield of California Grant, May, 1990.

15. M Battagliola, "Making employees better health care consumers," *Business and Health,* June 1992

Part 11

INTEGRATING WELLNESS INTO THE COST CONTROL STRATEGY

46.   A Low-Cost Wellness Program
Shari Caudron

Incentives and targeted health promotion activities have helped the City of Glendale, Arizona, encourage employees stay healthy without a fat budget.

During the last 10 years, the City of Glendale, Arizona, has had only three rate hikes from its health insurance carrier, the highest increase being a 5 percent adjustment last year. Moreover, the city received one rate reduction, as well as three refunds totalling more than a million dollars—something virtually unheard-of in today's health care climate.

The City of Glendale attributes these accomplishments to a wellness program that combines well-placed incentives with targeted health promotion activities. Established in 1982, the wellness program also is credited with reducing absenteeism and cutting the actual number of on-the-job accidents in half during a time in which the size of the city's work force tripled.

You'd think such extraordinary success would require an extraordinary budget. But in 1991, the City of Glendale spent just $148,000 on health promotion activities for its 1,400 employees and 800 insured spouses, demonstrating it's possible to develop a successful wellness program without spending a fortune (see Exhibit 1).

Glendale's program is unusual, in that it was developed under the direction of Allen Iampaglia, a risk manager who had had no previous experience in wellness or human resources. With a background in property and casualty insurance, he was hired by the city in 1980 to find ways to save money in

---

1991 Costs of the City of Glendale, Arizona's Wellness Program:

1.   Contract with Health Advancement Services for health screenings, education, lab work, literature and a full-time nurse: $105,000
2.   Contract for use of fitness center at Glendale Community College: $25,000
3.   *Vitality* magazine (distributed free to employees every month): $6,000
4.   On-site mobile mammography: $12,000

   Total cost of program: $148,000

   Cost per participant, based on 1,400 employees
       and 800 insured spouses: $67.27

Glendale's self-insured property and liability program. When his efforts proved successful, he also was given the worker's compensation program to manage, and within a year had saved the city more than a million dollars in the combined costs of both programs.

"The city managers 'rewarded' me," he says, "by giving me responsibility for employee benefits, including a health insurance plan that had been experiencing rate increases of 40 to 50 percent."

Iampaglia's first step was to apply risk management, or "risk avoidance" techniques to the city's health care program. "With $90 million in real estate and more than $200 million in equipment, the city had good risk management in other areas," he explains. "For example, we rotated tires on the police cars every 4,000 miles, we changed the oil every 3,000 miles and we made sure the wheels were always in balance.

"Unfortunately, we were doing all these things in preventive maintenance but were allowing an overweight, out-of-shape, stressed-out police officer to drive the car at 90 miles per hour because someone went through a red light."

After reviewing the city's loss history, Iampaglia determined that prevention had to apply to employees as well as equipment. "This is where we were really losing money," he says, "and as a risk manager, saving money is what I care about."

When Iampaglia began to research wellness as a way of avoiding expensive health costs, he was confronted with resistance from consultants who encouraged him to try higher deductibles, higher co-payments and other cost-shifting techniques as a way to reduce the city's health care tab. But Iampaglia believes that cost shifting only changes an organization's level on a cost spiral that will continue to rise.

Furthermore, he believes cost shifting increases the financial burden on employees to the point at which they can't afford health care at all. "What have you really accomplished," asks Iampaglia, "if an employee refuses to seek prenatal care because it's too expensive and winds up with a $50,000 hospital bill for a premature birth?

"Besides, I don't want to know what to do with an individual who has had a heart attack, I want to know who that individual is probably going to be. That's what risk avoidance is all about."

As a government entity, the City of Glendale didn't have the funds to launch headlong into the development of a comprehensive wellness program. Instead, the city contracted with Health Advancement Services, a local health services firm, to conduct a health risk assessment that would reveal specific employee health needs. About 40 percent of the employees participated in the initial voluntary screening, which consisted of a lifestyle questionnaire, complete blood work-up, flexibility testing, hearing and vision exams, skin inspection, body-fat measurement, lung function testing, blood pressure screening and step-pulse recovery rate.

Despite the high turnout for a voluntary program, Iampaglia says the initial screening was unsuccessful, because there was no emphasis on education, nor was there assistance available to employees who wanted to make healthy lifestyle changes. Rather than scrap the screening altogether, the city modified it, making a health nurse available for consultation and education.

"Instead of telling employees only what's wrong with them," Iampaglia says, "now a nurse is there to explain why their conditions are harmful and to provide suggestions for change."

The City of Glendale also offered a valuable out-of-pocket incentive: For employees who participate in the screening program, the city's $150 health insurance deduction is waived; if the spouse participates, the $300 family deductible is waived. This incentive has been credited with increasing the rate of employee participation up to 98 percent.

Furthermore, the city began to use the results from these screenings to develop a series of targeted health promotion programs. For instance, when the initial assessment revealed that many of the city's employees were out of shape or overweight, the city contracted for use of the fitness facilities at Glendale Community College, giving Glendales's employees a free and convenient place in which to work out. When it was discovered that the city's fire fighters had poor eating habits, nutritional seminars were conducted at each fire station. And when health screenings revealed that few female employees conducted regular breast exams, a mobile mammography unit was brought on-site and free mammograms were offered. Other programs developed in direct response to employee need include: stress reduction classes, water safety courses, on-site aerobics and back injury prevention.

"Our work force is so diverse that we have to target our wellness activities," Iampaglia says. "We've got more than 100 job categories ranging from a sanitation worker who operates an 86-ton piece of equipment in a landfill to a

PURITAN-BENNETT'S EMPLOYEE-DRIVEN WELLNESS PROGRAM

Mary Martha Stevens, manager of health and wellness for Puritan-Bennett Corp., doesn't regard her company's wellness program as an employee benefit. "Wellness is a way of life, and companies can't provide this," she says.

For this reason, instead of providing an array of expensive health promotion activities, Puritan-Bennett's Perfect Health wellness program is directed at creating a culture in which employees want to take care of their own health and well-being.

The program's wellness activities are based on what employees want, not what the company thinks they need. These activities—the result of ongoing employee surveys—include jogging and cycling clubs, soccer and bowling leagues, fishing tournaments and weight-lifting groups. "The idea is to draw people into fitness activities in a way that interests them," says Stevens.

In addition, all activities require some financial contribution form employees. The cost may be only $1, but Stevens believes people place a higher value on activities they have to pay for. Furthermore, all wellness activities are developed and managed by employees, creating the buy-in necessary for program success.

To date, the most expensive aspect of the company's wellness program is the Health Promotion Account, an experimental program that rewards efforts to improve health by reimbursing 50 percent of the cost of off-site health and wellness activities up to $150 per employee per year.

To become eligible, employees are required to complete a health risk assessment at the beginning of the year and a follow-up assessment at the end, and to maintain good participation in the program of their choice. Stevens says the account supports the company's goal of self-sufficiency, for employees have to show some initiative to receive the reimbursement.

Puritan-Bennett doesn't view wellness solely in terms of physical health; the emotional, social, and occupational well-being of employees are also considered. This is why programs, such as a sign language support group, non-denominational Bible study and a car-care clinic, are under the auspices of the wellness program.

The company's wellness efforts are part of its goal to apply for the Malcolm Baldrige National Quality Award. "Our reason for developing the Perfect Health Program was to create a positive company atmosphere, because the health and well-being of each individual is intertwined with the quality of our products," say Stevens.

Although rising health care costs had little to do with the reason Perfect Health was developed, Stevens admits there will be a long-term impact on costs. But right now, the company is content to measure results based on employee attitudes, which have improved dramatically during the past year. Surveys reveal that more employees place a value on wellness, and top management has recognized a change in the employee culture.

The development of Puritan-Bennett's wellness program began in 1989, but it wasn't fully implemented until January 1991. To date, only 600 of the company's 2,100 domestic employees based at its Kansas City, Kansas, headquarters have

access to wellness activities. In 1991, the program will be introduced to all
U.S.-based employees.

Cost figures for 1991 haven't yet been compiled; however, Stevens believes
the self-sufficiency model combined with the employees' contributions will keep
program costs to a minimum. Moreover, because employees have been given the
tools to take responsibility for themselves, costs should continue to decrease. Says
Stevens, "As Shakespeare says, 'Our remedies oft in ourselves do lie.' "

biochemist who has to make sure 185,000 people get quality drinking water each
day. These employees have got to feel good on the job because any mistakes they
make are irreversible."

Communication also is an important part of Glendale's program. All
employees receive a free copy of *Vitality* magazine each month, and wellness
issues are covered in the employee newsletter, in the city manager's newsletter,
as well as in bulletins and during staff meetings. Because 35 percent of the city's
workers speak English and Spanish, presentations are given in both English and
Spanish. Additionally, the city has its own television studio, in which wellness
presentations can be broadcast over cable to all city locations or videotaped for
playback at a later date.

The city's approach to communication is straightforward. "We haven't
fooled employees into thinking we offer wellness activities simply because we
care," Iampaglia says. "We do care, but we offer programs to save money in
benefits costs, and what we save, we can spend on salaries or additional benefits,"
Since the wellness program began, Glendale has added comprehensive dental and
vision care, long-term disability and additional life insurance to the benefits
package, using health insurance refunds to cover these expenses.

But lower health insurance costs and enhanced employee benefits are only
part of the harvest Glendale has reaped from its wellness program. Three times
as many employees are having half the actual number of on-the-job accidents,
wellness participants now have fewer worker' compensation claims than nonpar-
ticipants and absenteeism is down. Moreover, when the potential cost avoidance
of such events as heart attacks and mastectomies are figured in, Glendale sees an
estimated 10-to-one return on its wellness dollar.

Last year, when Iampaglia received word that the city's insurance company
was projecting an 8 percent increase in its health insurance premium, he invited
the underwriter to Arizona to have a firsthand look at Glendale's wellness
program. She did, and when the bill finally came, the increase had been held to
just 5 percent—a $135,000 savings, which, by itself, almost covers the annual
cost of wellness services.

"I understand insurance companies are in business to make a profit, but my
job is to make sure that profit is reasonable," Iampaglia explains.

To anyone who still isn't convinced that wellness makes good financial sense, Iampaglia will gladly tell the story of the most highly compensated Glendale employee. It isn't the city manager, he says, but a sanitation worker who cost the city almost $250,000 in hospital bills when his wife gave birth to a premature baby.

When Iampaglia researched the case, he discovered the employee's wife hadn't sought prenatal care. Why not? "This was her seventh baby," he says. "The first six came out fine."

By considering the cultural differences of its work force and targeting health promotion activities, Glendale's wellness program is designed to prevent this from ever happening again.

47. Are Wellness Incentives Incensing Employees?

Richard E. Miller

Tobacco-smoking, saturated fat-eating, scale-tipping employees lead lifestyles that generate doctor bills. Why should healthy employees make equal payments to a group health insurance plan when the premium is pumped-up by their unhealthy counterparts? The logic of providing incentives to the healthy and disincentives to the unhealthy is straight-forward and convincing. There is only one catch—is it really fair?

The sputtering ethics movement in corporate America is facing the controversy of rewarding and penalizing employees over health behaviors. There is considerable evidence that lifestyle behaviors are modifiable. Individuals can cut pounds, reduce alcohol intake, quit smoking, increase physical activity, and take up measures to control blood pressure and cholesterol levels. By doing so, they are eligible for incentives, rebates or financial discounts in some companies. For some individuals, however, lifestyle is not easily modified. Heredity plays a significant role in the management of body weight, blood pressure, and serum cholesterol. Once this is realized, employees will be incensed rather than "incented" regarding their wellness.

Given this controversy, the practice of using incentives, rebates, and insurance premium discounts needs closer examination. Employers may be elaborately reinforcing desirable behaviors in their employees only to fail in containing health care costs. Incentive programs involve tangible costs as well as less detectable expenses. Another major consideration is the impact of this system on employees' morale and sense of privacy. So if everything has a price, corporations may have a larger than expected bill to pay.

WELLNESS INCENTIVES

The rationale for wellness incentives is that valued outcomes can be ensured by investing more time and money in the process. Therefore, employers organize health activities in which successful employees earn social and tangible awards, prizes, and recognition. Honoring the healthy, active employee has been practiced by industrial recreation specialists since the start of the century. Tangible incentives seem to carry more weight, however. Merchandise such as athletic apparel and equipment motivate a hardy contingent of employees to scramble for personal bests. When companies like the Xerox Corporation led the corporate fitness movement in the late 1970s, achieving employee got their share of t-shirts, athletic wear, and stationary bicycles.

Wellness incentives remain an attractive feature of most corporate programs. Many work organizations, including public sector agencies, have taken wellness incentives a step forward by reimbursing employees for attending health education classes and behavioral modification sessions.

The nature of incentives has changed considerably in some companies. Employees (and sometimes dependents as well) can receive direct financial payments if they lose weight, reduce cholesterol levels, exercise more, or stop smoking. Although incentives are designed to lure employees towards healthy behaviors, experienced directors of corporate fitness and wellness programs caution about its overuse. This could be why only about a tenth of corporate health and fitness programs surveyed by the Office of Workplace Health Promotion of the Washington Business Group on Health operate a monetary wellness incentive system. Apparently, financial incentives, acting as positive and negative reinforcers, do not necessarily translate into permanent changes in fitness behavior. Even so, many companies are investing resources into this system of awarding the healthy.

Employees Can Change

The federal government has set national goals for changes in health habits. The Office of Disease Prevention and Health Promotion (US Public Health Service) has a goal of at least 35 percent of adult Americans to exercise weekly, but only 12 percent have answered the call. High blood pressure plagues 10 to 15 percent of white and 20 to 25 percent of black adults. The government's target is to have at least half of these adults maintain acceptable blood pressure levels, even though only about 16 percent have demonstrated control. Although workplace cigarette smoking has decreased, the Surgeon General wants the number of smoking blue collar workers reduced from 36 percent to 22 percent. In terms of girth, the government thinks the number of overweight Americans can be reduced from 25 percent to 20 percent.

Employees need to change. When it comes to risks of cardiovascular disease, medical evidence has replaced popular speculation. The very lifestyle practices identified above account for the leading causes of premature death and a vast amount of medical dollars. The University of Michigan's Fitness Research Center has reported that the combination of tobacco use, high blood pressure, and physical inactivity accounts for $600 to $700 per person in health care claims each year. So it is reasonable for employers to expect unhealthy employees to change their ways. But it is also understandable for employees to wonder what exactly needs to be changed.

Change What?

Life is a baseball game umpired by Kafka. The bat meets the ball and the player runs the baseline only to discover someone is moving the bases. Coping with life means adjusting to ever-changing medical care standards. In just a few years, the National Cholesterol Education Program (Heart, Lung and Blood Institute) has shifted recommended levels of 220 mg/dl to 200 mg/dl (milligrams of cholesterol per deciliter of blood). In actuality, the current recommendation is keeping levels between 170-180 mg/dl. This is quite a feat considering the body manufactures 85 percent of our cholesterol leaving only a 15 percent intake through diet. So when recommended levels are lowered, this lifestyle practice become less controllable. On top of that, a cholesterol level below 150 mg/dl is associated with cancer and cerebral hemorrhaging. That is a mighty narrow corridor for lifestyle modification.

Americans should keep their body weight within reasonable limits, but in reality this is not feasible. A recent National Institutes on Health panel, headed by Suzanne Fletcher, editor of the Annals of Internal Medicine, concluded that no matter what informal, therapeutic, or commercial weight reduction approach is employed (e.g., cutting back on calories, spending $30 billion a year on commercial diet programs, gulping vitamins and over-the-counter diet drugs), nothing succeeds in keeping weight off for good. Although dieters can typically cut 10 percent of their body weight, most is regained within a year and all comes back within five years. The more effective way is a combination of diet and exercise as well as viewing weight management as a life-long challenge. According to one researcher from Columbia University, individuals who have been successful in losing pounds and maintaining the loss require a graduated approach spanning 10 to 20 years! This realistic time frame does not fit into the short-term expectations of corporate wellness incentive programs.

Remember the annual physical, an American Medical Association tradition introduced at the turn of the century? In 1984, a 20-member Preventive Services

Task Force recommended that healthy persons without unexplained symptoms (e.g., pain, weight loss, bleeding, weakness, dizziness) need not visit a doctor periodically. The Task Force's *Guide to Clinical Preventive Services* evaluated nearly 170 medical tests and procedures and concluded that the focus of the encounter should be on the patient's own risk and habits, not on expensive tests to detect hidden illnesses. Among the recommendations were hypertension screening via blood pressure cuff every one to two years, and cholesterol screening every 5 years for adults (unless elevated cholesterol has been detected). Annual check-ups and cholesterol screenings are central health assessments in wellness incentive programs, especially those relying on individual health insurance risk-rating. There seems to be a contradiction between what is expected of employees in wellness incentives programs and the current standards of health care practice.

Risk Rating and Rebates

An increasingly popular means of incenting employee health behavior is individual risk rating. (Risk-rating is not a radical idea, considering automobile and life insurance plans have operated like this for years.) Through risk rating, health insurance premiums are based individuals' modifiable lifestyle behaviors. This is contrary to the traditional idea of insurance, which is to spread risk throughout the population to reduce costs borne by individual employees. Risk-rating is thought to predict the individual's future risk of illness and its related costs. It does this by adjusting an individual's share of premium according to lifestyle, thus shifting the responsibility for potential medical costs to the higher-risk individual. The intent is to reduce the need for and consumption of health care services by encouraging individuals to maintain or improve their health habits by the prospect of lower premiums. The National Association of Insurance Commissioners developed a model regulation that is intended to provide standards for certifying health plans and policies that authorize risk-rated insurance. (See Exhibit 1.)

The general rule is that employees have the option of participating in risk-rating. Clinical assessments and employee self-reports confirm eligibility for a financial incentive, which is pro-rated over the year. Usually, the incentive appears in the employee's paycheck and offsets a regular insurance premium deduction. If the employee improves from baseline measures of blood pressure, serum cholesterol, and carbon monoxide levels in the blood, essentially he/she will pay a discounted insurance premium while the nonparticipating employee continues on the regular payment schedule. *Unhealthy* employees—those not improving from baseline measures—also retain the regular payment schedule unless they choose to participate in health improvement programs, after which

---

Exhibit 1. Model Regulations for Healthy Lifestyle Behaviors

No Tobacco: No use of tobacco products at least six months before the issuance of the plan and while plan is in force.

Regular Exercise: Participating, 3 or more times per week, in an aerobic activity such as brisk walking, running, swimming, and bicycling, maintaining 60% of maximum heart rate for 20 minutes.

Moderate Alcohol Consumption: No more than 2 drinks in any 24 hour period and no more than 7 drinks in any week.

Blood Pressure Maintenance: Maintaining blood pressure equal to or less than 140/90 mm Hg, with or without physician-prescribed medications.

Weight Control: Maintaining desirable weight as determined by the 1983 Metropolitan Life Insurance Company lean body mass calculation, or skin fold measurements.

Non-abuse of Drugs: Complete avoidance of substances illegal under state or federal law, and ingestion or use of legend drugs only as prescribed by a physician.

Seat Belt Usage: Using seat belts in the manner prescribed by the manufacturer whenever riding in or driving a private passenger vehicle.

---

they receive partial financial incentives. This means, of course, that the employer picks up the balance.

An alternative to risk rating is awarding payroll bonuses or rebates that can be used in a flexible medical benefits plan. For example, Baker Hughes, Inc., a Texas-based firm, requires self-admitted smokers to pay an additional $10 dollar per month for medical coverage. They also have the opportunity for $100 pre-tax spending out of a flexible benefits account if they have an annual physical examination.

As another example, Southern California Edison, Inc., offers a $10 monthly rebate to employees and spouses covered under the flexible benefits plan. The rebates, which are included in regular paychecks, can be used to offset monthly health insurance premiums. To qualify, employees and spouses are screened at the workplace, at a $10 charge, for five modifiable risk factors: body weight mass (blood mass index), blood pressure, smoking (carbon monoxide level), cholesterol level, and blood sugar level. Measurements must fall within acceptable guidelines. (The company assures employees that the sample will not be used for other purposes such as drug testing). Edison's health care department analyzes the data to confirm employee eligibility for rebates. Those completing the screening, but not meeting the criteria, may still qualify by participating in medical treatment or educational programming designed to modify lifestyle.

United Power Association (Elk River, Minnesota) examines employees' self-reported tobacco use, weight or percent body fat, exercise, seat belt use, blood pressure, cholesterol, and alcohol/drug use. Results of a medical examination or health risk appraisal are also required. Thereafter, participants are placed in health risk categories: dangerous, poor, good, or excellent. Employees in the excellent health category have a $5 per month health insurance premium payment while those in the dangerous health must pay $75. Opportunities are available for employees to participate in educational programs to assist them in moving up from one health category to another.

The Group Health Cooperative (Puget Sound, Washington) awards a 15 percent discount membership fee in year one and 10 percent discount in subsequent years to healthy individual members of this health maintenance organization. The plan is not open to group members sponsored by employers. Individuals self-report their efforts at meeting healthy behavior criteria (similar to the ones listed in *Model Regulation of Healthy Lifestyle Behaviors*). The Group Health Cooperative validates employee health status by reviewing a sample of charts and analyzing health care utilization data.

Adolph Coors Company (Golden, Colorado) offers a reduction in co-payment from 15 percent to 10 percent for the healthy employees enrolled in the indemnity health insurance plan. To qualify, employees must submit acceptable "Health Hazard Appraisal" results, which are examined by the company's health educator. Opportunities to requalify are once every year.

Union Camp Corporation (Wayne, New Jersey) offers bonus pay to reimburse medical expenses not covered by the indemnity plan. The interesting twist here is that the program is administered by the company's insurance carrier. In addition, employees can pick up an extra $100 if they and their dependents are nonsmokers.

Mesa Corporation gained notoriety in the 1980s for requiring their employees to be members of the company's fitness program. Since then, the company has loosened its policy, recognizing that employees can participate in healthy physical activities outside the employer-sponsored program. Annually, the corporation provides direct financial compensation to employees ($474) and spouses ($228) for meeting health and fitness criteria. The company uses the health risk appraisal, and five semi-annual fitness tests to determine if employees qualify for bonus pay.

THE REAL PRICE

Incentives, risk-rating and rebates are investments by companies to drive down health care costs. But do companies realize all the costs connected with turning unhealthy employees into healthy ones? As mentioned earlier, annual health assessments such as medical examinations and cholesterol tests are unnecessary and superfluous expenditures of medical dollars. Yet some companies are bound to these criteria in determining the healthy employee. As an illustration, how is a person going to pay for the serum cholesterol test? Under most indemnity plans, this blood test is not reimbursable. So unless the employer sponsors the test and offers it to the workforce at a reduced price, the individual employee must enter the health care system annually and secure the test during a $40 to $125 medical office visit. With fingers crossed, the employee may have an acceptable cholesterol reading and therefore recoup some of the expenses through financial discounts and rebates. If the results indicate hypercholesteremia, the employee has to wait until next year to qualify for the financial awards. Of course, some companies give employees partial credit for participating in a health improvement program in the interim.

So, the healthiest employees—those qualifying for the rebates, discounts, and lump sums—are incented to re-enter the health care system annually. Several companies have occupational health services that perform the examinations and blood tests. However, the administrative overhead for in-house occupational health services adds up. In a comprehensive program offering a wide array of services, it could cost $15 just to pull a patient's chart. (This involves securing the employee's file from the medical records room, delivering it to and receiving it back from the medical care provider, inserting and checking any forms from the provider and laboratory, and then logging service information into a central-ized information system.) The actual price of the occupational health visit involves pro-rating (by the hour) services of an occupational health physician (at least $100), nurse practitioner ($60), registered nurse ($40). This does not include the extra charges for a medical assistant who may take blood pressure readings, height and weight information, and so forth. Putting it together, the annual health care visit amounts to $50 to $120. Under risk rating, this procedure would take place at least once a year.

Here is another cost issue: What if the wellness incentives are unnecessary? Employers may be paying employees to change habits when the employees were probably going to change on their own. For example, the American public has taken it upon itself to exert more control over hypertension. During the 1970s, only 6 percent of hypertensive adults demonstrated control (for two or more years); yet by the 1980s, this number had increased to 16 percent—without direct financial lures. As for tobacco habits, since the 1960s, almost half all living adults who have ever smoked have quit. Reports from many companies, as published in professional journals, show employee smoking rates as low as 8 to 11 percent compared to the general population of adults at 29 percent.

What if wellness incentives are more expensive than other ways of en-couraging health improvement? There is little evidence to date of the cost effectiveness and benefit of risk rating and rebates. On the other hand, there is substantial evidence that corporate fitness and wellness programs can offset their operational costs in terms of fewer medical dollars spent, reduced absenteeism, and shorter disability leaves. Companies touting these yields are Northern

Exhibit 2. Single Strategies Compared to Integration

Strategies	Reinforcement Source		Reinforcement Effect	
	Internal	External	Short-term	Long-term
Health Education	√	√	√	
Risk Rating		√	√	
Rebates		√		√
Integration Model	√	√	√	√

Telecom, The Travelers, Steelcase, GE Aircraft, Coca Cola, and Canadian Life Assurance Company.

So what if risk rating and rebates incense rather than incent employees? The cost of employees' loss of privacy is difficult to calculate, but may be a real dilemma when disgruntled employees question the fairness of program. Although participation is optional, employees cannot receive incentives unless they are in it. Depending on one's health assessment and medical test results, a number of people (other than provider and wellness staff) will be privy to one's health categorization—namely benefits specialists and payroll personnel.

Moreover, risk rating and rebates may frustrate screened employees whose cholesterol or blood pressure measures may be beyond their control. This is why a number of the companies have instituted an appeals process that involves employees submitting medical confirmation (another doctor visit) of their limitations.

IN ALL FAIRNESS

Companies that have incentive, risk-rating, and rebate programs have taken steps to ensure fairness to all. Generally, these financial reinforcers are applied in conjunction with employee health promotion and education programs. The combination of these strategies is known as integration.[1] Employee health education in the form of personal learning experiences to improve health and medical care decision-making will likely have the greatest impact on health care costs in the short-term. Risk rating is another short-term strategy in which an organization's health plan depends on the employee's health risk. A long-term strategy is employee rebates in which cash payments are available to employees for meeting predetermined organizational goals for health care costs. Taken individually, each strategy has limited value. Combined into an integrated plan, health education, risk rating, and rebate incentives offer an effective short- and long-term health promotion intervention. (See Exhibit 2.) Integration will probably have its greatest impact in self-insured or experience-rated indemnity plans. It is no coincidence that the companies profiled earlier meet this description.

Caution is advised if a company fragments the integration plan by focusing on single strategies in health care cost management. Along these lines, companies are short-sighted if they miss hidden costs to program. Incentives, risk rating, and rebates have the potential of conditioning healthy employees, but in the process, participants will make additional health care contacts. If these contacts result in identifying and modifying expensive risk factors, the employer has made a good investment. If these incentive programs primarily appeal to already healthy employees, subjecting them to additional tests and examinations, the employer is paying for something that does not drive down health care costs.

1. Golaszewski, Kaelin, Miller & Douma, "Combining Health Education, Risk-Rated Insurance and Employee Rebates into an Integrated Health Care Cost Containment Strategy," 1992 *Benefits Quarterly* 15, pp 41-50.

Part 12

INSURANCE ISSUES

48. Understanding the New Role of Insurance Carriers

Matthew Schwartz

Insurance companies are becoming health care managers involved in the delivery of health services. But insurers' role in managed care could be affected by a backlash against managed care programs.

As the 1990s progress, the business practices of health insurers entering the managed care market will gradually shift gears. These companies, insurance industry sources say, will ultimately become managers—in addition to their primary role as administrators—of health services, signaling a fundamental change in the nation's delivery of health care.

Although industry sources insist that they have emerged as one of the most effective ways of stemming soaring health care costs, managed care programs have met resistance from the medical profession and from state legislatures, who have enacted laws that could stall the development of such programs.

Traditionally, insurance companies have "paid claims, managed money and served employers," said Anthony Masso, director of managed care and insurance products at the Health Insurance Association of America.

In 1992 and beyond, however, insurers will be "compelled to change into health care managers involved in the delivery" of health services, said Mr. Masso.

Insurers' functions as deliverers of health care will include establishing physician and hospital networks; developing discount rates for doctors in return for increased patient volume; and mounting utilization management programs to assure that appropriate services are provided to a plan's membership.

Figures obtained from HIAA show that the number of health insurers embracing managed care has been accelerating over the past few years.

In 1986 for example, 26 percent of HIAA member companies offered a PPO plan and 5 percent offered an HMO. In 1990, the same figures had increased to 59 percent and 18 percent, respectively.

Moreover, the vast majority of Americans—perhaps up to 80 percent—will be enrolled in some type of managed care network by 1997, according to Mr. Masso.

Undoubtedly, there is some initial trepidation among consumers when choosing a doctor from a managed care network, said Pamela Jones, a consultant in the health and welfare unit of Towers & Perrin, the employee benefits consulting firm.

Studies show, however, that after an average of four years, there is a "high level" of satisfaction with providers among individuals enrolled in various types of managed care programs, she said.

However, some feel that with the proliferation of managed care programs, the doctor/patient relationship could be jeopardized.

"Managed care is one of a number of approaches that have a potential for slowing the growth in health care costs, but if the programs are overly aggressive, managed care can disrupt the physician/patient relationship and reduce access to [health] services that are needed," said a spokesman for the American Medical Association.

"Whether it's through utilization review or heavy financial penalties on physicians who exceed pre-set utilization targets, managed care programs can act as a strong incentive to underserve patients," said the AMA spokesman.

Representatives from the insurance industry disagree. "One of the areas where managed care has been successful in the past has been limiting the inappropriate use of the hospital, particularly through management of the lengths of stay," said Chip Sharkey, senior vice president, national marketing for Cigna Employee Benefits Companies, a leading provider of health benefit programs and insurance services that has a heavy presence in the managed care market. "Utilization managment ultimately controls an employer's health care costs," he said.

Mr. Sharkey stressed that insurers marketing managed care maintain a "local focus." "Health care delivery is a very local type of exercise," said Mr. Sharkey, adding that "success with managed care is dependent on the insurer's emphasis on preventive medicine."

And although a growing number of insurers—and an increasing amount of employers—have been courting managed care programs, state legislatures have apparently been reticent to pass legislation that would facilitate the expansion of such programs.

According to the HIAA, during the 1991 session, for instance, 195 pieces of legislation have been introduced or enacted in statehouses across the country that could "cripple" the growth of managed care.

49.   The Health Management Network

David J. Blume   Raymond A. Lenhardt

*Few industries are undergoing as much change as quickly as the health manage-
ment industry. And this rate of change can be expected to increase through the
1990s, especially in the areas of benefits management and services, networking
of services and technology application. An insurer's ability to predict and prepare
for change will be its key to leadership in tomorrow's health management
industry, particularly in light of the emergence of the health management network—the most dramatic change in the health management industry and the roles
of its players.*

The health management network will consist of the individuals and organizations that, through their relationships, provide, finance and manage
the delivery of health care. These relationships may be personal (in-
sured/physician) or professional (insurer/hospital). Professional relationships can
be termed *networks* when they involve the transfer of information via technology
among network players—the insured, employers, providers, independent vendors, insurers and government. The traditional roles of these key players are
becoming blurred, while new relationships are beginning to form, in part to help
manage costs.

But players' roles are not the only changing elements in the new health
management network. The health management environment as we know it is
evolving to a new structure with new characteristics. Traditionally, hospitals have
been the center for all services not performed in the general practitioner's office,
and insurance companies have been the primary source for group insurance. In
addition, typical health insurance organizations have been large, centralized

Best's Review, January 1992. © A.M. Best Company — used with permission.

offices with functional departments that provide indemnity products and services. Indemnity coverage has been the dominant product in the marketplace, and most products have provided full coverage with few cost controls.

Insurers have focused on claim payment processing. In the traditional health insurance process, the insured has received service, the insured or the provider has submitted the claim and the insurer has paid and/or reimbursed for the claim. All of this information has been exchanged primarily on paper.

NEW TRENDS

But as the health management industry evolves, new patterns emerge. For example, the old and the very old soon will outnumber the young in the United States. As the population ages, health care liabilities will increase. In addition, health care costs are rising faster than the rate of inflation. With these rising costs comes mounting dissatisfaction from customers and the government. In response, the government is expected to offer some form of guaranteed health care and cost incentives as costs grow to more than 15 percent of the gross national product and the population of the uninsured and underinsured increases. In addition, the government is beginning to play a more active role in health issues, as evidenced by the forum on health care administrative costs hosted by the Secretary of Health and Human Services.

Other likely trends in the health management industry include these:

- A focus on benefits, cost and quality measurement in the delivery of health care.
- A move toward nationally planned, regionally administered and locally managed organizations. Insurers will restructure to be more responsive to customers and will decentralize operations along market or geographic lines.
- A change in the roles of industry players. Care centers will specialize, focusing on acute care rather than outpatient services. A new role will emerge in the form of the "services integrator" of health and related benefits. New entrants to the industry will be major financial institutions experimenting with services to the health management network.
- The growth of managed care. Managed care organizations will consolidate and expand. As the number of managed care companies falls, the percentage of the population covered by managed care will rise. In fact, 80 to 90 percent of coverage will be managed care by the year 2000
- An increased focus on product integration. Procedure protocols, utilization review and quality assessment, as well as cost sharing, will be the norm. Management of both the total cost cycle and quality of care will improve, and point-of-service products will dominate.
- Growing use of electronic communication among network players. Medical credit cards will be provided by benefits managers or financial intermediaries.

Centralized payment processing operations with electronic direct payment procedures will evolve. Full electronic data interchange will be required by key players in the network.

- A focus on quality measurement. There will be a movement toward the best, most cost-effective practices in the delivery of health care, including procedure protocols and incentives.

One result of these changes in the health management industry is that the traditional role of the insurer will evolve into multiple roles that address specific network functions. These three roles, which may be played by single or multiple organizations within the network, are the case manager, the risk assumer and the health services integrator.

Case Manager

The case benefits manager will assume activities ranging from the provider's request for procedure authorization to the communication of insurance benefits supplied. Advancing beyond a simple claims processing system, the case manager will plan benefit products, authorize procedures, track cases to monitor progress and perform utilization and care quality reviews. Organizations that assume this role will focus on managing the delivery of health care to control costs and to service purchasers of benefits services.

To fulfill this role, an organization must have knowledge workers who can use new information processing technologies and who have immediate access to information that is organized to support flexibility. The case manager will interface with the health management network, inputting fees, enrollments, claims, diagnoses, case utilization information, quality of care information and case status information. He or she will supply the network with authorization for benefits, quality statistics, utilization statistics, risk analysis and procedure protocols.

Risk Assumer

The organization that assumes this role will take on the risk associated with benefits being managed. This specialized role will enable the separation of risk management from case management. The risk assumer will evaluate risk and determine fees to be charged. Today this role is taken by insurers, reinsurers or self-insurers. By the year 2000, the risk assumer will hold its own distinct role in the network.

Purchasers, case management organizations or other network players may assume this role, but the risk assumer will be required to make quick decisions regarding the risk in each particular relationship. This will require sophisticated information access and analysis capabilities. The risk assumer will receive inputs of utilization information, risk analysis and premiums. The outputs from the risk assumer to the network will be payments and risk limitations.

Health Services Integrator

This role will be the focal point of the network for both business relationships and telecommunications. The health services integrator will serve as a facilitator of health management services and will bring together those services needed to meet the unique requirements of purchasers.

As a technology vendor, the health services integrator will maintain the communications network essential for the on-line, interactive data exchange required by the network. The organization that assumes the role of health services integrator may be a stand-alone organization or some other player in the network.

The health service integrator must be able to bring together "suites" of players that can demonstrate cost efficiency and care quality. This will require immediate access to large amounts of information and rapid analysis of complex alternatives. The organization in this role must have efficient and reliable telecommunications and message processing of both voice and data for a potentially large number of different player combinations in the managed care network.

MANAGING BENEFITS

The health services integrator will establish contractual relationships, maintain the communication network, manage the exchange of information among other network players, evaluate the effectiveness of the relationships to reduce costs and meet quality goals.

These roles—case manager, risk assumer, health services integrator—together will address the management of benefits. As these new network functions emerge, the insurer's current role will evolve into a combination of roles in the not-so-distant future. Organizations that maintain positions as industry leaders will be the ones that understand the role of network players and the business processes that support each role. More than that, they will be prepared to modify their business strategies to conform to the changes.

The ability to demonstrate product flexibility and service quality will be key to successfully marketing benefits management services. Products and services must reflect local needs, but they also must by planned and administered through regional and national networking and operations. In other words, organizations must be flexible.

DEVELOPING A STRATEGY

The need for flexibility and efficiency will require industry leaders to improve the capabilities of their business processes, people and systems by organizing to respond quickly to market needs, improving employees' skills and successfully integrating new technologies into business processes. Before doing any of this, however, an organization will need a strategic planning process that assesses the environment and determines objectives. Within the strategic planning process, a migration plan for managing change will need to be developed.

To develop a migration plan, a company must organize a business migration management team to communicate the organization's vision. This team will coordinate the initiatives of process, people and technology to implement the vision statement.

The migration plan—the insurer's strategy for change—must consider changes in all facets of the organization: business processes, personnel and technologies. The completed migration plan will be integrated into a business integration plan to ensure that resources will be used effectively. To do this, an organization must take the following steps:

- Assess its direction—develop a vision statement. The organization determines what role it sees itself playing in the network. Then it defines a vision statement, created by executive management and communicated throughout the organization.
- Develop goals, objectives and strategies. The organization must evaluate the current environment by collecting competitor data and analyzing the gaps between today's environment and the goals defined in the vision statement.
- Compile a business integration plan. The business integration plan focuses on a reengineering process that pursues people, process and technology initiatives that support the organization's new role in the network. People initiatives include organization transformation and skill-base development. Process initiatives include process planning or business strategy integration, process engineering or reengineering and technology assimilation. Technology initiatives include information integration, software reengineering and incremental software development employing client/server and knowledge-based technologies.
- Implement integrated plans. Implementation is the actual transformation of the organization. An organization must communicate information about business goals clearly to all personnel because success depends on the acceptance of these goals. Furthermore, credit for progress in the effort must be diffused throughout the organization, offering ownership and pride in the integration project at all personnel levels. The organization also must be persistent, pursuing objectives aggressively. It must not punish risk-taking, but rather foster an environment open to new approaches.

- Monitor ongoing operations. Throughout the migration planning and implementation process, the organization must continue tracking results, providing feedback and fostering continuous improvement.

The migration plan is a means of anticipating and preparing for the future. It is an active response that will prepare an organization for the many changes the health management industry will experience before the year 2000.

Several trends affecting the industry's structure already are clear:

1. There will be significant changes to the health management industry's structure, business processes and supporting technologies.
2. Networks of business relationships that facilitate telecommunications will form the basic industry structure.
3. Players in the network will assume roles that require flexible, skilled organizations and the ability to embrace new technologies.
4. Transitioning from today's environment will require creative approaches to managing organization process change and technology change.

In the year 2000, those who succeed in the new roles of the health management network will find improved cost management, quality and cash flow. In many cases, these players will become vendors or consumers of services that will be coordinated by a health services integrator. Business relationships will be firmly established, with the health services integrator functioning at the hub. These business relationships will be fostered by a telecommunications network that will enable the sharing of information and will serve as a means for network operations.

In addition to changes in professional relationships in the industry, other changes must be made to complete the network and achieve its benefits. For example, the information of communication networks lags behind the development of business relationships. To achieve parity in this regard, both physical and philosophical barriers to communicating information must be broken down. In other words, not only must the industry adopt methods to transport information across systems, but players also must become comfortable revealing information that historically has been considered confidential.

CHALLENGING TRADITION

This health management network is one way to envision the future for the health management industry. This vision may not match traditional expectations for the future of the industry, but the possibility of an emerging health management network may challenge the traditional view of the industry in coming years.

Whatever the perspective, it will take a dramatic change in thinking and vision to be a player in the health management industry in the year 2000. To take advantage of future opportunities, insurers must embrace change by revitalizing business processes, re-educating personnel and renewing technologies—key components of an effective migration plan.

50. Rate Guarantees for Managed Care Contracts

Bruce Shutan

Rate guarantees under managed care contracts have come a long way, baby, since 1988, when Allied-Signal negotiated its pioneering three-year deal with CIGNA capping the employer's health benefits outlays. For one thing, today they're mostly called "risk-sharing" arrangements or "trend guarantees."

The all-or-nothing deal between Allied-Signal and CIGNA, through which the insurer had borne all the risk and gain, has spawned new variations of an old theme, explains Joseph Duva, who helped negotiate guarantees for Allied-Signal.

Benefit consultants say today's contracts usually stipulate that both parties share in the risk and potential for gain.

SIZE BRINGS LEVERAGE

Duva, now a partner at Ernst & Young specializing in managed care, says some guarantees are more aggressive than others, depending on the strength and size of an employer's preferred provider network. He says the arrangements are confined to large employers that bring with them tremendous leverage to the negotiating table.

Reprinted from *Employee Benefit News*, Vol 5, No 7, with permission.

But don't expect to see any time soon the same sweeping guarantees that Allied-Signal walked away with, according to Elizabeth A. Dudek, a managing consultant with Noble Lowndes in Philadelphia.

Dudek tried to negotiate an Allied-Signal style guarantee for a client, but says CIGNA clearly had no intention of offering another deal like it. She says she was surprised to learn that CIGNA included a rate guarantee in its recent managed care contract with the Black & Decker Corp.

Bruce T. Davidson, a Simsbury, Conn.-based independent employee benefits and managed care consultant who recently retired from The Travelers, also expressed surprise that the carrier would entertain such a move with anyone other than Allied-Signal.

While details of Allied-Signal's original contract with CIGNA have remained under wraps, it's widely believed the employer received assurances that its in-network health care costs would be held to high single-digit increases.

Industry observers also say CIGNA initially may have lost money on the deal, which expired in March, but was compensated by the publicity that was generated. CIGNA has maintained that the arrangement was profitable.

Efforts are still under way to extend a new contract, which replaced the original three-year deal, beyond the end of this year, when it is set to expire.

BLACK & DECKER'S DEAL

Neither CIGNA nor Black & Decker would divulge specifics of their contract, but indications are that it's vastly different from the original Allied-Signal model. Even B&D's director of benefits, Raymond J. Brusca, concedes that Allied-Signal benefitted from a "once-in-a-lifetime deal." In fact, those initial guarantees for Allied-Signal have been scaled back in the contract's second phase (see March 1991 *Employee Benefit News,* p. 11).

Rate guarantees are "much more sophisticated now than when we did the first one with Allied-Signal," notes Chip Sharkey, senior vice president, national marketing for CIGNA in Hartford, Conn.

"The main difference is that they are constructed to more specifically reflect the performance of managing the care of the program," he explains, "whereas the Allied-Signal arrangement in its early form applied to both the managed care and indemnity portions, including people who lived outside the network's service area for whom there really was no management of care."

Today's rate guarantees are structured so that there's an even split of the risks and savings, according to Sharkey. What varies, he says, is the annual health care cost containment targets and quality of claims data from the employer's previous carriers and provider arrangements.

Dudek says watered-down "trend guarantees" have appeared to replace full-fledged guarantees. Under a managed care contract, she says medical inflation, changing technology and utilization patterns may be factored into the rate guarantee to reflect cost trends.

These trend factors in turn may add, for example, 20 percent to an annual $1 million cost-containment target on in-network care, she explains. That is, claims could rise by an additional $200,000 without exceeding the "trend guarantee" limit.

In a year in which a company enjoys good claims experience, a company probably would break even with a trend guarantee, but come out ahead with a rate guarantee, Dudek says. In a poor year, she says a company stands to lose more with a trend guarantee.

Brusca, offering a glimpse into the structure of B&D's deal with CIGNA, says the Towson, MD.-based power tool maker entertained bids from five major carriers and the Blues. He says all the proposed guarantees were virtually identical, though CIGNA's was slightly superior.

Generally, the contracts stipulated that risks and gains be shared equally. If claims were 3 percent higher or lower than the targeted guarantee, B&D would absorb the cost or savings. Risks would be shared equally for all claims between 103 percent and 120 percent of the target. Likewise, savings would be split if claims were between 80 percent and 97 percent of the target.

Stephen C. Caulfield, a managing director of William M. Mercer, Inc. in Boston, the consulting firm that helped B&D strike its deal with CIGNA, says the best rate guarantees contain three essential elements:

First, he says they should stipulate that 60 percent of the health care dollars flow through the network in the first year, with the figure reaching 65 percent in the second year and 70 percent in the third year. "This puts pressure on insurers to get the right hospitals and doctors into the network," he notes.

Other key points would include ways to manage network utilization and determine health care cost trends. The latter should be based on price contracts that allow insurers to negotiate rates that guarantee hospitals a profit margin and high volume, according to Caulfield.

Before signing onto a rate guarantee, he advises employers to carefully define the terms and methodology of the contract. For example, projections should be based on credible claims data incurred during a set period of time to which both parties can agree. Also, companies need to consider employee demographics, the number of people receiving care in an HMO setting, admission rates, etc.

He believes the rate guarantee component of Allied-Signal's contract with CIGNA "really was overplayed," adding that the deal was more about establishing a quality-driven system that targeted inappropriate care and network accountability.

LOOKING AHEAD

In the future, "rate guarantees may be used as a bargaining tool" in negotiations with insurers, says Davidson. He believes employers could threaten to take their business elsewhere without them.

Dudek, however, believes insurers are in a position to be choosy about the kind of guarantees they agree to and knows from experience that they will turn down business. This is not surprising considering they tend to steer clear of any arrangement that's not predictable, she adds.

"I think it's one of those situations where all the employers want them, but most of the vendors would prefer not to give them," Caulfield says.

Is it possible that the market will see a return to the winner-take-all Allied-Signal-style guarantee?

Dudek doesn't think so. Down the road, it's likely that employers will want the entire potential savings pie, Sharkey opines. Eventually, though, he thinks "the demand for risk-sharing arrangements will abate and possibly disappear, altogether."

Once the marketplace has five to seven years of aggressive managed care experience under its belt, Brusca says, carriers probably will be more forthcoming about offering such guarantees. That is, he adds, as long as they know with some degree of certainty that the deals won't be a financial drain.

The growth of rate guarantees will depend on the extent to which managed care becomes a buyer's market for employers, Caulfield predicts. In the years ahead, he believes insurers reluctantly will agree to the arrangements, which will be prevalent among large, national employers that "have the kind of numbers that are workable" for the carrier.

Like performance guarantees, Caulfield says rate guarantees will be an integral part of the managed care contract of tomorrow and offer both parties a chance for mutual gain.

Duva warns that rate guarantees should not be considered a panacea to the health care cost crisis facing employers. "You really don't need to have risk contracts," he says, adding that a well-designed managed care program is one that "rewards providers for quality of carte and accountability, not just volume," and encourages preventive care.

Index